# *FACTS PLUS*™

## *An Almanac of Essential Information*

by Susan C. Anthony

Instructional Resources Company
Anchorage, Alaska

Quantity discounts are available for educational institutions. For information write:

    Instructional Resources Company
    1013 E. Dimond Blvd. #188
    Anchorage, Alaska 99515

First Edition, January, 1991

ISBN 1-879478-00-5

Printed in the United States of America on recycled paper.

# INTRODUCTION

The idea for *Facts Plus* came on one of the most frustrating days of my life, as I attempted to teach reference skills to a class using a standard almanac. It may have been one of the most frustrating days of my students' lives, too, as they struggled to extract the information they needed from multi-column tables with small type, abbreviations and numbers carried to several decimal places.

I couldn't blame them. The almanac was simply and truly too difficult for them. I sometimes had difficulty with it myself. As I analyzed the problem, the idea came. Why not a simplified reference book, "user-friendly" enough for students, yet authoritative enough for use by anyone? It seemed a practical idea, and the brainstorming began.

This was the beginning of six years of research and writing. The more I read and did research for this book, the more I realized that truth can be stranger than fiction. Not only are facts fascinating and useful, they are relatively difficult to remember. I began using *Facts Plus* as a memory aid for myself, a sort of storage place for statistics and details.

I wanted *Facts Plus* to be more than a collection of unrelated information. I worked to present in a concise and understandable format the basic core of information taught in most schools. It includes much information considered necessary by E. D. Hirsch for "cultural literacy"—familiarity with facts and information generally understood by educated Americans. This book is a foundation for further learning, a basic outline which can serve to help organize further knowledge.

I consulted countless reference books in the preparation of this book, and located primary sources of information whenever possible. Facts were carefully checked and cross-checked for accuracy, and specialists asked to comment on sections relating to their areas of expertise. Although I cannot personally guarantee the accuracy of all facts included, every effort has been made to find and use the best sources of information possible.

A partial bibliography of sources appears on pages 232. These represent the books from which most substantive information was taken. Numerous others were consulted. See pages 229-231 for explanatory notes by page number and sources of some specific facts. Information in the notes can also be accessed through the index.

*Facts Plus* was prepared on a Macintosh SE using Microsoft Word, Adobe Illustrator, and Aldus Pagemaker.

More thanks than I can ever express go to Mike and Jeanne Bradner, Thor and Nancy Brandt-Erichsen, Phyllis Hamann, Alan Hastings, Sue Keith, Fred and Jeannette Kent, Mary Kay Sambo, Beverly Wheeler, and especially Dennis Weston for help on this project. Thanks also to the librarians at Loussac and Samson-Dimond Public Libraries, and at the University of Alaska Anchorage Consortium Library. Special thanks to Dr. Glenn Shaw and Dr. David Stone of the University of Alaska Fairbanks Geophysical Institute for their review and comments on the science section. Shannon Weiss, Earl Kubaskie, Kim Sandford, Earl Stirling, and personnel at the UAA Learning Center provided invaluable and much needed computer-related assistance. I am deeply grateful to others too numerous to mention who have offered ideas, encouragement and support through the past six years.

# SUGGESTIONS FOR USING *FACTS PLUS*

## STUDENTS

—Keep *Facts Plus* in your desk or study area at home as a quick source of reference information for reports, writing, math or other homework.

—Look up answers to questions as they occur to you. Take advantage of an easy opportunity to extend your knowledge.

—Impress others by learning fascinating facts that few people know.

—Use the maps to locate places you hear or read about.

—Use *Facts Plus* to help you review and recall what you've been taught.

## PARENTS

—Model using *Facts Plus*, the dictionary and other reference books to answer questions as they occur to you or others in the family. Keep it available near the dinner table, in the living room, or wherever it's most likely to be used.

—Discuss television programs as a family. Use the maps to locate places, the time line to put historical events into perspective, and the index to find related information.

—Use *Facts Plus* as an aid in teaching children how to be courteous, how to use the telephone, how to write thank-you notes, and so on.

—Help children learn to rely on *Facts Plus* and other reference books to answer their questions, rather than depending on you. Assist them in using the index, finding the appropriate page, and skimming and scanning to find the information. They can use the same skills with the telephone book and the cookbook.

## TEACHERS

—Use it as an authentic reference book in a whole language classroom. Help children learn reference skills by doing, in connection with every area of the curriculum.

—Keep a copy in the classroom for instant reference. Use it to take advantage of "teachable moments" when student interest in a question or topic is high.

—Use it as an aid to studying the newspaper and current events.

—Have students use the statistics and information to create their own math problems.

—Use *Facts Plus* as an aid in planning mini-lessons to suit your own and your students' needs. Procedures and guidelines for interviewing, taking standardized tests, or doing research reports may be useful at different times of the year.

—Challenge students to memorize for extra credit—the preamble to the Constitution, the countries of the world, and the manual alphabet are some good challenges.

—Use the addresses for classroom letter-writing projects.

—Introduce report topics using *Facts Plus*. Each notable person, Indian tribe, and National Park, for example, has an individual article in a standard school encyclopedia.

—Have students manipulate statistics and other information. Graph population densities of countries, make a time line of communication inventions, or rank states by per capita income.

—Write Instructional Resources Company, 1013 E. Dimond Blvd. #188, Anchorage, AK 99515 for information on quantity discounts for classroom sets.

# TABLE OF CONTENTS

# TIME
# AND
# SPACE

# TIME AND CLOCKS

Long ago, people began measuring time by keeping track of the regular cycles of nature, such as the movement of the sun, the phases of the moon, and the seasons. The cycle of the sun came to be called a **day**, the cycle of the moon was a **month**, and the cycle of the seasons was a **year**. People tried for hundreds of years to make a calendar which fit both the cycle of the moon and the cycle of the seasons, but nothing worked. The calendar we use today was based on the year, and what we call "months" are divisions of the year which have no relation to the phases of the moon. Some groups of people still use calendars based on the moon.

The seven-day **week** is from the Bible, which says God created the universe in six days, and rested on the seventh.

Ancient people divided both the day and night into twelve equal parts, which together make a 24 **hour** day. They also divided the circle into 360 equal degrees. The compass is based on this division, as are the lines of latitude and longitude. Each degree of the circle was further divided into 60 **minutes** and 60 **seconds**. Later, clockmakers borrowed the idea of 60 minutes and 60 seconds. By the 1700's, clocks were correct to the minute.

## CONVERSIONS

| | | | |
|---|---|---|---|
| 60 | seconds | = | 1 minute |
| 60 | minutes | = | 1 hour |
| 24 | hours | = | 1 day |
| 7 | days | = | 1 week |
| 365¼ | days | = | 1 year |
| 52 | weeks | = | 1 year |
| 12 | months | = | 1 year |
| 10 | years | = | 1 decade |
| 100 | years | = | 1 century |
| 1000 | years | = | 1 millennium |

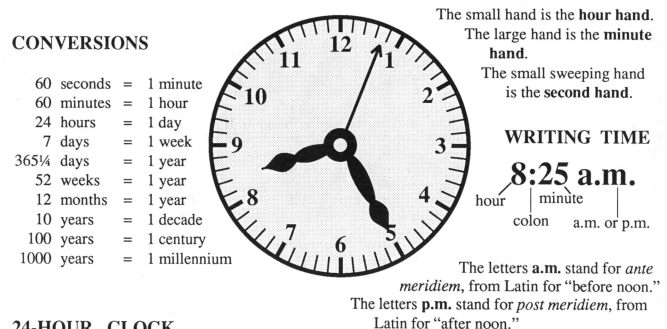

The small hand is the **hour hand**. The large hand is the **minute hand**. The small sweeping hand is the **second hand**.

## WRITING TIME

# 8:25 a.m.

hour — minute
colon — a.m. or p.m.

The letters **a.m.** stand for *ante meridiem*, from Latin for "before noon." The letters **p.m.** stand for *post meridiem*, from Latin for "after noon."

## 24-HOUR CLOCK

Because there are two times of the day called 9:00, there must be some way to tell the difference. One way is to use **a.m.** and **p.m.** Another way is to use a **24-hour clock**, as does the military.

| 1:00 a.m. | 0100 hours | 7:00 a.m. | 0700 hours | 1:00 p.m. | 1300 hours | 7:00 p.m. | 1900 hours |
|---|---|---|---|---|---|---|---|
| 2:00 a.m. | 0200 hours | 8:00 a.m. | 0800 hours | 2:00 p.m. | 1400 hours | 8:00 p.m. | 2000 hours |
| 3:00 a.m. | 0300 hours | 9:00 a.m. | 0900 hours | 3:00 p.m. | 1500 hours | 9:00 p.m. | 2100 hours |
| 4:00 a.m. | 0400 hours | 10:00 a.m. | 1000 hours | 4:00 p.m. | 1600 hours | 10:00 p.m. | 2200 hours |
| 5:00 a.m. | 0500 hours | 11:00 a.m. | 1100 hours | 5:00 p.m. | 1700 hours | 11:00 p.m. | 2300 hours |
| 6:00 a.m. | 0600 hours | 12:00 p.m. | 1200 hours | 6:00 p.m. | 1800 hours | 12:00 a.m. | 2400 hours |

# TIME ZONES

**Noon** is the middle of the day. Because the earth turns, and half of the earth is always in darkness, the middle of the day comes to different places at different times. A little over a century ago, every place set its own time by the sun. This was confusing for travelers, who never knew what time it was from place to place. The railroads had a terrible time writing their schedules. It was the railroad companies who first divided the United States into four time zones in 1883. The next year, the entire world was divided into standard time zones, based on the meridians, or lines of longitude. Whenever a traveler crosses into a new time zone, she must change her watch by one hour. Traveling from east to west, the time gets earlier, and traveling west to east it gets later.

A person crossing the International Date Line in the Pacific Ocean loses or gains not an hour, but a whole day! Traveling east to west across the Pacific, it becomes a day later. Going west to east, it becomes a day earlier. It is very possible for travelers to arrive in San Francisco earlier than they left Tokyo, Japan!

A few things make using time zones complicated. Many places use Daylight Saving, a plan in which clocks are set an hour ahead of standard time for a certain period, usually in the summer. Time zone maps do not show which places use Daylight Saving and when it is in effect. Lines between time zones are not straight because they are drawn to keep cities, communities, and even states and countries from having two zones. In some places, the time changes by two hours rather than one. A few countries, including India, use a half-hour rather than a full hour change, and Saudi Arabia does not use standard time zones at all.

## STANDARD TIME ZONES OF THE WORLD

| 165° W | 150° W | 135° W | 120° W | 105° W | 90° W | 75° W | 60° W | 45° W | 30° W | 15° W | 0° | 15° E | 30° E | 45° E | 60° E | 75° E | 90° E | 105° E | 120° E | 135° E | 150° E | 165° E | 180° |
|---|---|---|---|---|---|---|---|---|---|---|---|---|---|---|---|---|---|---|---|---|---|---|---|

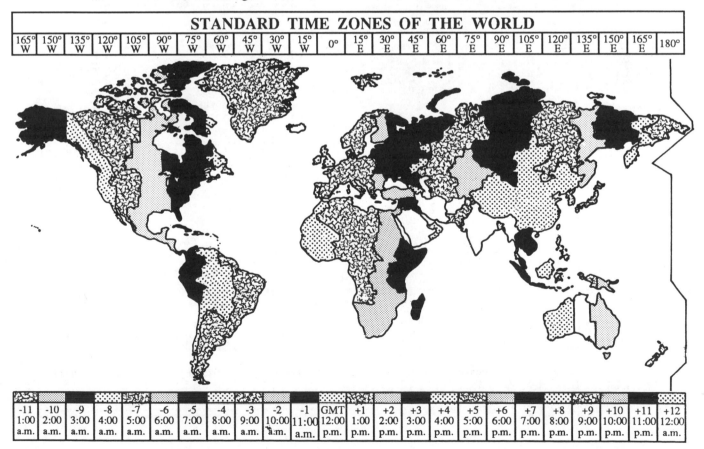

| -11 | -10 | -9 | -8 | -7 | -6 | -5 | -4 | -3 | -2 | -1 | GMT | +1 | +2 | +3 | +4 | +5 | +6 | +7 | +8 | +9 | +10 | +11 | +12 |
|---|---|---|---|---|---|---|---|---|---|---|---|---|---|---|---|---|---|---|---|---|---|---|---|
| 1:00 a.m. | 2:00 a.m. | 3:00 a.m. | 4:00 a.m. | 5:00 a.m. | 6:00 a.m. | 7:00 a.m. | 8:00 a.m. | 9:00 a.m. | 10:00 a.m. | 11:00 a.m. | 12:00 p.m. | 1:00 p.m. | 2:00 p.m. | 3:00 p.m. | 4:00 p.m. | 5:00 p.m. | 6:00 p.m. | 7:00 p.m. | 8:00 p.m. | 9:00 p.m. | 10:00 p.m. | 11:00 p.m. | 12:00 a.m. |

# PERPETUAL CALENDAR

| | | | | | | |
|---|---|---|---|---|---|---|
| 1763—7 | 1806—4 | 1849—2 | 1892—13 | 1935—3 | 1978—1 | 2021—6 |
| 1764—8 | 1807—5 | 1850—3 | 1893—1 | 1936—11 | 1979—2 | 2022—7 |
| 1765—3 | 1808—13 | 1851—4 | 1894—2 | 1937—6 | 1980—10 | 2023—1 |
| 1766—4 | 1809—1 | 1852—12 | 1895—3 | 1938—7 | 1981—5 | 2024—9 |
| 1767—5 | 1810—2 | 1853—7 | 1896—11 | 1939—1 | 1982—6 | 2025—4 |
| 1768—13 | 1811—3 | 1854—1 | 1897—6 | 1940—9 | 1983—7 | 2026—5 |
| 1769—1 | 1812—11 | 1855—2 | 1898—7 | 1941—4 | 1984—8 | 2027—6 |
| 1770—2 | 1813—6 | 1856—10 | 1899—1 | 1942—5 | 1985—3 | 2028—14 |
| 1771—3 | 1814—7 | 1857—5 | 1900—2 | 1943—6 | 1986—4 | 2029—2 |
| 1772—11 | 1815—1 | 1858—6 | 1901—3 | 1944—14 | 1987—5 | 2030—3 |
| 1773—6 | 1816—9 | 1859—7 | 1902—4 | 1945—2 | 1988—13 | 2031—4 |
| 1774—7 | 1817—4 | 1860—8 | 1903—5 | 1946—3 | 1989—1 | 2032—12 |
| 1775—1 | 1818—5 | 1861—3 | 1904—13 | 1947—4 | 1990—2 | 2033—7 |
| 1776—9 | 1819—6 | 1862—4 | 1905—1 | 1948—12 | 1991—3 | 2034—1 |
| 1777—4 | 1820—14 | 1863—5 | 1906—2 | 1949—7 | 1992—11 | 2035—2 |
| 1778—5 | 1821—2 | 1864—13 | 1907—3 | 1950—1 | 1993—6 | 2036—10 |
| 1779—6 | 1822—3 | 1865—1 | 1908—11 | 1951—2 | 1994—7 | 2037—5 |
| 1780—14 | 1823—4 | 1866—2 | 1909—6 | 1952—10 | 1995—1 | 2038—6 |
| 1781—2 | 1824—12 | 1867—3 | 1910—7 | 1953—5 | 1996—9 | 2039—7 |
| 1782—3 | 1825—7 | 1868—11 | 1911—1 | 1954—6 | 1997—4 | 2040—8 |
| 1783—4 | 1826—1 | 1869—6 | 1912—9 | 1955—7 | 1998—5 | 2041—3 |
| 1784—12 | 1827—2 | 1870—7 | 1913—4 | 1956—8 | 1999—6 | 2042—4 |
| 1785—7 | 1828—10 | 1871—1 | 1914—5 | 1957—3 | 2000—14 | 2043—5 |
| 1786—1 | 1829—5 | 1872—9 | 1915—6 | 1958—4 | 2001—2 | 2044—13 |
| 1787—2 | 1830—6 | 1873—4 | 1916—14 | 1959—5 | 2002—3 | 2045—1 |
| 1788—10 | 1831—7 | 1874—5 | 1917—2 | 1960—13 | 2003—4 | 2046—2 |
| 1789—5 | 1832—8 | 1875—6 | 1918—3 | 1961—1 | 2004—12 | 2047—3 |
| 1790—6 | 1833—3 | 1876—14 | 1919—4 | 1962—2 | 2005—7 | 2048—11 |
| 1791—7 | 1834—4 | 1877—2 | 1920—12 | 1963—3 | 2006—1 | 2049—6 |
| 1792—8 | 1835—5 | 1878—3 | 1921—7 | 1964—11 | 2007—2 | 2050—7 |
| 1793—3 | 1836—13 | 1879—4 | 1922—1 | 1965—6 | 2008—10 | 2051—1 |
| 1794—4 | 1837—1 | 1880—12 | 1923—2 | 1966—7 | 2009—5 | 2052—9 |
| 1795—5 | 1838—2 | 1881—7 | 1924—10 | 1967—1 | 2010—6 | 2053—4 |
| 1796—13 | 1839—3 | 1882—1 | 1925—5 | 1968—9 | 2011—7 | 2054—5 |
| 1797—1 | 1840—11 | 1883—2 | 1926—6 | 1969—4 | 2012—8 | 2055—6 |
| 1798—2 | 1841—6 | 1884—10 | 1927—7 | 1970—5 | 2013—3 | 2056—14 |
| 1799—3 | 1842—7 | 1885—5 | 1928—8 | 1971—6 | 2014—4 | 2057—2 |
| 1800—4 | 1843—1 | 1886—6 | 1929—3 | 1972—14 | 2015—5 | 2058—3 |
| 1801—5 | 1844—9 | 1887—7 | 1930—4 | 1973—2 | 2016—13 | 2059—4 |
| 1802—6 | 1845—4 | 1888—8 | 1931—5 | 1974—3 | 2017—1 | 2060—12 |
| 1803—7 | 1846—5 | 1889—3 | 1932—13 | 1975—4 | 2018—2 | 2061—7 |
| 1804—8 | 1847—6 | 1890—4 | 1933—1 | 1976—12 | 2019—3 | 2062—1 |
| 1805—3 | 1848—14 | 1891—5 | 1934—2 | 1977—7 | 2020—11 | 2063—2 |

## 1

**JANUARY**

| S | M | T | W | T | F | S |
|---|---|---|---|---|---|---|
| 1 | 2 | 3 | 4 | 5 | 6 | 7 |
| 8 | 9 | 10 | 11 | 12 | 13 | 14 |
| 15 | 16 | 17 | 18 | 19 | 20 | 21 |
| 22 | 23 | 24 | 25 | 26 | 27 | 28 |
| 29 | 30 | 31 | | | | |

**FEBRUARY**

| S | M | T | W | T | F | S |
|---|---|---|---|---|---|---|
| | | | 1 | 2 | 3 | 4 |
| 5 | 6 | 7 | 8 | 9 | 10 | 11 |
| 12 | 13 | 14 | 15 | 16 | 17 | 18 |
| 19 | 20 | 21 | 22 | 23 | 24 | 25 |
| 26 | 27 | 28 | | | | |

**MARCH**

| S | M | T | W | T | F | S |
|---|---|---|---|---|---|---|
| | | | 1 | 2 | 3 | 4 |
| 5 | 6 | 7 | 8 | 9 | 10 | 11 |
| 12 | 13 | 14 | 15 | 16 | 17 | 18 |
| 19 | 20 | 21 | 22 | 23 | 24 | 25 |
| 26 | 27 | 28 | 29 | 30 | 31 | |

**APRIL**

| S | M | T | W | T | F | S |
|---|---|---|---|---|---|---|
| | | | | | | 1 |
| 2 | 3 | 4 | 5 | 6 | 7 | 8 |
| 9 | 10 | 11 | 12 | 13 | 14 | 15 |
| 16 | 17 | 18 | 19 | 20 | 21 | 22 |
| 23 | 24 | 25 | 26 | 27 | 28 | 29 |
| 30 | | | | | | |

**MAY**

| S | M | T | W | T | F | S |
|---|---|---|---|---|---|---|
| | 1 | 2 | 3 | 4 | 5 | 6 |
| 7 | 8 | 9 | 10 | 11 | 12 | 13 |
| 14 | 15 | 16 | 17 | 18 | 19 | 20 |
| 21 | 22 | 23 | 24 | 25 | 26 | 27 |
| 28 | 29 | 30 | 31 | | | |

**JUNE**

| S | M | T | W | T | F | S |
|---|---|---|---|---|---|---|
| | | | | 1 | 2 | 3 |
| 4 | 5 | 6 | 7 | 8 | 9 | 10 |
| 11 | 12 | 13 | 14 | 15 | 16 | 17 |
| 18 | 19 | 20 | 21 | 22 | 23 | 24 |
| 25 | 26 | 27 | 28 | 29 | 30 | |

**JULY**

| S | M | T | W | T | F | S |
|---|---|---|---|---|---|---|
| | | | | | | 1 |
| 2 | 3 | 4 | 5 | 6 | 7 | 8 |
| 9 | 10 | 11 | 12 | 13 | 14 | 15 |
| 16 | 17 | 18 | 19 | 20 | 21 | 22 |
| 23 | 24 | 25 | 26 | 27 | 28 | 29 |
| 30 | 31 | | | | | |

**AUGUST**

| S | M | T | W | T | F | S |
|---|---|---|---|---|---|---|
| | | 1 | 2 | 3 | 4 | 5 |
| 6 | 7 | 8 | 9 | 10 | 11 | 12 |
| 13 | 14 | 15 | 16 | 17 | 18 | 19 |
| 20 | 21 | 22 | 23 | 24 | 25 | 26 |
| 27 | 28 | 29 | 30 | 31 | | |

**SEPTEMBER**

| S | M | T | W | T | F | S |
|---|---|---|---|---|---|---|
| | | | | | 1 | 2 |
| 3 | 4 | 5 | 6 | 7 | 8 | 9 |
| 10 | 11 | 12 | 13 | 14 | 15 | 16 |
| 17 | 18 | 19 | 20 | 21 | 22 | 23 |
| 24 | 25 | 26 | 27 | 28 | 29 | 30 |

**OCTOBER**

| S | M | T | W | T | F | S |
|---|---|---|---|---|---|---|
| 1 | 2 | 3 | 4 | 5 | 6 | 7 |
| 8 | 9 | 10 | 11 | 12 | 13 | 14 |
| 15 | 16 | 17 | 18 | 19 | 20 | 21 |
| 22 | 23 | 24 | 25 | 26 | 27 | 28 |
| 29 | 30 | 31 | | | | |

**NOVEMBER**

| S | M | T | W | T | F | S |
|---|---|---|---|---|---|---|
| | | | 1 | 2 | 3 | 4 |
| 5 | 6 | 7 | 8 | 9 | 10 | 11 |
| 12 | 13 | 14 | 15 | 16 | 17 | 18 |
| 19 | 20 | 21 | 22 | 23 | 24 | 25 |
| 26 | 27 | 28 | 29 | 30 | | |

**DECEMBER**

| S | M | T | W | T | F | S |
|---|---|---|---|---|---|---|
| | | | | | 1 | 2 |
| 3 | 4 | 5 | 6 | 7 | 8 | 9 |
| 10 | 11 | 12 | 13 | 14 | 15 | 16 |
| 17 | 18 | 19 | 20 | 21 | 22 | 23 |
| 24 | 25 | 26 | 27 | 28 | 29 | 30 |
| 31 | | | | | | |

## 2

**JANUARY**

| S | M | T | W | T | F | S |
|---|---|---|---|---|---|---|
| | 1 | 2 | 3 | 4 | 5 | 6 |
| 7 | 8 | 9 | 10 | 11 | 12 | 13 |
| 14 | 15 | 16 | 17 | 18 | 19 | 20 |
| 21 | 22 | 23 | 24 | 25 | 26 | 27 |
| 28 | 29 | 30 | 31 | | | |

**FEBRUARY**

| S | M | T | W | T | F | S |
|---|---|---|---|---|---|---|
| | | | | 1 | 2 | 3 |
| 4 | 5 | 6 | 7 | 8 | 9 | 10 |
| 11 | 12 | 13 | 14 | 15 | 16 | 17 |
| 18 | 19 | 20 | 21 | 22 | 23 | 24 |
| 25 | 26 | 27 | 28 | | | |

**MARCH**

| S | M | T | W | T | F | S |
|---|---|---|---|---|---|---|
| | | | | 1 | 2 | 3 |
| 4 | 5 | 6 | 7 | 8 | 9 | 10 |
| 11 | 12 | 13 | 14 | 15 | 16 | 17 |
| 18 | 19 | 20 | 21 | 22 | 23 | 24 |
| 25 | 26 | 27 | 28 | 29 | 30 | 31 |

**APRIL**

| S | M | T | W | T | F | S |
|---|---|---|---|---|---|---|
| 1 | 2 | 3 | 4 | 5 | 6 | 7 |
| 8 | 9 | 10 | 11 | 12 | 13 | 14 |
| 15 | 16 | 17 | 18 | 19 | 20 | 21 |
| 22 | 23 | 24 | 25 | 26 | 27 | 28 |
| 29 | 30 | | | | | |

**MAY**

| S | M | T | W | T | F | S |
|---|---|---|---|---|---|---|
| | | 1 | 2 | 3 | 4 | 5 |
| 6 | 7 | 8 | 9 | 10 | 11 | 12 |
| 13 | 14 | 15 | 16 | 17 | 18 | 19 |
| 20 | 21 | 22 | 23 | 24 | 25 | 26 |
| 27 | 28 | 29 | 30 | 31 | | |

**JUNE**

| S | M | T | W | T | F | S |
|---|---|---|---|---|---|---|
| | | | | | 1 | 2 |
| 3 | 4 | 5 | 6 | 7 | 8 | 9 |
| 10 | 11 | 12 | 13 | 14 | 15 | 16 |
| 17 | 18 | 19 | 20 | 21 | 22 | 23 |
| 24 | 25 | 26 | 27 | 28 | 29 | 30 |

**JULY**

| S | M | T | W | T | F | S |
|---|---|---|---|---|---|---|
| 1 | 2 | 3 | 4 | 5 | 6 | 7 |
| 8 | 9 | 10 | 11 | 12 | 13 | 14 |
| 15 | 16 | 17 | 18 | 19 | 20 | 21 |
| 22 | 23 | 24 | 25 | 26 | 27 | 28 |
| 29 | 30 | 31 | | | | |

**AUGUST**

| S | M | T | W | T | F | S |
|---|---|---|---|---|---|---|
| | | | 1 | 2 | 3 | 4 |
| 5 | 6 | 7 | 8 | 9 | 10 | 11 |
| 12 | 13 | 14 | 15 | 16 | 17 | 18 |
| 19 | 20 | 21 | 22 | 23 | 24 | 25 |
| 26 | 27 | 28 | 29 | 30 | 31 | |

**SEPTEMBER**

| S | M | T | W | T | F | S |
|---|---|---|---|---|---|---|
| | | | | | | 1 |
| 2 | 3 | 4 | 5 | 6 | 7 | 8 |
| 9 | 10 | 11 | 12 | 13 | 14 | 15 |
| 16 | 17 | 18 | 19 | 20 | 21 | 22 |
| 23 | 24 | 25 | 26 | 27 | 28 | 29 |
| 30 | | | | | | |

**OCTOBER**

| S | M | T | W | T | F | S |
|---|---|---|---|---|---|---|
| | 1 | 2 | 3 | 4 | 5 | 6 |
| 7 | 8 | 9 | 10 | 11 | 12 | 13 |
| 14 | 15 | 16 | 17 | 18 | 19 | 20 |
| 21 | 22 | 23 | 24 | 25 | 26 | 27 |
| 28 | 29 | 30 | 31 | | | |

**NOVEMBER**

| S | M | T | W | T | F | S |
|---|---|---|---|---|---|---|
| | | | | 1 | 2 | 3 |
| 4 | 5 | 6 | 7 | 8 | 9 | 10 |
| 11 | 12 | 13 | 14 | 15 | 16 | 17 |
| 18 | 19 | 20 | 21 | 22 | 23 | 24 |
| 25 | 26 | 27 | 28 | 29 | 30 | |

**DECEMBER**

| S | M | T | W | T | F | S |
|---|---|---|---|---|---|---|
| | | | | | | 1 |
| 2 | 3 | 4 | 5 | 6 | 7 | 8 |
| 9 | 10 | 11 | 12 | 13 | 14 | 15 |
| 16 | 17 | 18 | 19 | 20 | 21 | 22 |
| 23 | 24 | 25 | 26 | 27 | 28 | 29 |
| 30 | 31 | | | | | |

## 3

**JANUARY**

| S | M | T | W | T | F | S |
|---|---|---|---|---|---|---|
| | | 1 | 2 | 3 | 4 | 5 |
| 6 | 7 | 8 | 9 | 10 | 11 | 12 |
| 13 | 14 | 15 | 16 | 17 | 18 | 19 |
| 20 | 21 | 22 | 23 | 24 | 25 | 26 |
| 27 | 28 | 29 | 30 | 31 | | |

**FEBRUARY**

| S | M | T | W | T | F | S |
|---|---|---|---|---|---|---|
| | | | | | 1 | 2 |
| 3 | 4 | 5 | 6 | 7 | 8 | 9 |
| 10 | 11 | 12 | 13 | 14 | 15 | 16 |
| 17 | 18 | 19 | 20 | 21 | 22 | 23 |
| 24 | 25 | 26 | 27 | 28 | | |

**MARCH**

| S | M | T | W | T | F | S |
|---|---|---|---|---|---|---|
| | | | | | 1 | 2 |
| 3 | 4 | 5 | 6 | 7 | 8 | 9 |
| 10 | 11 | 12 | 13 | 14 | 15 | 16 |
| 17 | 18 | 19 | 20 | 21 | 22 | 23 |
| 24 | 25 | 26 | 27 | 28 | 29 | 30 |
| 31 | | | | | | |

**APRIL**

| S | M | T | W | T | F | S |
|---|---|---|---|---|---|---|
| | 1 | 2 | 3 | 4 | 5 | 6 |
| 7 | 8 | 9 | 10 | 11 | 12 | 13 |
| 14 | 15 | 16 | 17 | 18 | 19 | 20 |
| 21 | 22 | 23 | 24 | 25 | 26 | 27 |
| 28 | 29 | 30 | | | | |

**MAY**

| S | M | T | W | T | F | S |
|---|---|---|---|---|---|---|
| | | | 1 | 2 | 3 | 4 |
| 5 | 6 | 7 | 8 | 9 | 10 | 11 |
| 12 | 13 | 14 | 15 | 16 | 17 | 18 |
| 19 | 20 | 21 | 22 | 23 | 24 | 25 |
| 26 | 27 | 28 | 29 | 30 | 31 | |

**JUNE**

| S | M | T | W | T | F | S |
|---|---|---|---|---|---|---|
| | | | | | | 1 |
| 2 | 3 | 4 | 5 | 6 | 7 | 8 |
| 9 | 10 | 11 | 12 | 13 | 14 | 15 |
| 16 | 17 | 18 | 19 | 20 | 21 | 22 |
| 23 | 24 | 25 | 26 | 27 | 28 | 29 |
| 30 | | | | | | |

**JULY**

| S | M | T | W | T | F | S |
|---|---|---|---|---|---|---|
| | 1 | 2 | 3 | 4 | 5 | 6 |
| 7 | 8 | 9 | 10 | 11 | 12 | 13 |
| 14 | 15 | 16 | 17 | 18 | 19 | 20 |
| 21 | 22 | 23 | 24 | 25 | 26 | 27 |
| 28 | 29 | 30 | 31 | | | |

**AUGUST**

| S | M | T | W | T | F | S |
|---|---|---|---|---|---|---|
| | | | | 1 | 2 | 3 |
| 4 | 5 | 6 | 7 | 8 | 9 | 10 |
| 11 | 12 | 13 | 14 | 15 | 16 | 17 |
| 18 | 19 | 20 | 21 | 22 | 23 | 24 |
| 25 | 26 | 27 | 28 | 29 | 30 | 31 |

**SEPTEMBER**

| S | M | T | W | T | F | S |
|---|---|---|---|---|---|---|
| 1 | 2 | 3 | 4 | 5 | 6 | 7 |
| 8 | 9 | 10 | 11 | 12 | 13 | 14 |
| 15 | 16 | 17 | 18 | 19 | 20 | 21 |
| 22 | 23 | 24 | 25 | 26 | 27 | 28 |
| 29 | 30 | | | | | |

**OCTOBER**

| S | M | T | W | T | F | S |
|---|---|---|---|---|---|---|
| | | 1 | 2 | 3 | 4 | 5 |
| 6 | 7 | 8 | 9 | 10 | 11 | 12 |
| 13 | 14 | 15 | 16 | 17 | 18 | 19 |
| 20 | 21 | 22 | 23 | 24 | 25 | 26 |
| 27 | 28 | 29 | 30 | 31 | | |

**NOVEMBER**

| S | M | T | W | T | F | S |
|---|---|---|---|---|---|---|
| | | | | | 1 | 2 |
| 3 | 4 | 5 | 6 | 7 | 8 | 9 |
| 10 | 11 | 12 | 13 | 14 | 15 | 16 |
| 17 | 18 | 19 | 20 | 21 | 22 | 23 |
| 24 | 25 | 26 | 27 | 28 | 29 | 30 |

**DECEMBER**

| S | M | T | W | T | F | S |
|---|---|---|---|---|---|---|
| 1 | 2 | 3 | 4 | 5 | 6 | 7 |
| 8 | 9 | 10 | 11 | 12 | 13 | 14 |
| 15 | 16 | 17 | 18 | 19 | 20 | 21 |
| 22 | 23 | 24 | 25 | 26 | 27 | 28 |
| 29 | 30 | 31 | | | | |

## 4

**JANUARY**

| S | M | T | W | T | F | S |
|---|---|---|---|---|---|---|
| | | | 1 | 2 | 3 | 4 |
| 5 | 6 | 7 | 8 | 9 | 10 | 11 |
| 12 | 13 | 14 | 15 | 16 | 17 | 18 |
| 19 | 20 | 21 | 22 | 23 | 24 | 25 |
| 26 | 27 | 28 | 29 | 30 | 31 | |

**FEBRUARY**

| S | M | T | W | T | F | S |
|---|---|---|---|---|---|---|
| | | | | | | 1 |
| 2 | 3 | 4 | 5 | 6 | 7 | 8 |
| 9 | 10 | 11 | 12 | 13 | 14 | 15 |
| 16 | 17 | 18 | 19 | 20 | 21 | 22 |
| 23 | 24 | 25 | 26 | 27 | 28 | |

**MARCH**

| S | M | T | W | T | F | S |
|---|---|---|---|---|---|---|
| | | | | | | 1 |
| 2 | 3 | 4 | 5 | 6 | 7 | 8 |
| 9 | 10 | 11 | 12 | 13 | 14 | 15 |
| 16 | 17 | 18 | 19 | 20 | 21 | 22 |
| 23 | 24 | 25 | 26 | 27 | 28 | 29 |
| 30 | 31 | | | | | |

**APRIL**

| S | M | T | W | T | F | S |
|---|---|---|---|---|---|---|
| | | 1 | 2 | 3 | 4 | 5 |
| 6 | 7 | 8 | 9 | 10 | 11 | 12 |
| 13 | 14 | 15 | 16 | 17 | 18 | 19 |
| 20 | 21 | 22 | 23 | 24 | 25 | 26 |
| 27 | 28 | 29 | 30 | | | |

**MAY**

| S | M | T | W | T | F | S |
|---|---|---|---|---|---|---|
| | | | | 1 | 2 | 3 |
| 4 | 5 | 6 | 7 | 8 | 9 | 10 |
| 11 | 12 | 13 | 14 | 15 | 16 | 17 |
| 18 | 19 | 20 | 21 | 22 | 23 | 24 |
| 25 | 26 | 27 | 28 | 29 | 30 | 31 |

**JUNE**

| S | M | T | W | T | F | S |
|---|---|---|---|---|---|---|
| 1 | 2 | 3 | 4 | 5 | 6 | 7 |
| 8 | 9 | 10 | 11 | 12 | 13 | 14 |
| 15 | 16 | 17 | 18 | 19 | 20 | 21 |
| 22 | 23 | 24 | 25 | 26 | 27 | 28 |
| 29 | 30 | | | | | |

**JULY**

| S | M | T | W | T | F | S |
|---|---|---|---|---|---|---|
| | | 1 | 2 | 3 | 4 | 5 |
| 6 | 7 | 8 | 9 | 10 | 11 | 12 |
| 13 | 14 | 15 | 16 | 17 | 18 | 19 |
| 20 | 21 | 22 | 23 | 24 | 25 | 26 |
| 27 | 28 | 29 | 30 | 31 | | |

**AUGUST**

| S | M | T | W | T | F | S |
|---|---|---|---|---|---|---|
| | | | | | 1 | 2 |
| 3 | 4 | 5 | 6 | 7 | 8 | 9 |
| 10 | 11 | 12 | 13 | 14 | 15 | 16 |
| 17 | 18 | 19 | 20 | 21 | 22 | 23 |
| 24 | 25 | 26 | 27 | 28 | 29 | 30 |
| 31 | | | | | | |

**SEPTEMBER**

| S | M | T | W | T | F | S |
|---|---|---|---|---|---|---|
| | 1 | 2 | 3 | 4 | 5 | 6 |
| 7 | 8 | 9 | 10 | 11 | 12 | 13 |
| 14 | 15 | 16 | 17 | 18 | 19 | 20 |
| 21 | 22 | 23 | 24 | 25 | 26 | 27 |
| 28 | 29 | 30 | | | | |

**OCTOBER**

| S | M | T | W | T | F | S |
|---|---|---|---|---|---|---|
| | | | 1 | 2 | 3 | 4 |
| 5 | 6 | 7 | 8 | 9 | 10 | 11 |
| 12 | 13 | 14 | 15 | 16 | 17 | 18 |
| 19 | 20 | 21 | 22 | 23 | 24 | 25 |
| 26 | 27 | 28 | 29 | 30 | 31 | |

**NOVEMBER**

| S | M | T | W | T | F | S |
|---|---|---|---|---|---|---|
| | | | | | | 1 |
| 2 | 3 | 4 | 5 | 6 | 7 | 8 |
| 9 | 10 | 11 | 12 | 13 | 14 | 15 |
| 16 | 17 | 18 | 19 | 20 | 21 | 22 |
| 23 | 24 | 25 | 26 | 27 | 28 | 29 |
| 30 | | | | | | |

**DECEMBER**

| S | M | T | W | T | F | S |
|---|---|---|---|---|---|---|
| | 1 | 2 | 3 | 4 | 5 | 6 |
| 7 | 8 | 9 | 10 | 11 | 12 | 13 |
| 14 | 15 | 16 | 17 | 18 | 19 | 20 |
| 21 | 22 | 23 | 24 | 25 | 26 | 27 |
| 28 | 29 | 30 | 31 | | | |

## 5

**JANUARY**

| S | M | T | W | T | F | S |
|---|---|---|---|---|---|---|
| | | | | 1 | 2 | 3 |
| 4 | 5 | 6 | 7 | 8 | 9 | 10 |
| 11 | 12 | 13 | 14 | 15 | 16 | 17 |
| 18 | 19 | 20 | 21 | 22 | 23 | 24 |
| 25 | 26 | 27 | 28 | 29 | 30 | 31 |

**FEBRUARY**

| S | M | T | W | T | F | S |
|---|---|---|---|---|---|---|
| 1 | 2 | 3 | 4 | 5 | 6 | 7 |
| 8 | 9 | 10 | 11 | 12 | 13 | 14 |
| 15 | 16 | 17 | 18 | 19 | 20 | 21 |
| 22 | 23 | 24 | 25 | 26 | 27 | 28 |

**MARCH**

| S | M | T | W | T | F | S |
|---|---|---|---|---|---|---|
| 1 | 2 | 3 | 4 | 5 | 6 | 7 |
| 8 | 9 | 10 | 11 | 12 | 13 | 14 |
| 15 | 16 | 17 | 18 | 19 | 20 | 21 |
| 22 | 23 | 24 | 25 | 26 | 27 | 28 |
| 29 | 30 | 31 | | | | |

**APRIL**

| S | M | T | W | T | F | S |
|---|---|---|---|---|---|---|
| | | | 1 | 2 | 3 | 4 |
| 5 | 6 | 7 | 8 | 9 | 10 | 11 |
| 12 | 13 | 14 | 15 | 16 | 17 | 18 |
| 19 | 20 | 21 | 22 | 23 | 24 | 25 |
| 26 | 27 | 28 | 29 | 30 | | |

**MAY**

| S | M | T | W | T | F | S |
|---|---|---|---|---|---|---|
| | | | | | 1 | 2 |
| 3 | 4 | 5 | 6 | 7 | 8 | 9 |
| 10 | 11 | 12 | 13 | 14 | 15 | 16 |
| 17 | 18 | 19 | 20 | 21 | 22 | 23 |
| 24 | 25 | 26 | 27 | 28 | 29 | 30 |
| 31 | | | | | | |

**JUNE**

| S | M | T | W | T | F | S |
|---|---|---|---|---|---|---|
| | 1 | 2 | 3 | 4 | 5 | 6 |
| 7 | 8 | 9 | 10 | 11 | 12 | 13 |
| 14 | 15 | 16 | 17 | 18 | 19 | 20 |
| 21 | 22 | 23 | 24 | 25 | 26 | 27 |
| 28 | 29 | 30 | | | | |

**JULY**

| S | M | T | W | T | F | S |
|---|---|---|---|---|---|---|
| | | | 1 | 2 | 3 | 4 |
| 5 | 6 | 7 | 8 | 9 | 10 | 11 |
| 12 | 13 | 14 | 15 | 16 | 17 | 18 |
| 19 | 20 | 21 | 22 | 23 | 24 | 25 |
| 26 | 27 | 28 | 29 | 30 | 31 | |

**AUGUST**

| S | M | T | W | T | F | S |
|---|---|---|---|---|---|---|
| | | | | | | 1 |
| 2 | 3 | 4 | 5 | 6 | 7 | 8 |
| 9 | 10 | 11 | 12 | 13 | 14 | 15 |
| 16 | 17 | 18 | 19 | 20 | 21 | 22 |
| 23 | 24 | 25 | 26 | 27 | 28 | 29 |
| 30 | 31 | | | | | |

**SEPTEMBER**

| S | M | T | W | T | F | S |
|---|---|---|---|---|---|---|
| | | 1 | 2 | 3 | 4 | 5 |
| 6 | 7 | 8 | 9 | 10 | 11 | 12 |
| 13 | 14 | 15 | 16 | 17 | 18 | 19 |
| 20 | 21 | 22 | 23 | 24 | 25 | 26 |
| 27 | 28 | 29 | 30 | | | |

**OCTOBER**

| S | M | T | W | T | F | S |
|---|---|---|---|---|---|---|
| | | | | 1 | 2 | 3 |
| 4 | 5 | 6 | 7 | 8 | 9 | 10 |
| 11 | 12 | 13 | 14 | 15 | 16 | 17 |
| 18 | 19 | 20 | 21 | 22 | 23 | 24 |
| 25 | 26 | 27 | 28 | 29 | 30 | 31 |

**NOVEMBER**

| S | M | T | W | T | F | S |
|---|---|---|---|---|---|---|
| 1 | 2 | 3 | 4 | 5 | 6 | 7 |
| 8 | 9 | 10 | 11 | 12 | 13 | 14 |
| 15 | 16 | 17 | 18 | 19 | 20 | 21 |
| 22 | 23 | 24 | 25 | 26 | 27 | 28 |
| 29 | 30 | | | | | |

**DECEMBER**

| S | M | T | W | T | F | S |
|---|---|---|---|---|---|---|
| | | 1 | 2 | 3 | 4 | 5 |
| 6 | 7 | 8 | 9 | 10 | 11 | 12 |
| 13 | 14 | 15 | 16 | 17 | 18 | 19 |
| 20 | 21 | 22 | 23 | 24 | 25 | 26 |
| 27 | 28 | 29 | 30 | 31 | | |

## 6

**JANUARY**

| S | M | T | W | T | F | S |
|---|---|---|---|---|---|---|
| | | | | | 1 | 2 |
| 3 | 4 | 5 | 6 | 7 | 8 | 9 |
| 10 | 11 | 12 | 13 | 14 | 15 | 16 |
| 17 | 18 | 19 | 20 | 21 | 22 | 23 |
| 24 | 25 | 26 | 27 | 28 | 29 | 30 |
| 31 | | | | | | |

**FEBRUARY**

| S | M | T | W | T | F | S |
|---|---|---|---|---|---|---|
| | 1 | 2 | 3 | 4 | 5 | 6 |
| 7 | 8 | 9 | 10 | 11 | 12 | 13 |
| 14 | 15 | 16 | 17 | 18 | 19 | 20 |
| 21 | 22 | 23 | 24 | 25 | 26 | 27 |
| 28 | | | | | | |

**MARCH**

| S | M | T | W | T | F | S |
|---|---|---|---|---|---|---|
| | 1 | 2 | 3 | 4 | 5 | 6 |
| 7 | 8 | 9 | 10 | 11 | 12 | 13 |
| 14 | 15 | 16 | 17 | 18 | 19 | 20 |
| 21 | 22 | 23 | 24 | 25 | 26 | 27 |
| 28 | 29 | 30 | 31 | | | |

**APRIL**

| S | M | T | W | T | F | S |
|---|---|---|---|---|---|---|
| | | | | 1 | 2 | 3 |
| 4 | 5 | 6 | 7 | 8 | 9 | 10 |
| 11 | 12 | 13 | 14 | 15 | 16 | 17 |
| 18 | 19 | 20 | 21 | 22 | 23 | 24 |
| 25 | 26 | 27 | 28 | 29 | 30 | |

**MAY**

| S | M | T | W | T | F | S |
|---|---|---|---|---|---|---|
| | | | | | | 1 |
| 2 | 3 | 4 | 5 | 6 | 7 | 8 |
| 9 | 10 | 11 | 12 | 13 | 14 | 15 |
| 16 | 17 | 18 | 19 | 20 | 21 | 22 |
| 23 | 24 | 25 | 26 | 27 | 28 | 29 |
| 30 | 31 | | | | | |

**JUNE**

| S | M | T | W | T | F | S |
|---|---|---|---|---|---|---|
| | | 1 | 2 | 3 | 4 | 5 |
| 6 | 7 | 8 | 9 | 10 | 11 | 12 |
| 13 | 14 | 15 | 16 | 17 | 18 | 19 |
| 20 | 21 | 22 | 23 | 24 | 25 | 26 |
| 27 | 28 | 29 | 30 | | | |

**JULY**

| S | M | T | W | T | F | S |
|---|---|---|---|---|---|---|
| | | | | 1 | 2 | 3 |
| 4 | 5 | 6 | 7 | 8 | 9 | 10 |
| 11 | 12 | 13 | 14 | 15 | 16 | 17 |
| 18 | 19 | 20 | 21 | 22 | 23 | 24 |
| 25 | 26 | 27 | 28 | 29 | 30 | 31 |

**AUGUST**

| S | M | T | W | T | F | S |
|---|---|---|---|---|---|---|
| 1 | 2 | 3 | 4 | 5 | 6 | 7 |
| 8 | 9 | 10 | 11 | 12 | 13 | 14 |
| 15 | 16 | 17 | 18 | 19 | 20 | 21 |
| 22 | 23 | 24 | 25 | 26 | 27 | 28 |
| 29 | 30 | 31 | | | | |

**SEPTEMBER**

| S | M | T | W | T | F | S |
|---|---|---|---|---|---|---|
| | | | 1 | 2 | 3 | 4 |
| 5 | 6 | 7 | 8 | 9 | 10 | 11 |
| 12 | 13 | 14 | 15 | 16 | 17 | 18 |
| 19 | 20 | 21 | 22 | 23 | 24 | 25 |
| 26 | 27 | 28 | 29 | 30 | | |

**OCTOBER**

| S | M | T | W | T | F | S |
|---|---|---|---|---|---|---|
| | | | | | 1 | 2 |
| 3 | 4 | 5 | 6 | 7 | 8 | 9 |
| 10 | 11 | 12 | 13 | 14 | 15 | 16 |
| 17 | 18 | 19 | 20 | 21 | 22 | 23 |
| 24 | 25 | 26 | 27 | 28 | 29 | 30 |
| 31 | | | | | | |

**NOVEMBER**

| S | M | T | W | T | F | S |
|---|---|---|---|---|---|---|
| | 1 | 2 | 3 | 4 | 5 | 6 |
| 7 | 8 | 9 | 10 | 11 | 12 | 13 |
| 14 | 15 | 16 | 17 | 18 | 19 | 20 |
| 21 | 22 | 23 | 24 | 25 | 26 | 27 |
| 28 | 29 | 30 | | | | |

**DECEMBER**

| S | M | T | W | T | F | S |
|---|---|---|---|---|---|---|
| | | | 1 | 2 | 3 | 4 |
| 5 | 6 | 7 | 8 | 9 | 10 | 11 |
| 12 | 13 | 14 | 15 | 16 | 17 | 18 |
| 19 | 20 | 21 | 22 | 23 | 24 | 25 |
| 26 | 27 | 28 | 29 | 30 | 31 | |

**Directions:** All of the possible calendars are shown on these two pages. Look for the year on the chart to the left, and use the number listed beside it to find the correct calendar.

## 7

| JANUARY | FEBRUARY | MARCH | APRIL |
|---|---|---|---|
| S M T W T F S | S M T W T F S | S M T W T F S | S M T W T F S |

| MAY | JUNE | JULY | AUGUST |
|---|---|---|---|

| SEPTEMBER | OCTOBER | NOVEMBER | DECEMBER |
|---|---|---|---|

## 8

| JANUARY | FEBRUARY | MARCH | APRIL |
|---|---|---|---|

| MAY | JUNE | JULY | AUGUST |
|---|---|---|---|

| SEPTEMBER | OCTOBER | NOVEMBER | DECEMBEER |
|---|---|---|---|

## 9

| JANUARY | FEBRUARY | MARCH | APRIL |
|---|---|---|---|

| MAY | JUNE | JULY | AUGUST |
|---|---|---|---|

| SEPTEMBER | OCTOBER | NOVEMBER | DECEMBER |
|---|---|---|---|

## 10

| JANUARY | FEBRUARY | MARCH | APRIL |
|---|---|---|---|

| MAY | JUNE | JULY | AUGUST |
|---|---|---|---|

| SEPTEMBER | OCTOBER | NOVEMBER | DECEMBER |
|---|---|---|---|

## 11

| JANUARY | FEBRUARY | MARCH | APRIL |
|---|---|---|---|

| MAY | JUNE | JULY | AUGUST |
|---|---|---|---|

| SEPTEMBER | OCTOBER | NOVEMBER | DECEMBER |
|---|---|---|---|

## 12

| JANUARY | FEBRUARY | MARCH | APRIL |
|---|---|---|---|

| MAY | JUNE | JULY | AUGUST |
|---|---|---|---|

| SEPTEMBER | OCTOBER | NOVEMBER | DECEMBER |
|---|---|---|---|

## 13

| JANUARY | FEBRUARY | MARCH | APRIL |
|---|---|---|---|

| MAY | JUNE | JULY | AUGUST |
|---|---|---|---|

| SEPTEMBER | OCTOBER | NOVEMBER | DECEMBER |
|---|---|---|---|

## 14

| JANUARY | FEBRUARY | MARCH | APRIL |
|---|---|---|---|

| MAY | JUNE | JULY | AUGUST |
|---|---|---|---|

| SEPTEMBER | OCTOBER | NOVEMBER | DECEMBER |
|---|---|---|---|

# 1991

### January
| S | M | T | W | T | F | S |
|---|---|---|---|---|---|---|
|   |   | **1** | 2 | 3 | 4 | 5 |
| 6 | 7 | 8 | 9 | 10 | 11 | 12 |
| 13 | 14 | 15 | 16 | 17 | 18 | 19 |
| 20 | **21** | 22 | 23 | 24 | 25 | 26 |
| 27 | 28 | 29 | 30 | 31 |   |   |

### February
| S | M | T | W | T | F | S |
|---|---|---|---|---|---|---|
|   |   |   |   |   | 1 | **2** |
| 3 | 4 | 5 | 6 | 7 | 8 | 9 |
| 10 | 11 | **12** | 13 | **14** | 15 | 16 |
| 17 | **18** | 19 | 20 | 21 | 22 | 23 |
| 24 | 25 | 26 | 27 | 28 |   |   |

### March
| S | M | T | W | T | F | S |
|---|---|---|---|---|---|---|
|   |   |   |   |   | 1 | 2 |
| 3 | 4 | 5 | 6 | 7 | 8 | 9 |
| 10 | 11 | 12 | 13 | 14 | 15 | 16 |
| **17** | 18 | 19 | **20** | 21 | 22 | 23 |
| 24 | 25 | 26 | 27 | 28 | **29** | 30 |
| **31** |   |   |   |   |   |   |

### April
| S | M | T | W | T | F | S |
|---|---|---|---|---|---|---|
|   | 1 | 2 | 3 | 4 | 5 | 6 |
| 7 | 8 | 9 | 10 | 11 | 12 | 13 |
| 14 | 15 | 16 | 17 | 18 | 19 | 20 |
| 21 | 22 | 23 | 24 | 25 | 26 | 27 |
| 28 | 29 | 30 |   |   |   |   |

### May
| S | M | T | W | T | F | S |
|---|---|---|---|---|---|---|
|   |   |   | 1 | 2 | 3 | 4 |
| 5 | 6 | 7 | 8 | 9 | 10 | 11 |
| **12** | 13 | 14 | 15 | 16 | 17 | 18 |
| 19 | 20 | 21 | 22 | 23 | 24 | 25 |
| 26 | **27** | 28 | 29 | 30 | 31 |   |

### June
| S | M | T | W | T | F | S |
|---|---|---|---|---|---|---|
|   |   |   |   |   |   | 1 |
| 2 | 3 | 4 | 5 | 6 | 7 | 8 |
| 9 | 10 | 11 | 12 | 13 | **14** | 15 |
| **16** | 17 | 18 | 19 | 20 | **21** | 22 |
| 23 | 24 | 25 | 26 | 27 | 28 | 29 |
| 30 |   |   |   |   |   |   |

### July
| S | M | T | W | T | F | S |
|---|---|---|---|---|---|---|
|   | 1 | 2 | 3 | **4** | 5 | 6 |
| 7 | 8 | 9 | 10 | 11 | 12 | 13 |
| 14 | 15 | 16 | 17 | 18 | 19 | 20 |
| 21 | 22 | 23 | 24 | 25 | 26 | 27 |
| 28 | 29 | 30 | 31 |   |   |   |

### August
| S | M | T | W | T | F | S |
|---|---|---|---|---|---|---|
|   |   |   |   | 1 | 2 | 3 |
| 4 | 5 | 6 | 7 | 8 | 9 | 10 |
| 11 | 12 | 13 | 14 | 15 | 16 | 17 |
| 18 | 19 | 20 | 21 | 22 | 23 | 24 |
| 25 | 26 | 27 | 28 | 29 | 30 | 31 |

### September
| S | M | T | W | T | F | S |
|---|---|---|---|---|---|---|
| 1 | **2** | 3 | 4 | 5 | 6 | 7 |
| 8 | 9 | 10 | 11 | 12 | 13 | 14 |
| 15 | 16 | 17 | 18 | 19 | 20 | 21 |
| 22 | **23** | 24 | 25 | 26 | 27 | 28 |
| 29 | 30 |   |   |   |   |   |

### October
| S | M | T | W | T | F | S |
|---|---|---|---|---|---|---|
|   |   | 1 | 2 | 3 | 4 | 5 |
| 6 | 7 | 8 | 9 | 10 | 11 | 12 |
| 13 | **14** | 15 | 16 | 17 | 18 | 19 |
| 20 | 21 | 22 | 23 | 24 | 25 | 26 |
| 27 | 28 | 29 | 30 | **31** |   |   |

### November
| S | M | T | W | T | F | S |
|---|---|---|---|---|---|---|
|   |   |   |   |   | 1 | 2 |
| 3 | 4 | **5** | 6 | 7 | 8 | 9 |
| 10 | **11** | 12 | 13 | 14 | 15 | 16 |
| 17 | 18 | 19 | 20 | 21 | 22 | 23 |
| 24 | 25 | 26 | 27 | **28** | 29 | 30 |

### December
| S | M | T | W | T | F | S |
|---|---|---|---|---|---|---|
| 1 | 2 | 3 | 4 | 5 | 6 | 7 |
| 8 | 9 | 10 | 11 | 12 | 13 | 14 |
| 15 | 16 | 17 | 18 | 19 | 20 | 21 |
| **22** | 23 | 24 | **25** | 26 | 27 | 28 |
| 29 | 30 | 31 |   |   |   |   |

# 1992

### January
| S | M | T | W | T | F | S |
|---|---|---|---|---|---|---|
|   |   |   | **1** | 2 | 3 | 4 |
| 5 | 6 | 7 | 8 | 9 | 10 | 11 |
| 12 | 13 | 14 | 15 | 16 | 17 | 18 |
| 19 | **20** | 21 | 22 | 23 | 24 | 25 |
| 26 | 27 | 28 | 29 | 30 | 31 |   |

### February
| S | M | T | W | T | F | S |
|---|---|---|---|---|---|---|
|   |   |   |   |   |   | 1 |
| **2** | 3 | 4 | 5 | 6 | 7 | 8 |
| 9 | 10 | 11 | **12** | 13 | **14** | 15 |
| 16 | **17** | 18 | 19 | 20 | 21 | 22 |
| 23 | 24 | 25 | 26 | 27 | 28 | 29 |

### March
| S | M | T | W | T | F | S |
|---|---|---|---|---|---|---|
| 1 | 2 | 3 | 4 | 5 | 6 | 7 |
| 8 | 9 | 10 | 11 | 12 | 13 | 14 |
| 15 | 16 | **17** | 18 | 19 | **20** | 21 |
| 22 | 23 | 24 | 25 | 26 | 27 | 28 |
| 29 | 30 | 31 |   |   |   |   |

### April
| S | M | T | W | T | F | S |
|---|---|---|---|---|---|---|
|   |   |   | 1 | 2 | 3 | 4 |
| 5 | 6 | 7 | 8 | 9 | 10 | 11 |
| 12 | 13 | 14 | 15 | 16 | **17** | 18 |
| **19** | 20 | 21 | 22 | 23 | 24 | 25 |
| 26 | 27 | 28 | 29 | 30 |   |   |

### May
| S | M | T | W | T | F | S |
|---|---|---|---|---|---|---|
|   |   |   |   |   | 1 | 2 |
| 3 | 4 | 5 | 6 | 7 | 8 | 9 |
| **10** | 11 | 12 | 13 | 14 | 15 | 16 |
| 17 | 18 | 19 | 20 | 21 | 22 | 23 |
| 24 | **25** | 26 | 27 | 28 | 29 | 30 |
| 31 |   |   |   |   |   |   |

### June
| S | M | T | W | T | F | S |
|---|---|---|---|---|---|---|
|   | 1 | 2 | 3 | 4 | 5 | 6 |
| 7 | 8 | 9 | 10 | 11 | 12 | 13 |
| **14** | 15 | 16 | 17 | 18 | 19 | **20** |
| **21** | 22 | 23 | 24 | 25 | 26 | 27 |
| 28 | 29 | 30 |   |   |   |   |

### July
| S | M | T | W | T | F | S |
|---|---|---|---|---|---|---|
|   |   |   | 1 | 2 | 3 | **4** |
| 5 | 6 | 7 | 8 | 9 | 10 | 11 |
| 12 | 13 | 14 | 15 | 16 | 17 | 18 |
| 19 | 20 | 21 | 22 | 23 | 24 | 25 |
| 26 | 27 | 28 | 29 | 30 | 31 |   |

### August
| S | M | T | W | T | F | S |
|---|---|---|---|---|---|---|
|   |   |   |   |   |   | 1 |
| 2 | 3 | 4 | 5 | 6 | 7 | 8 |
| 9 | 10 | 11 | 12 | 13 | 14 | 15 |
| 16 | 17 | 18 | 19 | 20 | 21 | 22 |
| 23 | 24 | 25 | 26 | 27 | 28 | 29 |
| 30 | 31 |   |   |   |   |   |

### September
| S | M | T | W | T | F | S |
|---|---|---|---|---|---|---|
|   |   | 1 | 2 | 3 | 4 | 5 |
| 6 | **7** | 8 | 9 | 10 | 11 | 12 |
| 13 | 14 | 15 | 16 | 17 | 18 | 19 |
| 20 | 21 | **22** | 23 | 24 | 25 | 26 |
| 27 | 28 | 29 | 30 |   |   |   |

### October
| S | M | T | W | T | F | S |
|---|---|---|---|---|---|---|
|   |   |   |   | 1 | 2 | 3 |
| 4 | 5 | 6 | 7 | 8 | 9 | 10 |
| 11 | **12** | 13 | 14 | 15 | 16 | 17 |
| 18 | 19 | 20 | 21 | 22 | 23 | 24 |
| 25 | 26 | 27 | 28 | 29 | 30 | **31** |

### November
| S | M | T | W | T | F | S |
|---|---|---|---|---|---|---|
| 1 | 2 | **3** | 4 | 5 | 6 | 7 |
| 8 | 9 | 10 | **11** | 12 | 13 | 14 |
| 15 | 16 | 17 | 18 | 19 | 20 | 21 |
| 22 | 23 | 24 | 25 | **26** | 27 | 28 |
| 29 | 30 |   |   |   |   |   |

### December
| S | M | T | W | T | F | S |
|---|---|---|---|---|---|---|
|   |   | 1 | 2 | 3 | 4 | 5 |
| 6 | 7 | 8 | 9 | 10 | 11 | 12 |
| 13 | 14 | 15 | 16 | 17 | 18 | 19 |
| 20 | **21** | 22 | 23 | 24 | **25** | 26 |
| 27 | 28 | 29 | 30 | 31 |   |   |

# 1993

### January
```
S  M  T  W  T  F  S
            1  2
3  4  5  6  7  8  9
10 11 12 13 14 15 16
17 18 19 20 21 22 23
24 25 26 27 28 29 30
31
```

### February
```
S  M  T  W  T  F  S
   1  2  3  4  5  6
7  8  9  10 11 12 13
14 15 16 17 18 19 20
21 22 23 24 25 26 27
28
```

### March
```
S  M  T  W  T  F  S
   1  2  3  4  5  6
7  8  9  10 11 12 13
14 15 16 17 18 19 20
21 22 23 24 25 26 27
28 29 30 31
```

### April
```
S  M  T  W  T  F  S
            1  2  3
4  5  6  7  8  9  10
11 12 13 14 15 16 17
18 19 20 21 22 23 24
25 26 27 28 29 30
```

### May
```
S  M  T  W  T  F  S
                  1
2  3  4  5  6  7  8
9  10 11 12 13 14 15
16 17 18 19 20 21 22
23 24 25 26 27 28 29
30 31
```

### June
```
S  M  T  W  T  F  S
      1  2  3  4  5
6  7  8  9  10 11 12
13 14 15 16 17 18 19
20 21 22 23 24 25 26
27 28 29 30
```

### July
```
S  M  T  W  T  F  S
            1  2  3
4  5  6  7  8  9  10
11 12 13 14 15 16 17
18 19 20 21 22 23 24
25 26 27 28 29 30 31
```

### August
```
S  M  T  W  T  F  S
1  2  3  4  5  6  7
8  9  10 11 12 13 14
15 16 17 18 19 20 21
22 23 24 25 26 27 28
29 30 31
```

### September
```
S  M  T  W  T  F  S
      1  2  3  4
5  6  7  8  9  10 11
12 13 14 15 16 17 18
19 20 21 22 23 24 25
26 27 28 29 30
```

### October
```
S  M  T  W  T  F  S
               1  2
3  4  5  6  7  8  9
10 11 12 13 14 15 16
17 18 19 20 21 22 23
24 25 26 27 28 29 30
31
```

### November
```
S  M  T  W  T  F  S
   1  2  3  4  5  6
7  8  9  10 11 12 13
14 15 16 17 18 19 20
21 22 23 24 25 26 27
28 29 30
```

### December
```
S  M  T  W  T  F  S
         1  2  3  4
5  6  7  8  9  10 11
12 13 14 15 16 17 18
19 20 21 22 23 24 25
26 27 28 29 30 31
```

| HOLIDAY | 1991 | 1992 | 1993 |
|---|---|---|---|
| New Years Day | Tuesday, January 1 | Wednesday, January 1 | Friday, January 1 |
| Martin Luther King, Jr. Day* | Monday, January 21 | Monday, January 20 | Monday, January 18 |
| Ground Hog Day | Saturday, February 2 | Sunday, February 2 | Tuesday, February 2 |
| Lincoln's Birthday | Tuesday, February 12 | Wednesday, February 12 | Friday, February 12 |
| Valentine's Day | Thursday, February 14 | Friday, February 14 | Sunday, February 14 |
| Washington's Birthday* | Monday, February 18 | Monday, February 17 | Monday, February 15 |
| St. Patrick's Day | Sunday, March 17 | Tuesday, March 17 | Wednesday, March 17 |
| First Day of Spring | Wednesday, March 20 | Friday, March 20 | Saturday, March 20 |
| Good Friday | Friday, March 29 | Friday, April 17 | Friday, April 9 |
| Easter | Sunday, March 31 | Sunday, April 19 | Sunday, April 11 |
| Mother's Day | Sunday, May 12 | Sunday, May 10 | Sunday, May 9 |
| Memorial Day* | Monday, May 27 | Monday, May 25 | Monday, May 31 |
| Flag Day | Friday, June 14 | Sunday, June 14 | Monday, June 14 |
| Father's Day | Sunday, June 16 | Sunday, June 21 | Sunday, June 20 |
| First Day of Summer | Friday, June 21 | Saturday, June 20 | Monday, June 21 |
| Independence Day | Thursday, July 4 | Saturday, July 4 | Sunday, July 4 |
| Labor Day | Monday, September 2 | Monday, September 7 | Monday, September 6 |
| First Day of Autumn | Monday, September 23 | Tuesday, September 22 | Wednesday, September 22 |
| Columbus Day* | Monday, October 14 | Monday, October 12 | Monday, October 11 |
| Halloween | Thursday, October 31 | Saturday, October 31 | Sunday, October 31 |
| Election Day | Tuesday, November 5 | Tuesday, November 3 | Tuesday, November 2 |
| Veterans Day | Monday, November 11 | Wednesday, November 11 | Thursday, November 11 |
| Thanksgiving | Thursday, November 28 | Thursday, November 26 | Thursday, November 25 |
| First Day of Winter | Sunday, December 22 | Monday, December 21 | Tuesday, December 21 |
| Christmas | Wednesday, December 25 | Friday, December 25 | Saturday, December 25 |

*Legal holiday observed

# MAJOR HOLIDAYS AND SPECIAL DAYS

The word "holiday" comes from "holy day." Originally, all holidays were religious celebrations but now the word means any special day, particularly when people do not have to work. A "legal holiday" is the day a holiday is celebrated to allow workers to have long weekends. Since 1971, Washington's Birthday, Memorial Day and Columbus Day have been celebrated on Mondays. The holidays listed below are those most commonly observed in the United States. People of religions other than Christianity celebrate a number of other important holidays.

**NEW YEAR'S DAY**—January 1. In Roman times, the first day of the new year was the special day of the god Janus, who had two faces, one looking forward to the future, and one looking back to the past.

P. Hamann

**MARTIN LUTHER KING JR.'S BIRTHDAY**—January 15. This holiday, first celebrated in 1986, honors the famous civil rights leader who was assassinated in 1968. He was born on January 15, 1929. The legal holiday is the third Monday in January.

**GROUND HOG DAY**—February 2. The ground hog, or woodchuck, supposedly awakens from its winter sleep on this day. It sticks its head out of its burrow and looks around. If it is sunny and it sees its shadow, it is frightened and goes back into its hole to sleep. This means there will be another six weeks of wintery weather. If the day is cloudy and the ground hog cannot see its shadow, it comes out of its hole, and spring weather will come soon. There is no scientific basis for this bit of folklore.

**LINCOLN'S BIRTHDAY**—February 12. President Abraham Lincoln was born on  February 12, 1809. He was president of the United States during the Civil War, and his leadership kept the country from splitting apart. His birthday has been observed since 1866.

**VALENTINE'S DAY**—February 14. The patron saint of this day is St. Valentine. Valentine's Day is usually celebrated by exchanging Valentine's cards and candy with sweethearts and friends. The Valentine's Day colors are red and pink.

**WASHINGTON'S BIRTHDAY**—February 22. President George Washington, the first president of the United States, was born on February 22, 1732. His birthday has been celebrated since 1796. The legal holiday is celebrated on the third Monday in February.

**LEAP YEAR DAY**—February 29. A year is the amount of time it takes the earth to revolve around the sun. It takes almost exactly 365¼ days. Because of the ¼ day, every fourth year has an extra day added onto February, the 29th. Years in which February has 29 days can be divided by the number 4 and are called "Leap Years". See page 12 for more about Leap Year.

**ST. PATRICK'S DAY**—March 17. The patron saint of Ireland, St. Patrick, has been honored on this day since the United States began. The day is celebrated by wearing green, and by the St. Patrick's Day Parade in New York City. The shamrock is the symbol of St. Patrick's Day and green is the color.

**FIRST DAY OF SPRING**—March 20 or 21. On this day, the hours of daylight and the hours of darkness are equal. Between now and the year 2000, the first day of spring each year will be March 20.

**GOOD FRIDAY**—The Friday before Easter. This is the day observed by Christians as the anniversary of Christ's death on the cross.

**EASTER**—Easter is celebrated the Sunday after the first full moon on or after March 21. It is always between March 22 and April 25, but the actual date is different each year. This

Christian holiday is to remember the Resurrection of Jesus Christ. It is frequently celebrated with special church services. One common tradition is the dying of hard-boiled eggs, which may be hidden by the "Easter bunny." Children search for the eggs Easter morning. Easter colors are usually pastel pink, blue, and yellow and the Easter lily is the flower. Below are dates for Easter between 1989 and 2000:

| 1989 | March 26 | 1995 | April 16 |
| 1990 | April 15 | 1996 | April 7 |
| 1991 | March 31 | 1997 | March 30 |
| 1992 | April 19 | 1998 | April 12 |
| 1993 | April 11 | 1999 | April 4 |
| 1994 | April 3 | 2000 | April 23 |

**DAYLIGHT SAVING TIME BEGINS**—First Sunday in April. On this day, clocks are moved forward one hour. This means people must get up one hour earlier. Daylight Saving is a period of time during which all clocks are set ahead of standard time by one hour. This means that, according to the clocks, the sun rises and sets an hour earlier, "saving" that hour of daylight for the evening. Daylight Saving was first used during World War I. In 1967, a Congressional act went into effect which proclaimed Daylight

Saving for the whole country. It begins the first Sunday in April and ends the last Sunday in October. To remember which way to change the clock: "Spring forward, fall back."

**MOTHER'S DAY**—The second Sunday in May. Mother's Day was first observed in 1907, and is a day to honor all mothers.

**MEMORIAL DAY**—May 31. Memorial Day, or Decoration Day, was first observed in 1866 to honor the memory of those who died in the Civil War by decorating their graves with flowers. It is now to remember all loved ones who have passed away, including those who have died in service to their country. The legal holiday is the last Monday in May.

**FLAG DAY**—June 14. On this day in 1777,  the Stars and Stripes was adopted as the United States flag. Flag Day is frequently observed by flying the U.S. flag from homes and businesses.

**FATHER'S DAY**—Third Sunday in June. Father's Day was first celebrated in 1910 as a day to honor all fathers.

**FIRST DAY OF SUMMER**—June 20 or 21. This is the longest day of the year in the northern hemisphere. Summer will begin on June 20 in 1992, 1996 and 2000. All other years until 2000, it will begin on June 21.

**INDEPENDENCE DAY**—July 4. This holiday is also called the Fourth of July. The Declaration of Independence was signed on this date in 1776. People frequently celebrate with picnics and fireworks displays.

**LABOR DAY**—First Monday in September. Labor Day honors those who labor — the working people of America. It was first celebrated in 1882, sponsored by the Central Labor Union of New York. It marks the end of summer and the beginning of the school year.

**FIRST DAY OF AUTUMN**—September 22 or 23. On this day, the hours of daylight and the hours of darkness are equal. Autumn will begin on September 23 in 1991, 1994, 1995 and 1999. All other years until 2000 it will begin September 22.

**COLUMBUS DAY**—October 12. On this holiday, people remember Columbus' discovery of America on October 12, 1492. The legal holiday is celebrated the second Monday in October.

**DAYLIGHT SAVING TIME ENDS**—Last Sunday in October. Clocks are moved back one hour on this day. This means people get an extra hour of sleep.

**HALLOWEEN**—October 31. Halloween is the eve of All Saint's Day, November 1. Halloween is commonly celebrated by wearing costumes, visiting haunted houses, telling ghost  stories and partying. Many people hollow out pumpkins and carve them into Jack-o-Lanterns which are lit from inside with a candle. Orange and black are the Halloween colors.

**ELECTION DAY**—First Tuesday after the first Monday in November. Since 1845, Presidential elections have been held on this date. State elections may also be held on this day.

**VETERANS DAY**—November 11. In 1918, the Armistice was signed ending World War I, which at that time was thought to be the "war to end all wars." The holiday was called "Armistice Day" until 1954, when it was changed to Veterans Day. It is now a day to honor the veterans of all wars.

**THANKSGIVING**—Fourth Thursday in November. Traditionally, Thanksgiving in the United States dates to the time of the Pilgrims in Plymouth Colony, who held a feast in 1621 to celebrate their first harvest after a long and difficult winter. Indians were invited and brought wild turkeys. Thanksgiving is  celebrated with large feasts, which usually have turkey as the main dish. The illustration shows a cornucopia, which is a symbol of nature's productivity. Thanksgiving is a time to give thanks for food and all the blessings of nature.

**FIRST DAY OF WINTER**—December 21 or 22. This is the shortest day of the year in the northern hemisphere. Winter will begin on December 22 in 1991, 1995 and 1999. In other years until 2000, it will begin December 21.

**CHRISTMAS**—December 25. Christmas celebrates the birth of Jesus Christ and is the most widely observed Christian holiday. Many people decorate their homes with wreaths, holly and poinsettias. Christmas trees are trimmed with tinsel and ornaments, and gifts are placed underneath to be exchanged and opened Christmas Eve or Christmas day. Children hang stockings to be filled with candy and small gifts by Santa Claus, a legendary old man who visits homes and delivers gifts on Christmas Eve while children sleep. During the Christmas season, people sing carols and send cards and letters to friends and relatives. Red and dark green are the Christmas colors.

# DAYS

The earth's axis is an imaginary line running from the North Pole to the South Pole through the center of the earth. The earth rotates, or spins, on its axis once every 24 hours. It is **daytime** for the half of the earth facing the sun and **nighttime** for the half facing away from the sun.

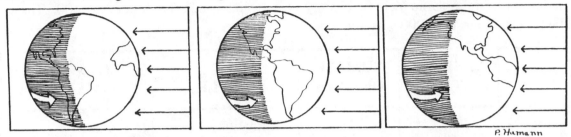

P. Humann

The earth is spinning very fast. A person standing still on the equator would be spinning with the earth at the speed of nearly 1,038 miles per hour (17 miles per minute).

| | | THE NAMES OF THE DAYS | | |
|---|---|---|---|---|
| DAY | ABBREVI-ATION | PLANET | LATIN NAME | SAXON NAME |
| Sunday | Sun. | Sun | Dies Solis | Sun's Day |
| Monday | Mon. | Moon | Dies Lunae | Moon's Day |
| Tuesday | Tues. | Mars | Dies Martis | Tiw's Day |
| Wednesday | Wed. | Mercury | Dies Mercurii | Woden's Day |
| Thursday | Thurs. | Jupiter | Dies Jovis | Thor's Day |
| Friday | Fri. | Venus | Dies Veneris | Frigg's Day |
| Saturday | Sat. | Saturn | Dies Saturni | Seterne's Day |

The Romans named the days of the week for the Sun, the Moon, and the five planets known at that time. The planets were named after Roman gods. The Anglo-Saxons later renamed the days by substituting the Norse gods for the Roman gods. For example, Mars is the Roman god of war, Tiw is the Norse god of war. Jupiter is the Roman god of thunder, Thor is the Norse god of thunder. Venus is the Roman goddess of love, Frigg is the Norse goddess of love. The English names of the days are based on the Anglo-Saxon names.

| NAMES OF THE DAYS IN FOREIGN LANGUAGES | | | | |
|---|---|---|---|---|
| ENGLISH | FRENCH | ITALIAN | SPANISH | GERMAN |
| Sunday | dimanche | domenica | domingo | Sonntag |
| Monday | lundi | lunedi | lunes | Montag |
| Tuesday | mardi | martedi | martes | Dienstag |
| Wednesday | mercredi | mercoledi | miercoles | Mittwoch |
| Thursday | jeudi | giovedi | jueves | Donnerstag |
| Friday | vendredi | venedri | viernes | Freitag |
| Saturday | samedi | sabato | sabado | Sonnabend |

NOTE: Names of the days are not capitalized in some languages.

# MONTHS

The calendar we use was drawn up by Pope Gregory XIII in 1582, and is called the Gregorian calendar. It has 12 months. Before then, people used the Julian Calendar, drawn up by Julius Caesar. The Julian calendar was almost the same as the Gregorian calendar. The main change Pope Gregory made was skipping Leap Year on century years which cannot be divided by 400. The year 2000 will be a Leap Year, but 1900 was not.

| MONTH | ABBREVI-ATION | NUMBER OF DAYS | FLOWER | GEM BIRTHSTONE |
|---|---|---|---|---|
| January | Jan. | 31 | Carnation Snowdrop | Garnet |
| February | Feb. | 28* | Primrose | Amethyst |
| March | Mar. | 31 | Violet | Aquamarine Bloodstone |
| April | Apr. | 30 | Daisy Sweet Pea | Diamond |
| May | May | 31 | Lily of the Valley Hawthorne | Emerald |
| June | June | 30 | Rose | Pearl Alexandrite |
| July | July | 31 | Water Lily | Ruby Star Ruby |
| August | Aug. | 31 | Poppy Gladiolus | Sardonyx Peridot |
| September | Sept. | 30 | Morning-Glory | Sapphire Star Sapphire |
| October | Oct. | 31 | Calendula | Opal Tourmaline |
| November | Nov. | 30 | Chrysanthemum | Topaz |
| December | Dec. | 31 | Holly Narcissus Poinsettia | Turquoise Zircon Lapis lazuli |

*Every fourth year is a "leap year," which means February has 29 days instead of 28. Leap years are those years evenly divisible by four, except century years unless they are divisible by 400.

This poem may be helpful in remembering how many days are in each month:

> Thirty days hath September,
> April, June and November.
> All the rest have thirty-one,
> Except February, which has 28.

# THE NAMES OF THE MONTHS

**January** was named after the Roman god Janus, the god of gates and doors. Janus had two faces, one looking into the past and one into the future.

**February** is from *februare,* a Latin word meaning "to purify."

**March** was named after Mars, the Roman god of war.

**April** is from *Aprilis,* which comes from a Latin word meaning "to open."

**May** is named after Maia, the Roman goddess of spring and growth.

**June** is named after Juno, the goddess of marriage.

**July** was named after the Roman emperor Julius Caesar, who was born during that month. Before then, it was *Quintilis,* or "fifth."*

**August** was named after the Roman emperor Augustus Caesar. It was originally *Sextilis,* which means "sixth."*

**September** is from *septum,* the Latin word meaning "seven." *

**October** is from the Latin word *octo,* meaning "eight."*

**November** is from the Latin word *novem,* meaning "nine."*

**December** is from *decem,* the Latin word for "ten."*

*The earliest Latin calendar began on March 1. Thus, July was the fifth month, August the sixth, September the seventh, October the eighth, November the ninth, and December the tenth. January and February were the last two months of the year. Julius Caesar changed the calendar in 46 B.C., beginning the year on January 1.

# WORLD CALENDARS

The **Gregorian calendar** is now the most widely used calendar in the world. It dates from the birth of Christ, in what is considered the year 0. The year 1990 is 1,990 years after Christ was born, and is correctly written 1990 A.D. A.D. stands for *anno Domini,* which is Latin for "in the year of our Lord." The years before Christ was born are counted backwards, and are followed by the letters B.C., which stands for "before Christ." Thus, 10 B.C. is 2 years earlier than 8 B.C. People of many religions, including those who do not believe in Christ, now use the Gregorian calendar. Instead of the letters B.C. and A.D., non-Christians often use C.E. and B.C.E., which stands for "common era" and "before common era."

The **Hebrew calendar** is used by people of the Jewish religion. It dates from the time they believe the earth was created, which is 3,760 years and three months before the common era. The year 1991 in the Hebrew calendar is 5751.

The Hebrew calendar has 12 months with different names than those we use. It is based on the moon.

The **Islamic calendar** is used by people of the Moslem religion. It dates from the year that Mohammed, the founder of the religion, escaped from Mecca to Medina, which is 622 A.D. in the Gregorian calendar. 1991 is the year 1369 in the Islamic countries. The Islamic calendar is based on the moon.

The **Chinese calendar** begins in 2637 B.C. of the Gregorian calendar, which is the year it was supposedly invented. The years are counted in cycles of 60. Each year is assigned one of twelve animal names, *rat, ox, tiger, hare, dragon, snake, horse, sheep, monkey, fowl, dog,* or *pig.* The Chinese calendar is based on the moon, so Chinese New Year changes each year. It is always between January 20 and February 20. The year 1991 is 4628 in China.

# SEASONS

Seasons occur because the earth's axis is tilted at a 23½° angle.  As the earth orbits the sun, there is a time when the North Pole is tilted toward the sun and the South Pole is tilted away from it.  At this time, the northern hemisphere receives more sunlight and is warmer, while the southern hemisphere receives less sunlight and is cooler.  It is **summer** in the north and **winter** in the south.

Six months later, when the earth has traveled half-way around the sun, the opposite is true.  The northern hemisphere is tilted away from the sun and has **winter**.  The southern hemisphere is tilted toward the sun and has **summer**.

During **spring** and **autumn**, both hemispheres receive about the same amount of sunlight.

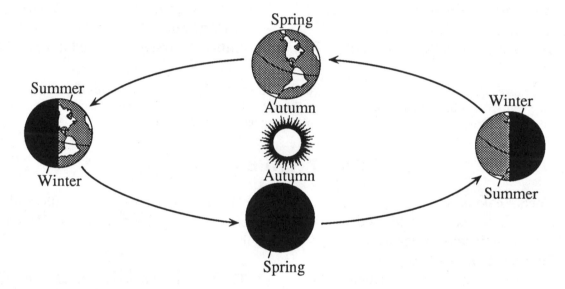

The earth revolves all the way around the sun, a distance of more than 575 million miles, in 365¼ days (one year).  Its average speed in orbit exceeds 17½ miles per second, or about 64,000 miles per hour!

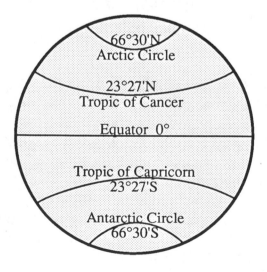

North of the **Arctic Circle** and south of the **Antarctic Circle** the sun stays above the horizon for at least one day a year, the first day of summer.

Between the **Tropic of Cancer** and the **Tropic of Capricorn** the sun will shine down from directly overhead for at least one day a year.  On the summer solstice, June 20 or 21, it shines directly over the Tropic of Cancer.  On the winter solstice, December 21 or 22, it shines directly over the Tropic of Capricorn.  On the vernal and autumnal equinoxes, March 20 or 21 and September 22 or 23 respectively, it shines directly over the equator.

# THE UNIVERSE

The **universe** is everything that exists. Scientists think the universe began up to 20 billion years ago with an incredible explosion that is still going on. The universe is still expanding outwards in all directions.

**Astronomy** is the scientific study of the universe, especially the stars, galaxies, planets, comets, and so on.

A **light year** is the distance light travels in a year at the speed of 186,282 miles per second—about 5.88 trillion miles. Because space is so vast, the light year is the most common unit used to measure distance in astronomy.

**Quasars** are the most distant objects astronomers have discovered. Some are as far away as sixteen billion light years and are moving away from us at up to 150,000 miles per second. Quasars give off tremendous amounts of energy, about 100,000 billion times as much as the sun, and more than 100 times as much as all the stars in the sky.

**Nebulae** are huge clouds of dust and gas, from which scientists think stars and galaxies are born.

**Black holes** are invisible, but have such strong gravity that all nearby objects are pulled in, and nothing, not even light, can escape.

A **galaxy** is a group of several billion stars. Scientists know about millions of galaxies and think there are many more. Nearly all we see in the sky belongs to our galaxy, the Milky Way. Only three other galaxies can possibly be seen without a telescope—on a *very* dark night.

The **Milky Way galaxy** contains our own sun and solar system. It is a spiral galaxy about 100,000 light years across and 10,000 light years thick. Our sun is one of about 100 billion stars in the Milky Way. The sun and solar system travel around the center of the Milky Way every 225 million years at the speed of about 156 miles per second (561,600 mph).

**Stars** are balls of gas, kept hot by nuclear explosions in their centers. Stars can be as small as 10 miles in diameter, or as large as 1,000,000,000 miles in diameter. Our sun has a diameter of 865,000 miles and is an average sized star. It looks larger to us than other stars because it is so much closer. The closest star other than our own sun is Proxima Centauri, 4.3 light years away. Below is a chart of some of the brightest stars and their distances from us in light years.

| Star | Light years | Star | Light years |
|---|---|---|---|
| Sirius | 8.8 | Betelgeuse | 300 |
| Canopus | 98 | Archernar | 114 |
| Alpha Centauri | 4.3 | Beta Centari | 490 |
| Arcturus | 36 | Altair | 16 |
| Vega | 26 | Alpha Crucis | 370 |
| Capella | 46 | Aldebaran | 68 |
| Rigel | 900 | Spica | 300 |
| Procyon | 11 | Antares | 400 |

**Constellations** are groups of stars within a definite region of the sky. They were named by ancient astronomers after figures the stars seemed to form in the sky. Some important constellations are the **Big Dipper**, **Orion**, and the **Southern Cross**.

# THE SOLAR SYSTEM

The **solar system** consists of the sun at the center, nine planets and their moons, comets, asteroids and meteors (space rocks).

Our **sun** is one of the billions of stars in the Milky Way galaxy. Like other stars, it is a glowing ball of hot gases. The temperature on the sun's surface is more than 10,000° Fahrenheit. Its energy is produced by nuclear fusion.

The sun is an average of 93 million miles away from the earth. It takes light from the sun about eight minutes and twenty seconds to reach the earth at the speed of 186,282 miles per second.

The sun is 865,000 miles in diameter, about 109 times the diameter of earth. If the earth were one inch in diameter, the sun would be nine feet in diameter. It would take 1.3 million earths to equal the size of the sun.

The sun revolves around the center of the Milky Way at the speed of about 156 miles per second. It rotates completely on its axis about once every 22 days.

Nine **planets** revolve around the sun. Some, such as earth and Mars, are rocky, while others, such as Jupiter and Saturn, are balls of gas. Planets can be seen only because they reflect light from the sun.

Other objects in our solar system include a belt of **asteroids**, very small rocky planets, between Mars and Jupiter. The largest is Ceres, which is 600 miles in diameter. Only thirty asteroids have diameters greater than 120 miles. Asteroids often collide and break into smaller pieces. Some pieces occasionally reach the earth and burn as they fall through the atmosphere, forming "falling stars", or **meteors**.

Some meteors are so large that they don't burn up in the atmosphere. These hit the earth, and are called **meteorites.** They form craters in the earth's surface. The moon is covered with craters because it has no atmosphere and is constantly being hit with meteors.

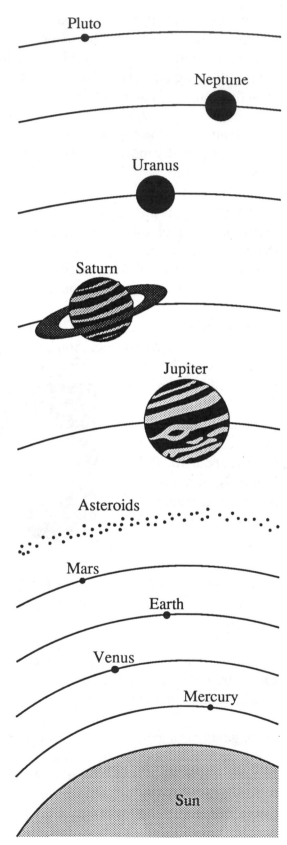

**Comets** travel in long elliptical orbits around the sun. They are probably like dirty snowballs, made of frozen gases and dust. Comets can be seen when they are close enough to the sun to reflect light. They often have "tails" which are made up of parts of the comet being blown away by the solar wind. **Halley's Comet** is the best known comet. It appears every 76 to 79 years. It last appeared in 1986.

| PLANETS OF THE SOLAR SYSTEM | | | | | | | |
|---|---|---|---|---|---|---|---|
| **PLANET** | **Distance from Sun** (millions of miles) | **Diameter** (miles) | **Average Speed in Orbit** (miles per second) | **Length of Year** (earth days) | **Length of Day** (earth time) | **Range of Temperatures** (degrees Fahrenheit) | **Number of Moons** |
| Mercury | 36 | 3,031 | 30 | 88 | 59 days | -315°/+648° | 0 |
| Venus | 67 | 7,520 | 22 | 225 | 243 days | +850° | 0 |
| Earth | 93 | 7,926 | 19 | 365 | 24 hours | -127°/+136° | 1 |
| Mars | 142 | 4,200 | 15 | 687 | 24 hours, 37 min. | -191°/-24° | 2 |
| Jupiter | 484 | 88,700 | 8 | 4,333 | 9 hours, 55 min. | -236° | 16 |
| Saturn | 885 | 74,600 | 6 | 10,759 | 10 hours, 39 min. | -285° | 23 |
| Uranus | 1,781 | 31,570 | 4 | 30,685 | 16-28 hrs. | -357° | 15 |
| Neptune | 2,793 | 30,800 | 3 | 60,188 | 16 hrs. | -400° | 8 |
| Pluto | 3,660 | 1,420 | 3 | 90,700 | 6 days | -342°/-369° | 1 |

The orbit of Pluto is much longer and narrower than that of any other planet. Every 248 years, Pluto crosses the orbit of Neptune, and is closer to the sun than Neptune. This happened on January 23, 1979. Neptune will be the most distant planet until March 15, 1999, when Pluto will cross outside Neptune's orbit. The distances from the sun given in the chart above are average distances.

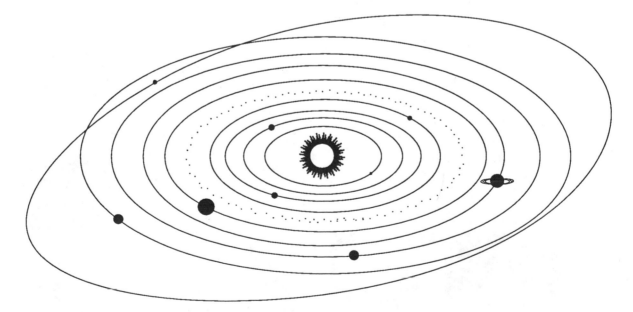

# THE MOON

The **moon** is the earth's only natural satellite. It is about one-fourth the size of the earth, with a diameter of 2,160 miles. It revolves around the earth every 29½ days and is an average distance of 238,857 miles away. The same side of the moon always faces the earth.

The moon has no atmosphere, water, wind or weather. It gets as hot as 260° Fahrenheit during the lunar day and as cold as -400° Fahrenheit in some craters near the poles.

Two major features on the moon's surface are **marias** and **craters**. Marias are large dark areas which are more or less flat. They are also knows as "seas" although there is no water. Craters were formed when meteors, or space rocks, hit the surface of the moon.

The first man to set foot on the moon was Neil A. Armstrong, on July 20, 1969. His first words were, "That's one small step for man, one giant leap for mankind."

## PHASES OF THE MOON

The moon shines because it reflects light from the sun. Every 29½ days, we see the moon seem to change size and shape as it goes through **phases**. Although one-half of the moon is always lit by the sun's rays, we can see only the part of the lighted half which faces the earth. Starting with a new moon, where none of the lighted side faces earth, the moon **waxes** to a crescent, a half moon, and a full moon. It then **wanes** to a half moon, a crescent, and back to a new moon.

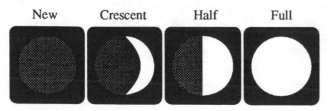

| New | Crescent | Half | Full |

## TIDES

**Tides** are the rise and fall of ocean water. They are caused by the gravitational pull of the moon and the sun on the waters of the earth. There are two high tides and two low tides each day, approximately six hours apart.

Some high tides are higher than others. These are called **spring tides** and are caused by the moon and the sun being lined up in their pull on the water. This can happen in two ways.

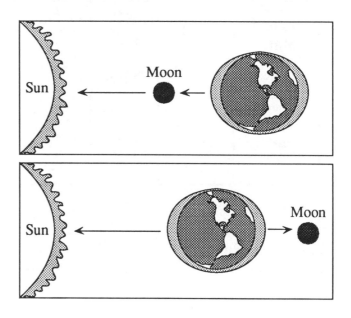

When the moon and sun are pulling in different directions, they cancel each other's effect to some degree, and the tides are not so high or low. These are called **neap tides**.

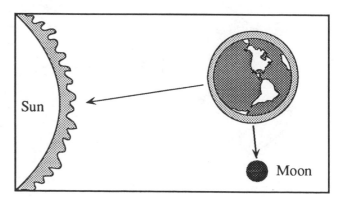

# ECLIPSES

During a **lunar eclipse**, the moon's light is eclipsed (hidden) by the earth's shadow.

During a **solar eclipse**, the sun's light is eclipsed (hidden) by the moon's shadow.

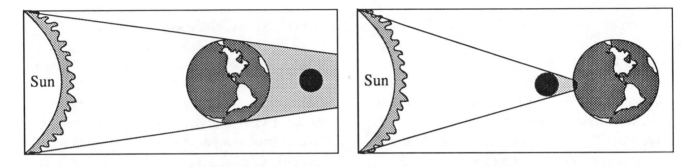

Only a few eclipses are **total eclipses**, where the sun or moon is totally hidden. Most are **partial eclipses**. Another type of solar eclipse is the **annular eclipse**, in which the moon passes directly in front of the sun, but does not completely cover it. A thin outer ring of the sun's disk is not covered by the dark disk of the moon.

Eclipses are usually visible in some parts of the world and not others. A total eclipse can usually be seen best in certain areas, and may appear to be a partial eclipse in other places.

## SOLAR AND LUNAR ECLIPSES

January 15-16, 1991 ..... Annular solar eclipse.
July 11, 1991 ................. Total solar eclipse.
December 21, 1991 ...... Partial lunar eclipse.
January 4-5, 1992 ......... Annular solar eclipse.
June 15, 1992 ................. Partial lunar eclipse.
June 30, 1992 ................. Total solar eclipse.
December 10, 1992 ...... Total lunar eclipse.
December 24, 1992 ...... Partial solar eclipse.
May 21, 1993 ................. Partial solar eclipse.
June 4, 1993 ................... Total lunar eclipse.
November 13, 1993 ...... Partial solar eclipse.
November 29, 1993 ...... Total lunar eclipse.
May 10, 1994 ................. Annular solar eclipse.
May 25, 1994 ................. Partial lunar eclipse.
November 3, 1994 ........ Total solar eclipse.
April 15, 1995 .............. Partial lunar eclipse.
April 29, 1995 .............. Annular solar eclipse.
October 24, 1995 ......... Total solar eclipse.
April 4, 1996 ................ Total lunar eclipse.
April 17, 1996 .............. Partial solar eclipse.
September 27, 1996 ...... Total lunar eclipse.

## FACTS ABOUT THE MOON

✳ The moon has a diameter of 2,160 miles, about one-fourth that of earth. It is the fifth largest moon in the solar system

✳ A person would weigh about one-sixth as much on the moon as on earth.

✳ Because the moon has no atmosphere, the sky looks black and stars can be seen even during the moon's daytime.

✳ The footprints of astronauts who have walked on the moon will probably remain exactly the same for billions of years.

✳ To escape from the moon's gravity, a spaceship must travel 5,400 miles per hour, compared to 25,000 mph to escape earth, and 52,200 mph to escape the sun's gravity.

# THE SPACE AGE

The **space age** began on October 4, 1957, when the Soviet Union launched the first artificial satellite to orbit the earth.  This began a "space race" between the United States and Russia.

## NOTABLE EVENTS IN THE SPACE AGE

October 4, 1957—Russia launched *Sputnik I*, the first earth-orbiting satellite.

January 31, 1958—*Explorer I* became the first U.S. earth-orbiting satellite.

September 12, 1959—Russia launched *Luna 2*, the first spacecraft to hit the moon.

April 12, 1961—Yuri A. Gagarin, Soviet cosmonaut, became the first man to orbit the earth.

May 5,  1961—Alan B. Shepard, Jr., became the first American in space.

February 20, 1962—John Glenn, Jr., became the first American to orbit the earth.

July 10, 1962—*Telstar I* relayed the first satellite TV between the U.S. and Europe.

June 16, 1963—Valentina V. Tereshkova of Russia was the first female in space.

March 18, 1965—Alexei A. Leonov, Russian cosmonaut, took the first space walk.

January 27, 1967—Three American Apollo astronauts were killed in a spacecraft fire: Virgil I. Grissom, Edward White II, and Roger B. Chaffee.

December 24-25, 1968—U.S. astronauts Frank Borman, William A. Anders and James A. Lovell, Jr. orbited the moon 10 times.

July 20, 1969—Americans Neil A. Armstrong and Edwin A. Aldrin, Jr., took man's first walk on the moon.  Michael Collins piloted the Command Module.

May 25, 1973—America launched *Skylab*, the first orbiting space station.

July 15, 1975—*Apollo*  and *Soyuz*  spacecraft took off for a U.S.-Soviet linkup in space.

August 20, 1977—*Voyager 2*  was launched to photograph planets in the outer solar system, Jupiter, Saturn, Uranus and Neptune.

September 5, 1977—*Voyager 1*  was launched.

April 12, 1981—U.S. astronauts John W. Young and Robert L. Crippen took off on the maiden voyage of space shuttle *Columbia*.

June 18, 1983—Sally K. Ride became the first American woman in space in the space shuttle *Challenger*.

January 28, 1986—Space shuttle *Challenger* exploded 73 seconds after takeoff, killing all seven people aboard, including American schoolteacher Christa McAuliffe.

September 29, 1988—Space shuttle *Discovery* blasted off on the first U.S. manned space mission after the *Challenger* disaster.

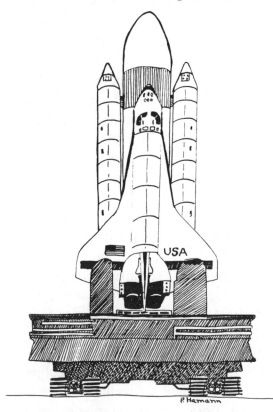

National Aeronautics and Space Administration
600 Independence Avenue
Washington, DC 20546

# SCIENCE
# AND
# HEALTH

# THE ATMOSPHERE AND WEATHER

The **atmosphere** is the air that surrounds the earth. 99% of the air is within 25 miles of the earth's surface. The atmosphere is divided into four layers, called the troposphere, stratosphere, mesosphere and thermosphere. Above the troposphere, air is too thin to support life.

## AIR

**Air** is made up of gases, moisture, and particles such as dust. Water (moisture) gets into the air by the process of **evaporation**. The amount of water in the air is **humidity**.

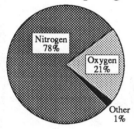

Nitrogen 78%
Oxygen 21%
Other 1%

## CLOUDS

There are four basic types of **clouds**: cirrus, nimbus, cumulus and stratus. They frequently combine to make clouds with such names as cirrostratus, cumulonimbus, and stratocumulus.

1. **Cirrus** clouds are delicate wispy clouds made of ice crystals which form very high in the atmosphere.
2. **Stratus** clouds look like layers or sheets and are usually near the earth. Drizzle often falls from stratus clouds.
3. **Cumulus** clouds are piled up heaps of white clouds, often flat on the bottom.
4. **Nimbus** clouds are very dark rain clouds.

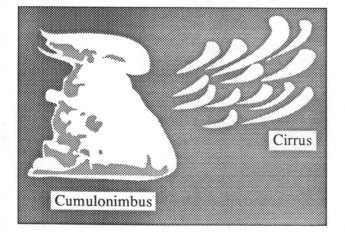

Cirrus

Cumulonimbus

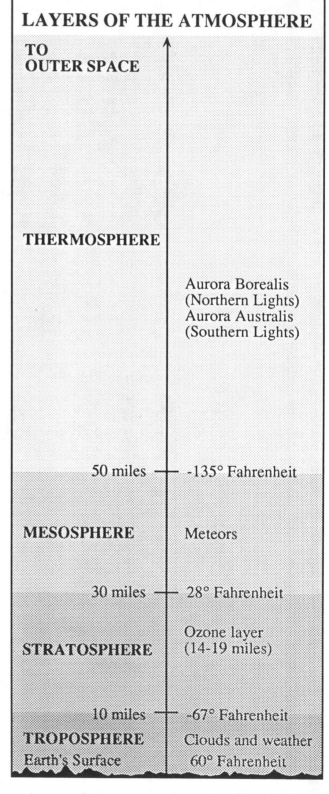

## LAYERS OF THE ATMOSPHERE

TO
OUTER SPACE

THERMOSPHERE

Aurora Borealis
(Northern Lights)
Aurora Australis
(Southern Lights)

50 miles — -135° Fahrenheit

MESOSPHERE          Meteors

30 miles — 28° Fahrenheit

Ozone layer
(14-19 miles)
STRATOSPHERE

10 miles — -67° Fahrenheit
TROPOSPHERE        Clouds and weather
Earth's Surface        60° Fahrenheit

# THE WATER CYCLE

The **water cycle** shows how water travels from place to place.

Water vapor gets into the air by **evaporation** from oceans, lakes, rivers and other bodies of water. **Transpiration** is the release of water into the air by plants.

Clouds form and travel, eventually releasing **precipitation**—rain, snow, sleet or hail. This water either soaks into the ground or runs off toward the ocean in rivers or streams.

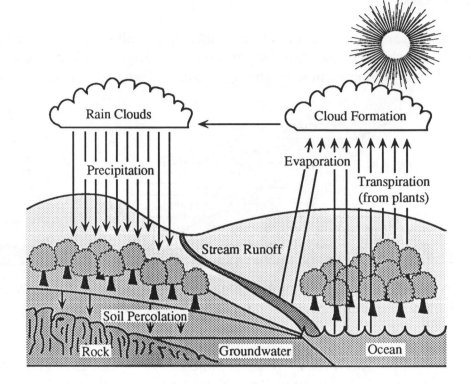

# WIND CHILL

**Wind chill** is the freezing effect of the combination of cold temperature and wind speed. For example, at a temperature of 10° Fahrenheit with a wind speed of 15 miles per hour, the freezing effect is the same as a temperature of -18° Fahrenheit with no wind. Wind has little additional freezing effect at speeds above 45 miles per hour.

| Wind speed (mph) | Thermometer reading (degrees Fahrenheit) | | | | | | | | | | | | | |
|---|---|---|---|---|---|---|---|---|---|---|---|---|---|---|
| | **35** | **30** | **25** | **20** | **15** | **10** | **5** | **0** | **-5** | **-10** | **-15** | **-20** | **-25** | **-30** |
| **5** | 32 | 27 | 22 | 16 | 11 | 6 | 0 | -5 | -10 | -15 | -21 | -26 | -31 | -36 |
| **10** | 22 | 16 | 10 | 3 | -3 | -9 | -15 | -22 | -27 | -34 | -40 | -46 | -52 | -58 |
| **15** | 16 | 9 | 2 | -5 | -11 | -18 | -25 | -31 | -38 | -45 | -51 | -58 | -65 | -72 |
| **20** | 12 | 4 | -3 | -10 | -17 | -24 | -31 | -39 | -46 | -53 | -60 | -67 | -74 | -81 |
| **25** | 8 | 1 | -7 | -15 | -22 | -29 | -36 | -44 | -51 | -59 | -66 | -74 | -81 | -88 |
| **30** | 6 | -2 | -10 | -18 | -25 | -33 | -41 | -49 | -56 | -64 | -71 | -79 | -86 | -93 |
| **35** | 4 | -4 | -12 | -20 | -27 | -35 | -43 | -52 | -58 | -67 | -74 | -82 | -89 | -97 |
| **40** | 3 | -5 | -13 | -21 | -29 | -37 | -45 | -53 | -60 | -69 | -76 | -84 | -92 | -100 |
| **45** | 2 | -6 | -14 | -22 | -30 | -38 | -46 | -54 | -62 | -70 | -78 | -85 | -93 | -102 |

# STORMS

**Storms** are often the result of a cold mass of air colliding with a warm mass of air.  A **cold front** occurs when the cold air moves in and may be accompanied by thundershowers and high winds.  A **warm front** moves in more slowly, and may cause rains that last many days.

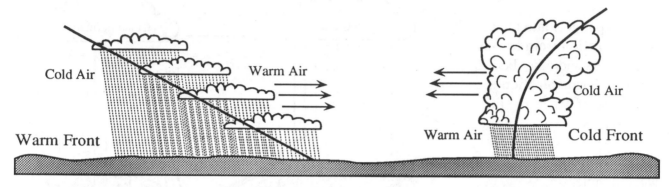

Cold Air

Warm Air

Warm Front

Cold Air

Warm Air    Cold Front

**Weather maps** shows storms and moving fronts that may signal that storms are coming.  The most violent storms are **hurricanes, tornados** and **thunderstorms**.

**Hurricanes** are caused by a low pressure area which forms over warm ocean waters. Hurricanes are 200 to 300 miles in diameter and have winds up to 150 miles per hour. Hurricane-type storms may also be called **cyclones**, or, in the western Pacific Ocean, **typhoons.**  They rotate counterclockwise in the northern hemisphere, and clockwise in the southern.

**Tornados** are twisting funnel clouds that extend downward from a mass of dark clouds. Winds may reach up to 280 miles per hour or more.  Few tornadoes last more than an hour, but they can cause great damage in populated areas.  Tornados may also be called **cyclones, twisters** or **waterspouts** (when over lakes or oceans).

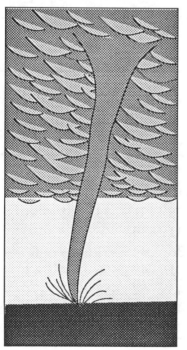

**Thunderstorms** occur in tall cumulonimbus clouds that have built up an electric charge. Lightning is a giant spark that travels within a cloud, between clouds, or between a cloud and the ground.  Flashes of lightning between clouds can be up to 90 miles long.  Lightning strikes the ground somewhere about 100 times each second.  The sound of thunder is caused by the quick expansion of air heated by lightning. Because light travels almost 900,000 times faster than sound, we see lightning before we hear thunder.  Light travels 186,282 miles per second and sound travels only 1,116 feet per second in air. Sound travels about one mile every five seconds.  To estimate how far lightning is from where you stand, count the seconds from the time you see the lightning until you hear the thunder and divide by five.  The lightning is that many miles from you.

# COMMON WEATHER INSTRUMENTS

**Anemometers** measure **wind speed.**

**Barometers** measure **atmospheric pressure,** which can be thought of as the weight of the air. Changing air pressure usually means changing weather, with low pressure bringing cloudy weather and high pressure bringing clear weather. Barometers measure air pressure in inches or millibars of mercury. A simple barometer is a glass tube of mercury upside down in a cup of mercury. The pressure of the atmosphere will hold 29.92 inches (1013 millibars) in the tube when the temperature is 59° Fahrenheit at sea level. Barometric pressure is lower at high altitudes. At 10,000 feet above sea level, the true pressure is 21.03 inches, and at 30,000 feet, it is only 9.07 inches. Scientists adjust barometric pressure readings to compare to the standard value of 29.92 at sea level at 59° Fahrenheit.

**Hygrometers** measure **relative humidity,** or the amount of water vapor in the air compared to the amount it can hold at a certain temperature. Relative humidity is written as a percentage. If the air has half the amount of water vapor it can hold, the relative humidity is 50%. When the air can hold no more water vapor, it is **saturated** and there is 100% humidity.

**Rain gauges** measure rainfall.

**Thermometers** measure the **temperature.** See page 207 for an illustration.

# WEATHER AND TEMPERATURE EXTREMES

**Highest recorded temperature on earth:** 136° F. in the shade at El Azizia, Libya, Africa, on September 13, 1922.

**Highest recorded temperature in the United States:** 134° F. in Death Valley, California, on July 10, 1913.

**Lowest recorded temperature on earth:** -129° F. in Vostok, Antarctica, on July 21, 1983.

**Lowest recorded temperature in the United States:** -80° F at Prospect Creek, Alaska, on January 23, 1971.

**Greatest one-minute rainfall on earth:** 1.23 inches in Unionville, Maryland, on July 4, 1956.

**Greatest 24-hour rainfall on earth:** 74 inches on the island of Réunion in the Indian Ocean on March 15-16, 1952.

**Greatest 24-hour rainfall in the United States:** 43 inches in Alvin, Texas on July 25-26, 1979.

**Greatest 12-month rainfall on earth:** 1,042 inches in Cherrapunji, India between August 1860 and August 1861.

**Greatest 12-month rainfall in the United States:** 739 inches on the island of Maui, Hawaii between December 1981 and December 1982.

**Greatest 24-hour snowfall in the United States:** 76 inches in Silver Lake, Colorado on April 14-15, 1921.

**Greatest 12-month snowfall in the United States:** 1,122 inches at Rainier Paradise Ranger Station, Washington, 1971-1972.

**Largest hailstone on record:** 17.5 inches around at Coffeyville, Kansas on September 3, 1979. It weighed 1⅔ pounds.

**Driest place on earth:** The Atacama Desert in northern Chile. Little rain fell for 400 years.

**Fastest recorded winds:** 280 miles per hour in a tornado at Wichita Falls, Texas on April 2, 1958.

# CLIMATES

The air in the atmosphere is always moving. The sun's rays heat air at the equator more than air at the poles. Warm air rises, forming areas of low pressure, and cooler air moves in underneath. Cold air at the poles sinks, forming areas of high pressure. Masses of air are always moving across the surface of the earth, as shown in the wind diagram below.

The area between the North Pole and the Arctic Circle has an **arctic climate.**

The area between the Arctic Circle and the Tropic of Cancer has a **temperate climate.**

The area around the equator, between the Tropic of Cancer and the Tropic of Capricorn has a **tropical climate.**

The area between the Tropic of Capricorn and the Antarctic Circle has a **temperate climate.**

The area between the Antarctic Circle and the South Pole has an **arctic climate.**

**Climate** is the average weather of an area over a long period of time. There are six basic types of climates.

1. The **tropics** are near the equator. They receive the most direct rays of the sun. A **tropical wet** climate has heavy rain throughout the year.

2. A **tropical wet and dry** climate has two seasons. During part of the year, there are heavy **monsoon rains**. The rest of the year is dry.

3. The **temperate zone** has moderate temperatures and four seasons: summer, autumn, winter and spring. Temperature and humidity vary according to seasons. Most of the United States is in the temperate zone.

4. The **arctic** climates are nearly always cold. Summers are short and chilly. Winters are long and very dry. Nearly all precipitation is snow.

5. **Highland** areas, or mountains, usually have a cooler and wetter climate than surrounding areas. The temperature falls by an average of about 1° Fahrenheit for every 275 feet of altitude.

6. A **desert** climate is very dry, and temperature may change from very hot in the day to very cold at night. Some deserts have so little water that almost nothing can live.

# GEOLOGY

## FORMATION OF THE EARTH

Scientists think the solar system, of which the earth is part, formed about 4½ billion years ago from a cloud of gas and dust.  The central part of the cloud became the sun and swirls in the cloud eventually became the planets.

According to the scientific theory, the earth was first made of gas, but slowly it condensed and became hot and molten.  Gradually, as the earth cooled, a thin solid crust formed over the top.  The earth is still cooling, and the inside is still molten or partially molten rock.

## INSIDE THE EARTH

In the very center of the earth is a **core** of molten rock which is about 2,200 miles thick.  The temperature of the core is around 9,000° Fahrenheit in the deepest parts.

The **mantle** surrounds the core, and is about 1,800 miles thick.  It is mostly solid, with temperatures between 1,600° and 4,000° Fahrenheit.

A solid **crust** covers the mantle.  Its thickness ranges from 5 to 25 miles.

## FORMATION OF CONTINENTS

Scientists think that long ago, all the land in the world was together in one big land mass called **Pangaea**.  The present continents are parts of this land mass which have broken apart.  **Continental plates** are huge portions of the earth's surface which slide around in relation to each other over a layer of partially molten rock.  This is called **continental drift.**  The plates move 1½ to 4 inches a year.  Most earthquakes and volcanoes occur along the boundaries of the plates, especially along the **Ring of Fire** around the Pacific Ocean.

Pangaea, 200 million years ago.

The continents today.

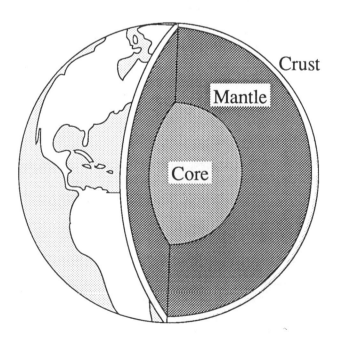

## GEOLOGICAL PERIODS AND EVENTS

| ERA | PERIOD | LENGTH (millions of yrs.) | BEGINNING (millions of yrs. ago) | MAJOR EVENTS |
|---|---|---|---|---|
| **Cenezoic** *Age of Mammals* | Quaternary  Holocene | 10,000 years ago to now | | Modern times |
| | Pleistocene | 2 | 2 | Early man, recent ice ages |
| | Tertiary  Pliocene | 10 | 12 | Fruits & grasses |
| | Miocene | 13 | 25 | Himalayas and Alps forming |
| | Oligocene | 11 | 36 | First large mammals, apes |
| | Eocene | 18 | 54 | Rocky Mountains forming |
| | Paleocene | 11 | 65 | Much volcanic activity |
| **Mesozoic** *Age of Reptiles* | Cretaceous | 70 | 135 | Dinosaurs extinct at the end  Flowering plants  Giant sea turtles  South America cut from Africa |
| | Jurassic | 55 | 190 | First birds  Dinosaurs reached largest size |
| | Triassic | 35 | 225 | Early dinosaurs  First mammals  Arizona's Petrified Forest  Pangaea began to split |
| **Paleozoic** *Age of Fishes* | Permian | 55 | 280 | Trilobites became extinct  First cone-bearing trees  Appalachians forming |
| | Pennsylvanian | 40 | 320 | Extensive formation of coal  Many clams and snails  Many large insects |
| | Mississippian | 25 | 345 | First known reptiles  Dense swampy forests  Many amphibians and sharks |
| | Devonian | 55 | 400 | First amphibians and insects  First forests |
| | Silurian | 30 | 430 | First land plants  First air breathing animals |
| | Ordovician | 70 | 500 | Sea over most of N. America  First vertebrates—jawless fish |
| | Cambrian | 100 | 600 | Trilobites, blue-green algae  Many marine invertebrates |
| **Precambrian** | | | 4,000 | Earth formed  First life, invertebrates |

# FORCES WHICH BUILD THE EARTH

## VOLCANOES

**Volcanoes** begin as molten rock forms gas and builds up pressure in a chamber of melted rock (magma chamber) under the earth. This pressure causes a volcano to blast or melt a path to the earth's surface. The explosion caused by this pressure being released is a **volcanic eruption**. Some volcanic eruptions are very violent and release huge clouds of gas, dust, rocks and lava. Others are relatively quiet and release a gentle flow of molten rock. Most volcanoes are on continental plate boundaries.

There are three kinds of volcanoes—shield volcanoes, cinder cones and composite volcanoes. Shield volcanoes are low, broad, dome-shaped mountains consisting mostly of gentle lava flows. Cinder cones are steep and cone-shaped, and made mostly of cinders with little lava. Composite volcanoes are a combination of lava and tephra (ash, dust and rocks) as shown in the diagram.

Some volcanoes are **active**, or constantly erupting. Others are **intermittent** and explode fairly regularly. Still others are **dormant**, which means they have not erupted in a very long time but may erupt again. **Extinct** volcanoes have not erupted since the beginning of recorded history and are not likely to erupt again.

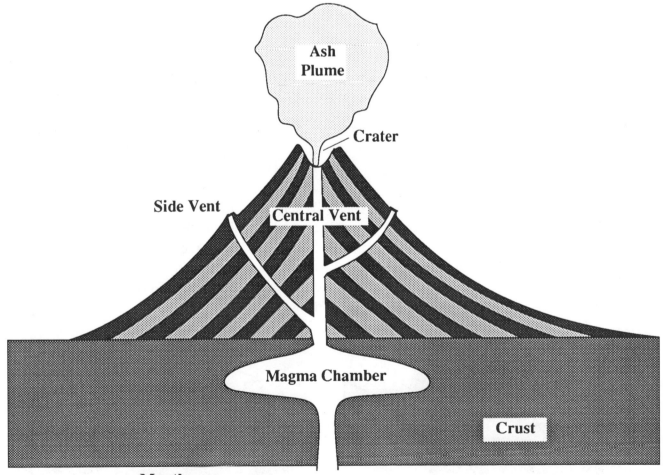

## MAJOR VOLCANOES OF THE WORLD

| Volcano | Location | Last Erupted | Elevation (feet) | Interesting Facts |
|---------|----------|--------------|------------------|-------------------|
| Aconcagua | Argentina | Extinct | 22,831 | Highest mountain in the western hemisphere. |
| Cotopaxi | Ecuador | Active | 19,347 | Perhaps the highest active volcano in the world. |
| Katmai | Alaska | Erupted 1912 | 6,715 | Largest eruption of the 20th century. |
| Kilauea | Hawaii | Active | 4,090 | On the side of Mauna Loa. |
| Krakatoa | Indonesia | Active | 1,972 | 1883 explosion caused one of the world's worst disasters. |
| Lassen Peak | California | Erupted 1921 | 10,453 | In Lassen Volcanic National Park. |
| Mauna Loa | Hawaii | Active | 13,680 | Discharges more lava than any other volcano. |
| Mont Pelee | Martinique | Active | 4,583 | Eruption in 1902 destroyed. the city of St. Pierre and killed 38,000 people. |
| Mount Etna | Sicily, Italy | Active | 11,122 | In Mediterranean Sea. |
| Mount Fuji | Japan | Dormant | 12,388 | Highest mountain in Japan. Considered sacred. |
| Mt. St. Helens | Washington | Erupted May 18, 1980 | 9,677 | 60 persons died in 1980 eruption. |
| Paricutin | Mexico | Erupted 1952 | 9,213 | First appeared in a cornfield in February 1943. A 140 foot cone grew in one week. |
| Stromboli | Mediterranean | Active | 3,031 | Constantly erupting. |
| Vesuvius | Italy | Active | 4,190 | City of Pompeii buried in 79 A.D. in history's most famous volcanic eruption. |

## FAULTING

**Faults** are cracks in the earth's surface where rocks have broken and are sliding past one another. One side of the fault may move up and the other down, forming a mountain. The San Andreas Fault in California is well-known. The Sierra Nevadas are fault-block mountains.

## FOLDING

When rocks are pressured from two sides toward the middle, they will **fold**. This forms mountains. Some mountain ranges formed by folding are the Himalayas, the Alps, the Rocky Mountains, the Andes and the Appalachian Mountains.

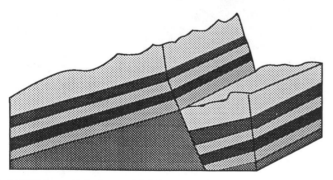

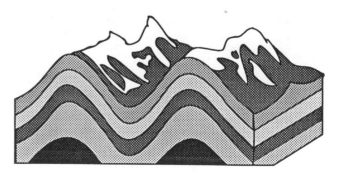

# EARTHQUAKES

**Earthquakes** are caused by forces inside the earth which cause sudden movement in the rocks. Volcanoes, faulting and folding result in earthquakes. The **Richter Scale** is used to measure the magnitude, or force, of an earthquake. Thousands of earthquakes occur each day with a magnitude of less than five. These are considered minor. Often people do not even notice them. Each number on the Richter Scale represents ten times more vertical ground movement than the last number. An earthquake with a magnitude of 6 has ten times more up and down ground movement than one with a magnitude of 5! The highest magnitude ever recorded was 8.9, in Japan in 1933 and in the Pacific Ocean near South America in 1906. The **epicenter** is directly above the earthquake.

## THE RICHTER SCALE

1  Detected by scientific instruments only.
2  Felt when everything is quiet by a few people and some animals.
3  Felt by most people near the epicenter.
4  Felt by everyone near the epicenter.
5  May cause walls to crack and things to fall off of shelves.
6  Tall structures may fall. Destructive in crowded areas.
7  Lives are lost and buildings are destroyed.
8  A major disaster.
9  No earthquake has yet measured 9 on this scale.

## SOME FAMOUS EARTHQUAKES

**San Francisco**, California, April 18, 1906. Earthquake measuring 8.3 killed 500 people.
**Alaska**, March 27, 1964. Strongest earthquake in North America, measuring 8.5, killed 117.
**China**, July 28, 1976. Earthquake measuring 8.2 killed 242,000 people. This is the highest death toll in modern times.

# FORCES WHICH WEAR DOWN THE EARTH

Mountains are constantly being built by volcanoes, faulting and folding. They are also constantly being worn away, or **eroded**. Three forces that break mountains apart and wear them down are **weathering**, **erosion**, and **mass movement**.

**Weathering** is the first step. Some minerals in rocks may be dissolved in rainwater. Because rocks expand when heated by the sun and contract when cooled, cracks form. Water in these cracks may freeze and expand, enlarging them. Eventually, soil may get into the cracks and plants start to grow. The roots of the plants cause the cracks to spread wider, eventually causing the rock to break apart. Weathering breaks rocks into small enough pieces that erosion can occur.

**Erosion** moves weathered material, called **sediment**, from one place to another. **Rainwater** washes sand and soil into creeks, which carry the material into rivers and lakes or the sea. It settles there and piles up. Heat and pressure eventually change it back into rock— sedimentary rock.

**Glaciers** are rivers of ice which grind through mountains and scrape up underlying rock, moving it to the end of the glacier where it piles up as the glacier melts.

**Waves** erode the shoreline and **wind** wears down rocks by constantly blowing sand against them.

Beautiful natural features formed by wind and water erosion are natural arches, badlands, and canyons, such as the Grand Canyon.

**Mass movements** are landslides and mudslides.

# ROCKS

**Igneous** rocks are formed from cooling magma (molten rock) which comes from deep inside the earth. Sometimes this happens when the magma comes outside the earth, as from a volcano. Often the magma slowly rises inside the earth and cools before it reaches the surface. Some igneous rocks are *granite, obsidian* and *pumice*.

**Sedimentary** rocks are formed when eroded materials pile up and are changed back into rock by heat and pressure. Some common sedimentary rocks are *sandstone, limestone, shale, conglomerate* and *chalk*. Sedimentary rocks often contain **fossils**, which are traces of animals or plants which died and were buried under the layers of sediment as they piled up.

**Metamorphic** rocks are rocks which have been changed and partially melted by the heat and pressure of mountain building. Some common metamorphic rocks are *marble, slate* and *schist*.

The basic building blocks of rocks are **minerals**, which were formed into **crystals** as molten rock cooled. Some common minerals are *gold, pyrite, graphite, mica, quartz, salt* and many gems. **Gems** are stones or minerals that are used for ornament. Some well-known gems are *diamonds, opals, rubies, sapphires, emeralds, turquoise* and *jade*. Scientists use **Mohs Hardness Scale** to help identify minerals.

| Mineral | Hardness | Easy Tests |
|---------|----------|------------|
| Talc | 1 | Scratched by a fingernail |
| Gypsum | 2 | |
| Calcite | 3 | Scratched by a copper coin |
| Fluorite | 4 | Scratched by window glass or a knife blade |
| Apatite | 5 | |
| Feldspar | 6 | Scratches window glass or a knife blade |
| Quartz | 7 | |
| Topaz | 8 | |
| Corundum | 9 | |
| Diamond | 10 | Scratches all other minerals |

# FOSSIL FUELS

There are three primary fossil fuels which people use for energy: **coal, oil** and **natural gas**. All are found under the earth and are made of the remains of plants and animals that lived millions of years ago. All are **nonrenewable**, which means once they are used, they cannot be replaced.

**Coal** was formed from plants which lived in swampy areas one million to 440 million years ago. The plants died and their remains piled up. As other things piled on top of them, heat and pressure turned the layer of plant material into **peat**, then **lignite** (soft coal), and finally to **bituminous** and **anthracite** coal. Anthracite is very hard coal which burns cleanly. There is not much of it in the world. Coal is mined and sold to heat houses, run factories, and create electricity.

**Natural gas** and **oil** (petroleum) were likely formed from the remains of tiny plants and animals that lived in the sea millions of years ago. These animals and plants sank to the bottom of the sea when they died and were covered by sediments. Through millions of years, the heat and pressure of the sediments turned the animal and plant remains into oil and natural gas. Oil and gas move through layers of sedimentary rock until they are trapped by a layer of rock through which they cannot move. Often they form "reservoirs" in folded rock.

**Oil shale** is a form of oil which is trapped in sedimentary rock. The rock has to be heated to more than 900° Fahrenheit in order for the oil to vaporize out of the rock. Because of this, it is quite expensive as a fuel source.

Alternate sources of energy, which do not depend on nonrenewable fossil fuels, include solar, wood, wind, hydroelectric, nuclear, and geothermal.

# ENERGY

**Energy** is a word for the ability to do work. Energy can be either **potential** (stored), such as the energy in a gallon of gasoline, or **kinetic**, such as the movement of an automobile, the heat of its engine, and the sound of the motor.

There are seven **forms of energy**:

1. Electricity
2. Heat
3. Light
4. Motion
5. Nuclear
6. Sound
7. Chemical

Energy is always changing from one form to another. For example, *nuclear* energy makes the *light* of the sun, which plants use to make food, stored as *chemical* energy. People eat the food, which then turns into *heat* to warm their bodies, *motion* such as walking, and *sound* as they speak. Another example is the potential energy stored by water in a dam. The kinetic *motion* of the water through turbines creates *electrical* energy, which travels to homes and is changed to *light,* the *heat* of an electric stove, and the *sound* of a radio.

While energy is the ability to do work, a **machine** is a device that does work. Although most machines consist of a number of parts that work together, they are all based in some way on six types of **simple machines:** the **lever**, the **wheel and axle**, the **pulley**, the **inclined plane**, the **wedge**, and the **screw**.

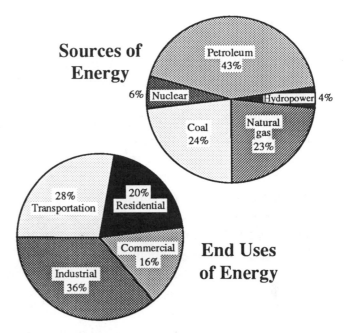

Sources of Energy

End Uses of Energy

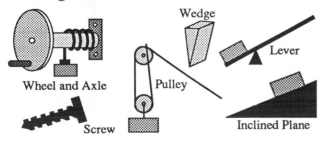

Wheel and Axle

Wedge

Lever

Pulley

Screw

Inclined Plane

## DECIBELS

The loudness of sound energy is measured in **decibels** (dB). Each number on the decibel scale below represents a loudness ten times as great at the number just below it. The 120 dB rating for a rock concert is a million times louder than normal conversation. Damage to ears begins at about 100 dB.

| | |
|---|---|
| 140 | Lightning or dynamite at close range |
| 130 | Jet plane takeoff nearby |
| 120 | Amplified rock and roll band |
| | Impossible to communicate by voice |
| 110 | Rock and roll band, loud shout in ear |
| 100 | Chain saw, fireworks, screaming near ear |
| 90 | Vacuum cleaner, shouting or screaming |
| 80 | TV on high, loud yelling and laughing |
| 70 | Car horn, louder than average talking |
| 60 | Large store, loud conversation |
| 50 | Soft music, average conversation |
| 40 | Refrigerator, quiet conversation |
| 30 | Turning pages, soft whisper |
| 20 | Cat purring very softly |
| 10 | Soft rustling of leaves |
| 0 | Low threshold of normal hearing |

# MATTER

## ATOMS

**Matter** is anything that takes up space. All matter is made of **atoms**. Democritus, an ancient Greek, developed the idea of the atom. He defined an atom as the smallest unit of matter, which could be split no more. In fact, the word "atom" means "uncuttable." It was found in 1897, however, that atoms had smaller parts called **electrons**. Later, at the famous Cavendish Laboratory in England, it was discovered that atoms contain nuclei made of **protons** and **neutrons**. There are also many other small particles in the atom. The model of the atom shown in the illustration was developed by Ernest Rutherford in 1911 and revised in 1913 by Niels Bohr. The revision reflected the theory that electrons could only travel in certain specific orbits.

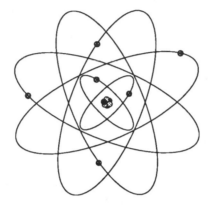

Atoms are extremely small. More than a million side by side would be only as thick as a hair. The particles which make up atoms, however, are much, much smaller. If a hydrogen atom were enlarged to a mile in diameter, the nucleus would be less than an inch in diameter. The electrons would be so small they could not be seen. All matter, including our bodies, is mostly empty space! It is the tremendous speed of electrons which makes matter behave as though it were solid.

## ELEMENTS, COMPOUNDS AND MIXTURES

When a substance has only one kind of atom in it, it is known as an **element**. There are about 107 known elements. Each has a name, a chemical symbol, an atomic number, and an atomic weight. The **chemical symbol** is used as an abbreviation. The **atomic number** equals the number of electrons in the atom, which is the same as the number of protons. The **atomic weight** is the relative weight, and is almost the same as the sum of the number of protons and neutrons. Scientists organize the elements into what is known as the **Periodic Table of the Elements**. The alphabetical list shows some common elements.

## ELEMENTS

| NAME | SYMBOL | ATOMIC NUMBER |
|---|---|---|
| Aluminum | Al | 13 |
| Argon | Ar | 18 |
| Arsenic | As | 33 |
| Bromine | Br | 35 |
| Cadmium | Cd | 48 |
| Calcium | Ca | 20 |
| Carbon | C | 6 |
| Chlorine | Cl | 17 |
| Chromium | Cr | 24 |
| Copper | Cu | 29 |
| Fluorine | F | 9 |
| Gold | Au | 79 |
| Helium | He | 2 |
| Hydrogen | H | 1 |
| Iodine | I | 53 |
| Iron | Fe | 26 |
| Lead | Pb | 82 |
| Magnesium | Mg | 12 |
| Manganese | Mn | 25 |
| Mercury | Hg | 80 |
| Molybdenum | Mo | 42 |
| Neon | Ne | 10 |
| Nickel | Ni | 28 |
| Nitrogen | N | 7 |
| Oxygen | O | 8 |
| Phosphorous | P | 15 |
| Platinum | Pt | 78 |
| Plutonium | Pu | 94 |
| Potassium | K | 19 |
| Radium | Ra | 88 |
| Radon | Rn | 86 |
| Silver | Ag | 47 |
| Sodium | Na | 11 |
| Strontium | Sr | 38 |
| Sulfur | S | 16 |
| Tin | Sn | 50 |
| Tungsten | W | 74 |
| Uranium | U | 92 |
| Zinc | Zn | 30 |

When two atoms combine, or join together, they form **molecules**. The oxygen in the air is made of molecules consisting of two oxygen atoms joined together ($O_2$).

**Compounds** are formed when atoms of two or more different elements join together. Some common compounds are: water ($H_2O$), carbon dioxide ($CO_2$), salt (NaCl), sugar ($C_{12}H_{22}O_{11}$), ammonia ($NH_3$), baking soda ($NaHCO_3$) and rust ($3Fe_2O_3H_2O$). Rust is formed when water and the oxygen in the air combine with iron.

**Mixtures** are formed when elements mix but the atoms do not combine. Brass is an alloy (mixture) of copper and zinc. Bronze is an alloy of copper and tin.

## STATES OF MATTER

There are three **states of matter**: solid, liquid, and gas. In a **solid**, the atoms or molecules are close together and are arranged in regular patterns. Solids are hard and rigid, and they always take up a fixed amount of space and have a fixed shape. In a **liquid**, the atoms or molecules are further apart and move more freely than in the solid state. A liquid always takes up a fixed amount of space, but it has no shape of its own and takes the shape of the container into which it is poured. In a **gas**, the atoms or molecules are far apart and move freely. A gas has neither a fixed shape nor a fixed volume. It will fill any container into which it is placed, and take the container's shape.

When matter is heated, the molecules move more quickly and move further apart. If enough heat is added, the state of matter will change. A substance **melts** when it changes from solid to liquid, and **boils** when it changes from liquid to gas. For example, when ice is heated, it changes from a solid to a liquid at its **melting point** of 32° F (0° C). If heated further, it will change

from a liquid to a gas, water vapor, at its **boiling point** of 212° F (100° C). Different substances melt and boil at different temperatures, and all substances can be in any state depending on the temperature. For example, copper, which is normally a solid, will melt at 1981° F (1083° C) and boil at about 4653° F (2567° C). The boiling point depends on the atmospheric pressure. At sea level, water boils at 212° F (100° C) but at 10,000 feet above sea level, it boils at about 162°F (72° C). This means that at higher altitudes, food must be boiled longer than at sea level in order to be completely cooked.

When matter is cooled, the molecules slow down and move closer together. If cooled enough, the state of matter will change. A substance **condenses** when it changes from a gas to a liquid and **freezes** when it changes from liquid to solid. When water is cooled, it will change from a liquid to a solid at its **freezing point** of 32° F (0° C). Different substances condense and freeze at different temperatures. For example, air, which is normally a gas, will become liquid at −310° F (-190° C). Liquid air will boil if poured over ice.

## MELTING POINTS AND BOILING POINTS

| Element | Melting Point | Boiling Point |
|---|---|---|
| Aluminum | 1220°F | 4473°F |
| Calcium | 1542°F | 2703°F |
| Copper | 1981°F | 4653°F |
| Gold | 1947°F | 5086°F |
| Hydrogen | -434°F | -423°F |
| Iron | 2795°F | 4982°F |
| Mercury | −38°F | 675°F |
| Nickel | 2647°F | 4950°F |
| Nitrogen | −346°F | −321°F |
| Oxygen | −360°F | −297°F |
| Silver | 1764°F | 4014°F |
| Tin | 450°F | 4118°F |
| Uranium | 2070°F | 6904°F |

# PLANTS AND ANIMALS

Living things are divided into two groups: **plants** and **animals**. Plants are important because they are the basis of all life on earth. They use sunlight to produce food, and they give off oxygen which animals breathe. Animals supply carbon dioxide and water which plants need.

## CELLS

The basic unit of all life is the **cell**. All living things are made up of cells, which are so small  they can be seen only under a microscope. The smallest living things are made of only a single cell. The human body has more than ten trillion cells (10,000,000,000,000).

Although there are many different types and shapes of cells, they all have many things in common. Every cell has the same basic parts, a cell membrane, cytoplasm, and a nucleus. The **cell membrane** is a thin covering which encloses each cell. The **cytoplasm** is everything in the cell except the nucleus. The **nucleus** is the control center which directs the activities of the cell. It contains **chromosomes** which hold the **genes** that determine the type of living thing, and the thousands of characteristics which make it distinct from other living things. Each cell performs all the functions of life, such as breathing, taking in food, and giving off wastes. Cells grow, reproduce themselves by dividing in two, and eventually die. About three billion cells in your body die every minute. During the same minute, about three billion new cells form to replace them. In about seven years, almost all the cells in your body have been replaced. The only cells which cannot be replaced are nerve cells and brain cells, but these can live for about 100 years. Some cells reproduce fairly quickly. It takes skin cells only ten hours to divide into two.

## PLANTS

Plants make food through a process called **photosynthesis**. Light from the sun is absorbed by the green **chlorophyll** in plants. The light causes carbon dioxide to combine with the hydrogen in water to make sugar. Oxygen is given off in the process. The chemical formula is:

$$6CO_2 + 6H_2O \xrightarrow[\text{light}]{\text{chlorophyll}} C_6H_{12}O_6 + 6O_2$$

Many plants have the same basic parts. The **root** anchors the plant to the ground and absorbs water and minerals from the soil. The **stem** supports the plant's leaves and flowers. The **leaves**, which can be needles, make food through photosynthesis. The **flowers** contain the reproductive parts of flowering plants. The **seeds** contain all the genetic information needed for the growth of a new plant.

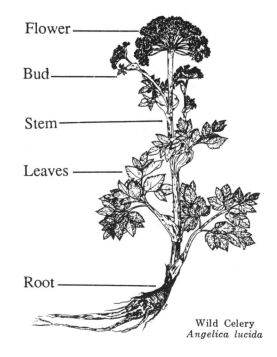

Flower

Bud

Stem

Leaves

Root

Wild Celery
*Angelica lucida*

# ANIMALS

Animals are divided into two main groups, **vertebrates**, animals with backbones, and **invertebrates**, animals without backbones. Some of the vertebrates are mammals, birds, reptiles, amphibians and fish. Invertebrates include insects, shellfish, jellyfish, crabs and microscopic animals. Over a million species of invertebrates and more than 50,000 species of vertebrates are known.

Animals may be warm-blooded or cold-blooded. **Warm-blooded** animals have about the same body temperature all the time, regardless of the temperature outside. Birds and mammals are warm-blooded. **Cold-blooded** animals have body temperatures which are hot in hot weather and cold in cold weather. Fish, reptiles, amphibians, insects and invertebrates are cold-blooded.

## OUTLINE OF TYPES OF ANIMALS

I. **VERTEBRATES** (backbone)

   A. **Mammals** (warm–blooded vertebrates which have hair and nurse their young)
     1. Herbivores (plant–eating mammals such as rabbits, cows and beavers)
     2. Carnivores (meat–eating mammals such as dogs, lions and seals)
     3. Insectivores (insect–eating mammals such as bats and shrews)
     4. Omnivores (mammals which eat both plants and animals, such as human beings and bears)

   B. **Birds** (warm–blooded vertebrates with wings and feathers which lay eggs)
     1. Songbirds (robins, crows)
     2. Birds of prey (eagles, hawks, owls)
     3. Water birds (loons, ducks, geese)
     4. Shorebirds (gulls, sandpipers)
     5. Fowl (chickens, pheasants)
     6. Flightless birds (ostrich, penguins)

   C. **Reptiles** (cold–blooded vertebrates which have scaly skin, produce eggs, and breathe with lungs)
     1. Lizards, snakes
     2. Turtles
     2. Crocodilians (alligators, crocodiles, caymans)

   D. **Amphibians** (cold–blooded vertebrates without scaly skins which develop from eggs into adult animals through metamorphosis, and which live part of their lives in water and part on land)
     1. Frogs and toads
     2. Salamandars
     3. Caecilians

   E. **Fish** (cold–blooded vertebrates which live in water)
     1. Bony fish (bass, catfish, salmon)
     2. Fish with skeletons of cartilage (sharks, rays, chimaeras)
     3. Lampreys and hagfish

II. **INVERTEBRATES** (no backbone)

   A. Annelida (worms with segments)
   B. Mollusca (animals with shells)
   C. Echinodermata (starfish, sea urchins)
   D. Arthropoda (joint-legged animals)
     1. Insecta (insects)
     2. Arachnida (spiders, scorpions, ticks)
     3. Crustacae (crabs, lobsters, shrimp)
   G. Coelenterata (jellyfish, corals)
   H. Porifera (sponges)
   I. Protozoa (one-celled animals)

## ANIMAL INFORMATION

| ANIMAL | MALE | FEMALE | YOUNG | GROUP | SPEED (mph) | GESTATION PERIOD |
|---|---|---|---|---|---|---|
| Antelope | buck | doe | kid | herd | 61 | 9 months |
| Bear | boar | sow | cub | sloth | 30 | 7-9 months |
| Cat | tom | puss | kitten | clowder | 30 | 9 weeks |
| Cattle | bull | cow | calf | herd | -- | 9 months |
| Chicken | rooster | hen | chick | flock | 9 | 21 days |
| Deer | buck | doe | fawn | herd | 35 | 6-9 months |
| Dog | dog | bitch | pup | kennel | 45 | 9 weeks |
| Duck | drake | duck | duckling | brace | 72 | 23-30 days |
| Elephant | bull | cow | calf | herd | 25 | 18-23 months |
| Fox | dog | vixen | cub | skulk | 42 | 49-79 days |
| Goat | billy | nanny | kid | herd | -- | 151 days |
| Goose | gander | goose | gosling | gaggle | 88 | 28-32 days |
| Hog | boar | sow | piglet | herd | 11 | 114 days |
| Horse | stallion | mare | foal colt (male) filly (female) | herd | 45 | 11 months |
| Human | man | woman | child | group | 20 | 9 months |
| Lion | lion | lioness | cub | pride | 50 | 108 days |
| Rabbit | buck | doe | bunny | warren | 40 | 26-30 days |
| Seal | bull | cow | pup | herd | 10 | 8-12 months |
| Sheep | ram | ewe | lamb | flock | -- | 5 months |
| Swan | cob | pen | cygnet | flock | 55 | 30-35 days |
| Whale | bull | cow | calf | herd | 30 | 10-16 months |

## AMAZING PLANT AND ANIMAL FACTS

**Smallest plants:** Diatoms—as small as one ten-thousandth of an inch.

**Largest plant:** General Sherman sequoia tree—274.9 feet high and 82 feet around.

**Oldest plant:** Methuselah, a bristlecone pine—4,700 years old. Oldest living thing on earth.

**Largest animal:** Blue whale—up to 110 feet long, 2½ times as long as a railroad boxcar. It is the largest animal which ever lived.

**Largest land animal:** African elephant—6.5 tons.

**Largest fish:** Whale shark—up to 15 tons.

**Largest bird:** African ostrich—up to 9 feet tall and 345 pounds. Egg can weigh 3.88 pounds.

**Largest snake:** Anaconda—500 pounds.

**Largest reptile:** Salt-water crocodile—up to 1,150 pounds and 16 feet long.

**Largest insects:** Goliath beetle—more than four inches long, and Hercules moth, with a wingspread of about 11 inches.

**Tallest animal:** Giraffe—up to 20 feet tall.

**Greatest traveler:** Arctic tern—migrates 11,000 miles each way from nesting grounds in the Arctic to winter homes in Antarctica.

**Highest flying bird:** Bar-headed goose—can fly at 25,000 feet above sea level.

**Fastest animal:** Peregrine falcon—217 mph.

**Fastest land animal:** Cheetah—63 mph.

**Loudest sound:** Blue whale—188 decibels, can be detected 530 miles away.

# ENDANGERED SPECIES

All animals and plants are classified into **species**. Members of a species are different from all other forms of life in one or more ways, and can breed and produce young of the same species. Scientists know of more than 350,000 species of plants and over a million species of animals. More are being discovered every year. A number of species which lived on the earth in the past, such as dinosaurs, are now **extinct**, or no longer in existence. Due to the changes man has made in the natural environment and the destruction of wildlife **habitat**, a very large number of plant and animal species are now **endangered**, or in danger of becoming extinct. Scientists think that unless this trend is reversed, a different species will disappear permanently from the earth every minute in the 1990's.

## ENDANGERED LARGE ANIMALS

American crocodile
Bald eagle
Blue whale
Brown pelican
California condor
Cheetah
Chimpanzee
Elephant
Florida panther
Giant catfish
Gorilla
Gray wolf
Grizzly bear
Indian python
Jaguar
Leopard
Orangutan
Peregrine falcon
Rhinoceros
Snow leopard
Tiger

# ECOLOGY AND ENVIRONMENT

**Ecology** is the study of the relationship living things have to each other and to their **environment**, or surroundings. Animals depend on plants for food and plants depend on the soil. The soil is fertilized by both plant and animal wastes and decaying bodies which are broken down into simple nutrients which can be used by plants. The diagram illustrates a very simple food chain. **Producers**, or plants, are eaten by **first–order consumers**, such as rabbits. These, in turn, are eaten by the **second–order consumers**, such as wolves. When any living thing produces waste or dies, the waste material is broken down by **decomposers**, such as mold, yeast and bacteria, and recycled into material which is usable by plants in the soil. The ocean has a similar food chain.

## FOOD PYRAMID

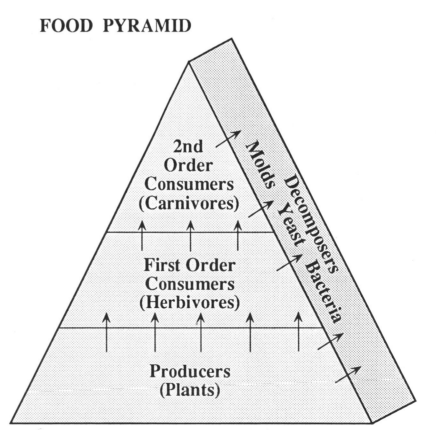

# HUMAN BODY SYSTEMS

The human body consists of nine major **body systems**. Each carries out a different activity, and consists of a number of parts, or **organs**. Only the major parts of the systems are shown in the illustrations. The urinary, endocrine and reproductive systems are not shown.

## SKELETAL SYSTEM

The **skeletal system** consists of all the bones in the body. The skeleton gives the body shape, protects and supports vital organs, and together with the muscles, allows the body to move.

The adult human skeleton has about 206 bones. They are joined to each other by **joints**. Joints may be immovable, such as the joints in the skull, or movable, such as the hinge joint of the elbow, or the ball and socket joint of the shoulder.

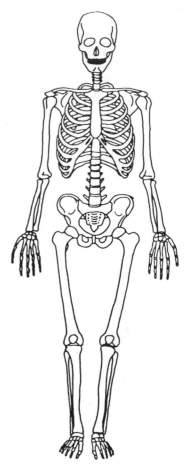

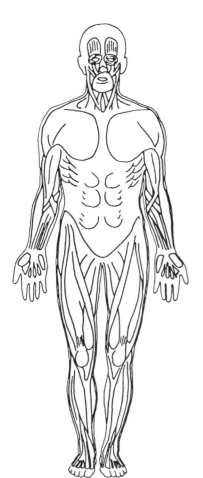

## MUSCULAR SYSTEM

The **muscular system** consists of all the muscles in the body. Skeletal muscles are **voluntary muscles**. They move the bones of the skeleton and are controlled by thoughts. The heart muscle is an **involuntary muscle** which pumps blood through the body. Smooth muscles are also involuntary, or not controlled by thought. They move food through the digestive system and help blood circulate.

An adult's body has about 656 skeletal muscles, which make up between ⅓ and ½ of a person's weight.

# CIRCULATORY SYSTEM

The **circulatory system** consists of the heart, the blood vessels and the blood. Its purpose is to supply all the cells of the body with oxygen and nutrients from food, and to carry away carbon dioxide and other wastes produced by the cells.

The heart of a resting adult beats about 70 times, and pumps about five quarts of blood, each minute. The number of times a person's heart beats each minute is called the **pulse**. In ten years, a human heart beats about 368 million times, pumping over 6 million gallons of blood. That's enough to fill 522 tank trucks! An average adult has about five quarts of blood. It **circulates**, or makes the round trip from the heart to the cells and back, then to the lungs and back, every sixty seconds.

The blood vessels include **arteries**, which carry blood from the heart to the cells, **veins**, which carry blood from the cells to the heart, and **capillaries**, which are tiny vessels which connect the arteries to the veins. There are about 60,000 miles of blood vessels connected to the heart, enough to wrap around the world almost two and a half times.

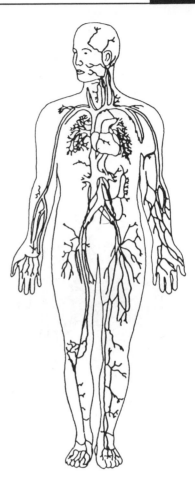

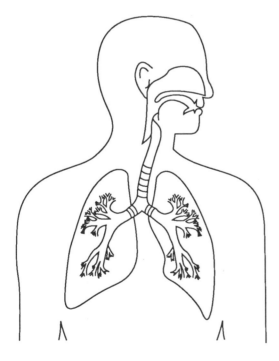

# RESPIRATORY SYSTEM

The **respiratory system** consists of the lungs and other organs of breathing. Its purpose is to take in oxygen from the air and transfer it to the blood for circulation to the cells. The lungs also take waste carbon dioxide from the blood and release it into the air.

A resting adult breathes about twelve times each minute, taking in about 2,620 gallons of air each day. In a normal lifetime, that will amount to over 70 million gallons of air!

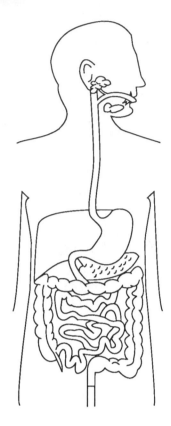

# DIGESTIVE SYSTEM

The **digestive system** consists of the alimentary canal and other organs such as the gall bladder and liver. The **alimentary canal** contains the mouth, esophagus, stomach, small intestine and large intestine. The purpose of the digestive system is to take in food and break it down into simple nutrients which are carried by the blood to the cells for use.

Digestion begins in the **mouth**, where food is chewed and mixed with saliva. Food then passes through a tube called the **esophagus** to the **stomach**, where it is stored and further broken down. The **small intestine**, which is about 22 feet long, finishes digestion and passes the nutrients into the bloodstream. The **large intestine** eliminates undigestible food from the body.

An average American will eat at least 60,000 pounds, or 30 tons, of food in a lifetime. That is about as much as the combined weight of five elephants!

# NERVOUS SYSTEM

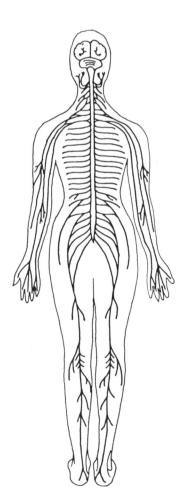

The **nervous system** consists of the brain, the spinal cord, the nerves and the sense organs. Our five **senses** are sight, hearing, smell, taste and touch. The purpose of the nervous system is to control and regulate the activities of all the body systems. The brain receives information brought by the nerves from the sense organs, analyzes it, and decides on a response. Messages then travel through the spinal cord and nerves to direct the muscles or other organs on what action to take.

The brain weighs about three pounds and has two halves, or hemispheres. The right side of the brain controls the left side of the body and vice versa. In general, the left side of the brain is better at logical thinking and understands time and numbers. The right side of the brain is better at creative thinking.

The spinal cord is a large bundle of nerves which is protected by the backbone. It is about one–half inch wide and weighs one ounce. Nearly 45 miles of nerves travel from the brain to all parts of the body, many of them through the spinal cord.

# NUTRITION

Good food is necessary for good health. Food is our source of energy, and of the materials that make up our bodies. The amount of energy in food is measured in calories. A calorie is a unit of heat that will warm one gram of water 1° Centigrade.

Our bodies need five important nutrients from food: carbohydrates, fats, proteins, minerals and vitamins.

**Carbohydrates** are sugars and starches. They are the body's main source of energy and should make up about 45% of the calories in a person's diet. Nearly all foods have some carbohydrates in them. Some good sources are: fruits, bread, corn, potatoes and rice.

**Fats** should make up about 40% of the calories in a person's diet. They are needed for energy as well as growth and maintenance of the body. Some good sources are: butter, salad oil, milk, nuts, and meat.

**Proteins** are necessary for the growth and maintenance of the body. Bones, muscles and skin are made of protein. About 12% to 15% of the calories in a person's diet should be from proteins. Good sources are cheese, eggs, fish, meat and milk.

**Vitamins** and **minerals** do not have calories, but are necessary for the correct functioning of parts of the body.

To insure correct nutrition, it is important to eat a **balanced diet**. Choose foods each day from each of the Basic Four Food Groups.

## BASIC FOUR FOOD GROUPS

**Meat, Poultry, Fish, Beans**

| | |
|---|---|
| Sources: | meat, poultry and eggs, fish and shellfish, dry beans, dry peas, soybeans, lentils, nuts |
| Servings: | two 3-ounce servings a day |
| Provides: | protein, vitamins, minerals |

**Milk and Cheese**

| | |
|---|---|
| Sources: | milk, cheese, cottage cheese, cream cheese, ice cream, yogurt |
| Servings: | 3-4 eight ounce cups a day |
| Provides: | calcium, protein, vitamins |

**Vegetables and Fruits**

| | |
|---|---|
| Sources: | all vegetables and fruits, including citrus fruits, green leafy vegetables tomatoes and potatoes |
| Servings: | 4 or more servings a day. Choose foods high in vitamin A and C whenever possible. |
| Provides: | vitamins and minerals, fiber |

**Bread and Cereal**

| | |
|---|---|
| Sources: | all breads and cereals, including rice |
| Servings: | 4 or more servings a day. Use whole grain or enriched products. |
| Provides: | protein, iron, vitamins and food energy |

# CHART OF VITAMINS

**Vitamin A**
Needed for: eyes, normal growth, skin, bones & teeth
Deficiency: night blindness, stunted growth, dry, scaly skin
Good sources: liver, carrots, dark green leafy vegetables
Recommended daily allowance: 5000 IU

**Vitamin B-1 (Thiamine)**
Needed for: energy, appetite, muscle tone, mental attitude
Deficiency: tiredness, beriberi
Good sources: lean pork, peanuts
Recommended daily allowance: 1.4 mg.

**Vitamin B-2 (Riboflavin)**
Needed for: chemical reactions during oxidation of foods
Deficiency: sore mouth and tongue, chapped lips
Good sources: liver, kidney, heart, almonds, cheese, eggs
Recommended daily allowance: 1.7 mg.

**Vitamin B-6**
Needed for: body chemistry
Deficiency: skin problems, weakness, irritability
Good sources: bran, sunflower seeds, avocados, bananas, corn
Recommended daily allowance: 2.2 mg.

**Vitamin B-12**
Needed for: bone marrow, nerves, digestive system
Deficiency: sore tongue, weakness, loss of weight, back pains
Good sources: meat, fish, eggs, cheese
Recommended daily allowance: 3.0 mcg.

**Vitamin C (Ascorbic Acid)**
Needed for: healing wounds, bones

Deficiency: bleeding gums, brittle bones, scurvy
Good sources: citrus fruits and juices, rose hips, green leafy vegetables, tomatoes
Recommended daily allowance: 60 mg.

**Vitamin D**
Needed for: bones and teeth
Deficiency: rickets (bowed legs, knocked knees)
Good sources: sunlight, fatty fish, egg yolks, vitamin D milk
Recommended daily allowance: 400 IU

**Vitamin E**
Needed for: intestines and tissue
Deficiency: often no symptoms
Good sources: salad and cooking oil, margarine, nuts, oatmeal
Recommended daily allowance: 14.90 IU

**Vitamin K**
Needed for: blood clotting
Deficiency: slow clotting of blood
Good sources: green tea, green leafy vegetables, beef liver
Recommended daily allowance: 140 mcg.

**Niacin**
Needed for: body chemistry
Deficiency: pellagra, skin problems, anxiety or depression
Good sources: liver, kidney, lean meats, poultry, fish, nuts
Recommended daily allowance: 18 mg.

**Folic Acid**
Needed for: cell division, hemoglobin
Deficiency: anemia
Good sources: liver, kidney, avocados, beans, eggs, fish
Recommended daily allowance: 400 mcg.

# CHART OF MINERALS

## Calcium
| | |
|---|---|
| Needed for: | bones and teeth |
| Deficiency: | stunted growth, rickets |
| Good sources: | cheese, blackstrap molasses, milk, nuts, green leafy vegetables, ice cream, yogurt, cottage cheese |

Recommended daily allowance: maximum recommended is 1200 mg.

## Phosphorus
| | |
|---|---|
| Needed for: | bones and teeth, muscles |
| Deficiency: | weakness, loss of appetite, bone pain |
| Good sources: | cocoa powder, pumpkin and squash seeds, rice bran, soybean flour, sunflower seeds, wheat bran, meat, cheese, nuts |

Recommended daily allowance: 1200 mg.

## Sodium
| | |
|---|---|
| Needed for: | balanced body chemistry |
| Deficiency: | poor growth, loss of weight, muscle cramps, headache, nausea |
| Good sources: | bacon, bologna, bran cereal, butter and margarine |

Recommended daily allowance: 900-2,700 mg.

## Magnesium
| | |
|---|---|
| Needed for: | bones and teeth, relaxes nerves |
| Deficiency: | muscle spasms, rapid heartbeat, confusion |
| Good sources: | instant coffee, cocoa powder, sesame seeds, wheat germ |

Recommended daily allowance: 400 mg.

## Potassium
| | |
|---|---|
| Needed for: | cells, relaxing heart |
| Deficiency: | rapid, irregular heartbeat, weakness, irritability |
| Good sources: | dehydrated fruits, molasses, rice bran, seaweed, soybean flour, spices, sunflower seeds, wheat bran, meat |

Recommended daily allowance: 1,875-5,625 mg.

## Iodine
| | |
|---|---|
| Needed for: | thyroid gland |
| Deficiency: | goiter, obesity, high blood cholesterol |
| Good sources: | iodized salt, seafood |

Recommended daily allowance: 150 mcg.

## Iron
| | |
|---|---|
| Needed for: | blood, red blood cells which carry oxygen |
| Deficiency: | anemia |
| Good sources: | kidneys, blackstrap molasses, chicken giblets, cocoa powder, liver, oysters, spices, wheat bran |

Recommended daily allowance: 18 mg.

## Zinc
| | |
|---|---|
| Needed for: | normal skin, bones, hair |
| Deficiency: | loss of appetite, stunted growth, skin changes |
| Good sources: | beef, liver, oysters, spices, wheat bran |

Recommended daily allowance: 15 mg.

### ABBREVIATIONS
| | |
|---|---|
| IU | International Units |
| mg. | milligrams |
| mcg. | micrograms |

# DRUGS AND ALCOHOL

Drugs are a very valuable tool for doctors. They are used to prevent and treat diseases, some of which might otherwise result in death. Many people live longer and healthier lives than would otherwise be possible because of helpful drugs.

A **drug** is any chemical substance which affects the functioning of the body. Drugs can be helpful or harmful depending on their use. Even the safest and most helpful of drugs can cause sickness or death if misused or abused.

**Alcohol**, although legal, is one of the most widely abused drugs. Many people who use alcohol become addicted to it. **Addiction** is when a person's body needs a drug so badly that pain or sickness results when the drug is not used regularly. Addicts often need larger and larger doses of a drug as they become accustomed to using it. An adult can become an **alcoholic**, or a person addicted to alcohol, in one to eighteen years. A teenager can become addicted in one to eighteen months.

There are many other kinds of drugs, both helpful and harmful. They are classified according to the effect they have on the body. The outline lists some major classifications of drugs with examples of each.

## OUTLINE OF TYPES OF DRUGS

I. **Narcotics.** These depress or numb the nervous system and are addicting.
   A. Natural—opium, morphine, codeine
   B. Semisynthetic—heroin
   C. Synthetic—Methodone (used to treat heroin addicts), Demerol, Darvon

II. **Nonprescription analgesics.**
   A. Aspirin
   B. Tylenol

III. **Stimulants,** or "uppers." These speed up the nervous system, creating alertness and/or edginess.
   A. Amphetamines—diet pills, pep pills
   B. Cocaine
   C. Caffeine—in coffee, tea, chocolate, cola drinks
   D. Nicotine—in cigarettes, cigars, snuff and chewing tobacco

IV. **Sedatives,** also called depressnts or "downers." These slow down, sedate and depress the nervous system.
   A. Alcohol—beer, wine, distilled spirits
   B. Tranquilizers—Valium, Benadryl
   C. Barbiturates—sleeping pills

V. **Cannabis** is legally a narcotic, but acts sometimes as a hallucinogen or depressant.
   A. THC
   B. Hashish
   C. Marijuana

VI. **Hallucinogens,** or psychedelic drugs. These distort sight and sound, and are mind-altering.
   A. L.S.D. (lysergic acid diethylamide-25)
   B. Mescaline
   C. Peyote

VII. **Volatile Inhalants.** These depress the body's breathing mechanism.
   A. Gasoline
   B. Aerosol Spray
   C. Glue
   D. Paint

# THE EARTH AND ITS PEOPLE

# WATERS OF THE WORLD

More than 70% of the earth's surface is covered by water. There are four large oceans as well as numerous seas, bays, gulfs, channels, lakes, and rivers.

## THE OCEANS

| Ocean | Area (square miles) | Average Depth (feet) | Deepest Point (feet) |
|---|---|---|---|
| Pacific | 63,800,000 | 14,000 | 36,198 |
| Atlantic | 31,530,000 | 14,000 | 28,374 |
| Indian | 28,356,000 | 12,785 | 25,344 |
| Arctic | 3,662,000 | 4,362 | 17,880 |

The deepest place in any ocean is the Mariana Trench. The bottom of the ocean there is 36,198 feet below the surface of the Pacific Ocean. No light shines into the deepest parts of the ocean, but some unusual fish live there, eating remains of dead plants and animals that drift down from above.

The deeper into the ocean you go, the more pressure there is from the weight of the water above. The pressure would crush an unprotected human. Fish which live deep in the ocean must have pressure inside their bodies to equal the pressure outside. Scientists have gone as deep as 35,000, over six miles, into the ocean in a special submarine called a **bathyscape**.

## DEPTH & PRESSURE CHART

| DEPTH | Pounds per sq. in. pressure |
|---|---|
| Surface | 14.7 (from atmosphere) |
| 600 feet | 282 pounds |
| 1,200 feet | 549 pounds |
| 3,000 feet | 1,351 pounds |
| 7,200 feet | 3,222 pounds |
| 18,000 feet | 8,033 pounds |
| 30,000 feet | 13,378 pounds |
| 36,198 feet | 16,139 pounds |

## LAKES OF THE WORLD

| LAKE | LOCATION | AREA (square miles) | LENGTH (miles) | GREATEST DEPTH (feet) |
|---|---|---|---|---|
| Caspian Sea* | Asia | 143,630 | 750 | 3,363 |
| Lake Superior | North America | 31,700 | 350 | 1,333 |
| Lake Victoria | Africa | 26,828 | 200 | 270 |
| Aral Sea* | Asia (U.S.S.R.) | 25,660 | 270 | 223 |
| Lake Huron | North America | 23,050 | 206 | 750 |
| Lake Michigan | North America | 22,300 | 307 | 923 |
| Lake Tanganyika | Africa | 12,700 | 420 | 4,708 |
| Great Bear Lake | North America | 12,275 | 232 | 1,350 |
| Lake Baikal | Asia (U.S.S.R.) | 12,162 | 395 | 5,315 |
| Lake Nyasa | Africa | 11,100 | 350 | 2,300 |
| Great Slave Lake | North America | 10,980 | 298 | 2,015 |
| Lake Erie | North America | 9,910 | 240 | 210 |
| Lake Winnipeg | North America | 9,416 | 258 | 70 |
| Lake Ontario | North America | 7,550 | 193 | 802 |
| Lake Chad | Africa | 6,300 | Varies | 22 |
| Great Salt Lake* | North America | 1,700 | 75 | 44 |

*Salt water.

## SEAS OF THE WORLD

| SEA | AREA (sq. mi.) | LOCATION |
|---|---|---|
| Adriatic | 41,440 | Mediterranean, near Italy |
| Aegean | 69,110 | Mediterranean, near Greece |
| Arabian | 1,490,000 | Indian Ocean, near Saudi Arabia |
| Azoz | 14,000 | Southern Russia, near Black Sea |
| Baltic | 162,930 | Between Russia and northern Europe |
| Banda | 285,020 | Near Indonesia |
| Barents | 529,096 | North of eastern Norway and Russia |
| Bering | 956,700 | Between Alaska and Siberia |
| Black | 175,960 | Between Russia and Turkey |
| Caribbean | 758,400 | East of Central America |
| Dead | 395 | Middle East, between Israel & Jordan |
| East China | 281,850 | Between Korea, Japan and China |
| Ionian | --- | Mediterranean, between southern Italy & Greece |
| Irish | 40,000 | Separates Ireland from England |
| Japan | 389,200 | Separates Japan and Korea |
| Java | 120,000 | Near Indonesia |
| Marmara | 4,300 | Between Mediterranean and Black Seas |
| Mediterannean | 967,230 | Between Europe and Africa |
| North | 222,000 | Between Great Britain and mainland of Europe |
| Okhotsk | 589,961 | East of U.S.S.R. |
| Red | 169,112 | Between Africa and Asia |
| South China | 894,980 | East of southeast Asia |
| Sulu | 100,386 | Between Philippines and Borneo |
| Tasman | 888,030 | Between Australia and New Zealand |
| Timor | 173,745 | Northwest of Australia |
| Tyrrhenian | 60,000 | Mediterranean, west of Italy |
| White | 36,680 | North of U.S.S.R. |
| Yellow | 180,000 | Between China and Korea |

## WATERFALLS OF THE WORLD

| WATERFALL | LOCATION | Height (feet) | WATERFALL | LOCATION | Height (feet) |
|---|---|---|---|---|---|
| Angel | Venezuela | 3,212 | Vettisfoss | Norway | 1,200 |
| Tugela | South Africa | 3,110 | Widow's Tears | California | 1,170 |
| Cuquenán | Venezuela | 2,000 | Feather | California | 640 |
| Sutherland | New Zealand | 1,904 | Bridalveil | California | 620 |
| Ribbon | California | 1,612 | Multnomah | Oregon | 620 |
| Upper Yosemite | California | 1,430 | Victoria | Southeast Africa | 343 |
| Gavarnie | France | 1,385 | Lower Yellowstone | Wyoming | 308 |
| Takkakaw | Canada | 1,200 | Niagara | New York | 167 |

## IMPORTANT RIVERS OF THE WORLD

| RIVER | LOCATION | LENGTH (miles) | OTHER FACTS |
|---|---|---|---|
| Amazon | South America | 4,000 | Most water of any river |
| Arkansas | North America | 1,459 | Carved Royal Gorge |
| Colorado | North America | 1,450 | Carved Grand Canyon |
| Congo (Zaire) | Central Africa | 2,900 | Explored by Stanley in 1877 |
| Ganges | Asia | 1,540 | Sacred river for Hindus |
| Indus | Asia | 1,800 | Used heavily for irrigation |
| Irtysh | Asia (U.S.S.R.) | 2,640 | Frozen December to March |
| MacKenzie | North America | 1,071 | Longest Canadian river |
| Mekong | Southeast Asia | 2,600 | Longest river in SE Asia |
| Mississippi | North America | 2,348 | Longest U.S. river |
| Missouri | North America | 2,315 | Second longest U.S. river |
| Niger | Africa | 2,600 | Source is 150 miles from ocean |
| Nile | Northern Africa | 4,145 | Longest river in the world |
| Ob | Asia (U.S.S.R.) | 2,268 | Frozen October to June |
| Paraná | South America | 2,485 | Second longest in S. America |
| Rio Grande | North America | 1,885 | Border of U.S. and Mexico |
| St. Lawrence | North America | 800 | Links Atlantic & Great Lakes |
| Volga | Europe (Russia) | 2,194 | Longest river in Europe |
| Yangtze Kiang | Asia | 3,915 | Longest river in China |
| Yellow (Huang He) | Asia | 2,903 | Many terrible floods |
| Yenisey | Asia (U.S.S.R.) | 2,543 | Flows into Arctic Ocean |
| Yukon | North America | 1,979 | Famous for Klondike Gold Rush |

### The Continents and Oceans

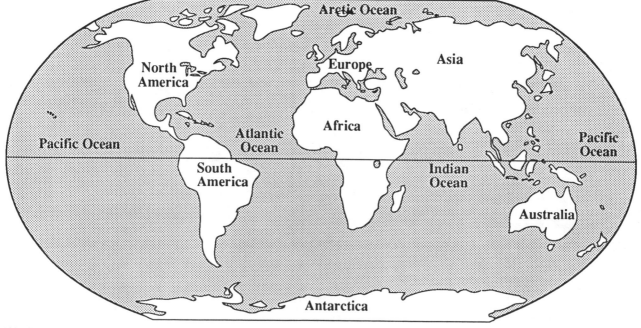

# LAND AREAS OF THE WORLD

About 30% of the earth's surface is **land.** Seven **continents** make up most of the land area. There are also thousands of islands.

## CONTINENTS

| Continent | Area (square miles) | Population | Highest Point (feet) | Lowest Point (feet) | No. of Indep. Countries |
|---|---|---|---|---|---|
| Africa | 11,683,000 | 643,000,000 | Kilimanjaro 19,340 | Lake Assali -509 | 51 |
| Antarctica | 5,400,000 | — | Vinson Massif 16,864 | sea level | 0 |
| Asia | 17,006,000 | 3,172,000,000 | Mt. Everest 29,028 | Dead Sea -1,310 | 42 |
| Australia | 2,966,150 | 16,365,000 | Mt. Kosciusko 7,310 | Lake Eyre -52 | 1 |
| Europe | 4,061,000 | 693,221,000 | Mt. Elbrus 18,481 | Caspian Sea -92 | 33 |
| North America | 9,358,000 | 427,000,000 | Mt. McKinley 20,320 | Death Valley -282 | 23 |
| South America | 6,880,000 | 297,000,000 | Aconcagua 22,831 | Valdes Peninsula -131 | 12 |

**% of Land Area**

21%  30%  9%  12%  16%  7%  5%

**% of Population**

12%  6%  8%  7%  60%

- Africa
- Asia
- Australia
- Europe
- North America
- South America
- Antarctica

Note: Australia has less than 1% of the world's population

## DESERTS OF THE WORLD

| DESERT | LOCATION | APPROXIMATE SIZE |
|---|---|---|
| Arabian | E. of Africa | 500,000 sq. mi. |
| Atacama | S. America | 600 miles long |
| Australian | Australia | 660,000 sq. mi. |
| Gobi | Asia | 500,000 sq. mi. |
| Kalahari | Africa | 190,000 sq. mi. |
| Sahara | Africa | 3,500,000 sq. mi. |

## ISLANDS OF THE WORLD

| ISLAND | LOCATION | AREA (sq. miles) |
|---|---|---|
| Greenland | N. Atlantic | 840,004 |
| New Guinea | SW Pacific | 311,737 |
| Borneo | W. mid-Pacific | 288,151 |
| Madagascar | Indian Ocean | 226,658 |
| Baffin | North Atlantic | 195,927 |
| Sumatra | NE Indian Ocean | 182,860 |
| Honshu | Sea of Japan | 87,805 |
| Great Britain | West of Europe | 84,550 |
| Victoria | Arctic Ocean | 83,896 |
| Ellesmere | Arctic Ocean | 75,767 |

## MOUNTAIN RANGES OF THE WORLD

| RANGE | LOCATION | TALLEST PEAK | LENGTH (miles) |
|---|---|---|---|
| Alaska | Alaska | Mount McKinley | 600 |
| Alps | Europe | Mont Blanc | 750 |
| Andes | West coast of South America | Aconcagua | 4,500 |
| Appalachian | Eastern United States | Mount Mitchell | 1,500 |
| Atlas | Northern Africa | Jebel Toubkal | 1,500 |
| Cascades | West Coast of North America | Mount Rainier | 700 |
| Himalayas | Asia | Mount Everest | 1,500 |
| Rockies | Western United States | Mount Elbert | 3,000 |

Of the 100 tallest peaks in the world, 59 are in the Himalayas and 14 others are in nearby mountain ranges. The remaining 27 are in the Andes of South America.

## IMPORTANT MOUNTAIN PEAKS

| PEAK | LOCATION | HEIGHT (feet) | OTHER INFORMATION |
|---|---|---|---|
| Aconcagua | Andes | 22,831 | Highest in western hemisphere |
| Communism Peak | U.S.S.R. | 24,590 | Highest in Russia, 49th in world |
| Cook | New Zealand | 12,319 | Highest in New Zealand |
| Cotopaxi | Andes | 19,347 | Highest active volcano in world |
| Elbert | Rockies | 14,433 | Highest in Rocky Mountains |
| Elbrus | Alps | 18,481 | Highest in Europe |
| Everest | Himalayas | 29,028 | Highest mountain in the world |
| Fuji | Japan | 12,388 | Considered sacred by Japanese |
| Godwin Austen (K-2) | Himalayas | 28,250 | 2nd highest in the world |
| Jebel Toubkal | Atlas | 13,665 | Highest in Atlas Mountains |
| Kanchenjunga | Himalayas | 28,208 | 3rd highest in the world |
| Kenya | Africa | 17,058 | Second highest in Africa |
| Kilimanjaro | Africa | 19,340 | Highest in Africa |
| Kosciusko | Australia | 7,310 | Highest in Australia |
| Logan | Canada | 19,524 | Highest in Canada |
| Matterhorn | Alps | 14,692 | Steep and pyramid-shaped |
| Mauna Kea | Hawaii | 13,796 | Highest island peak in world |
| McKinley | Alaska | 20,320 | Highest in North America, 103rd in world |
| Mitchell | Appalachians | 6,684 | Highest in Appalachians |
| Mont Blanc | Alps | 15,771 | Highest in Alps |
| Pikes Peak | Rockies | 14,110 | Gold rush slogan, "Pikes Peak or Bust" |
| Rainier | Cascades | 14,410 | Highest in Cascades |
| Vinson Massif | Antarctica | 16,864 | Highest in Antarctica |

# GEOGRAPHIC TERMS

Following is a list of geographic terms which are used to refer to areas or features of land and water.

**archipelago:** a group or chain of many islands

**bay:** part of a body of water which indents the shoreline

**butte:** a steep hill standing alone in a plain

**canyon:** a long valley between high cliffs, usually narrow and with a stream flowing through it

**channel:** a body of water joining two larger bodies of water

**coastline:** the outline of a coast, or seashore

**continent:** any of the seven main large land areas of the earth

**delta:** a deposit of sand and soil, usually triangular, at the mouth of a river

**desert:** a hot, dry region which receives little rainfall and supports little plant and animal life

**glacier:** a large mass of ice which is moving slowly downhill

**gulf:** a large area of ocean reaching into land which is larger than a bay

**hill:** a raised part of the earth's surface which is usually rounded and smaller than a mountain

**inlet:** a narrow strip of water extending into land or between islands

**island:** a land mass smaller than a continent which is surrounded by water

**isthmus:** a narrow strip of land with water on both sides which connects two larger bodies of land

**lake:** a body of usually fresh water which is surrounded by land

**mesa:** a small, flat tableland or high plateau with steep sides

**mountain:** a natural raised part of the earth's surface, usually steep and larger than a hill

**mountain range:** a group of connected mountains

**ocean:** any of the four large bodies of salt water which cover most of the earth's surface

**peak:** the highest point of a mountain

**peninsula:** a land area connected to the mainland, but surrounded almost completely by water

**plains:** a large area of level country

**plateau:** a high area of more or less level land

**reef:** a ridge of rock, coral or sand at or near the surface of the water

**reservoir:** a lake or pond, usually man-made, where water is collected and stored for use

**river:** a natural stream of water, larger than a creek or stream, which empties into another river or into a large body of water such as an ocean

**sea:** a large body of salt water partially or completely enclosed by land

**sound:** a long inlet or a wide strait connecting larger bodies of water

**strait:** a narrow waterway connecting two large bodies of water

**swamp:** an area of wet, marshy land

**tributary:** a river or stream which flows into a larger river or stream

**valley:** an area of low land between hills or mountains, usually with a stream flowing through it

## Kodiak Archipelago
Alaska

Kuprano Strait

Karluk River and tributaries

Kodiak Island

Karluk Lake

Gulf of Alaska

Aliulik Peninsula

Geese Channel

Trinity Islands

# COUNTRIES OF THE WORLD

## AFGHANISTAN
**Capital:** Kabul (1,127,417)
**Area:** 250,000 sq. mi.
**Language:** Pashtu and Dari Persian
**Currency:** afghani
**Population:** 15,862,000
**Population Growth Rate:** 2.6%
**Population Density:** 63
**Per Capita GNP:** $200
**Average Life Expectancy:** 41
**Infant Mortality Rate:** 182
**Literacy Rate:** 12%
**Location:** Southern Asia
**Latitude-Longitude:** 33°N 65°E

## ALBANIA
**Capital:** Tiranë (215,857)
**Area:** 11,100 sq. mi.
**Language:** Albanian
**Currency:** lek
**Population:** 3,273,000
**Population Growth Rate:** 2.0%
**Population Density:** 295
**Per Capita GNP:** $1200
**Average Life Expectancy:** 71
**Infant Mortality Rate:** 28
**Literacy Rate:** 75%
**Location:** Southern Europe
**Latitude-Longitude:** 41°N 20°E

## ALGERIA
**Capital:** Algiers (1,721,607)
**Area:** 919,590 sq. mi.
**Language:** Arabic, French
**Currency:** Algerian dinar
**Population:** 25,567,000
**Population Growth Rate:** 3.1%
**Population Density:** 28
**Per Capita GNP:** $2,450
**Average Life Expectancy:** 60
**Infant Mortality Rate:** 74
**Literacy Rate:** 52%
**Location:** Northern Africa
**Latitude-Longitude:** 28°N 3°E

## ANDORRA
**Capital:** Andorra la Vella (16,200)
**Area:** 180 sq. mi.
**Language:** Catalan, French,
Spanish

**Currency:** French franc and
Spanish peseta
**Population:** 52,000
**Population Growth Rate:** 0.8%
**Population Density:** 289
**Per Capita GNP:** Not available
**Average Life Expectancy:** 77
**Infant Mortality Rate:** 4
**Literacy Rate:** 100%
**Location:** Southern Europe
**Latitude-Longitude:** 42°N 1°E

## ANGOLA
**Capital:** Luanda (1,200,000)
**Area:** 481,350 sq. mi.
**Language:** Portuguese, Bantu
**Currency:** kwanza
**Population:** 8,534,000
**Population Growth Rate:** 2.7%
**Population Density:** 18
**Per Capita GNP:** $600
**Average Life Expectancy:** 45
**Infant Mortality Rate:** 137
**Literacy Rate:** 41%
**Location:** Central Africa
**Latitude-Longitude:** 12°S 18°E

## ANTIGUA AND BARBUDA
**Capital:** St. John's (36,000)
**Area:** 170 sq. mi.
**Language:** English
**Currency:** East Caribbean dollar
**Population:** 64,000
**Population Growth Rate:** 1.0%
**Population Density:** 377
**Per Capita GNP:** $2,800
**Average Life Expectancy:** 71
**Infant Mortality Rate:** 24
**Literacy Rate:** 90%
**Location:** Caribbean Sea
**Latitude-Longitude:** 17°N 61°W

## ARGENTINA
**Capital:** Buenos Aires (2,922,829)
**Area:** 1,068,300 sq. mi.
**Language:** Spanish
**Currency:** austral
**Population:** 32,291,000
**Population Growth Rate:** 1.3%

**Population Density:** 30
**Per Capita GNP:** $2,640
**Average Life Expectancy:** 71
**Infant Mortality Rate:** 32
**Literacy Rate:** 94%
**Location:** South America
**Latitude-Longitude:** 34°S 64°W

## AUSTRALIA
**Capital:** Canberra (273,600)
**Area:** 2,967,900 sq. mi.
**Language:** English
**Currency:** Australian dollar
**Population:** 17,083,000
**Population Growth Rate:** 0.8%
**Population Density:** 6
**Per Capita GNP:** $12,390
**Average Life Expectancy:** 76
**Infant Mortality Rate:** 9
**Literacy Rate:** 99%
**Location:** Oceania
**Latitude-Longitude:** 25°S 135°E

## AUSTRIA
**Capital:** Vienna (1,531,346)
**Area:** 32,370 sq. mi.
**Language:** German
**Currency:** Austrian schilling
**Population:** 7,623,000
**Population Growth Rate:** 0.1%
**Population Density:** 235
**Per Capita GNP:** $15,560
**Average Life Expectancy:** 75
**Infant Mortality Rate:** 8
**Literacy Rate:** 98%
**Location:** Western Europe
**Latitude-Longitude:** 47°N 14°E

## THE BAHAMAS
**Capital:** Nassau (110,000)
**Area:** 5,380 sq. mi.
**Language:** English
**Currency:** Bahamian dollar
**Population:** 246,000
**Population Growth Rate:** 1.5%
**Population Density:** 46
**Per Capita GNP:** $10,570
**Average Life Expectancy:** 71
**Infant Mortality Rate:** 22
**Literacy Rate:** 95%

**Location:** Caribbean Sea
**Latitude-Longitude:** 24°N 76°W

## BAHRAIN

**Capital:** Manama (108,684)
**Area:** 240 sq. mi.
**Language:** Arabic, English, French
**Currency:** Bahraini dinar
**Population:** 520,000
**Population Growth Rate:** 2.3%
**Population Density:** 2,172
**Per Capita GNP:** $6,610
**Average Life Expectancy:** 67
**Infant Mortality Rate:** 24
**Literacy Rate:** 40%
**Location:** Western Asia
**Latitude-Longitude:** 26°N 50°E

## BANGLADESH

**Capital:** Dhaka (3,458,602)
**Area:** 55,600 sq. mi.
**Language:** Bangla, English
**Currency:** taka
**Population:** 114,783,000
**Population Growth Rate:** 2.5%
**Population Density:** 2,064
**Per Capita GNP:** $170
**Average Life Expectancy:** 54
**Infant Mortality Rate:** 120
**Literacy Rate:** 29%
**Location:** Southern Asia
**Latitude-Longitude:** 24°N 90°E

## BARBADOS

**Capital:** Bridgetown (7,466)
**Area:** 170 sq. mi.
**Language:** English
**Currency:** Barbadian dollar
**Population:** 257,000
**Population Growth Rate:** 0.7%
**Population Density:** 1,548
**Per Capita GNP:** $5,990
**Average Life Expectancy:** 75
**Infant Mortality Rate:** 16
**Literacy Rate:** 99%
**Location:** Caribbean Sea
**Latitude-Longitude:** 13°N 59°W

## BELGIUM

**Capital:** Brussels (973,499)
**Area:** 11,750 sq. mi.
**Language:** Dutch, French
**Currency:** Belgian franc

**Population:** 9,893,000
**Population Growth Rate:** 0.2%
**Population Density:** 842
**Per Capita GNP:** $14,550
**Average Life Expectancy:** 74
**Infant Mortality Rate:** 9
**Literacy Rate:** 98%
**Location:** Western Europe
**Latitude-Longitude:** 50°N 4°E

## BELIZE

**Capital:** Belmopan (4,500)
**Area:** 8,860 sq. mi.
**Language:** English, Spanish
**Currency:** Belizean dollar
**Population:** 220,000
**Population Growth Rate:** 3.1%
**Population Density:** 25
**Per Capita GNP:** $1,460
**Average Life Expectancy:** 69
**Infant Mortality Rate:** 36
**Literacy Rate:** 93%
**Location:** Central America
**Latitude-Longitude:** 17°N 89°W

## BENIN

**Capital:** Porto-Novo (144,000)
**Area:** 43,480 sq. mi.
**Language:** French, African
  languages
**Currency:** CFA franc
**Population:** 4,741,000
**Population Growth Rate:** 3.2%
**Population Density:** 109
**Per Capita GNP:** $340
**Average Life Expectancy:** 47
**Infant Mortality Rate:** 110
**Literacy Rate:** 26%
**Location:** Western Africa
**Latitude-Longitude:** 9°N 2°E

## BHUTAN

**Capital:** Thimphu (15,000)
**Area:** 18,150 sq. mi.
**Language:** Dzongkha
**Currency:** ngultrum
**Population:** 1,565,000
**Population Growth Rate:** 2.1%
**Population Density:** 86
**Per Capita GNP:** $150
**Average Life Expectancy:** 48
**Infant Mortality Rate:** 128
**Literacy Rate:** 5%

**Location:** Southern Asia
**Latitude-Longitude:** 27°N 90°E

## BOLIVIA

**Capital:** La Paz (992,592)
**Area:** 424,160 sq. mi.
**Language:** Spanish, Quéchua,
  Aymara
**Currency:** boliviano
**Population:** 7,277,000
**Population Growth Rate:** 2.6%
**Population Density:** 17
**Per Capita GNP:** $570
**Average Life Expectancy:** 53
**Infant Mortality Rate:** 110
**Literacy Rate:** 63%
**Location:** South America
**Latitude-Longitude:** 17°S 65°W

## BOTSWANA

**Capital:** Gaborone (94,705)
**Area:** 231,800 sq. mi.
**Language:** English, Setswana
**Currency:** pula
**Population:** 1,225,000
**Population Growth Rate:** 2.9%
**Population Density:** 5
**Per Capita GNP:** $1,050
**Average Life Expectancy:** 59
**Infant Mortality Rate:** 64
**Literacy Rate:** 60%
**Location:** Southern Africa
**Latitude-Longitude:** 22°S 24°E

## BRAZIL

**Capital:** Brasília (1,576,657)
**Area:** 3,286,470 sq. mi.
**Language:** Portuguese
**Currency:** nova cruzado
**Population:** 150,368,000
**Population Growth Rate:** 1.9%
**Population Density:** 46
**Per Capita GNP:** $2,280
**Average Life Expectancy:** 65
**Infant Mortality Rate:** 63
**Literacy Rate:** 76%
**Location:** South America
**Latitude-Longitude:** 9°S 53°W

## BRUNEI

**Capital:** Bandar Scri Bcgawan
**Area:** 2,230 sq. mi.
**Language:** Malay, Chinese, English

Currency: Bruneian dollar
Population: 257,000
Population Growth Rate: 2.5%
Population Density: 115
Per Capita GNP: $14,120
Average Life Expectancy: 71
Infant Mortality Rate: 11
Literacy Rate: 45%
Location: Southeast Asia
Latitude-Longitude: 4°N 114°E

## BULGARIA

Capital: Sofia (1,114,759)
Area: 42,820 sq. mi.
Language: Bulgarian
Currency: lev
Population: 8,934,000
Population Growth Rate: 0.1%
Population Density: 209
Per Capita GNP: $5,710
Average Life Expectancy: 72
Infant Mortality Rate: 14
Literacy Rate: 95%
Location: Eastern Europe
Latitude-Longitude: 43°N 25°E

## BURKINA FASO

Capital: Ouagadougou (441,515)
Area: 105,870 sq. mi.
Language: French, African languages
Currency: CFA franc
Population: 9,078,000
Population Growth Rate: 3.2%
Population Density: 86
Per Capita GNP: $230
Average Life Expectancy: 51
Infant Mortality Rate: 126
Literacy Rate: 13%
Location: Western Africa
Latitude-Longitude: 13°N 2°W

## BURUNDI

Capital: Bujumbura (172,201)
Area: 10,750 sq. mi.
Language: Kirundi, French
Currency: Burundi franc
Population: 5,646,000
Population Growth Rate: 3.2%
Population Density: 525
Per Capita GNP: $230
Average Life Expectancy: 51
Infant Mortality Rate: 114

Literacy Rate: 34%
Location: Eastern Africa
Latitude-Longitude: 3°S 30°E

## CAMBODIA

Capital: Phnom Penh (700,000)
Area: 69,900 sq. mi.
Language: Khmer, French
Currency: riel
Population: 6,991,000
Population Growth Rate: 2.2%
Population Density: 100
Per Capita GNP: $130
Average Life Expectancy: 49
Infant Mortality Rate: 128
Literacy Rate: 48%
Location: Southeast Asia
Latitude-Longitude: 13°N 105°E

## CAMEROON

Capital: Yaoundé (650,000)
Area: 183,570 sq. mi.
Language: French, English, African languages
Currency: CFA franc
Population: 11,092,000
Population Growth Rate: 2.6%
Population Density: 60
Per Capita GNP: $1,010
Average Life Expectancy: 50
Infant Mortality Rate: 125
Literacy Rate: 56%
Location: Central Africa
Latitude-Longitude: 6°N 12°E

## CANADA

Capital: Ottawa, Ontario (295,160)
Area: 3,851,790 sq. mi.
Language: English, French
Currency: Canadian dollar
Population: 26,560,000
Population Growth Rate: 0.7%
Population Density: 7
Per Capita GNP: $16,760
Average Life Expectancy: 77
Infant Mortality Rate: 7
Literacy Rate: 99%
Location: North America
Latitude-Longitude: 60°N 95°W

## CAPE VERDE

Capital: Praia (57,748)
Area: 1,560 sq. mi.

Language: Portuguese, Crioulo
Currency: Cape Verdean escudo
Population: 379,000
Population Growth Rate: 2.8%
Population Density: 244
Per Capita GNP: $494
Average Life Expectancy: 61
Infant Mortality Rate: 66
Literacy Rate: 48%
Location: Atlantic Ocean west of Africa
Latitude-Longitude: 16°N 24°W

## CENTRAL AFRICAN REPUBLIC

Capital: Bangui (473,817)
Area: 240,530 sq. mi.
Language: French, Sangho, Arabic, Hunsa, Swahili
Currency: CFA franc
Population: 2,877,000
Population Growth Rate: 2.5%
Population Density: 12
Per Capita GNP: $390
Average Life Expectancy: 46
Infant Mortality Rate: 143
Literacy Rate: 40%
Location: Central Africa
Latitude-Longitude: 7°N 21°E

## CHAD

Capital: N'Djamena (402,000)
Area: 495,750 sq. mi.
Language: French, Arabic, tribal languages
Currency: CFA franc
Population: 5,017,000
Population Growth Rate: 2.5%
Population Density: 10
Per Capita GNP: $160
Average Life Expectancy: 46
Infant Mortality Rate: 132
Literacy Rate: 25%
Location: Central Africa
Latitude-Longitude: 15°N 19°E

## CHILE

Capital: Santiago (4,318,305)
Area: 292,260 sq. mi.
Language: Spanish
Currency: Chilean peso
Population: 13,173,000
Population Growth Rate: 1.7%

Population Density: 45
Per Capita GNP: $1,510
Average Life Expectancy: 71
Infant Mortality Rate: 19
Literacy Rate: 94%
Location: South America
Latitude-Longitude: 30°S 71°W

## CHINA

Capital: Beijing (5,970,000)
Area: 3,705,390 sq. mi.
Language: Chinese (many dialects)
Currency: yuan
Population: 1,119,877,000
Population Growth Rate: 1.4%
Population Density: 302
Per Capita GNP: $330
Average Life Expectancy: 68
Infant Mortality Rate: 37
Literacy Rate: 75%
Location: East Asia
Latitude-Longitude: 35°N 105°E

## COLOMBIA

Capital: Bogotá (3,982,941)
Area: 439,730 sq. mi.
Language: Spanish
Currency: Colombian peso
Population: 31,819,000
Population Growth Rate: 2.0%
Population Density: 72
Per Capita GNP: $1,240
Average Life Expectancy: 66
Infant Mortality Rate: 46
Literacy Rate: 88%
Location: South America
Latitude-Longitude: 4°N 72°W

## COMOROS

Capital: Moroni (17,267)
Area: 690 sq. mi.
Language: Shaafi Islam, Malagasy, French
Currency: Comoran franc
Population: 460,000
Population Growth Rate: 3.4%
Population Density: 663
Per Capita GNP: $440
Average Life Expectancy: 55
Infant Mortality Rate: 94
Literacy Rate: 15%
Location: East of Africa
Latitude-Longitude: 12°S 44°E

## CONGO

Capital: Brazzaville (596,200)
Area: 132,050 sq. mi.
Language: French, Lingala, Kikongo
Currency: CFA franc
Population: 2,242,000
Population Growth Rate: 3.0%
Population Density: 17
Per Capita GNP: $930
Average Life Expectancy: 53
Infant Mortality Rate: 113
Literacy Rate: 63%
Location: Central Africa
Latitude-Longitude: 1°S 15°E

## COSTA RICA

Capital: San José (274,832)
Area: 19,580 sq. mi.
Language: Spanish
Currency: Costa Rican colón
Population: 3,033,000
Population Growth Rate: 2.5%
Population Density: 155
Per Capita GNP: $1,760
Average Life Expectancy: 76
Infant Mortality Rate: 17
Literacy Rate: 93%
Location: Central America
Latitude-Longitude: 10°N 84°W

## CUBA

Capital: Havana (2,036,799)
Area: 44,220 sq. mi.
Language: Spanish
Currency: Cuban peso
Population: 10,620,000
Population Growth Rate: 1.2%
Population Density: 240
Per Capita GNP: $2,000
Average Life Expectancy: 75
Infant Mortality Rate: 12
Literacy Rate: 99%
Location: Caribbean Sea
Latitude-Longitude: 21°N 80°W

## CYPRUS

Capital: Nicosia (124,300)
Area: 3,570 sq. mi.
Language: Greek, Turkish, English
Currency: Cypriot pound
Population: 702,000
Population Growth Rate: 1.0%

Population Density: 197
Per Capita GNP: $6,260
Average Life Expectancy: 76
Infant Mortality Rate: 11
Literacy Rate: 99%
Location: Mediterranean Sea
Latitude-Longitude: 35°N 33°E

## CZECHOSLOVAKIA

Capital: Prague (1,189,828)
Area: 49,370 sq. mi.
Language: Czech, Slovak, Hungarian
Currency: koruna
Population: 15,638,000
Population Growth Rate: 0.2%
Population Density: 318
Per Capita GNP: $7,878
Average Life Expectancy: 71
Infant Mortality Rate: 12
Literacy Rate: 99%
Location: Eastern Europe
Latitude-Longitude: 49°N 17°E

## DENMARK

Capital: Copenhagen (478,615)
Area: 16,630 sq. mi.
Language: Danish
Currency: krone
Population: 5,135,000
Population Growth Rate: 0.0%
Population Density: 309
Per Capita GNP: $18,470
Average Life Expectancy: 75
Infant Mortality Rate: 8
Literacy Rate: 99%
Location: Northern Europe
Latitude-Longitude: 56°N 10°E

## DJIBOUTI

Capital: Djibouti (200,000)
Area: 8,490 sq. mi.
Language: French, Arabic, Afar, Somali
Currency: Djibouti franc
Population: 406,000
Population Growth Rate: 3.0%
Population Density: 48
Per Capita GNP: $1,070
Average Life Expectancy: 47
Infant Mortality Rate: 122
Literacy Rate: 20%
Location: Eastern Africa
Latitude-Longitude: 11°N 43°E

## DOMINICA
**Capital:** Roseau (8,346)
**Area:** 290 sq. mi.
**Language:** English and French patois
**Currency:** East Caribbean dollar
**Population:** 85,000
**Population Growth Rate:** 2.1%
**Population Density:** 294
**Per Capita GNP:** $1,650
**Average Life Expectancy:** 75
**Infant Mortality Rate:** 14
**Literacy Rate:** 80%
**Location:** Caribbean Sea
**Latitude-Longitude:** 15°N 61°W

## DOMINICAN REPUBLIC
**Capital:** Santo Domingo (1,313,172)
**Area:** 18,810 sq. mi.
**Language:** Spanish
**Currency:** Dominican peso
**Population:** 7,170,000
**Population Growth Rate:** 2.5%
**Population Density:** 381
**Per Capita GNP:** $680
**Average Life Expectancy:** 66
**Infant Mortality Rate:** 65
**Literacy Rate:** 74%
**Location:** Caribbean Sea
**Latitude-Longitude:** 19°N 71°W

## ECUADOR
**Capital:** Quito (1,093,278)
**Area:** 109,480 sq. mi.
**Language:** Spanish, Quéchua
**Currency:** sucre
**Population:** 10,737,000
**Population Growth Rate:** 2.5%
**Population Density:** 98
**Per Capita GNP:** $1,080
**Average Life Expectancy:** 65
**Infant Mortality Rate:** 63
**Literacy Rate:** 85%
**Location:** South America
**Latitude-Longitude:** 2°S 77°W

## EGYPT
**Capital:** Cairo (5,875,000)
**Area:** 386,660 sq. mi.
**Language:** Arabic
**Currency:** Egyptian pound
**Population:** 54,706,000
**Population Growth Rate:** 2.9%

**Population Density:** 141
**Per Capita GNP:** $650
**Average Life Expectancy:** 60
**Infant Mortality Rate:** 90
**Literacy Rate:** 45%
**Location:** Northern Africa
**Latitude-Longitude:** 27°N 30°E

## EL SALVADOR
**Capital:** San Salvador (452,614)
**Area:** 8,260 sq. mi.
**Language:** Spanish, Nahua
**Currency:** colón
**Population:** 5,310,000
**Population Growth Rate:** 2.7%
**Population Density:** 643
**Per Capita GNP:** $950
**Average Life Expectancy:** 62
**Infant Mortality Rate:** 54
**Literacy Rate:** 65%
**Location:** Central America
**Latitude-Longitude:** 14°N 89°W

## EQUATORIAL GUINEA
**Capital:** Malabo (15,253)
**Area:** 10,830 sq. mi.
**Language:** Spanish, Fang, Bubi
**Currency:** CFA franc
**Population:** 369,000
**Population Growth Rate:** 2.6%
**Population Density:** 34
**Per Capita GNP:** $350
**Average Life Expectancy:** 50
**Infant Mortality Rate:** 120
**Literacy Rate:** 40%
**Location:** Central Africa
**Latitude-Longitude:** 2°N 9°E

## ETHIOPIA
**Capital:** Addis Ababa (1,464,901)
**Area:** 471,780 sq. mi.
**Language:** Amharic, Tigrinya, Orominga
**Currency:** birr
**Population:** 51,667,000
**Population Growth Rate:** 2.0%
**Population Density:** 110
**Per Capita GNP:** $120
**Average Life Expectancy:** 41
**Infant Mortality Rate:** 154
**Literacy Rate:** 55%
**Location:** Eastern Africa
**Latitude-Longitude:** 9°N 39°E

## FIJI
**Capital:** Suva (69,481)
**Area:** 7,050 sq. mi.
**Language:** English, Fijian, Hindustani
**Currency:** Fijian dollar
**Population:** 764,000
**Population Growth Rate:** 2.2%
**Population Density:** 108
**Per Capita GNP:** $1,540
**Average Life Expectancy:** 63
**Infant Mortality Rate:** 21
**Literacy Rate:** 80%
**Location:** Oceania
**Latitude-Longitude:** 18°S 178°E

## FINLAND
**Capital:** Helsinki (487,521)
**Area:** 130,130 sq. mi.
**Language:** Finnish, Swedish
**Currency:** markka
**Population:** 4,984,000
**Population Growth Rate:** 0.3%
**Population Density:** 38
**Per Capita GNP:** $18,610
**Average Life Expectancy:** 75
**Infant Mortality Rate:** 6
**Literacy Rate:** 99%
**Location:** Northern Europe
**Latitude-Longitude:** 64°N 26°E

## FRANCE
**Capital:** Paris (2,188,960)
**Area:** 211,210 sq. mi.
**Language:** French
**Currency:** French franc
**Population:** 56,367,000
**Population Growth Rate:** 0.4%
**Population Density:** 267
**Per Capita GNP:** $16,080
**Average Life Expectancy:** 77
**Infant Mortality Rate:** 8
**Literacy Rate:** 99%
**Location:** Western Europe
**Latitude-Longitude:** 46°N 2°E

## GABON
**Capital:** Libreville (251,400)
**Area:** 103,350 sq. mi.
**Language:** French and Bantu dialects
**Currency:** CFA franc
**Population:** 1,171,000

**Population Growth Rate:** 2.2%
**Population Density:** 11
**Per Capita GNP:** $2,970
**Average Life Expectancy:** 52
**Infant Mortality Rate:** 103
**Literacy Rate:** 62%
**Location:** Central Africa
**Latitude-Longitude:** 1°S  12°E

## THE GAMBIA
**Capital:** Banjul (44,188)
**Area:** 4,360 sq. mi.
**Language:** English, African
   languages
**Currency:** dalasi
**Population:** 858,000
**Population Growth Rate:** 2.6%
**Population Density:** 197
**Per Capita GNP:** $220
**Average Life Expectancy:** 43
**Infant Mortality Rate:** 143
**Literacy Rate:** 25%
**Location:** Western Africa
**Latitude-Longitude:** 13°N  16°W

## GERMANY
**Capital:** Berlin (1,223,309)
**Area:** 137,810 sq. mi.
**Language:** German
**Currency:** deutsche mark
**Population:** 79,544,000
**Population Growth Rate:** 0.0%
**Population Density:** 577
**Per Capita GNP:** $16,781
**Average Life Expectancy:** 75
**Infant Mortality Rate:** 8
**Literacy Rate:** 99%
**Location:** Eastern Europe
**Latitude-Longitude:** 51°N  9°E

## GHANA
**Capital:** Accra (964,879)
**Area:** 92,100 sq. mi.
**Language:** English, native tongues
**Currency:** cedi
**Population:** 15,020,000
**Population Growth Rate:** 3.1%
**Population Density:** 163
**Per Capita GNP:** $400
**Average Life Expectancy:** 55
**Infant Mortality Rate:** 86
**Literacy Rate:** 53%
**Location:** Western Africa
**Latitude-Longitude:** 8°N  2°W

## GREECE
**Capital:** Athens (885,737)
**Area:** 50,940 sq. mi.
**Language:** Greek
**Currency:** drachma
**Population:** 10,050,000
**Population Growth Rate:** 0.2%
**Population Density:** 197
**Per Capita GNP:** $4,790
**Average Life Expectancy:** 77
**Infant Mortality Rate:** 11
**Literacy Rate:** 95%
**Location:** Southern Europe
**Latitude-Longitude:** 39°N  22°E

## GRENADA
**Capital:** St. George's (7,500)
**Area:** 130 sq. mi.
**Language:** English
**Currency:** East Caribbean dollar
**Population:** 84,000
**Population Growth Rate:** 3.0%
**Population Density:** 641
**Per Capita GNP:** $1,370
**Average Life Expectancy:** 71
**Infant Mortality Rate:** 30
**Literacy Rate:** 85%
**Location:** Caribbean Sea
**Latitude-Longitude:** 12°N  62°W

## GUATEMALA
**Capital:** Guatemala City (754,243)
**Area:** 42,040 sq. mi.
**Language:** Spanish, Indian dialects
**Currency:** quetzal
**Population:** 9,197,000
**Population Growth Rate:** 3.1%
**Population Density:** 219
**Per Capita GNP:** $880
**Average Life Expectancy:** 63
**Infant Mortality Rate:** 59
**Literacy Rate:** 50%
**Location:** Central America
**Latitude-Longitude:** 15°N  90°W

## GUINEA
**Capital:** Conakry (1,110,000)
**Area:** 94,930 sq. mi.
**Language:** French, native tongues
**Currency:** Guinean franc
**Population:** 7,269,000
**Population Growth Rate:** 2.5%
**Population Density:** 77

**Per Capita GNP:** $350
**Average Life Expectancy:** 42
**Infant Mortality Rate:** 147
**Literacy Rate:** 48%
**Location:** Western Africa
**Latitude-Longitude:** 11°N  10°W

## GUINEA-BISSAU
**Capital:** Bissau (109,214)
**Area:** 13,950 sq. mi.
**Language:** Portuguese
**Currency:** Guinea-Bissau peso
**Population:** 987,000
**Population Growth Rate:** 2.1%
**Population Density:** 71
**Per Capita GNP:** $160
**Average Life Expectancy:** 45
**Infant Mortality Rate:** 132
**Literacy Rate:** 34%
**Location:** Western Africa
**Latitude-Longitude:** 12°N  15°W

## GUYANA
**Capital:** Georgetown (72,049)
**Area:** 83,000 sq. mi.
**Language:** English, Amerindian
   dialects
**Currency:** Guyanese dollar
**Population:** 765,000
**Population Growth Rate:** 1.9%
**Population Density:** 9
**Per Capita GNP:** $410
**Average Life Expectancy:** 67
**Infant Mortality Rate:** 30
**Literacy Rate:** 85%
**Location:** South America
**Latitude-Longitude:** 5°N  59°W

## HAITI
**Capital:** Port-au-Prince (461,464)
**Area:** 10,710 sq. mi.
**Language:** French, Creole
**Currency:** gourde
**Population:** 6,504,000
**Population Growth Rate:** 2.2%
**Population Density:** 607
**Per Capita GNP:** $360
**Average Life Expectancy:** 53
**Infant Mortality Rate:** 122
**Literacy Rate:** 23%
**Location:** Caribbean Sea
**Latitude-Longitude:** 19°N  72°W

## HONDURAS
**Capital:** Tegucigalpa (597,512)
**Area:** 43,280 sq. mi.
**Language:** Spanish, Indian dialects
**Currency:** lempira
**Population:** 5,138,000
**Population Growth Rate:** 3.1%
**Population Density:** 119
**Per Capita GNP:** $850
**Average Life Expectancy:** 63
**Infant Mortality Rate:** 63
**Literacy Rate:** 56%
**Location:** Central America
**Latitude-Longitude:** 15°N 86°W

## HUNGARY
**Capital:** Budapest (2,075,990)
**Area:** 35,920 sq. mi.
**Language:** Hungarian
**Currency:** forint
**Population:** 10,569,000
**Population Growth Rate:** -0.2%
**Population Density:** 294
**Per Capita GNP:** $2,460
**Average Life Expectancy:** 70
**Infant Mortality Rate:** 16
**Literacy Rate:** 99%
**Location:** Eastern Europe
**Latitude-Longitude:** 47°N 20°E

## ICELAND
**Capital:** Reykjavik (91,497)
**Area:** 39,770 sq. mi.
**Language:** Icelandic
**Currency:** króna
**Population:** 260,000
**Population Growth Rate:** 1.1%
**Population Density:** 7
**Per Capita GNP:** $20,160
**Average Life Expectancy:** 78
**Infant Mortality Rate:** 6
**Literacy Rate:** 100%
**Location:** Northern Europe
**Latitude-Longitude:** 65°N 18°W

## INDIA
**Capital:** New Delhi (273,036)
**Area:** 1,269,340 sq. mi.
**Language:** Hindi, English, Bengali,
Telgu, Marathi, Tamil, Urdu,
Gujarati, Malayalam, Kannada,
Oriya, Punjabi, Assamese,
Kashmiri, Sindhi, Sanskrit
**Currency:** Indian rupee
**Population:** 853,373,000
**Population Growth Rate:** 2.1%
**Population Density:** 672
**Per Capita GNP:** $330
**Average Life Expectancy:** 57
**Infant Mortality Rate:** 95
**Literacy Rate:** 36%
**Location:** Southern Asia
**Latitude-Longitude:** 20°N 77°E

## INDONESIA
**Capital:** Jakarta (7,600,000)
**Area:** 735,360 sq. mi.
**Language:** Bahasa Indonesia,
Dutch, English, regional
languages
**Currency:** Indonesian rupiah
**Population:** 189,399,000
**Population Growth Rate:** 1.8%
**Population Density:** 258
**Per Capita GNP:** $430
**Average Life Expectancy:** 59
**Infant Mortality Rate:** 89
**Literacy Rate:** 62%
**Location:** Southeast of Asia
**Latitude-Longitude:** 5°S 120°E

## IRAN
**Capital:** Teheran (6,022,029)
**Area:** 636,290 sq. mi.
**Language:** Farsi (Persian), Turkic,
Kurdish
**Currency:** Rial
**Population:** 55,647,000
**Population Growth Rate:** 3.6%
**Population Density:** 87
**Per Capita GNP:** $1,800
**Average Life Expectancy:** 63
**Infant Mortality Rate:** 91
**Literacy Rate:** 48%
**Location:** Southern Asia
**Latitude-Longitude:** 32°N 53°E

## IRAQ
**Capital:** Baghdad (3,844,608)
**Area:** 167,920 sq. mi.
**Language:** Arabic, Kurdish
**Currency:** Iraqi dinar
**Population:** 18,782,000
**Population Growth Rate:** 3.9%
**Population Density:** 112
**Per Capita GNP:** $1,940
**Average Life Expectancy:** 67
**Infant Mortality Rate:** 67
**Literacy Rate:** 60%
**Location:** Western Asia
**Latitude-Longitude:** 33°N 44°E

## IRELAND
**Capital:** Dublin (915,115)
**Area:** 27,140 sq. mi.
**Language:** Irish, English
**Currency:** Irish pound
**Population:** 3,538,000
**Population Growth Rate:** 0.6%
**Population Density:** 130
**Per Capita GNP:** $7,480
**Average Life Expectancy:** 74
**Infant Mortality Rate:** 10
**Literacy Rate:** 99%
**Location:** Western Europe
**Latitude-Longitude:** 53°N 8°W

## ISRAEL
**Capital:** Jerusalem (457,700)
**Area:** 8,020 sq. mi.
**Language:** Hebrew, Arabic, English
**Currency:** new Israeli shekel
**Population:** 4,586,000
**Population Growth Rate:** 1.6%
**Population Density:** 572
**Per Capita GNP:** $8,650
**Average Life Expectancy:** 75
**Infant Mortality Rate:** 10
**Literacy Rate:** 87%
**Location:** Western Asia
**Latitude-Longitude:** 31°N 35°E

## ITALY
**Capital:** Rome (2,815,457)
**Area:** 116,310 sq. mi.
**Language:** Italian
**Currency:** Italian lira
**Population:** 57,664,000
**Population Growth Rate:** 0.1%
**Population Density:** 496
**Per Capita GNP:** $13,320
**Average Life Expectancy:** 75
**Infant Mortality Rate:** 10
**Literacy Rate:** 93%
**Location:** Southern Europe
**Latitude-Longitude:** 43°N 13°E

## IVORY COAST
**Capital:** Abidjan (1,423,323)
**Area:** 124,500 sq. mi.

**Language:** French and African
languages
**Currency:** CFA franc
**Population:** 12,596,000
**Population Growth Rate:** 3.7%
**Population Density:** 101
**Per Capita GNP:** $740
**Average Life Expectancy:** 53
**Infant Mortality Rate:** 96
**Literacy Rate:** 43%
**Location:** Western Africa
**Latitude-Longitude:** 8°N 5°W

## JAMAICA
**Capital:** Kingston (104,041)
**Area:** 4,240 sq. mi.
**Language:** English, Creole
**Currency:** Jamaican dollar
**Population:** 2,441,000
**Population Growth Rate:** 1.7%
**Population Density:** 575
**Per Capita GNP:** $1,080
**Average Life Expectancy:** 76
**Infant Mortality Rate:** 16
**Literacy Rate:** 74%
**Location:** Caribbean Sea
**Latitude-Longitude:** 18°N 77°W

## JAPAN
**Capital:** Tokyo (11,680,282)
**Area:** 143,750 sq. mi.
**Language:** Japanese
**Currency:** yen
**Population:** 123,638,000
**Population Growth Rate:** 0.4%
**Population Density:** 860
**Per Capita GNP:** $21,040
**Average Life Expectancy:** 79
**Infant Mortality Rate:** 5
**Literacy Rate:** 99%
**Location:** East Asia
**Latitude-Longitude:** 38°N 137°E

## JORDAN
**Capital:** Amman (812,500)
**Area:** 37,740 sq. mi.
**Language:** Arabic, English
**Currency:** Jordanian dinar
**Population:** 4,123,000
**Population Growth Rate:** 3.5%
**Population Density:** 109
**Per Capita GNP:** $1,500
**Average Life Expectancy:** 69
**Infant Mortality Rate:** 54

**Literacy Rate:** 71%
**Location:** Western Asia
**Latitude-Longitude:** 31°N 36°E

## KENYA
**Capital:** Nairobi (1,162,189)
**Area:** 224,960 sq. mi.
**Language:** Swahili, English, Bantu,
Kikuyu, other African languages
**Currency:** Kenyan shilling
**Population:** 24,639,000
**Population Growth Rate:** 3.8%
**Population Density:** 110
**Per Capita GNP:** $360
**Average Life Expectancy:** 63
**Infant Mortality Rate:** 62
**Literacy Rate:** 59%
**Location:** Eastern Africa
**Latitude-Longitude:** 1°N 38°E

## KIRIBATI
**Capital:** Tarawa (21,393)
**Area:** 278 sq. mi.
**Language:** English, Gilbertese
**Currency:** Australian dollar
**Population:** 70,000
**Population Growth Rate:** 2.1%
**Population Density:** 252
**Per Capita GNP:** $650
**Average Life Expectancy:** 55
**Infant Mortality Rate:** 65
**Literacy Rate:** 90%
**Location:** Oceania
**Latitude-Longitude:** 0° 174°E

## KOREA, NORTH
**Capital:** P'yongyang (1,500,000)
**Area:** 46,540 sq. mi.
**Language:** Korean
**Currency:** North Korean won
**Population:** 21,293,000
**Population Growth Rate:** 2.1%
**Population Density:** 458
**Per Capita GNP:** $1,240
**Average Life Expectancy:** 70
**Infant Mortality Rate:** 33
**Literacy Rate:** 95%
**Location:** East Asia
**Latitude-Longitude:** 40°N 127°E

## KOREA, SOUTH
**Capital:** Seoul (9,639,110)
**Area:** 38,020 sq. mi.

**Language:** Korean
**Currency:** South Korean won
**Population:** 42,789,000
**Population Growth Rate:** 1.0%
**Population Density:** 1,125
**Per Capita GNP:** $3,530
**Average Life Expectancy:** 68
**Infant Mortality Rate:** 30
**Literacy Rate:** 92%
**Location:** East Asia
**Latitude-Longitude:** 38°N 127°E

## KUWAIT
**Capital:** Kuwait (44,335)
**Area:** 6,880 sq. mi.
**Language:** Arabic and English
**Currency:** Kuwaiti dinar
**Population:** 2,143,000
**Population Growth Rate:** 2.5%
**Population Density:** 311
**Per Capita GNP:** $13,680
**Average Life Expectancy:** 73
**Infant Mortality Rate:** 16
**Literacy Rate:** 71%
**Location:** Western Asia
**Latitude-Longitude:** 29°N 48°E

## LAOS
**Capital:** Vientiane (176,637)
**Area:** 91,430 sq. mi.
**Language:** Lao, French, English
**Currency:** new kip
**Population:** 4,024,000
**Population Growth Rate:** 2.5%
**Population Density:** 44
**Per Capita GNP:** $180
**Average Life Expectancy:** 47
**Infant Mortality Rate:** 110
**Literacy Rate:** 85%
**Location:** Southeast Asia
**Latitude-Longitude:** 18°N 105°E

## LEBANON
**Capital:** Beirut (1,500,000)
**Area:** 4,020 sq. mi.
**Language:** Arabic, French,
Armenian, English
**Currency:** Lebanese pound
**Population:** 3,339,000
**Population Growth Rate:** 2.1%
**Population Density:** 832
**Per Capita GNP:** $700
**Average Life Expectancy:** 68

Infant Mortality Rate: 49
Literacy Rate: 75%
Location: Western Asia
Latitude-Longitude: 34°N 36°E

## LESOTHO

Capital: Maseru (80,250)
Area: 11,720 sq. mi.
Language: Sesotho, English
Currency: loti
Population: 1,774,000
Population Growth Rate: 2.8%
Population Density: 151
Per Capita GNP: $410
Average Life Expectancy: 56
Infant Mortality Rate: 100
Literacy Rate: 59%
Location: Southern Africa
Latitude-Longitude: 29°S 28°E

## LIBERIA

Capital: Monrovia (421,058)
Area: 43,000 sq. mi.
Language: English and tribal languages
Currency: Liberian dollar
Population: 2,640,000
Population Growth Rate: 3.2%
Population Density: 61
Per Capita GNP: $450
Average Life Expectancy: 56
Infant Mortality Rate: 83
Literacy Rate: 35%
Location: Western Africa
Latitude-Longitude: 6°N 10°W

## LIBYA

Capital: Tripoli (481,295)
Area: 679,360 sq. mi.
Language: Arabic
Currency: Libyan dinar
Population: 4,221,000
Population Growth Rate: 3.1%
Population Density: 6
Per Capita GNP: $5,410
Average Life Expectancy: 66
Infant Mortality Rate: 69
Literacy Rate: 55%
Location: Northern Africa
Latitude-Longitude: 27°N 17°E

## LIECHTENSTEIN

Capital: Vaduz (4,927)

Area: 62 sq. mi.
Language: German
Currency: Swiss franc
Population: 28,000
Population Growth Rate: 0.6%
Population Density: 452
Per Capita GNP: $16,500
Average Life Expectancy: 74
Infant Mortality Rate: 3
Literacy Rate: 100%
Location: Western Europe
Latitude-Longitude: 47°N 9°E

## LUXEMBOURG

Capital: Luxembourg (78,900)
Area: 990 sq. mi.
Language: Luxembourgish, French, German
Currency: Luxembourg franc
Population: 371,000
Population Growth Rate: 0.2%
Population Density: 374
Per Capita GNP: $22,600
Average Life Expectancy: 75
Infant Mortality Rate: 9
Literacy Rate: 100%
Location: Western Europe
Latitude-Longitude: 50°N 6°E

## MADAGASCAR

Capital: Antananarivo (406,366)
Area: 226,660 sq. mi.
Language: Malagasy, French
Currency: Malagasy franc
Population: 11,980,000
Population Growth Rate: 3.2%
Population Density: 53
Per Capita GNP: $180
Average Life Expectancy: 54
Infant Mortality Rate: 120
Literacy Rate: 68%
Location: East of Africa
Latitude-Longitude: 19°S 46°E

## MALAWI

Capital: Lilongwe (75,000)
Area: 45,750 sq. mi.
Language: English and Chichewa
Currency: kwacha
Population: 9,158,000
Population Growth Rate: 3.4%
Population Density: 200
Per Capita GNP: $160

Average Life Expectancy: 49
Infant Mortality Rate: 130
Literacy Rate: 41%
Location: Eastern Africa
Latitude-Longitude: 13°S 34°E

## MALAYSIA

Capital: Kuala Lumpur (919,610)
Area: 127,320 sq. mi.
Language: Malay, English, Chinese, tribal languages
Currency: ringgit
Population: 17,858,000
Population Growth Rate: 2.5%
Population Density: 140
Per Capita GNP: $1,870
Average Life Expectancy: 68
Infant Mortality Rate: 30
Literacy Rate: 65%
Location: Southeast of Asia
Latitude-Longitude: 4°N 102°E

## MALDIVES

Capital: Malé (46,334)
Area: 120 sq. mi.
Language: rufiyaa
Currency: Maldivian rupee
Population: 218,000
Population Growth Rate: 3.7%
Population Density: 1,882
Per Capita GNP: $410
Average Life Expectancy: 61
Infant Mortality Rate: 76
Literacy Rate: 36%
Location: South of Asia
Latitude-Longitude: 3°N 73°E

## MALI

Capital: Bamako (404,000)
Area: 478,760 sq. mi.
Language: French, Bambara, African languages
Currency: CFA franc
Population: 8,142,000
Population Growth Rate: 3.0%
Population Density: 17
Per Capita GNP: $230
Average Life Expectancy: 45
Infant Mortality Rate: 117
Literacy Rate: 18%
Location: Western Africa
Latitude-Longitude: 17°N 4°W

## MALTA
**Capital:** Valletta (9,302)
**Area:** 120 sq. mi.
**Language:** Maltese and English
**Currency:** Maltese lira
**Population:** 352,000
**Population Growth Rate:** 0.8%
**Population Density:** 2,849
**Per Capita GNP:** $5,050
**Average Life Expectancy:** 75
**Infant Mortality Rate:** 8
**Literacy Rate:** 83%
**Location:** Mediterranean Sea
**Latitude-Longitude:** 36°N 14°E

## MAURITANIA
**Capital:** Nouakchott (134,986)
**Area:** 397,950 sq. mi.
**Language:** Arabic, French
**Currency:** ouguyia
**Population:** 2,024,000
**Population Growth Rate:** 2.7%
**Population Density:** 5
**Per Capita GNP:** $480
**Average Life Expectancy:** 46
**Infant Mortality Rate:** 127
**Literacy Rate:** 17%
**Location:** Western Africa
**Latitude-Longitude:** 20°N 12°W

## MAURITIUS
**Capital:** Port Louis (136,323)
**Area:** 790 sq. mi.
**Language:** English, French, Creole, Hindi, Urdu
**Currency:** Mauritian rupee
**Population:** 1,070,000
**Population Growth Rate:** 1.3%
**Population Density:** 1,354
**Per Capita GNP:** $1,810
**Average Life Expectancy:** 68
**Infant Mortality Rate:** 25
**Literacy Rate:** 83%
**Location:** Eastern Africa
**Latitude-Longitude:** 18°S 58°E

## MEXICO
**Capital:** Mexico City (8,831,079)
**Area:** 761,600 sq. mi.
**Language:** Spanish
**Currency:** Mexican peso
**Population:** 88,598,000
**Population Growth Rate:** 2.4%

**Population Density:** 116
**Per Capita GNP:** $1,820
**Average Life Expectancy:** 68
**Infant Mortality Rate:** 50
**Literacy Rate:** 88%
**Location:** Central America
**Latitude-Longitude:** 23°N 102°W

## MONACO
**Capital:** Monaco (27,063)
**Area:** 1 sq. mi.
**Language:** French, English, Monégasque, Italian
**Currency:** French franc
**Population:** 29,000
**Population Growth Rate:** 0.0%
**Population Density:** 29,000
**Per Capita GNP:** Not available
**Average Life Expectancy:** 76
**Infant Mortality Rate:** 9
**Literacy Rate:** 99%
**Location:** Western Europe
**Latitude-Longitude:** 44°N 7°E

## MONGOLIA
**Capital:** Ulaanbaatar (511,100)
**Area:** 604,250 sq. mi.
**Language:** Khalkha Mongol
**Currency:** tughrik
**Population:** 2,160,000
**Population Growth Rate:** 2.8%
**Population Density:** 4
**Per Capita GNP:** $880
**Average Life Expectancy:** 65
**Infant Mortality Rate:** 50
**Literacy Rate:** 80%
**Location:** East Asia
**Latitude-Longitude:** 47°N 104°E

## MOROCCO
**Capital:** Rabat (808,007)
**Area:** 172,410 sq. mi.
**Language:** Arabic, Berber, French, Spanish
**Currency:** Moroccan dirham
**Population:** 25,630,000
**Population Growth Rate:** 2.6%
**Population Density:** 149
**Per Capita GNP:** $750
**Average Life Expectancy:** 61
**Infant Mortality Rate:** 82
**Literacy Rate:** 28%
**Location:** Northern Africa
**Latitude-Longitude:** 32°N 6°W

## MOZAMBIQUE
**Capital:** Maputo (1,006,765)
**Area:** 309,490 sq. mi.
**Language:** Portuguese, Bantu languages
**Currency:** metical
**Population:** 15,663,000
**Population Growth Rate:** 2.7%
**Population Density:** 51
**Per Capita GNP:** $100
**Average Life Expectancy:** 47
**Infant Mortality Rate:** 141
**Literacy Rate:** 38%
**Location:** Eastern Africa
**Latitude-Longitude:** 18°S 35°E

## MYANMAR (BURMA)
**Capital:** Rangoon (2,458,712)
**Area:** 261,220 sq. mi.
**Language:** Burmese
**Currency:** kyat
**Population:** 41,277,000
**Population Growth Rate:** 2.0%
**Population Density:** 158
**Per Capita GNP:** $280
**Average Life Expectancy:** 55
**Infant Mortality Rate:** 97
**Literacy Rate:** 78%
**Location:** Southeast Asia
**Latitude-Longitude:** 22°N 98°E

## NAMIBIA
**Capital:** Windhoek
**Area:** 318,260 sq. mi.
**Language:** Afrikaans, German, English
**Currency:** South African rand
**Population:** 1,453,000
**Population Growth Rate:** 3.2%
**Population Density:** 5
**Per Capita GNP:** $1,245
**Average Life Expectancy:** 56
**Infant Mortality Rate:** 106
**Literacy Rate:** 25%
**Location:** Southern Africa
**Latitude-Longitude:** 22°S 17°E

## NAURU
**Capital:** Yaren
**Area:** 8 sq. mi.
**Language:** Nauruan and English
**Currency:** Australian dollar
**Population:** 9,000

**Population Growth Rate:** 1.5%
**Population Density:** 987
**Per Capita GNP:** $10,000
**Average Life Expectancy:** 67
**Infant Mortality Rate:** 41
**Literacy Rate:** 99%
**Location:** Oceania
**Latitude-Longitude:** 0° 167°E

## NEPAL

**Capital:** Kathmandu (235,160)
**Area:** 54,360 sq. mi.
**Language:** Nepali, native languages
**Currency:** Nepalese rupee
**Population:** 19,146,000
**Population Growth Rate:** 2.5%
**Population Density:** 352
**Per Capita GNP:** $170
**Average Life Expectancy:** 52
**Infant Mortality Rate:** 112
**Literacy Rate:** 20%
**Location:** Southern Asia
**Latitude-Longitude:** 28°N 84°E

## THE NETHERLANDS

**Capital:** Amsterdam (677,360)
**Area:** 14,410 sq. mi.
**Language:** Dutch
**Currency:** Netherlands guilder
**Population:** 14,886,000
**Population Growth Rate:** 0.4%
**Population Density:** 1,033
**Per Capita GNP:** $14,530
**Average Life Expectancy:** 77
**Infant Mortality Rate:** 8
**Literacy Rate:** 99%
**Location:** Western Europe
**Latitude-Longitude:** 52°N 5°E

## NEW ZEALAND

**Capital:** Wellington (351,400)
**Area:** 103,740 sq. mi.
**Language:** English, Maori
**Currency:** New Zealand dollar
**Population:** 3,296,000
**Population Growth Rate:** 0.8%
**Population Density:** 32
**Per Capita GNP:** $9,620
**Average Life Expectancy:** 74
**Infant Mortality Rate:** 10
**Literacy Rate:** 99%
**Location:** Oceania
**Latitude-Longitude:** 41°S 174°E

## NICARAGUA

**Capital:** Managua (819,679)
**Area:** 50,190 sq. mi.
**Language:** Spanish
**Currency:** córdoba
**Population:** 3,856,000
**Population Growth Rate:** 3.3%
**Population Density:** 77
**Per Capita GNP:** $830
**Average Life Expectancy:** 62
**Infant Mortality Rate:** 69
**Literacy Rate:** 88%
**Location:** Central America
**Latitude-Longitude:** 13°N 85°W

## NIGER

**Capital:** Niamey (360,000)
**Area:** 489,190 sq. mi.
**Language:** French, Hausa, Djerma, Arabic
**Currency:** CFA franc
**Population:** 7,879,000
**Population Growth Rate:** 3.0%
**Population Density:** 16
**Per Capita GNP:** $310
**Average Life Expectancy:** 45
**Infant Mortality Rate:** 135
**Literacy Rate:** 14%
**Location:** Western Africa
**Latitude-Longitude:** 16°N 8°E

## NIGERIA

**Capital:** Lagos (1,060,848)
**Area:** 356,670 sq. mi.
**Language:** English and native tongues
**Currency:** naira
**Population:** 118,819,000
**Population Growth Rate:** 2.9%
**Population Density:** 333
**Per Capita GNP:** $290
**Average Life Expectancy:** 48
**Infant Mortality Rate:** 121
**Literacy Rate:** 42%
**Location:** Western Africa
**Latitude-Longitude:** 10°N 8°E

## NORWAY

**Capital:** Oslo (451,099)
**Area:** 125,180 sq. mi.
**Language:** Norwegian
**Currency:** Norwegian krone
**Population:** 4,247,000
**Population Growth Rate:** 0.3%

**Population Density:** 34
**Per Capita GNP:** $20,020
**Average Life Expectancy:** 76
**Infant Mortality Rate:** 8
**Literacy Rate:** 100%
**Location:** Northern Europe
**Latitude-Longitude:** 62°N 10°E

## OMAN

**Capital:** Muscat (50,000)
**Area:** 82,030 sq. mi.
**Language:** Arabic, English
**Currency:** Omani rial
**Population:** 1,468,000
**Population Growth Rate:** 3.3%
**Population Density:** 18
**Per Capita GNP:** $5,070
**Average Life Expectancy:** 55
**Infant Mortality Rate:** 100
**Literacy Rate:** 20%
**Location:** Western Asia
**Latitude-Longitude:** 21°N 57°E

## PAKISTAN

**Capital:** Islamabad (204,364)
**Area:** 310,400 sq. mi.
**Language:** Urdu, English, Punjabi, Sindhi, Pashtu, Balochi, others
**Currency:** Pakistani rupee
**Population:** 114,649,000
**Population Growth Rate:** 3.0%
**Population Density:** 369
**Per Capita GNP:** $350
**Average Life Expectancy:** 56
**Infant Mortality Rate:** 110
**Literacy Rate:** 26%
**Location:** Southern Asia
**Latitude-Longitude:** 30°N 70°E

## PANAMA

**Capital:** Panama City (424,204)
**Area:** 29,760 sq. mi.
**Language:** Spanish, English
**Currency:** balboa
**Population:** 2,418,000
**Population Growth Rate:** 2.2%
**Population Density:** 81
**Per Capita GNP:** $2,240
**Average Life Expectancy:** 72
**Infant Mortality Rate:** 23
**Literacy Rate:** 90%
**Location:** Central America
**Latitude-Longitude:** 9°N 80°W

## PAPUA NEW GUINEA
**Capital:** Port Moresby (145,300)
**Area:** 178,260 sq. mi.
**Language:** English, Melanesian pidgin, 715 native tongues
**Currency:** kina
**Population:** 4,011,000
**Population Growth Rate:** 2.7%
**Population Density:** 23
**Per Capita GNP:** $770
**Average Life Expectancy:** 54
**Infant Mortality Rate:** 59
**Literacy Rate:** 32%
**Location:** Oceania
**Latitude-Longitude:** 6°S 150°E

## PARAGUAY
**Capital:** Asunción (457,210)
**Area:** 157,050 sq. mi.
**Language:** Spanish, Guaraní
**Currency:** guaraní
**Population:** 4,277,000
**Population Growth Rate:** 2.8%
**Population Density:** 27
**Per Capita GNP:** $1,180
**Average Life Expectancy:** 67
**Infant Mortality Rate:** 42
**Literacy Rate:** 81%
**Location:** South America
**Latitude-Longitude:** 23°S 58°W

## PERU
**Capital:** Lima (5,008,400)
**Area:** 496,220 sq. mi.
**Language:** Spanish and Quéchua
**Currency:** inti
**Population:** 21,906,000
**Population Growth Rate:** 2.4%
**Population Density:** 44
**Per Capita GNP:** $1,440
**Average Life Expectancy:** 65
**Infant Mortality Rate:** 76
**Literacy Rate:** 80%
**Location:** South America
**Latitude-Longitude:** 10°S 76°W

## THE PHILIPPINES
**Capital:** Quezon City (1,728,441)
**Area:** 115,830 sq. mi.
**Language:** Pilipino, English
**Currency:** Philippine peso
**Population:** 66,117,000

**Population Growth Rate:** 2.6%
**Population Density:** 571
**Per Capita GNP:** $630
**Average Life Expectancy:** 64
**Infant Mortality Rate:** 48
**Literacy Rate:** 88%
**Location:** Southeast of Asia
**Latitude-Longitude:** 13°N 122°E

## POLAND
**Capital:** Warsaw (650,224)
**Area:** 120,730 sq. mi.
**Language:** Polish
**Currency:** zloty
**Population:** 37,777,000
**Population Growth Rate:** 0.6%
**Population Density:** 313
**Per Capita GNP:** $1,850
**Average Life Expectancy:** 71
**Infant Mortality Rate:** 16
**Literacy Rate:** 98%
**Location:** Eastern Europe
**Latitude-Longitude:** 52°N 19°E

## PORTUGAL
**Capital:** Lisbon (807,167)
**Area:** 35,550 sq. mi.
**Language:** Portuguese
**Currency:** Portuguese escudo
**Population:** 10,354,000
**Population Growth Rate:** 0.2%
**Population Density:** 291
**Per Capita GNP:** $3,670
**Average Life Expectancy:** 74
**Infant Mortality Rate:** 15
**Literacy Rate:** 83%
**Location:** Southern Europe
**Latitude-Longitude:** 39°N 8°W

## QATAR
**Capital:** Doha (217,294)
**Area:** 4,250 sq. mi.
**Language:** Arabic
**Currency:** Qatari riyal
**Population:** 491,000
**Population Growth Rate:** 2.3%
**Population Density:** 116
**Per Capita GNP:** $11,610
**Average Life Expectancy:** 69
**Infant Mortality Rate:** 25
**Literacy Rate:** 40%
**Location:** Western Asia
**Latitude-Longitude:** 25°N 51°E

## ROMANIA
**Capital:** Bucharest (1,989,823)
**Area:** 91,700 sq. mi.
**Language:** Romanian, Hungarian, German
**Currency:** leu
**Population:** 23,273,000
**Population Growth Rate:** 0.5%
**Population Density:** 254
**Per Capita GNP:** $3,445
**Average Life Expectancy:** 70
**Infant Mortality Rate:** 26
**Literacy Rate:** 98%
**Location:** Eastern Europe
**Latitude-Longitude:** 46°N 25°E

## RWANDA
**Capital:** Kigali (117,749)
**Area:** 10,170 sq. mi.
**Language:** Kinyarwanda, French
**Currency:** Rwandan franc
**Population:** 7,267,000
**Population Growth Rate:** 3.4%
**Population Density:** 715
**Per Capita GNP:** $310
**Average Life Expectancy:** 49
**Infant Mortality Rate:** 122
**Literacy Rate:** 47%
**Location:** Eastern Africa
**Latitude-Longitude:** 2°S 30°E

## ST. KITTS AND NEVIS
**Capital:** Basseterre (14,161)
**Area:** 140 sq. mi.
**Language:** English
**Currency:** East Caribbean dollar
**Population:** 40,000
**Population Growth Rate:** 1.3%
**Population Density:** 288
**Per Capita GNP:** $2,770
**Average Life Expectancy:** 68
**Infant Mortality Rate:** 40
**Literacy Rate:** 80%
**Location:** Caribbean Sea
**Latitude-Longitude:** 17°N 63°W

## ST. LUCIA
**Capital:** Castries (50,700)
**Area:** 240 sq. mi.
**Language:** English, French patois
**Currency:** East Caribbean dollar
**Population:** 153,000
**Population Growth Rate:** 2.2%

**Population Density:** 639
**Per Capita GNP:** $1,540
**Average Life Expectancy:** 71
**Infant Mortality Rate:** 22
**Literacy Rate:** 78%
**Location:** Caribbean Sea
**Latitude-Longitude:** 13°N 60°W

## ST. VINCENT AND THE GRENADINES

**Capital:** Kingstown (24,764)
**Area:** 150 sq. mi.
**Language:** English
**Currency:** East Caribbean dollar
**Population:** 113,000
**Population Growth Rate:** 1.9%
**Population Density:** 753
**Per Capita GNP:** $1,100
**Average Life Expectancy:** 72
**Infant Mortality Rate:** 25
**Literacy Rate:** 82%
**Location:** Caribbean Sea
**Latitude-Longitude:** 14°N 61°W

## SAN MARINO

**Capital:** San Marino (2,447)
**Area:** 24 sq mi.
**Language:** Italian
**Currency:** Italian lira
**Population:** 23,000
**Population Growth Rate:** 0.3%
**Population Density:** 958
**Per Capita GNP:** Not available
**Average Life Expectancy:** 76
**Infant Mortality Rate:** 14
**Literacy Rate:** 97%
**Location:** Southern Europe
**Latitude-Longitude:** 44°N 12°E

## SÃO TOMÉ AND PRINCIPÉ

**Capital:** São Tomé (40,000)
**Area:** 370 sq. mi.
**Language:** Portuguese
**Currency:** dobra
**Population:** 125,000
**Population Growth Rate:** 2.7%
**Population Density:** 337
**Per Capita GNP:** $280
**Average Life Expectancy:** 65
**Infant Mortality Rate:** 62
**Literacy Rate:** 50%

**Location:** Central Africa
**Latitude-Longitude:** 1°N 7°E

## SAUDI ARABIA

**Capital:** Riyadh (666,840)
**Area:** 830,000 sq. mi.
**Language:** Arabic
**Currency:** Saudi riyal
**Population:** 15,018,000
**Population Growth Rate:** 3.4%
**Population Density:** 18
**Per Capita GNP:** $6,170
**Average Life Expectancy:** 63
**Infant Mortality Rate:** 71
**Literacy Rate:** 52%
**Location:** Western Asia
**Latitude-Longitude:** 25°N 45°E

## SENEGAL

**Capital:** Dakar (798,792)
**Area:** 75,750 sq. mi.
**Language:** French, Wolof, Pulaar, Diola, Mandingo
**Currency:** CFA franc
**Population:** 7,369,000
**Population Growth Rate:** 2.7%
**Population Density:** 97
**Per Capita GNP:** $630
**Average Life Expectancy:** 46
**Infant Mortality Rate:** 128
**Literacy Rate:** 28%
**Location:** Western Africa
**Latitude-Longitude:** 14°N 14°W

## SEYCHELLES

**Capital:** Victoria (23,012)
**Area:** 110 sq. mi.
**Language:** English, French, Creole
**Currency:** Seychelles rupee
**Population:** 68,000
**Population Growth Rate:** 1.7%
**Population Density:** 629
**Per Capita GNP:** $3,800
**Average Life Expectancy:** 70
**Infant Mortality Rate:** 17
**Literacy Rate:** 60%
**Location:** East of Africa
**Latitude-Longitude:** 8°S 55°E

## SIERRA LEONE

**Capital:** Freetown (469,776)
**Area:** 27,700 sq. mi.

**Language:** English, Mende, Temne, Krio
**Currency:** leone
**Population:** 4,166,000
**Population Growth Rate:** 2.5%
**Population Density:** 150
**Per Capita GNP:** $240
**Average Life Expectancy:** 41
**Infant Mortality Rate:** 154
**Literacy Rate:** 31%
**Location:** Western Africa
**Latitude-Longitude:** 8°N 11°W

## SINGAPORE

**Capital:** Singapore (2,700,000)
**Area:** 220 sq. mi.
**Language:** Chinese, Malay, Tamil, English
**Currency:** Singapore dollar
**Population:** 2,727,000
**Population Growth Rate:** 1.5%
**Population Density:** 12,177
**Per Capita GNP:** $9,100
**Average Life Expectancy:** 73
**Infant Mortality Rate:** 7
**Literacy Rate:** 87%
**Location:** Southeast Asia
**Latitude-Longitude:** 1°N 104°E

## SOLOMON ISLANDS

**Capital:** Honiara (30,499)
**Area:** 10,980 sq. mi.
**Language:** Melanesian, pidgin, English, 120 native languages
**Currency:** Solomon Islands dollar
**Population:** 335,000
**Population Growth Rate:** 3.5%
**Population Density:** 30
**Per Capita GNP:** $430
**Average Life Expectancy:** 61
**Infant Mortality Rate:** 40
**Literacy Rate:** 60%
**Location:** Oceania
**Latitude-Longitude:** 8°S 159°E

## SOMALIA

**Capital:** Mogadishu (500,000)
**Area:** 246,200 sq. mi.
**Language:** Somali, Arabic, Italian, English
**Currency:** Somali shilling
**Population:** 8,424,000
**Population Growth Rate:** 3.1%

**Population Density:** 34
**Per Capita GNP:** $170
**Average Life Expectancy:** 45
**Infant Mortality Rate:** 132
**Literacy Rate:** 12%
**Location:** Eastern Africa
**Latitude-Longitude:** 10°N 49°E

## SOUTH AFRICA

**Capital:** Cape Town (776,617),
    Pretoria, Bloemfontein
**Area:** 471,440 sq. mi.
**Language:** Afrikaans, English,
    Bantu languages
**Currency:** rand
**Population:** 39,550,000
**Population Growth Rate:** 2.7%
**Population Density:** 84
**Per Capita GNP:** $2,290
**Average Life Expectancy:** 63
**Infant Mortality Rate:** 55
**Literacy Rate:** 75%
**Location:** Southern Africa
**Latitude-Longitude:** 30°S 26°E

## SOVIET UNION

**Capital:** Moscow (8,703,000)
**Area:** 8,649,500 sq. mi.
**Language:** Russian, more than 200
    regional languages
**Currency:** ruble
**Population:** 290,938,000
**Population Growth Rate:** 0.9%
**Population Density:** 34
**Per Capita GNP:** $9,211
**Average Life Expectancy:** 69
**Infant Mortality Rate:** 29
**Literacy Rate:** 99%
**Location:** Northern Asia
**Latitude-Longitude:** 60°N 80°E

## SPAIN

**Capital:** Madrid (3,217,461)
**Area:** 194,900 sq. mi.
**Language:** Castilian Spanish,
    Catalan, Galician, Basque
**Currency:** peseta
**Population:** 39,405,000
**Population Growth Rate:** 0.3%
**Population Density:** 202
**Per Capita GNP:** $7,740
**Average Life Expectancy:** 77
**Infant Mortality Rate:** 9

**Literacy Rate:** 97%
**Location:** Southern Europe
**Latitude-Longitude:** 40°N 4°W

## SRI LANKA

**Capital:** Colombo (683,000)
**Area:** 25,330 sq. mi.
**Language:** Sinhala, Tamil, English
**Currency:** Sri Lankan rupee
**Population:** 17,196,000
**Population Growth Rate:** 1.5%
**Population Density:** 679
**Per Capita GNP:** $420
**Average Life Expectancy:** 70
**Infant Mortality Rate:** 23
**Literacy Rate:** 87%
**Location:** Southern Asia
**Latitude-Longitude:** 8°N 81°E

## SUDAN

**Capital:** Khartoum (476,218)
**Area:** 967,490 sq. mi.
**Language:** Arabic, English, tribal
    languages and dialects
**Currency:** Sudanese pound
**Population:** 25,195,000
**Population Growth Rate:** 2.9%
**Population Density:** 26
**Per Capita GNP:** $340
**Average Life Expectancy:** 50
**Infant Mortality Rate:** 108
**Literacy Rate:** 31%
**Location:** Northern Africa
**Latitude-Longitude:** 15°N 30°E

## SURINAME

**Capital:** Paramaribo (180,000)
**Area:** 63,040 sq. mi.
**Language:** Dutch, Surinamese,
    English
**Currency:** Suriname guilder
**Population:** 397,000
**Population Growth Rate:** 2.0%
**Population Density:** 6
**Per Capita GNP:** $2,450
**Average Life Expectancy:** 68
**Infant Mortality Rate:** 40
**Literacy Rate:** 65%
**Location:** South America
**Latitude-Longitude:** 4°N 56°W

## SWAZILAND

**Capital:** Mbabane (38,636)

**Area:** 6,700 sq. mi.
**Language:** English, siSwati
**Currency:** lilangeni
**Population:** 779,000
**Population Growth Rate:** 3.1%
**Population Density:** 116
**Per Capita GNP:** $790
**Average Life Expectancy:** 50
**Infant Mortality Rate:** 130
**Literacy Rate:** 68%
**Location:** Southern Africa
**Latitude-Longitude:** 26°S 31°E

## SWEDEN

**Capital:** Stockholm (659,030)
**Area:** 173,730 sq. mi.
**Language:** Swedish
**Currency:** Swedish krona
**Population:** 8,527,000
**Population Growth Rate:** 0.2%
**Population Density:** 49
**Per Capita GNP:** $19,150
**Average Life Expectancy:** 77
**Infant Mortality Rate:** 6
**Literacy Rate:** 99%
**Location:** Northern Europe
**Latitude-Longitude:** 62°N 15°E

## SWITZERLAND

**Capital:** Bern (137,134)
**Area:** 15,940 sq. mi.
**Language:** German, French, Italian
**Currency:** Swiss franc
**Population:** 6,700,000
**Population Growth Rate:** 0.3%
**Population Density:** 420
**Per Capita GNP:** $27,260
**Average Life Expectancy:** 77
**Infant Mortality Rate:** 7
**Literacy Rate:** 99%
**Location:** Western Europe
**Latitude-Longitude:** 46°N 8°E

## SYRIA

**Capital:** Damascus (1,219,448)
**Area:** 71,500 sq. mi.
**Language:** Arabic, Kurdish,
    Armenian, Aramaic
**Currency:** Syrian pound
**Population:** 12,558,000
**Population Growth Rate:** 3.8%
**Population Density:** 176
**Per Capita GNP:** $1,670

**Average Life Expectancy:** 65
**Infant Mortality Rate:** 48
**Literacy Rate:** 49%
**Location:** Western Asia
**Latitude-Longitude:** 35°N 38°E

## TAIWAN
**Capital:** Taipei
**Area:** 12,460 sq. mi.
**Language:** Chinese (many dialects)
**Currency:** new Taiwan dollar
**Population:** 20,219,000
**Population Growth Rate:** 1.2%
**Population Density:** 1,623
**Per Capita GNP:** $6,000
**Average Life Expectancy:** 74
**Infant Mortality Rate:** 17
**Literacy Rate:** 94%
**Location:** East Asia
**Latitude-Longitude:** 23°N 121°E

## TANZANIA
**Capital:** Dar es Salaam (1,096,000)
**Area:** 364,900 sq. mi.
**Language:** Swahili, English
**Currency:** Tanzanian shilling
**Population:** 25,971,000
**Population Growth Rate:** 3.7%
**Population Density:** 71
**Per Capita GNP:** $160
**Average Life Expectancy:** 53
**Infant Mortality Rate:** 106
**Literacy Rate:** 79%
**Location:** Eastern Africa
**Latitude-Longitude:** 6°S 35°E

## THAILAND
**Capital:** Bangkok (4,697,071)
**Area:** 198,460 sq. mi.
**Language:** Thai, English
**Currency:** baht
**Population:** 55,702,000
**Population Growth Rate:** 1.5%
**Population Density:** 281
**Per Capita GNP:** $1,000
**Average Life Expectancy:** 66
**Infant Mortality Rate:** 39
**Literacy Rate:** 82%
**Location:** Southeast Asia
**Latitude-Longitude:** 15°N 100°E

## TOGO
**Capital:** Lomé (229,400)

**Area:** 21,930 sq. mi.
**Language:** Ewé, Mina, Kabyé,
Dagomba, French, many dialects
**Currency:** CFA franc
**Population:** 3,674,000
**Population Growth Rate:** 3.6%
**Population Density:** 168
**Per Capita GNP:** $370
**Average Life Expectancy:** 55
**Infant Mortality Rate:** 114
**Literacy Rate:** 41%
**Location:** Western Africa
**Latitude-Longitude:** 8°N 1°E

## TONGA
**Capital:** Nuku'alofa (28,899)
**Area:** 385 sq. mi.
**Language:** Tongan, English
**Currency:** pa'anga
**Population:** 101,000
**Population Growth Rate:** 2.5%
**Population Density:** 400
**Per Capita GNP:** $850
**Average Life Expectancy:** 71
**Infant Mortality Rate:** 24
**Literacy Rate:** 93%
**Location:** Oceania
**Latitude-Longitude:** 20°S 175°W

## TRINIDAD AND TOBAGO
**Capital:** Port-of-Spain (59,649)
**Area:** 1,980 sq. mi.
**Language:** English, Hindi
**Currency:** Trinidad and Tobago
dollar
**Population:** 1,345,000
**Population Growth Rate:** 2.0%
**Population Density:** 679
**Per Capita GNP:** $3,350
**Average Life Expectancy:** 70
**Infant Mortality Rate:** 14
**Literacy Rate:** 98%
**Location:** Caribbean Sea
**Latitude-Longitude:** 11°N 61°W

## TUNISIA
**Capital:** Tunis (596,654)
**Area:** 63,170 sq. mi.
**Language:** Arabic, French
**Currency:** Tunisian dinar
**Population:** 8,124,000
**Population Growth Rate:** 2.0%

**Population Density:** 129
**Per Capita GNP:** $1,230
**Average Life Expectancy:** 65
**Infant Mortality Rate:** 59
**Literacy Rate:** 62%
**Location:** Northern Africa
**Latitude-Longitude:** 34°N 9°E

## TURKEY
**Capital:** Ankara (2,235,035)
**Area:** 301,380 sq. mi.
**Language:** Turkish, Kurdish,
Arabic
**Currency:** Turkish lira
**Population:** 56,704,000
**Population Growth Rate:** 2.1%
**Population Density:** 188
**Per Capita GNP:** $1,280
**Average Life Expectancy:** 64
**Infant Mortality Rate:** 74
**Literacy Rate:** 70%
**Location:** Western Asia
**Latitude-Longitude:** 39°N 35°E

## TUVALU
**Capital:** Funafuti (2,810)
**Area:** 10 sq. mi.
**Language:** Tuvaluan, English
**Currency:** Australian dollar
**Population:** 9,000
**Population Growth Rate:** 2.0%
**Population Density:** 900
**Per Capita GNP:** $530
**Average Life Expectancy:** 63
**Infant Mortality Rate:** 33
**Literacy Rate:** 49%
**Location:** Oceania
**Latitude-Longitude:** 8°S 178°E

## UGANDA
**Capital:** Kampala (458,423)
**Area:** 91,140 sq. mi.
**Language:** English, Swahili,
Luganda
**Currency:** Ugandan shilling
**Population:** 17,960,000
**Population Growth Rate:** 3.6%
**Population Density:** 197
**Per Capita GNP:** $280
**Average Life Expectancy:** 49
**Infant Mortality Rate:** 107
**Literacy Rate:** 57%
**Location:** Eastern Africa
**Latitude-Longitude:** 1°N 32°E

## UNITED ARAB EMIRATES

**Capital:** Abu Dhabi (670,125)
**Area:** 32,280 sq. mi.
**Language:** Arabic, Farsi, English
**Currency:** Emirian dirham
**Population:** 1,588,000
**Population Growth Rate:** 1.9%
**Population Density:** 49
**Per Capita GNP:** $15,720
**Average Life Expectancy:** 71
**Infant Mortality Rate:** 26
**Literacy Rate:** 68%
**Location:** Western Asia
**Latitude-Longitude:** 24°N 54°E

## UNITED KINGDOM

**Capital:** London (6,775,200)
**Area:** 94,530 sq. mi.
**Language:** English, Welsh, Gaelic
**Currency:** Pound sterling (£)
**Population:** 57,410,000
**Population Growth Rate:** 0.2%
**Population Density:** 607
**Per Capita GNP:** $12,800
**Average Life Expectancy:** 75
**Infant Mortality Rate:** 10
**Literacy Rate:** 99%
**Location:** Western Europe
**Latitude-Longitude:** 54°N 2°W

## UNITED STATES

**Capital:** Washington, D.C.
**Area:** 3,615,100 sq. mi.
**Language:** English
**Currency:** Dollar
**Population:** 251,398,000
**Population Growth Rate:** 0.8%
**Population Density:** 70
**Per Capita GNP:** $19,780
**Average Life Expectancy:** 75
**Infant Mortality Rate:** 10
**Literacy Rate:** 99%
**Location:** North America
**Latitude-Longitude:** 38°N 97°W

## URUGUAY

**Capital:** Montevideo (1,247,920)
**Area:** 68,040 sq. mi.
**Language:** Spanish
**Currency:** new Uruguayan peso
**Population:** 3,037,000
**Population Growth Rate:** 0.8%
**Population Density:** 45
**Per Capita GNP:** $2,470
**Average Life Expectancy:** 71
**Infant Mortality Rate:** 22
**Literacy Rate:** 94%
**Location:** South America
**Latitude-Longitude:** 33°S 56°W

## VANUATU

**Capital:** Port Vila (140,154)
**Area:** 5,700 sq. mi.
**Language:** English, French, Bislama, many languages
**Currency:** vatu
**Population:** 165,000
**Population Growth Rate:** 3.2%
**Population Density:** 29
**Per Capita GNP:** $820
**Average Life Expectancy:** 69
**Infant Mortality Rate:** 36
**Literacy Rate:** 15%
**Location:** Oceania
**Latitude-Longitude:** 16°S 167°E

## VENEZUELA

**Capital:** Caracas (1,232,254)
**Area:** 352,140 sq. mi.
**Language:** Spanish
**Currency:** bolívar
**Population:** 19,636,000
**Population Growth Rate:** 2.3%
**Population Density:** 56
**Per Capita GNP:** $3,170
**Average Life Expectancy:** 70
**Infant Mortality Rate:** 33
**Literacy Rate:** 86%
**Location:** South America
**Latitude-Longitude:** 8°N 65°W

## VIETNAM

**Capital:** Hanoi (2,674,400)
**Area:** 127,240 sq. mi.
**Language:** Vietnamese, French, Chinese, English, Khmer, tribal languages
**Currency:** new dong
**Population:** 70,205,000
**Population Growth Rate:** 2.5%
**Population Density:** 552
**Per Capita GNP:** $215
**Average Life Expectancy:** 66
**Infant Mortality Rate:** 50
**Literacy Rate:** 78%
**Location:** Southeast Asia
**Latitude-Longitude:** 13°N 108°E

## WESTERN SAMOA

**Capital:** Apia (33,170)
**Area:** 1,100 sq. mi.
**Language:** Samoan, English
**Currency:** tala
**Population:** 171,000
**Population Growth Rate:** 2.8%
**Population Density:** 155
**Per Capita GNP:** $580
**Average Life Expectancy:** 66
**Infant Mortality Rate:** 48
**Literacy Rate:** 90%
**Location:** Oceania
**Latitude-Longitude:** 14°S 172°W

## YEMEN (ADEN)

**Capital:** Aden (271,590)
**Area:** 128,560 sq. mi.
**Language:** Arabic
**Currency:** Yemeni dinar
**Population:** 2,585,000
**Population Growth Rate:** 3.4%
**Population Density:** 20
**Per Capita GNP:** $430
**Average Life Expectancy:** 52
**Infant Mortality Rate:** 110
**Literacy Rate:** 25%
**Location:** Western Asia
**Latitude-Longitude:** 15°N 44°E

## YEMEN (SAN'A')

**Capital:** San'a' (277,818)
**Area:** 75,290 sq. mi.
**Language:** Arabic
**Currency:** Yemeni riyal
**Population:** 7,161,000
**Population Growth Rate:** 3.5%
**Population Density:** 95
**Per Capita GNP:** $650
**Average Life Expectancy:** 49
**Infant Mortality Rate:** 129
**Literacy Rate:** 15%
**Location:** Western Asia
**Latitude-Longitude:** 14°N 46°E

## YUGOSLAVIA

**Capital:** Belgrade (1,470,073)
**Area:** 98,760 sq. mi.

**Language:** Serbo-Croatian,
  Slovene, Macedonian
**Currency:** Yugoslav dinar
**Population:** 23,842,000
**Population Growth Rate:** 0.6%
**Population Density:** 241
**Per Capita GNP:** $2,680
**Average Life Expectancy:** 71
**Infant Mortality Rate:** 25
**Literacy Rate:** 91%
**Location:** Southern Europe
**Latitude-Longitude:** 44°N 19°E

## ZAIRE
**Capital:** Kinshasa (3,000,000)
**Area:** 905,560 sq. mi.
**Language:** French, African
  languages
**Currency:** zaire
**Population:** 36,589,000

**Population Growth Rate:** 3.3%
**Population Density:** 40
**Per Capita GNP:** $170
**Average Life Expectancy:** 53
**Infant Mortality Rate:** 108
**Literacy Rate:** 45%
**Location:** Central Africa
**Latitude-Longitude:** 1°S 25°E

## ZAMBIA
**Capital:** Lusaka (818,994)
**Area:** 290,580 sq. mi.
**Language:** English, African
  languages
**Currency:** Zambian kwacha
**Population:** 8,113,000
**Population Growth Rate:** 3.8%
**Population Density:** 28
**Per Capita GNP:** $290
**Average Life Expectancy:** 53

**Infant Mortality Rate:** 80
**Literacy Rate:** 76%
**Location:** Eastern Africa
**Latitude-Longitude:** 15°S 30°E

## ZIMBABWE
**Capital:** Harare (681,000)
**Area:** 150,800 sq. mi.
**Language:** English, Ndebele,
  Shona
**Currency:** Zimbabwean dollar
**Population:** 9,721,000
**Population Growth Rate:** 3.2%
**Population Density:** 64
**Per Capita GNP:** $660
**Average Life Expectancy:** 58
**Infant Mortality Rate:** 72
**Literacy Rate:** 74%
**Location:** Eastern Africa
**Latitude-Longitude:** 20°S 30°E

# REGIONS AND GROUPS OF COUNTRIES

**Balkans**—countries of the Balkan Peninsula: Yugoslavia, Bulgaria, Albania, Greece, Romania and a small part of Turkey.

**Central America**—the bridge of land between Mexico and South America. The Central American countries are Belize, Costa Rica, El Salvador, Guatemala, Honduras, Nicaragua, and Panama.

**European Community (Common Market)**—12 countries working to achieve a single European market by 1992: Belgium, Denmark, France, Germany, Greece, Ireland, Italy, Luxembourg, Netherlands, Portugal, Spain, and the United Kingdom.

**Far East**—the easternmost region of Asia, including China, Japan, Korea, Mongolia and eastern Siberia.

**Low Countries**—Netherlands, Belgium and Luxembourg.

**Middle East**—a region which covers parts of Africa, Asia and Europe. It includes Bahrain, Cyprus, Egypt, Iran, Iraq, Israel, Jordan, Kuwait, Lebanon, Oman, Qatar, Saudi Arabia, Sudan, Syria, Turkey, United Arab Emirates, Yemen (Aden), and Yemen (San'a').

**Oceania**—Pacific Islands. Main island groups are Melanesia, Micronesia and Polynesia.

**Scandinavia**—Denmark, Norway and Sweden.

**Southeast Asia**—the peninsula and islands east of India and south of China. It includes Brunei, Cambodia, Laos, Malaysia, Myanmar, Philippines, Singapore, Thailand, Vietnam and some of Indonesia.

**United Kingdom**—England, Scotland, Wales, Northern Ireland.

**Third World**—approximately 120 developing countries of Asia, Africa and South America.

# HISTORY

**History** is the study of past events. Scientists think people have lived on the earth for about three million years. Until the Ancient Egyptian civilization, which began about 5000 years ago, no written records were kept. Things which happened before that time are **prehistoric**.

A **generation** is the time it takes for an average person to grow up and have children. If a generation is considered to be 30 years, scientists say there have been 100,000 generations since the first people. Of that, 90,000 generations were spent in caves. If a generation is 30 years, it has been:

16,000 generations since man learned to control fire

8,300 generations since people crossed the Bering Strait from Asia into North America

250 generations since farming began

170 generations since written history began

67 generations since the birth of Christ

17 generations since Columbus came to America

7 generations since the United States began

4 generations since slavery was ended after the American Civil War

3 generations since electric lights were invented and cars were first manufactured

1 generation since man first set foot on the moon

In the past hundred years, more change has taken place on the earth than in all the years before, due to man's technology and exploding population. In 1990, the world population grew by more than 93,000,000. After deaths are taken into account, that amounts a net growth of approximately:

3 .....per second

178 .....per minute

10,668 .....per hour

256,043 .....per day, nearly as many as lived in Anchorage, the largest city in Alaska

1,797,224 .....per week, more than lived in Philadelphia the fifth largest city in the U.S.

7,787,792 .....per month, more than lived in New York City, the largest city in the United States

93,455,668 .....per year, or about 5 million more people than lived in Mexico, the eleventh most populous country in the world

## WORLD POPULATION GROWTH

World population began to grow rapidly in about 1630 A.D.
It reached:

1 billion in 1800
2 billion in 1930
3 billion in 1960
4 billion in 1975
5 billion in 1987

It is expected to reach:

6 billion in 1998
7 billion by 2008
8 billion by 2019

The estimated population for January 1991 is 5,368,000,000.

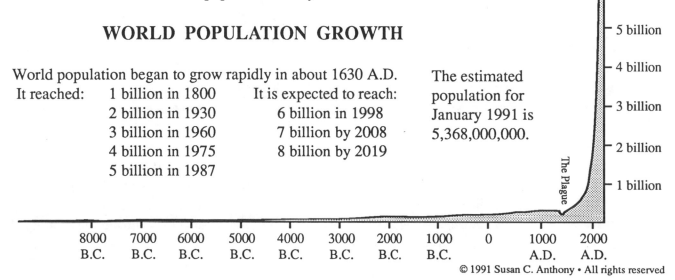

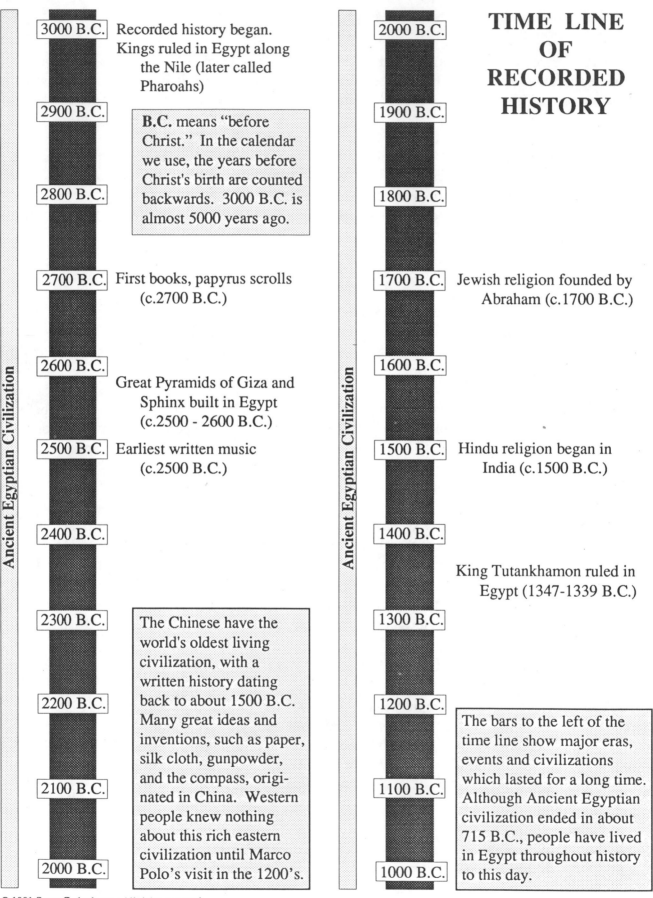

## TIME LINE OF RECORDED HISTORY

Ancient Egyptian Civilization

3000 B.C. — Recorded history began. Kings ruled in Egypt along the Nile (later called Pharoahs)

2900 B.C.

**B.C.** means "before Christ." In the calendar we use, the years before Christ's birth are counted backwards. 3000 B.C. is almost 5000 years ago.

2800 B.C.

2700 B.C. — First books, papyrus scrolls (c.2700 B.C.)

2600 B.C. — Great Pyramids of Giza and Sphinx built in Egypt (c.2500 - 2600 B.C.)

2500 B.C. — Earliest written music (c.2500 B.C.)

2400 B.C.

2300 B.C.

The Chinese have the world's oldest living civilization, with a written history dating back to about 1500 B.C. Many great ideas and inventions, such as paper, silk cloth, gunpowder, and the compass, originated in China. Western people knew nothing about this rich eastern civilization until Marco Polo's visit in the 1200's.

2200 B.C.

2100 B.C.

2000 B.C.

---

2000 B.C.

1900 B.C.

1800 B.C.

1700 B.C. — Jewish religion founded by Abraham (c.1700 B.C.)

1600 B.C.

1500 B.C. — Hindu religion began in India (c.1500 B.C.)

1400 B.C.

King Tutankhamon ruled in Egypt (1347-1339 B.C.)

1300 B.C.

1200 B.C.

The bars to the left of the time line show major eras, events and civilizations which lasted for a long time. Although Ancient Egyptian civilization ended in about 715 B.C., people have lived in Egypt throughout history to this day.

1100 B.C.

1000 B.C.

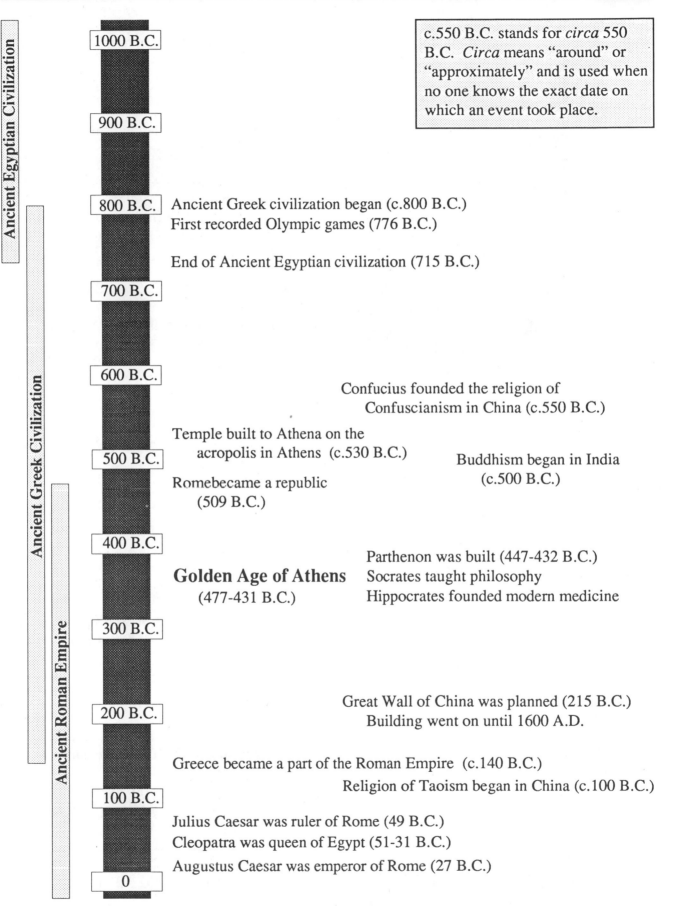

Ancient Egyptian Civilization

Ancient Greek Civilization

Ancient Roman Empire

1000 B.C.

900 B.C.

800 B.C.

700 B.C.

600 B.C.

500 B.C.

400 B.C.

300 B.C.

200 B.C.

100 B.C.

0

c.550 B.C. stands for *circa* 550 B.C. *Circa* means "around" or "approximately" and is used when no one knows the exact date on which an event took place.

Ancient Greek civilization began (c.800 B.C.)
First recorded Olympic games (776 B.C.)

End of Ancient Egyptian civilization (715 B.C.)

Confucius founded the religion of
    Confuscianism in China (c.550 B.C.)

Temple built to Athena on the
   acropolis in Athens (c.530 B.C.)

Buddhism began in India
(c.500 B.C.)

Romebecame a republic
(509 B.C.)

**Golden Age of Athens**
(477-431 B.C.)

Parthenon was built (447-432 B.C.)
Socrates taught philosophy
Hippocrates founded modern medicine

Great Wall of China was planned (215 B.C.)
    Building went on until 1600 A.D.

Greece became a part of the Roman Empire (c.140 B.C.)
Religion of Taoism began in China (c.100 B.C.)

Julius Caesar was ruler of Rome (49 B.C.)
Cleopatra was queen of Egypt (51-31 B.C.)
Augustus Caesar was emperor of Rome (27 B.C.)

**Ancient Roman Empire**

**Middle Ages**

**Arab Civilization**

| 0 | Birth of Jesus Christ was the beginning of the Christian religion (c.4 B.C.)

Crucifixion of Jesus Christ (c.30 A.D.)

Colosseum was built in Rome (71-80 A.D.)

| 100 A.D. |

Paper was invented in China (105 A.D.)

**Roman Empire at greatest power** (27 B.C.-180 A.D.)

| 200 A.D. |

Bubonic plague in Rome killed 5,000 people a day (262 A.D.)

**A.D.** means *anno Domini,* Latin for "in the year of our Lord." The calendar we use counts time from the birth of Christ. It is called the Gregorian calendar. See page 13 for more information.

| 300 A.D. | Christians granted freedom of religion in Roman Empire (c.300 A.D.)

Mayan civilization in North America (Classic Period 250-900 A.D.)

| 400 A.D. |

Rome was sacked (410 A.D.)

Rome was destroyed by Vandals (455 A.D.)
Fall of Roman Empire (476 A.D.)  Middle Ages began

| 500 A.D. |

King Arthur ruled in England (c.537 A.D.)

| 600 A.D. |

Mohammed founded Islam religion (622 A.D.)
Arab expansion began

Mound Builders in Mississippi Valley in North America (c.700 A.D.)

| 700 A.D. |

Charlemagne's empire in Western Europe (768-814 A.D.)

**Golden Age of Arab Culture** (786-809 A.D.)

| 800 A.D. |

A **century** is 100 years. The first century was from the birth of Christ to 100 A.D. The second century was from 100-200 A.D. 1990 is in the 20th century. The year 2000 will begin the 21st century.

| 900 A.D. |

| 1000 A.D. | Viking Leif Ericson discovered North America (c.1002 A.D.)

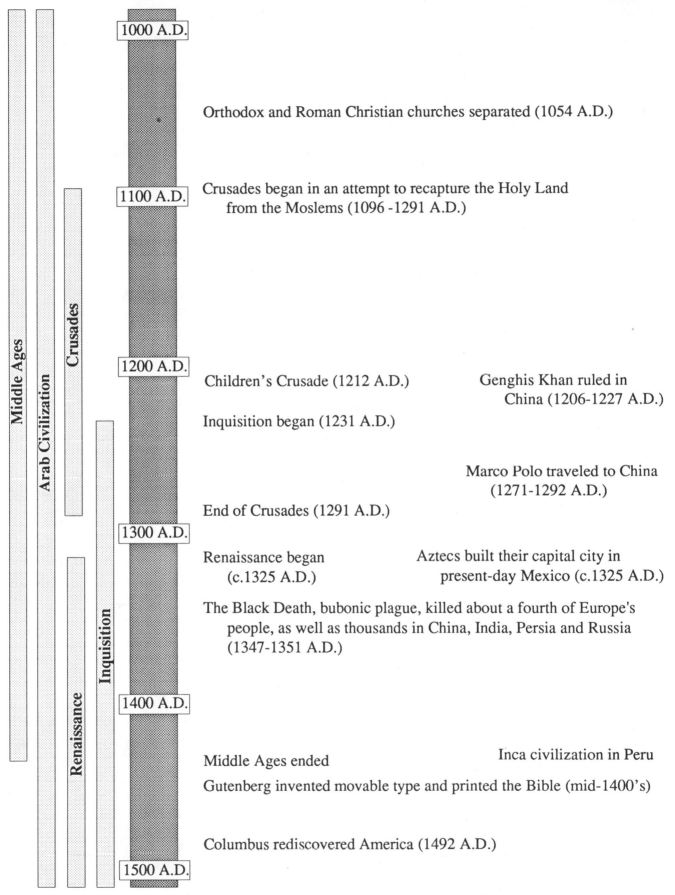

1000 A.D.

Orthodox and Roman Christian churches separated (1054 A.D.)

1100 A.D.

Crusades began in an attempt to recapture the Holy Land
from the Moslems (1096 -1291 A.D.)

1200 A.D.

Children's Crusade (1212 A.D.)        Genghis Khan ruled in
                                            China (1206-1227 A.D.)

Inquisition began (1231 A.D.)

                                  Marco Polo traveled to China
                                       (1271-1292 A.D.)

End of Crusades (1291 A.D.)

1300 A.D.

Renaissance began            Aztecs built their capital city in
    (c.1325 A.D.)                 present-day Mexico (c.1325 A.D.)

The Black Death, bubonic plague, killed about a fourth of Europe's
    people, as well as thousands in China, India, Persia and Russia
    (1347-1351 A.D.)

1400 A.D.

                                        Inca civilization in Peru

Middle Ages ended

Gutenberg invented movable type and printed the Bible (mid-1400's)

Columbus rediscovered America (1492 A.D.)

1500 A.D.

Middle Ages

Arab Civilization

Crusades

Inquisition

Renaissance

Renaissance

Arab Civilization

Inquisition

Age of Reason

1500 A.D.

Magellan's ship circled the globe (1519-1522 A.D.)

Hernando Cortés conquered the Aztecs in Mexico (1521 A.D.)

Pizzaro conquered the Incas in Peru (1533 A.D.)

Martin Luther began the Reformation, which split Protestant and Roman Catholic churches (1517 A.D.)

Copernicus said that the earth went around the sun (1543 A.D.)

Renaissance ended (c.1568 A.D.)

Pope Gregory worked out the modern calendar (1582 A.D.)

Spanish established first permanent settlement in present-day New Mexico (1598 A.D.)

1600 A.D. Age of Reason began. Shakespeare wrote plays in England (1590-1616)

Jamestown, Virginia, was the first permanent English colony in the present-day United States (1607 A.D.)

The Pilgrims came to America on the Mayflower (1620 A.D.)
First Thanksgiving in Plymouth Colony, Massachusetts (1621 A.D.)

French and Indian Wars (1689-1763 A.D.)

1700 A.D.

Arab civilization declined

| ORIGINAL THIRTEEN AMERICAN COLONIES |
|---|
| with dates of first permanent settlement |
| Virginia ................ 1607 |
| Massachusetts ...... 1620 |
| New Hampshire ... 1623 |
| New York ........... 1624 |
| Connecticut .......... 1633 |
| Maryland ............. 1634 |
| Rhode Island ........ 1636 |
| Delaware .............. 1638 |
| Pennsylvania ........ 1643 |
| North Carolina ..... 1653 |
| New Jersey ......... 1660 |
| South Carolina ..... 1670 |
| Georgia ................ 1733 |

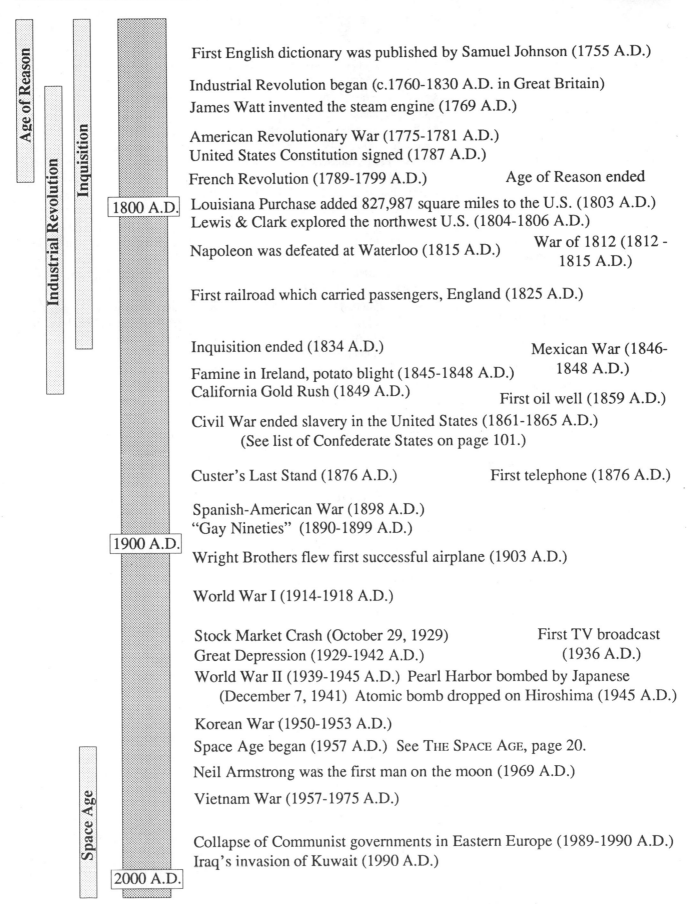

**Age of Reason**

**Industrial Revolution**

**Inquisition**

First English dictionary was published by Samuel Johnson (1755 A.D.)

Industrial Revolution began (c.1760-1830 A.D. in Great Britain)
James Watt invented the steam engine (1769 A.D.)

American Revolutionary War (1775-1781 A.D.)
United States Constitution signed (1787 A.D.)

French Revolution (1789-1799 A.D.)          Age of Reason ended

**1800 A.D.**   Louisiana Purchase added 827,987 square miles to the U.S. (1803 A.D.)
Lewis & Clark explored the northwest U.S. (1804-1806 A.D.)

Napoleon was defeated at Waterloo (1815 A.D.)    War of 1812 (1812 - 1815 A.D.)

First railroad which carried passengers, England (1825 A.D.)

Inquisition ended (1834 A.D.)              Mexican War (1846-
                                            1848 A.D.)
Famine in Ireland, potato blight (1845-1848 A.D.)
California Gold Rush (1849 A.D.)
                                        First oil well (1859 A.D.)
Civil War ended slavery in the United States (1861-1865 A.D.)
        (See list of Confederate States on page 101.)

Custer's Last Stand (1876 A.D.)           First telephone (1876 A.D.)

Spanish-American War (1898 A.D.)
"Gay Nineties" (1890-1899 A.D.)

**1900 A.D.**

Wright Brothers flew first successful airplane (1903 A.D.)

World War I (1914-1918 A.D.)

Stock Market Crash (October 29, 1929)          First TV broadcast
Great Depression (1929-1942 A.D.)                (1936 A.D.)
World War II (1939-1945 A.D.)  Pearl Harbor bombed by Japanese
    (December 7, 1941)  Atomic bomb dropped on Hiroshima (1945 A.D.)

Korean War (1950-1953 A.D.)
Space Age began (1957 A.D.)  See THE SPACE AGE, page 20.

Neil Armstrong was the first man on the moon (1969 A.D.)

Vietnam War (1957-1975 A.D.)

**Space Age**

Collapse of Communist governments in Eastern Europe (1989-1990 A.D.)
Iraq's invasion of Kuwait (1990 A.D.)

**2000 A.D.**

# NOTABLE PEOPLE

**Aaron**, Hank, American baseball player (1934- )

**Abernathy**, Ralph, American civil rights leader (1926- )

**Abraham**, founder of Jewish religion (c.1700 B.C.)

**Adams**, Ansel, American photographer (1902-1984)

**Adams**, John, second U.S. president (1735-1826)

**Adams**, John Quincy, sixth U.S. president (1767-1848)

**Adams**, Samuel, American patriot (1722-1803)

**Addams**, Jane, American social worker (1860-1935)

**Aesop**, Greek writer of fables (c. 600 B.C.)

**Alcott**, Louisa May, American author and war nurse (1832-1888)

**Alexander the Great**, Greek king and conqueror (356-323 B.C.)

**Ali**, Muhammad (Cassius Clay), American heavyweight boxing champion (1942- )

**Allen**, Ethan, American patriot and soldier (1738-1789)

**Allen**, Woody, American actor and comedian (1935- )

**Amundson**, Roald, Norwegian explorer of South Pole (1872-1928)

**Anderson**, Hans Christian, Danish author of fairy tales (1805-1875)

**Anderson**, Marian, American opera singer (1902- )

**Anthony**, Susan Brownell, American woman suffragist (1820-1906)

**Antony**, Mark, Roman statesman (83?-30 B.C.)

**Appleseed**, Johnny (John Chapman), American apple tree planter (1774-1845)

**Archimedes**, Greek inventor and mathematician (287?-212 B.C.)

**Aristotle**, Greek philosopher and scientist (384-322 B.C.)

**Armstrong**, Louis, American jazz musician (1901?-1971)

**Armstrong**, Neil, American astronaut (1930- )

**Arnold**, Benedict, American general and traitor (1741-1801)

**Arthur**, Chester A., twenty-first U.S. president (1829-1886)

**Arthur**, King, medieval English king (c. 500 A.D.)

**Astaire**, Fred, American dancer and actor (1899-1987)

**Atahualpa**, Inca chief (1500?- 1533)

**Attucks**, Cruspus, American patriot (1723?-1770)

**Audubon**, John James, American naturalist (1785-1851)

**Augustus Caesar** (Octavian), Roman emperor (63 B.C.-14 A.D.)

**Austin**, Stephen, American pioneer (1793-1836)

**Baca**, Elfego, American frontiersman (1865-1945)

**Bach**, Johann Sebastian, German composer (1685-1750)

**Baden-Powell**, Robert S., English founder of Boy Scouts (1857-1941)

**Balboa**, Vasco de, Spanish explorer (1475?-1519)

**Banneker**, Benjamin, American astronomer (1731-1806)

**Bannister**, Roger, British athlete and doctor (1929- )

**Bañuelos**, Romana Acosta, Mexican-American treasurer of U.S. (1925- )

**Barnum**, Phineas T., American circus showman (1810-1891)

**Barton**, Clara, American founder of Red Cross (1821-1912)

**Bass,** Sam, American outlaw (1851-1878)

**Bean**, Judge Roy, American frontiersman (1825?-1904)

**Beethoven**, Ludwig van, German composer (1770-1827)

**Bell**, Alexander Graham, American inventor of telephone (1847-1922)

**Bernhardt**, Sarah, French actress (1844-1923)

**Bethune**, Mary McLeod, American educator (1875-1955)

**Billy the Kid**, American outlaw (1859-1881)

**Black Hawk**, American Indian, Sauk tribe  (1767-1838)

**Black Kettle**, Cheyenne Indian chief (1803?-1868)

**Blackbeard**, British pirate (?-1718)

**Blackwell**, Antoinette Brown, first female American minister (1825-1921)

**Blackwell**, Elizabeth, first woman doctor in the U.S. (1821-1910)

**Bloomer**, Amelia, American woman's rights champion (1818-1894)

**Bluford**, Guion S., Jr., American astronaut (1942- )

**Bly**, Nellie, American newspaperwoman (1867?-1922)

**Bogart**, Humphrey, American actor (1899-1957)

**Bolivar**, Simon, South American general (1783-1830)

**Bonaparte**, Napoleon, French emperor (1769-1821)

**Boone**, Daniel, American frontiersman (1734-1820)

**Booth**, John Wilkes, American actor who assassinated Lincoln (1838-1865)

**Brahms**, Johannes, German composer (1833-1897)

**Braille**, Louis, French inventor of Braille (1809-1852)

**Brando**, Marlon, American actor (1924- )

**Brant**, Joseph, American Indian leader, Mohawk tribe (1742-1807)

**Brezhnev**, Leonid, Soviet leader (1906-1982)

**Bridger**, James, American frontiersman (1804-1881)

**Brown**, John, American abolitionist (1800-1859)

**Browning**, Elizabeth Barrett, English poet (1806-1861)

**Bryan**, William Jennings, American lawyer and political leader (1860-1925)

**Buchanan**, James, fifteenth U.S. president (1791-1868)

**Buddha**, Siddhartha Gautama, founder of Buddhist religion (563 B.C.?-483 B.C.?)

**Buffalo Bill Cody**, American army scout and Wild West showman (1846-1917)

**Burbank**, Luther, American plant breeder (1849-1926)

**Burns**, Robert, Scottish poet (1759-1796)

**Burr**, Aaron, American Revolutionary officer and political leader (1756-1836)

**Bush**, George Herbert Walker, forty-first U.S. president (1924- )

**Byrd**, Richard E., American polar explorer (1888-1957)

**Cabot**, John Sebastian, English explorer (1450?-1498?)

**Caesar**, Augustus (Octavian), Roman emperor (63 B.C.-A.D.14)

**Caesar**, Julius, Roman general (100?-44 B.C.)

**Calamity Jane**, American frontierswoman (1852?-1903)

**Calvin**, John, French religious leader (1509-1564)

**Capone**, Al, American gangster (1899-1947)

**Captain Jack**, American Indian leader, Modoc tribe (1837-1873)

**Carnegie**, Andrew, American industrialist (1835-1919)

**Carson**, Johnny, American entertainer (1925- )

**Carson**, Kit, American frontiersman (1809-1868)

**Carter**, James Earl, Jr., thirty-ninth U.S. president (1924- )

**Carver**, George Washington, American botanist (1864-1943)

**Castro**, Fidel, Cuban dictator (1926- )

**Castro**, Raul Hector, American governor and ambassador (1916- )

**Catherine the Great**, Empress of Russia (1729-1796)

**Champlain**, Samuel de, French explorer of America (1570?-1635)

**Chaplin**, Charles, English screen actor-director (1889-1977)

**Charlemagne**, French ruler (742-814)

**Charles**, Prince, British heir to the throne (1948- )

**Chavez**, Cesar Estrada, American labor union organizer (1927- )

**Chiang Kai-shek**, Nationalist Chinese leader (1887-1975)

**Chopin**, Frederic, Polish composer (1810?-1849)

**Churchill**, Sir Winston, British statesman (1874-1965)

**Cisneros**, Henry Gabriel, American mayor of San Antonio (1947- )

**Clark**, William, American explorer, leader of Lewis & Clark expedition (1770-1838)

**Clay**, Henry, American lawyer and statesman (1777-1852)

**Clemens**, Samuel L., also known as Mark Twain, American author (1835-1910)

**Cleopatra**, Egyptian queen (69-30 B.C.)

**Cleveland**, Grover, twenty-second and twenty-fourth U.S. president (1837-1908)

**Cochise**, Apache Indian chief (1800?-1874)

**Cody**, William Frederick, American army scout and Wild West showman, also known as Buffalo Bill (1846-1917)

**Columbus**, Christopher, Italian explorer and discoverer of America (1451-1506)

**Confucius**, Chinese philosopher (c. 551?-479? B.C.)

**Cook**, Captain James, British explorer of the Pacific (1728-1779)

**Coolidge**, Calvin, thirtieth U.S. president (1872-1933)

**Cooper**, James Fenimore, first American novelist (1789-1851)

**Copernicus**, Nicolaus, Polish scientist (1473-1543)

**Cornwallis**, Charles, English military leader (1738-1805)

**Cortés**, Hernando, Spanish conquistador who conquered the Aztecs in Mexico (1485-1547)

**Cortina**, Juan Nepomuceno, Mexican-American leader (1824-1894)

**Cosby**, Bill, American entertainer, author & TV producer (1937- )

**Cousteau**, Jacques-Yves, French oceanographer (1910- )

**Crazy Horse**, Cheyenne Indian chief (1844?-1877)

**Crockett**, Davy, American frontiersman (1786-1836)

**Curie**, Marie, Polish-French scientist (1867-1934)

**Curie**, Pierre, French physicist (1859-1906)

**Custer**, George Armstrong, American army officer (1839-1876)

**Dali**, Salvador, Spanish artist (1904-1989)

**Darwin**, Charles, English scientist (1809-1882)

**da Vinci**, Leonardo, Italian Renaissance artist and scientist (1452-1519)

**Davis**, Jefferson, President of Confederate States of America, (1808-1889)

**de Gaulle**, Charles, French military and political leader (1890-1970)

**Deloria**, Vine, Jr., American Indian leader (1933- )

**Demosthenes**, Greek orator (384?-322 B.C.)

**de Soto**, Hernando, Spanish explorer of America, discovered Mississippi River (1500?-1542)

**Dickens**, Charles, English novelist (1812-1870)

**Dickinson**, Emily, American poet (1830-1886)

**Diesel**, Rudolf, German inventor of diesel engine (1858-1913)

**Dillinger**, John, American gangster (1903-1934)

**Disney**, Walt, American cartoonist (1901-1966)

**Dix**, Dorothea, American social reformer (1802-1887)

**Dorion**, Marie, American Indian explorer, Iowa tribe (1790?-1850)

**Douglas**, Stephen A., American political leader (1813-1861)

**Douglass**, Frederick, American abolitionist (1818?-1895)

**Drake**, Sir Francis, English explorer (1540?-1596)

**Earhart**, Amelia, American aviator (1897-1937?)

**Earp**, Wyatt Berry Stapp, American frontiersman (1848-1929)

**Eastman**, George, American photograhic pioneer (1854-1932)

**Eddy**, Mary Baker, American founder of Christian Science (1821-1910)

**Edison**, Thomas Alva, American inventor (1847-1931)

**Einstein**, Albert, German-American physicist (1879-1955)

**Eisenhower**, Dwight D., thirty-fourth U.S. president (1890-1969)

**Ellington**, Duke, American jazz composer (1899-1974)

**Emerson**, Ralph Waldo, American philosopher (1803-1882)

**Ericson**, Leif, Norse explorer (980?-1025?)

**Fahrenheit**, Gabriel, German-Dutch physicist (1686-1736)

**Faraday**, Michael, English scientist and pioneer in electricity (1791-1867)

**Fermi**, Enrico, Italian physicist (1901-1954)

**Fields**, W. C., American entertainer (1879-1946)

**Fillmore**, Millard, thirteenth U.S. president (1800-1874)

**Fink**, Mike, American pioneer (1770-1823)

**Ford**, Gerald R., thirty-eighth U.S. president (1913- )

**Ford**, Henry, American automobile pioneer (1863-1947)

**Forten**, James, American abolitionist (1766-1842)

**Foster**, Stephen, American composer (1826-1864)

**Franco**, Francisco, dictator of Spain (1892-1975)

**Frank**, Anne, young Dutch writer (1929-1945)

**Franklin**, Benjamin, American statesman and inventor (1706-1790)

**Freud**, Sigmund, Austrian founder of psychoanalysis (1856-1939)

**Friedan**, Betty, American feminist (1921- )

**Frost**, Robert, American poet (1874-1963)

**Fulton**, Robert, American inventor (1765-1815)

**Gagarin**, Yuri, Soviet cosmonaut, first man in space (1934-1968)

**Galarza**, Ernesto, Mexican-American historian (1905-1984)

**Galilei**, Galileo, Italian scientist (1564-1642)

**Gall**, Sioux Indian leader (1840-1894)

**Gamio**, Manuel, Mexican-American anthropologist (1883-1960)

**Gandhi**, Indira, Prime Minister of India (1917-1984)

**Gandhi**, Mohandas (Mahatma Gandhi), leader of India (1869-1948)

**Garfield**, James A., twentieth U.S. president (1831-1881)

**Gauguin**, Paul, French artist (1848-1903)

**Gautama**, Siddhartha (Buddha), founder of Buddhism (563 B.C.?-483 B.C.?)

**Gehrig**, Lou, American baseball player (1903-1941)

**Genghis Khan**, Emperor of Mongolia (1162-1227)

**Geronimo**, Apache Indian chief (1829-1909)

**Giovanni**, Nikki, American poet (1943- )

**Glenn**, John, Jr., American astronaut and senator (1921- )

**Goddard**, Robert, American scientist (1882-1945)

**Gonzales**, Rodolfo (Corky), Mexican-American leader (1928- )

**Gorbachev**, Mikhail S., head of Communist Party in U.S.S.R. since 1985 (1931- )

**Goya**, Francisco, Spanish painter (1746-1828)

**Grant**, Ulysses S., Civil War general and eighteenth U.S. president (1822-1885)

**Greaves**, Captain, Scotch-Irish pirate (c. 1670)

**Greco**, El, Greek artist (1541?-1614)

**Greeley**, Horace, American newspaperman (1811-1872)

**Gutenberg**, Johannes, German inventor of movable type (1395?-1468?)

**Guthrie**, Woody, American folk singer (1912-1967)

**Gutiérrez**, José Angel, Mexican-American leader (1944- )

**Haile Selassie I**, emperor of Ethiopia (1892-1975)

**Hale**, Nathan, American patriot (1755-1776)

**Halley**, Edmund, English astronomer (1656-1742)

**Hamilton**, Alexander, American patriot (1755-1804)

**Hancock**, John, American patriot (1737-1793)

**Handel**, George Frideric, German-English composer (1685-1759)

**Handy**, W. C., American composer, Father of the Blues (1873-1958)

**Hannibal**, Carthaginian general and political leader (247-183 B.C.)

**Harding**, Warren G., twenty-ninth U.S. president (1865-1923)

**Harrison**, Benjamin, twenty-third U.S. president (1833-1901)

**Harrison**, William Henry, ninth U.S. president (1773-1841)

**Hawthorne**, Nathaniel, Ameican author (1804-1864)

**Haydn**, Joseph, Austrian composer (1732-1809)

**Hayes**, Rutherford B., nineteenth U.S. president (1822-1893)

**Hemingway**, Ernest, American author (1899-1961)

**Henry**, Patrick, American patriot (1736-1799)

**Hickok**, Wild Bill, American frontiersman (1837-1876)

**Hillary**, Sir Edmund, New Zealand mountain climber (1919- )

**Hippocrates**, Greek father of modern medicine (460?-380? B.C.)

**Hirohito**, Emperor of Japan (1901-1989)

**Hitchcock**, Sir Alfred, American director of suspense thriller films (1899-1980)

**Hitler**, Adolf, German dictator (1889-1945) (1889-1945)

**Ho Chi Minh**, Vietnamese revolutionary leader (1890-1969)

**Hogan**, Ben, American golfer (1912- )

**Holmes**, Oliver Wendell, Jr., American jurist (1841-1935)

**Homer**, Winslow, American artist (1836-1910)

**Hoover**, Herbert, thirty-first U.S. president (1874-1964)

**Hoover**, J. Edgar, American director of FBI (1895-1972)

**Hope**, Bob, American comedian (1903- )

**Houdini,** Harry (Erich Weiss), American magician and escape artist (1874-1926)

**Houston,** Samuel, American, political leader and soldier in Texas (1793-1863)

**Howe,** Elias, American inventor of sewing machine (1819-1867)

**Howe,** Julia Ward, American composer of "Battle Hymn of the Republic" (1819-1910)

**Hudson,** Henry, English navigator and explorer (?-1611)

**Hughes,** Howard, American industrialist (1905-1976)

**Hughes,** Langston, American poet (1902-1967)

**Irving,** Washington, American author (1783-1859)

**Jackson,** Andrew, seventh U.S. president (1767-1845)

**Jackson,** Rev. Jesse, American politician and minister (1941- )

**Jackson,** Stonewall, Southern general during U.S. Civil War (1824-1863)

**James,** Jesse, American outlaw (1847-1882)

**Jefferson,** Thomas, third U.S. president, author of Declaration of Independence (1743-1826)

**Joan of Arc,** French saint and heroine (1412?-1431?)

**Johnson,** Andrew, seventeenth U.S. president (1808-1875)

**Johnson,** Lyndon B., thirty-sixth U.S. president (1908-1973)

**Johnson,** Samuel, English writer of first dictionary (1709-1784)

**Jones,** Casey, American railroad engineer (1863-1900)

**Jones,** John Paul, Scottish-American naval hero (1747-1792)

**Joseph,** Chief, Nez Percé Indian chief (1840?-1904)

**Kamehameha I,** Hawaiian king (1758?-1819)

**Keats,** John, English poet (1795-1821)

**Keller,** Helen, American author and educator (1880-1968)

**Kennedy,** John, thirty-fifth U.S. president (1917-1963)

**Kepler,** Johannes, German astronomer and mathematician (1571-1630)

**Key,** Francis Scott, American composer of national anthem (1779-1843)

**Kidd,** William, Scottish pirate (1645?-1701)

**King,** Martin Luther, Jr., American civil rights leader (1929-1968)

**Kirkpatrick,** Jeane, American ambassador to United Nations (1926- )

**Kublai Khan,** Chinese ruler (1216-1294)

**Lafayette,** Marquis de, French soldier and statesman (1757-1834)

**Laffite,** Jean, French-American pirate (1780?-1826?)

**Landers,** Ann, American advice columnist (1918- )

**Lao-Tzu,** legendary Chinese philosopher (c. 500 B.C.)

**La Salle,** Sieur de, French explorer of Mississippi Valley (1643-1687)

**Lee,** Robert E., American Civil War general of the South (1807-1870)

**Leeuwenhoek,** Anton van, Dutch naturalist and "father of the microscope" (1632-1723)

**Lenin,** V. I., Soviet communist leader (1870-1924)

**Lewis,** Meriwether, American explorer—Lewis & Clark (1774-1809)

**Lincoln,** Abraham, sixteenth U.S. president (1809-1865)

**Lindbergh,** Charles, American aviator (1902-1974)

**Lister,** Sir Joseph, English surgeon (1827-1912)

**Liszt,** Franz, Hungarian composer (1811-1886)

**Livingston,** David, British explorer of Africa (1813-1873)

**Lloyd George,** David, British Prime Minister (1863-1945)

**Longfellow,** Henry Wadsworth, American poet (1807-1882)

**Low,** Juliette Gordon, American founder of Girl Scouts (1860-1927)

**Luther,** Martin, German religious leader of the Reformation (1483-1546)

**MacArthur,** Douglas, five-star U.S. general during WWII (1880-1964)

**Madison,** James, fourth U.S. president (1751-1836)

**Magellan,** Ferdinand, Portuguese explorer (1480?-1521)

**Mandela,** Nelson, South African black protest leader (1918- )

**Mann,** Horace, American educator (1796-1859)

**Mao Tse-tung,** Chinese Communist leader (1893-1976)

**Marconi,** Guglielmo, Italian physicist and inventor of the radio (1874-1937)

**Marshall,** Thurgood, U.S. Supreme Court Justice (1908- )

**Marx,** Karl, German philosopher and "father of Communism" (1818-1883)

**Massasoit,** Wampanoag Indian chief (1580?-1661)

**Maximilian,** Emperor of Mexico (1832-1867)

**McCormick,** Cyrus Hall, American inventor of the reaper (1809-1884)

**McKinley,** William, twenty-fifth U.S. president (1843-1901)

**Meir,** Golda, Israeli leader (1898-1978)

**Mendel,** Gregor, Austrian scientist (1822-1884)

**Mendelssohn,** Felix, German composer (1809-1847)

**Michelangelo** Buonarroti, Italian artist and architect (1475-1564)

**Milton,** John, English poet (1608-1674)

**Mohammed,** founder of Islam (570?-632 A.D.)

**Monet,** Claude, French artist (1840-1926)

**Monroe,** James, fifth U.S. president (1758-1831)

**Monroe,** Marilyn, American actress (1926-1962)

**Montessori,** Maria, Italian educator (1870-1952)

**Montezuma II,** Aztec emperor (1480?-1520)

**Montgolfier,** Jacques, French co-inventor of balloon (1745-1799)

**Montgolfier,** Joseph, French co-inventor of balloon (1740-1810)

**Morse**, Samuel F. B., American inventor (1791-1872)

**Moses**, Grandma (Anna Mary Moses), American artist (1860-1961)

**Mott**, Lucretia, American abolitionist and feminist (1793-1880)

**Mozart**, Wolfgang Amadeus, Austrian composer (1756-1791)

**Muir**, John, American naturalist (1838-1914)

**Mussolini**, Benito, Italian dictator (1883-1945)

**Nader**, Ralph, American lawyer and consumer advocate (1934- )

**Napoleon Bonaparte**, French emperor (1769-1821)

**Nash**, Ogden, American poet (1902-1971)

**Nation**, Carry, American temperance leader (1846-1911)

**Nero**, Roman emperor (37-68)

**Newton**, Sir Isaac, English scientist, philosopher and mathematician who discovered gravity (1642-1727)

**Nicholas II**, last czar of Russia (1868-1918)

**Nightingale**, Florence, English nurse (1820-1910)

**Nixon**, Richard M., thirty-seventh U.S. president (1913- )

**Nobel**, Alfred, Swedish industrialist and inventor of dynamite (1833-1896)

**Oakley**, Annie, American markswoman (1860-1926)

**O'Keeffe**, Georgia, American artist (1887-1986)

**Osceola**, Seminole Indian leader (1804?-1838)

**Owens**, Jesse, American athlete (1913-1980)

**Paine**, Thomas, American revolutionary writer (1737-1809)

**Parker**, Ely, American Indian leader, Seneca Iroquois (1828-1895)

**Parks**, Rosa Lee, American civil rights leader (1913- )

**Pasteur**, Louis, French scientist (1822-1895)

**Patton**, George Smith, Jr., American general (1885-1945)

**Peale**, Norman Vincent, American clergyman (1898- )

**Peary**, Robert, American Arctic explorer (1856-1920)

**Penn**, William, American founder of Pennsylvania (1644-1718)

**Philip**, King, Wampanoag Indian leader (?-1676)

**Picasso**, Pablo, Spanish-born French painter (1881-1973)

**Picotte**, Susan La Flesche, American Indian doctor, Omaha tribe (1865-1915)

**Pierce**, Franklin, fourteenth U.S. president (1804-1869)

**Pitcher**, Molly, American Revolutionary War heroine (1754?-1832)

**Pizarro**, Francisco, Spanish conquistador who conquered the Incas in Peru (1478?-1541)

**Plato**, Greek philosopher (427?-347? B.C.)

**Pocahontas**, Powhatan Indian princess (1595?-1617)

**Poe**, Edgar Allan, American writer (1809-1849)

**Polk**, James K., eleventh U.S. president (1795-1849)

**Polo**, Marco, Venetian explorer of the Far East (1254-1324?)

**Ponce de León**, Juan, Spanish explorer (1474-1521)

**Pontiac**, Ottawa Indian chief (1720?-1769)

**Post**, Wiley, American aviator (1899-1935)

**Powhatan**, Powhatan Indian chief (?-1618)

**Presley**, Elvis, American singer (1935-1977)

**Priestly**, Joseph, English scientist (1733-1804)

**Ptolemy**, Egyptian astronomer (100?-165?)

**Quayle**, J. Danforth, Vice-President of U.S. (1947- )

**Raleigh**, Sir Walter, English explorer (1552?-1618)

**Ramses II**, Egyptian pharoah (reigned 1290-1224 B.C.)

**Raphael**, Italian painter (1483-1520)

**Reagan**, Ronald, fortieth U.S. president (1911- )

**Reed**, Walter, American army physician and surgeon (1851-1902)

**Rembrandt** (Rembrandt Harmenszoon van Rijn), Dutch artist (1606-1669)

**Remington**, Frederic, American artist (1861-1909)

**Renoir**, Pierre, French painter (1841-1919)

**Revere**, Paul, American patriot (1735-1818)

**Rickenbacker**, Edward, American aviator (1890-1973)

**Ride**, Sally K., American astronaut (1951- )

**Robin Hood**, legendary English outlaw (c. 1300)

**Robinson**, Jackie, American baseball player (1919-1972)

**Rockefeller**, John D., American industrialist (1839-1937)

**Rockwell**, Norman, American illustrator (1894-1978)

**Roentgen**, Wilhelm Conrad, German discoverer of X-rays (1845-1923)

**Rogers**, Will, American humorist and author (1879-1935)

**Roosevelt**, Eleanor, American first lady and humanitarian (1884-1962)

**Roosevelt**, Franklin D., thirty-second U.S. president (1882-1945)

**Roosevelt**, Theodore, twenty-sixth U.S. president (1858-1919)

**Ross**, Betsy, American flagmaker (1752-1836)

**Ruth**, Babe (George Herman Ruth), American baseball hero (1895-1948)

**Sacagawea**, Shoshone Indian guide of Lewis & Clark expedition (1787?-1812?)

**Salk**, Jonas, American research scientist who developed the polio vaccine (1914- )

**Samoset**, Pemaquid Indian, friend of Pilgrims (1590?-1655)

**Sandburg**, Carl, American poet (1878-1967)

**Schubert**, Franz, Austrian composer (1797-1858)

**Schulz**, Charles, American cartoonist (1922- )

**Schweitzer**, Albert, German missionary (1875-1965)

**Sequoyah**, Cherokee Indian, invented system for writing (1760?-1843)

**Seward**, William H., American political leader and diplomat (1801-1872)

**Shackleton**, Sir Ernest Henry, Irish explorer (1874-1922)

**Shakespeare**, William, English dramatist and poet (1564-1616)

**Sinatra**, Frank, American singer (1915- )

**Sitting Bull**, Sioux Indian chief (1834?-1890)

**Smith**, John, English soldier who helped found Jamestown, Virginia, first permanent English colony in America (1580?-1631)

**Smith**, Joseph, American founder of Mormon Church (1805-1844)

**Socrates**, Greek philosopher (469?-399 B.C.)

**Sousa**, John Philip, American composer of marches (1854-1932)

**Squanto**, Patuxet Indian friend of Pilgrims (1585?-1622)

**Stalin**, Joseph, Soviet dictator (1879-1953)

**Stanley**, Henry Morton, English explorer of Africa (1841-1904)

**Stanton**, Elizabeth Cady, American reformer and suffragist (1815-1902)

**Stowe**, Harriet Beecher, American author and abolitionist (1811-1896)

**Strauss**, Johann, Austrian composer of waltzes (1825-1899)

**Strauss**, Richard, German composer (1864-1949)

**Stravinsky**, Igor, Russian composer (1882-1971)

**Taft**, William H., twenty-seventh U.S. president (1857-1930)

**Tallchief**, Maria, American ballerina (1925- )

**Taylor**, Zachary, twelfth U.S. president (1784-1850)

**Tchaikovsky**, Peter Ilich, Russian composer (1840-1893)

**Teasdale**, Sara, American poet (1884-1933)

**Tecumseh**, Shawnee Indian chief (1765?-1813)

**Temple**, Shirley, American child motion-picture star (1928- )

**Tennyson**, Alfred Lord, English poet (1809-1892)

**Teresa**, Mother, Roman Catholic nun and humanitarian (1910- )

**Tereshkova**, Valentina, Soviet cosmonaut, first woman in space (1937- )

**Thatcher**, Margaret, former British Prime Minister (1925- )

**Thoreau**, Henry David, American writer (1817-1862)

**Thorpe**, Jim, American football player (1887-1953)

**Tito**, Josip Broz, dictator of Yugoslavia (1892-1980)

**Trevino**, Lee, American golfer (1939- )

**Trotsky**, Leon, Russian Revolutionist (1879-1940)

**Trudeau**, Pierre, Canadian prime minister (1919- )

**Truman**, Harry S., thirty-third U.S. president (1884-1972)

**Truth**, Sojourner, American abolitionist (1797?-1883)

**Tubman**, Harriet, American abolitionist (1820?-1913)

**Turner**, Nat, American slave leader (1800-1831)

**Tutankhamon**, ancient Egyptian pharoah (1357?-1339 B.C.)

**Tutu,** Desmond, South African civil rights leader & archbishop (1931-)

**Twain**, Mark, pen name for Samuel Clemens, American author (1835-1910)

**Tyler**, John, tenth U.S. president (1790-1862)

**Van Buren**, Martin, eighth U.S. president (1782-1862)

**Van Gogh**, Vincent, Dutch painter (1853-1890)

**Vespucci**, Amerigo, Italian navigator and explorer, American continents were named after him (1454-1512)

**Villa**, Pancho, Mexican bandit leader (1877-1923)

**Von Braun**, Wernher, American rocket engineer (1912-1977)

**Wagner**, Richard, German composer of operas (1813-1883)

**Walesa**, Lech, Polish labor union leader (1943- )

**Washington**, Booker T., American educator (1856-1915)

**Washington**, George, first U.S. president, Revolutionary War general (1732-1799)

**Watie**, Stand, American Indian leader (1806-1871)

**Watt**, James, Scottish engineer and inventor (1736-1819)

**Webster**, Daniel, American statesman (1782-1852)

**Webster**, Noah, American writer of the dictionary (1758-1843)

**Wellington,** Duke of, British general who defeated Napoleon (1769-1852)

**Westinghouse**, George, American inventor and manufacturer (1846-1914)

**Wheatley**, Phyllis, black American poet (1753?-1784)

**Whistler**, James McNeill, American painter (1834-1903)

**Whitman**, Walt, American poet (1819-1892)

**Whitney**, Eli, American inventor of cotton gin (1765-1825)

**Whittier**, John Greenleaf, American poet (1807-1892)

**Wilkins**, Roy, American black leader (1901-1981)

**Williams**, Daniel Hale, American black surgeon (1856-1931)

**Williams**, Hank, American singer and composer (1923-1953)

**Wilson**, Woodrow, twenty-eighth U.S. president (1856-1924)

**Wonder**, Stevie, American musician (1950- )

**Wordsworth**, William, English poet (1770-1850)

**Wright**, Frank Lloyd, American architect (1867-1959)

**Wright**, Orville, American aviation pioneer (1871-1948)

**Wright**, Wilbur, American aviation pioneer (1867-1912)

**Wyeth**, Andrew, American painter (1917- )

**Young**, Brigham, American Mormon leader (1801-1877)

# INVENTIONS AND DISCOVERIES

**Inventions** come from ideas for doing something better or solving a problem. Some inventions are new combinations or uses of things which already exist. Others are new processes, or ways of doing things. Many are new devices, or things. Inventions often build upon one another as people improve on older ideas. It is difficult to give credit for the invention of the computer to a single person, for example. The first computers were nothing like those of today, which are the result of ideas from hundreds of people.

Some inventions were ahead of their time. Barthélemy Thimmonier invented the first sewing machine in France in the early 1800's, but a group of angry tailors destroyed his shop. They were afraid that the machines would put them out of work. Elias Howe is usually given credit for inventing the sewing machine in 1846, but it wasn't until Isaac Singer's improved machine in 1851 that sewing machines became popular.

Inventors who think they have an idea which could sell may take out a **patent** to keep others from copying the idea. Some inventors never patented or sold their good ideas, and so did not receive credit for them. Occasionally, it is the person who sold an idea to the public who is remembered. Johann Gutenberg is given credit for movable type, although the Chinese invented it almost 400 years earlier. Robert Fulton is often given credit for inventing the steamship, but patents were issued to three others before he launched the first successful steamship on the Mississippi River in 1807.

**Discoveries** are not inventions. People who discover something find out about it. For example, Sir Isaac Newton discovered gravity, but it existed before he learned about it.

## SOME IMPORTANT DISCOVERIES

| DISCOVERY | DATE | DISCOVERER | COUNTRY |
|---|---|---|---|
| Atomic structure, theory of | 1911 | Ernest Rutherford | England |
| Atomic theory, modern | 1803 | John Dalton | England |
| Bacteria | 1674 | Anton van Leewenhoek | Netherlands |
| Blood, circulation of | 1628 | William Harvey | England |
| $e=mc^2$ | 1905 | Albert Einstein | Switzerland |
| Earth goes around sun | 1543 | Nicolaus Copernicus | Poland |
| Electromagnetic induction | 1831 | Michael Faraday | England |
| Electron | 1897 | Sir Joseph J. Thomson | England |
| Falling bodies, law of | 1590 | Galileo Galilei | Italy |
| Gravity | 1665 | Sir Isaac Newton | England |
| Heredity, laws of | 1865 | Gregor Mendel | Austria |
| Light, speed of | 1675 | Olaus Roemer | Denmark |
| Neutron | 1932 | Sir James Chadwick | England |
| Penicillin | 1928 | Sir Alexander Fleming | United States |
| Planetary orbits | 1609 | Johannes Kepler | Germany |
| Proton | 1902 | Wilhelm Wien | Germany |
| X-rays | 1895 | Wilhelm Roentgen | Germany |

# IMPORTANT INVENTIONS

| INVENTION | DATE | INVENTOR | COUNTRY |
|---|---|---|---|
| Accordion | 1829 | Cyrillys Damian | Austria |
| Airplane | 1903 | Wilbur and Orville Wright | United States |
| Aluminum manufacture | 1886 | Charles M. Hall | United States |
| | | Paul L. T. Héroult | France |
| Anesthetic (on man) | 1842 | Crawford W. Long | United States |
| Antiseptic for surgery | 1865 | Sir Joseph Lister | England |
| Aspirin | 1853 | Charles Gerhardt | France |
| Automobile with gasoline engine | 1885 | Karl Benz | Germany |
| Balloon, hot air | 1783 | Joseph and Jacques Montgolfier | France |
| Barbed wire, machine for manufacture | 1874 | Joseph Glidden | United States |
| Barometer | 1643 | Evangelista Torricelli | Italy |
| Basketball | 1891 | James Naismith | United States |
| Battery, electric | c.1800 | Alessandro Volta | Italy |
| Bicycle | 1790 | Comte Mede de Sivrac | France |
| Braille | 1829 | Louis Braille | France |
| Brake, air | 1868 | George Westinghouse | United States |
| Bullet, conical | 1849 | Claude Minié | France |
| Camera, hand-held | 1888 | George Eastman | United States |
| Cash register | 1879 | James Ritty | United States |
| Cereal, Corn Flakes | 1894 | John Harvey Kellogg | United States |
| Cereal, Grape Nuts | 1897 | C. W. Post | United States |
| Clock, pendulum | 1656 | Christiaan Huygens | Netherlands |
| Coca-Cola | 1886 | Dr. John S. Pemberton | United States |
| Compass, magnetic | c.1088 | Unknown | China, Europe |
| Computer, electronic digital | 1946 | J. Presper Eckert, John Mauchly | United States |
| Computer, analog | 1930 | Vannevar Bush | United States |
| Cotton gin | 1793 | Eli Whitney | United States |
| Denim jeans | 1874 | Levi Strauss | United States |
| Dyes, chemical | 1856 | William Perkin | England |
| Dynamite | 1867 | Alfred Nobel | Sweden |
| Earmuffs | 1873 | Chester Greenwood | United States |
| Electromagnet | 1825 | William Sturgeon | England |
| Elevator | 1854 | Elisha Otis | United States |
| Engine, diesel | 1892 | Rudolf Diesel | Germany |
| Engine, 4-cycle gasoline | 1866 | Nikolaus Otto, Eugen Langen | Germany |
| Eyeglasses, bifocal | 1784 | Benjamin Franklin | United States |
| Ferris wheel | 1893 | George W. G. Ferris, Jr. | United States |
| Film, color photographic | 1935 | Leopold Godowsky, Leopold Mannes | United States |

| INVENTION | DATE | INVENTOR | COUNTRY |
|---|---|---|---|
| Food, canned | 1795 | Nicolas Appert | France |
| Food, quick frozen | 1925 | Clarence Birdseye | United States |
| Frisbee | 1948 | Walter Frederick Morrison | United States |
| Generator, electric | 1832 | Hippolyte Pixii | France |
| Gum, chewing | 1870 | Thomas Adams | United States |
| Gunpowder | c. 200 | Unknown | China |
| Helicopter, single rotor | 1939 | Igor Sikorsky | United States |
| Jet engine | 1930 | Frank Whittle | England |
| Jigsaw puzzles | 1767 | John Spilsbury | England |
| Laser | 1960 | Theodore H. Maiman | United States |
| Lawn mower | 1830 | Edwin Budding | England |
| Life Savers candy | 1913 | Clarence Crane | United States |
| Light bulb, incandescent (practical) | 1879 | Thomas Edison | United States |
| Light, fluorescent | 1867 | A. E. Becquerel | France |
| Lightning rod | 1752 | Benjamin Franklin | United States |
| Locomotive, steam | 1804 | Richard Trevithick | England |
| Loom, power | 1785 | Edmund Cartwright | England |
| Machine gun | 1718 | James Puckle | England |
| Match | 1816 | François Derosne | France |
| Microscope, compound | 1590 | Zacharias Janssen | Netherlands |
| Motion pictures | 1893 | Thomas Edison | United States |
| Motor, electric | 1822 | Michael Faraday | England |
| Motor, outboard | 1907 | Ole Evinrude | United States |
| Motorcycle | 1885 | Gottlieb Daimler | Germany |
| Nuclear reactor | 1942 | Enrico Fermi and others | United States |
| Nylon | 1935 | Wallace H. Carothers | United States |
| Paper | 105 | Ts'ai Lun | China |
| Parachute | 1783 | Sebastian Lenormand | France |
| Pen, ball-point | 1888 | John H. Loud | United States |
| Pencil, wooden | 1683 | J. Pettus | Germany |
| Phonograph | 1877 | Thomas A. Edison | United States |
| Photography, daguerreotype | 1837 | Louis Daguerre | France |
| Piano | 1709 | Bartolommeo Cristofori | Italy |
| Pin, safety | 1849 | Walter Hunt | United States |
| Plastic (celluloid) | 1869 | John Wesley Hyatt | United States |
| Potato chips | 1853 | George Crum | United States |
| Pressure cooker | 1679 | Denis Papin | France |
| Printing, movable type | 1045 | Bi Sheng | China |
| Printing, movable type | 1456 | Johann Gutenberg | Germany |
| Propeller, screw (successful) | 1836 | John Ericsson | Sweden/U.S. |
| Radar | 1904 | Christian Hülsmeyer | Germany |
| Radio, wireless | 1895 | Guglielmo Marconi | Italy |

| INVENTION | DATE | INVENTOR | COUNTRY |
|---|---|---|---|
| Reaper | 1834 | Cyrus Hall McCormick | United States |
| Revolver | 1835 | Samuel Colt | United States |
| Rifle, automatic | 1918 | John Browning | United States |
| Rocket | 1926 | Robert Goddard | United States |
| Roller skate (4-wheeled) | 1863 | James L. Plimpton | United States |
| Rubber bands | 1821 | Thomas Hancock | England |
| Rubber, vulcanized | 1839 | Charles Goodyear | United States |
| Saxophone | 1840 | Adolphe Sax | Belgium |
| Scuba gear (aqua-lung) | 1943 | Jacques-Yves Cousteau, Émile Gagnan | France |
| Seed drill | 1700 | Jethro Tull | England |
| Sewing machine | 1846 | Elias Howe | United States |
| Shopping cart | 1937 | Sylvan N. Goldman | United States |
| Shuttle, flying | 1733 | John Kay | England |
| Spinning jenny | 1764 | James Hargreaves | England |
| Spinning mule | 1779 | Samuel Crompton | England |
| Spinning wheel | c.500 B.C. | Unknown | India |
| Steam engine, modern | 1769 | James Watt | England |
| Steamship | 1783 | Claude de Jouffroy d'Abbans | France |
| Straws, drinking | 1888 | Marvin Stone | United States |
| Synthesizer (successful) | 1964 | Robert A. Moog | United States |
| Telegraph | 1837 | Samuel F. B. Morse | United States |
| Telephone | 1876 | Alexander Graham Bell | United States |
| Telescope | 1608 | Hans Lippershey | Netherlands |
| Television | 1925 | John Baird | Scotland |
| Television camera | 1927 | Philo T. Farnsworth | United States |
| Thermometer, mercury, Fahrenheit scale | 1714 | Gabriel D. Fahrenheit | Germany |
| Thermometer, Celsius scale | 1742 | Anders Celsius | Sweden |
| Tire, pneumatic | 1845 | Robert W. Thomson | Scotland |
| Toothbrush | 1770 | William Addis | England |
| Tractor, modern | 1900 | Benjamin Holt | United States |
| Trampoline, modern | 1936 | George Nissen | United States |
| Typewriter | 1867 | C. Latham Sholes and others | United States |
| Vaccine, smallpox | 1796 | Edward Jenner | United States |
| Vaccine, polio | 1953 | Jonas E. Salk | United States |
| Vacuum cleaner, home | 1908 | James Murray Spangler | United States |
| Velcro | 1956 | George de Mestral | Switzerland |
| Water skis | 1922 | Ralph Samuelson* | United States |
| Wheelbarrow | c.100 | Unknown | China |
| Xerography (copy machine) | 1938 | Chester F. Carlson | United States |
| Zipper | 1893 | Whitcomb Judson | United States |

*Patented by Fred Walker.

# MAN-MADE STRUCTURES

## IMPORTANT CANALS

| CANAL | LOCATION | LENGTH (miles) | NUMBER OF LOCKS | YEAR OPENED |
|---|---|---|---|---|
| Albert | Belgium | 81 | 6 | 1939 |
| Amsterdam-Rhine | Netherlands | 45 | 4 | 1952 |
| Chesapeake and Delaware | Maryland Delaware | 14 | 0 | 1829 |
| Chicago Sanitary and Ship | Illinois | 30 | 1 | 1900 |
| Erie* | New York | 363 | -- | 1825 |
| Houston | Texas | 51 | 0 | 1914 |
| New York State Barge System | New York | 524 | 57 | 1918 |
| Panama | Panama | 51 | 12 | 1914 |
| Saint Lawrence Seaway | New York Canada | 182 | 7 | 1959 |
| Suez | Egypt | 117 | 0 | 1869 |
| Volga-Baltic | U.S.S.R. | 528 | 7 | 1964 |
| Welland Ship | Canada | 26 | 8 | 1932 |

*The Erie Canal is part of the present-day New York State Barge System.

## IMPORTANT BRIDGES

| BRIDGE | LOCATION | TYPE | MAIN SPAN | YEAR OPENED |
|---|---|---|---|---|
| Humber | England | Suspension | 4,626 | 1981 |
| Verrazano-Narrows | New York | Suspension | 4,260 | 1964 |
| Golden Gate | California | Suspension | 4,200 | 1937 |
| Mackinac | Michigan | Suspension | 3,800 | 1957 |
| Minami Bisan-seto | Japan | Suspension | 3,609 | 1988 |
| Second Bosporus | Turkey | Suspension | 3,576 | 1988 |
| First Bosporus | Turkey | Suspension | 3,524 | 1973 |
| George Washington | New York-N.J. | Suspension | 3,500 | 1931 |
| 25th of April | Portugal | Suspension | 3,323 | 1966 |
| Quebec | Canada | Cantilever | 1,800 | 1917 |
| Forth | Scotland | Cantilever | 1,710 | 1890 |
| New River Gorge | West Virginia | Steel Arch | 1,700 | 1977 |
| Bayonne | New York-N.J. | Steel Arch | 1,675 | 1931 |
| Osaka Port | Japan | Cantilever | 1,673 | 1974 |
| Sydney Harbor | Australia | Steel Arch | 1,650 | 1932 |
| Commodore John Barry | Penn.-N.J. | Cantilever | 1,644 | 1974 |
| Brooklyn | New York | Suspension | 1,595 | 1883 |

The **Taj Mahal** is at Agra in northern India. An Indian ruler, Shah Jahan, had it built as a tomb for his wife Mumtaz Mahal, who died in 1629.

## IMPORTANT RAILROAD TUNNELS

| TUNNEL | LOCATION | LENGTH (miles) | YEAR OPENED |
|---|---|---|---|
| Seikan | Japan | 33.5 | 1988 |
| Channel | England, France | 30.6 | UC* |
| Ooshimizu | Japan | 13.8 | 1982 |
| Simplon I | Italy, Switzerland | 12.3 | 1906 |
| Simplon II | Italy, Switzerland | 12.3 | 1922 |
| Shin Kanmon | Japan | 11.6 | 1975 |
| Apennine | Italy | 11.5 | 1934 |
| Rokko | Japan | 10.1 | 1972 |
| Furka | Switzerland | 9.5 | UC* |
| St. Gotthard | Switzerland | 9.3 | 1882 |
| Lötschberg | Switzerland | 9.1 | 1913 |

*UC means "under construction."

## IMPORTANT MOTOR VEHICLE TUNNELS

| TUNNEL | LOCATION | LENGTH (miles) | YEAR OPENED |
|---|---|---|---|
| St. Gotthard | Switzerland | 10.1 | 1980 |
| Arlberg | Austria | 8.7 | 1978 |
| Fréjus | France, Italy | 8.1 | 1980 |
| Mt. Blanc | France, Italy | 7.3 | 1965 |
| Gran Sasso | Italy | 6.2 | 1976 |
| Seelisberg | Switzerland | 5.8 | UC* |
| Ena | Japan | 5.3 | 1976 |
| Rokko II | Japan | 4.3 | 1974 |
| San Bernardino | Switzerland | 4.1 | 1967 |
| Tauern | Austria | 4.0 | 1974 |

*UC means "under construction."

The **Golden Gate Bridge** is at the entrance to San Francisco Bay in California. It was the longest single span suspension bridge in the world between 1937 and 1964.

The **Arc de Triomphe** (Arch of Triumph) is in Paris, France. It was begun by Napoleon as a monument to his troups in 1806, and the names of 386 of his generals are on the inner walls.

©DG 1990

## IMPORTANT DAMS

| DAM | LOCATION | CAPACITY[1] | HEIGHT (feet) | YEAR COMPLETED |
|---|---|---|---|---|
| Afsluitdijk | Netherlands | 82,927 | -- | 1932 |
| Chicoasén | Mexico | -- | 869 | 1981 |
| Fort Peck | Montana | 125,628 | -- | 1940 |
| Grande Dixence | Switzerland | -- | 935 | 1962 |
| High Aswan | Egypt | 56,242 | -- | 1970 |
| Hoover | Arizona-Nevada | -- | 726 | 1936 |
| Mica | Canada | -- | 794 | 1972 |
| New Cornelia Tailings | Arizona | 274,016 | -- | 1973 |
| Nurek | U.S.S.R. | 75,861 | 984 | 1980 |
| Oahe | South Dakota | 92,000 | -- | 1960 |
| Oroville | California | 78,005 | 770 | 1968 |
| Rogun | U.S.S.R. | 98,750 | 1019 | 1985 |
| Tarbela | Pakistan | 159,20 | -- | 1976 |
| Tehri | India | -- | 856 | UC[2] |
| Vaiont | Italy | -- | 869 | 1961 |

[1]In thousands of cubic yards.   [2]UC means Under Construction.

## TALLEST SKYSCRAPERS

| SKYSCRAPER | LOCATION | STORIES | HEIGHT |
|---|---|---|---|
| Sears Tower | Chicago | 110 | 1,454 ft. |
| World Trade Center | New York City | 110 | 1,350 ft. |
| Empire State Building | New York City | 102 | 1,250 ft. |
| Amoco | Chicago | 80 | 1,136 ft. |
| John Hancock Center | Chicago | 100 | 1,127 ft. |
| First Interstate World Center | Los Angeles | 75 | 1,018 ft. |
| Texas Commerce Tower | Houston | 75 | 1,002 ft. |
| Bank of China | Hong Kong | 73 | 1,001 ft. |
| Allied Bank Plaza | Houston | 71 | 992 ft. |
| 311 South Wacker | Chicago | 65 | 970 ft. |
| Columbia Seafirst | Seattle | 76 | 954 ft. |
| Bank of Montreal | Toronto | 72 | 935 ft. |
| NCNB Plaza | Dallas | 72 | 921 ft. |
| Overseas Union Bank | Singapore | 60 | 919 ft. |
| Citicorp Center | New York City | 46 | 915 ft. |
| Scotia Plaza | Toronto | 68 | 906 ft. |
| Transco Tower | Houston | 64 | 901 ft. |

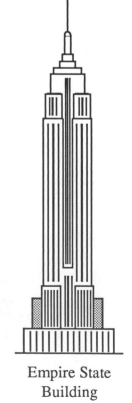

Empire State Building

# MAJOR WORLD RELIGIONS

**Religion** is an organized system of beliefs, ceremonies, traditions and values that center on the worship of divine power. The eight major world religions are listed in order of their founding.

## JUDAISM

Judaism was begun about 1700 B.C. by **Abraham**. Jews practice **monotheism**, or the worship of one God. The Holy Books are the **Torah**, which is the first five books of what Christians call the Old Testament, and the **Talmud**, a guide to Jewish laws. The Jewish holy day is the **Sabbath**, Saturday, which they believe is the day God rested after creating the earth. Jewish groups worship in a **synagogue**, or temple, led by a **rabbi**. About 18 million people are Jews. They live scattered throughout the world, with many in the countries of Israel, the United States, and the Soviet Union. The Jewish symbol is the **Star of David**.

## HINDUISM

Hinduism began about 1500 B.C. in India and developed gradually over thousands of years. Hindus are **polytheistic**, which means they worship many gods. All of the gods are considered part of the universal spirit **Brahman**. Hindus believe that a person's soul never dies, and if a he lives a good life, he will be **reincarnated**, or reborn, into a higher state of life. This is called **karma**. A person who lives a bad life may be reincarnated into a lower state, perhaps as an animal. Hindus do not kill animals. Reincarnation is thought to continue until a person reaches spiritual perfection. **Gurus** or **yogis** are considered near spiritual perfection and are followed by others. About 647,895,000 people are Hindu, and most live in

India. A symbol is the Sanskrit word **om**, which is used in meditation.

## BUDDHISM

Buddhism was begun in India about 500 B.C. by Siddhartha Gautama, the **Buddha**, or *Enlightened One*. Buddhists believe that life is filled with suffering, and the way to find **nirvana**, or a state of happiness and peace, is to become free from all desires and worldly attachments. Like Hindus, Buddhists believe in reincarnation and karma. Buddha is honored, but is not considered to be God. The book of scriptures is called the **Tripitika** and the spiritual leaders are **monks**. About 307,416,000 Buddhists live mostly in Sri Lanka, Southeast Asia and Japan. A symbol of Buddhism is the **Wheel of Life**, which represents the **Noble Eightfold Path**: right knowledge, right intention, right speech, right conduct, right livelihood, right effort, right mindfulness and right concentration.

## CONFUCIANISM

Confucianism was begun about 500 B.C. by **Confucius** in China. It does not teach the worship of a God or gods, but rather a way of living. Confucius stressed the importance of self-discipline, duty, moral living and respect for ancestors and authority. He taught that leaders must govern by high moral standards and serve as examples of good living for others to follow. His teachings are recorded in the **Five Classics**

and **Four Books**. For 2000 years, Confucianism was the basis of Chinese thought and government. Chinese communists opposed it until 1977 because they thought it looked too much to the past instead of the future. About 175,689,000 people practice Confucianism, mostly in China and Taiwan.

## TAOISM

Taoism was begun about 100 B.C. in reaction to Confucianism in China. It is based on the teachings in two books, the **Tao Te Ching** and **Chuang Tzu**. Taoists try to live simple, reflective lives close to nature, and to find their own unique way of being. **Tao** means "way." **Priests** are the spiritual leaders. About 29 million people, mostly in China, are Taoist. The symbol stands for what Taoists consider the two basic forces of the universe, **yin**, or female energy, and **yang**, or male energy. Yin is shown as white and yang as black.

## SHINTOISM

Shintoism developed in Japan from native folk beliefs. People worship spirits and demons they believe to live in animals, plants, mountains, and other parts of nature. The sun goddess is considered the highest god, and until the 1940's, the emperor of Japan was worshipped as a descendent of the sun goddess. About 3,487,000 Shintos live in Japan.

## CHRISTIANITY

Christianity began with **Jesus Christ** in Palestine, present-day Israel. Christians believe that Jesus is the Son of God, who came to earth, died on the Cross, and rose from the dead, thereby paying the

penalty for sin. The Christian religion teaches that those who accept Jesus Christ will be saved from sin and will have eternal life with God in Heaven after death. Christ told his followers to love God and one another, and to spread His teachings throughout the world. A major split between Christian churches came in 1054 A.D., when the Orthodox and Roman Catholic churches divided. In the 1500's, Martin Luther led another split called the Reformation which divided the Catholic and Protestant churches. A large number of Protestant churches now exist, including Congregationalist, Episcopal, Lutheran, Methodist and Presbyterian. The Holy Book is the **Bible**, including the **New Testament**. Christians worship on **Sunday**, the anniversary of Christ's resurrection, in **churches** or **cathedrals**. The spiritual leaders are **priests, ministers,** or **preachers**. About 1,455,053,000 Christians live throughout the world, mostly in Europe and the Americas.

## ISLAM

Islam was founded in the early 600's by **Mohammed**, who was believed by his followers to be a prophet of **Allah**, or God. Mohammed said he had visions in which he was commanded to preach the message of Allah to the Arabs, who at that time worshipped many gods. He wrote his message in the **Koran**, the Holy Book. Believers pray five times daily facing the Holy City of **Mecca**, give alms to the poor, fast during the daylight hours of the month of **Ramadan**, and make a pilgrimage, or **hajj**, to Mecca during their lifetime. Moslems gather for worship on **Fridays** in **mosques**, and are led by an **iman**. About 840,221,000 Moslems live mostly in the Middle East, North Africa, Bangladesh, Pakistan and Indonesia. Two major Moslem groups are the Shiites and Sunnites. The symbol is a crescent and star.

# THE
# UNITED
# STATES

# STATES OF THE UNION

## ALABAMA
**Capital:** Montgomery (177,857)
**Governor:** Guy Hunt (to January 1995)
**Entered Union (rank):** December 14, 1819 (22nd)
**Motto:** *Audemus jura nostra defendere* (We dare maintain our rights)
**State Song:** "Alabama"
**State Flower:** Camellia
**State Bird:** Yellowhammer
**State Tree:** Southern Longleaf Pine
**Nickname:** The Heart of Dixie
**Origin of Name:** May come from Choctaw meaning "thicket-clearers" or "vegetation-gatherers"
**Population (rank):** 4,062,608 (22)
**Population Density:** 79 per sq. mi.
**Per Capita Income:** $12,851
**Area (rank):** 51,705 sq. mi. (29th)
**Highest Point:** 2,405 feet
**Lowest Point:** Sea level

## ALASKA
**Capital:** Juneau (19,528)
**Governor:** Walter J. Hickel (to Dec. 1994)
**Entered Union (rank):** Jan. 3, 1959 (49th)
**Motto:** North to the Future
**State Song:** "Alaska's Flag"
**State Flower:** Forget-Me-Not
**State Bird:** Willow Ptarmigan
**State Tree:** Sitka Spruce
**Nicknames:** The Last Frontier, Land of the Midnight Sun
**Origin of Name:** From Aleut word meaning "great land"
**Population (rank):** 551,947 (49th)
**Population Density:** 0.9 per sq. mi.
**Per Capita Income:** $19,079
**Area (rank):** 591,004 sq. mi. (1st)
**Highest Point:** 20,320 feet
**Lowest Point:** Sea level

## ARIZONA
**Capital:** Phoenix (789,704)
**Governor:** Runoff: Terry Goddard or J. Fife Symington (to 1995)
**Entered Union (rank):** Feb 14, 1912 (48th)
**Motto:** *Ditat Deus* (God enriches)
**State Song:** "Arizona"
**State Flower:** Bossom of the Giant Saguaro Cactus
**State Bird:** Cactus Wren
**State Tree:** Palo Verde
**Nickname:** Grand Canyon State
**Origin of Name:** From Indian word "Arizonac," meaning "little spring"
**Population (rank):** 3,677,985 (24th)
**Population Density:** 32 per sq. mi.
**Per Capita Income:** $14,970
**Area (rank):** 114,000 sq. mi. (6th)
**Highest Point:** 12,633 feet
**Lowest Point:** 70 feet

## ARKANSAS
**Capital:** Little Rock (159,159)
**Governor:** Bill Clinton (to Jan. 1995)
**Entered Union (rank):** June 15, 1836 (25th)
**Motto:** *Regnat Populus* (The people rule)
**State Song:** "Arkansas"
**State Flower:** Apple Blossom
**State Bird:** Mockingbird
**State Tree:** Pine
**Nickname:** Land of Opportunity
**Origin of Name:** From the Quapaw Indians
**Population (rank):** 2,362,239 (33rd)
**Population Density:** 44 per sq. mi.
**Per Capita Income:** $12,219
**Area (rank):** 53,187 sq. mi. (27th)
**Highest Point:** 2,753 feet
**Lowest Point:** 55 feet

## CALIFORNIA
**Capital:** Sacramento (275,741)
**Governor:** Pete Wilson (to Jan. 1995)
**Entered Union (rank):** Sept. 9, 1850 (31st)
**Motto:** *Eureka* (I have found it)
**State Song:** "I Love You, California"
**State Flower:** Golden Poppy
**State Bird:** California Valley Quail
**State Tree:** California Redwood
**Nickname:** Golden State
**Origin of Name:** From a book by Garcia Ordóñez de Montalvo
**Population (rank):** 29,839,250 (1st)
**Population Density:** 188 per sq. mi.
**Per Capita Income:** $18,753
**Area (rank):** 158,706 sq. mi. (3rd)
**Highest Point:** 14,494 feet
**Lowest Point:** -282 feet

## COLORADO
**Capital:** Denver (492,686)
**Governor:** Roy Romer (to Jan. 1995)
**Entered Union (rank):** Aug. 1, 1876 (38th)
**Motto:** *Nil sine Numine* (Nothing without Providence)
**State Song:** "Where the Columbines Grow"
**State Flower:** Rocky Mountain Columbine
**State Bird:** Lark Bunting
**State Tree:** Colorado Blue Spruce
**Nickname:** Centennial State
**Origin of Name:** From Spanish meaning "reddish"
**Population (rank):** 3,307,912 (26th)
**Population Density:** 32 per sq. mi.
**Per Capita Income:** $16,463
**Area (rank):** 104,091 sq. mi. (8th)
**Highest Point:** 14,433 feet
**Lowest Point:** 3,350 feet

## CONNECTICUT
**Capital:** Hartford (136,392)
**Governor:** Lowell P. Weicker, Jr. (to Jan. 1995)
**Entered Union (rank):** Jan. 9, 1788 (5th)
**Motto:** *Qui transtulit sustinet* (He who transplanted still sustains)
**State Song:** "Yankee Doodle"
**State Flower:** Mountain Laurel
**State Bird:** American Robin
**State Tree:** White Oak
**Nickname:** Constitution State

**Origin of Name:** From a Quinnehtukqut Indian word meaning "beside the long tidal river"
**Population (rank):** 3,295,669 (27th)
**Population Density:** 657 per sq. mi.
**Per Capita Income:** $23,059
**Area (rank):** 5,018 sq. mi. (48th)
**Highest Point:** 2,380 feet
**Lowest Point:** Sea level

## DELAWARE

**Capital:** Dover (23,507)
**Governor:** Michael N. Castle (to Jan. 1993)
**Entered Union (rank):** Dec. 7, 1787 (1st)
**Motto:** Liberty and Independence
**State Song:** "Our Delaware"
**State Flower:** Peach Blossom
**State Bird:** Blue Hen Chicken
**State Tree:** American Holly
**Nicknames:** First State
**Origin of Name:** From Delaware River and Bay, named after Sir Thomas West, Lord De La Warr
**Population (rank):** 668,696 (46th)
**Population Density:** 327 per sq. mi.
**Per Capita Income:** $17,661
**Area (rank):** 2,045 sq. mi. (49th)
**Highest Point:** 442 feet
**Lowest Point:** Sea level

## FLORIDA

**Capital:** Tallahassee (81,548)
**Governor:** Lawton Chiles (to Jan. 1995)
**Entered Union (rank):** March 3, 1845 (27th)
**Motto:** In God We Trust
**State Song:** "Swanee River"
**State Flower:** Orange Blossom
**State Bird:** Mockingbird
**State Tree:** Sabal Palm
**Nickname:** Sunshine State
**Origin of Name:** From Spanish word meaning "feast of flowers"
**Population (rank):** 13,003,362 (4th)
**Population Density:** 222 per sq. mi.
**Per Capita Income:** $16,603
**Area (rank):** 58,664 sq. mi. (22th)
**Highest Point:** 345 feet
**Lowest Point:** Sea level

## GEORGIA

**Capital:** Atlanta (425,022)
**Governor:** Zell Miller (to Jan. 1995)
**Entered Union (rank):** Jan. 2, 1788 (4th)
**Motto:** Wisdom, Justice, and Moderation
**State Song:** "Georgia On My Mind"
**State Flower:** Cherokee Rose
**State Bird:** Brown Thrasher
**State Tree:** Live Oak
**Nicknames:** Empire State of the South, Peach State
**Origin of Name:** In honor of George II of England
**Population (rank):** 6,508,419 (11th)
**Population Density:** 110 per sq. mi.
**Per Capita Income:** $15,260
**Area (rank):** 58,910 sq. mi. (21st)
**Highest Point:** 4,784 feet
**Lowest Point:** Sea level

## HAWAII

**Capital:** Honolulu (365,048)
**Governor:** John Waihee (to Dec. 1994)
**Entered Union (rank):** Aug. 21, 1959 (50th)
**Motto:** *Ua Mau Ke Ea O Ka Aina I Ka Pono* (The life of the land is perpetuated in righteousness)
**State Song:** "Hawaii Ponoi"
**State Flower:** Hibiscus
**State Bird:** Nene (Hawaiian goose)
**State Tree:** Kukui Tree
**Nickname:** Aloha State
**Origin of Name:** Uncertain. Hawaii Loa is the traditional discoverer of the islands.
**Population (rank):** 1,115,274 (40th)
**Population Density:** 172 per sq. mi.
**Per Capita Income:** $16,753
**Area (rank):** 6,471 sq. mi. (47th)
**Highest Point:** 13,796 feet
**Lowest Point:** Sea level

## IDAHO

**Capital:** Boise (102,249)
**Governor:** Cecil D. Andrus (to Jan. 1995)
**Entered Union (rank):** July 3, 1890 (43rd)

**Motto:** *Esto perpetua* (Let it be perpetual)
**State Song:** "Here We Have Idaho"
**State Flower:** Syringa
**State Bird:** Mountain Bluebird
**State Tree:** Western White Pine
**Nicknames:** Gem State, Spud State, Panhandle State
**Origin of Name:** Means "Gem of the Mountains"
**Population (rank):** 1,011,986 (42)
**Population Density:** 12 per sq. mi.
**Per Capita Income:** $12,665
**Area (rank):** 83,564 sq. mi. (13th)
**Highest Point:** 12,662 feet
**Lowest Point:** 710 feet

## ILLINOIS

**Capital:** Springfield (100,054)
**Governor:** Jim Edgar (to Jan. 1995)
**Entered Union (rank):** Dec. 3, 1818 (21st)
**Motto:** State Sovereignty, National Union
**State Song:** "Illinois"
**State Flower:** Native Violet
**State Bird:** Cardinal
**State Tree:** White Oak
**Nickname:** Prairie State
**Origin of Name:** From Indian and French meaning "tribe of superior men"
**Population (rank):** 11,466,682 (6th)
**Population Density:** 204 per sq. mi.
**Per Capita Income:** $17,575
**Area (rank):** 56,345 sq. mi. (24th)
**Highest Point:** 1,235 feet
**Lowest Point:** 279 feet

## INDIANA

**Capital:** Indianapolis (700,807)
**Governor:** Evan Bayh (to Jan. 1993)
**Entered Union (rank):** Dec. 11, 1816 (19th)
**Motto:** Crossroads of America
**State Song:** "On the Banks of the Wabash, Far Away"
**State Flower:** Peony
**State Bird:** Cardinal
**State Tree:** Tulip Poplar
**Nickname:** Hoosier State

**Origin of Name:** Meaning is "land of Indians"
**Population (rank):** 5,564,228 (14th)
**Population Density:** 154 per sq. mi.
**Per Capita Income:** $14,924
**Area (rank):** 36,185 sq. mi. (38th)
**Highest Point:** 1,257 feet
**Lowest Point:** 320 feet

## IOWA

**Capital:** Des Moines (191,003)
**Governor:** Terry E. Branstad (to Jan. 1995)
**Entered Union (rank):** Dec. 28, 1846 (29th)
**Motto:** Our liberties we prize and our rights we will maintain
**State Song:** "The Song of Iowa"
**State Flower:** Wild Rose
**State Bird:** Eastern Goldfinch
**State Tree:** Oak
**Nickname:** Hawkeye State
**Origin of Name:** Probably from an Indian word meaning "this is the place" or "The Beautiful Land"
**Population (rank):** 2,787,424 (30th)
**Population Density:** 50 per sq. mi.
**Per Capita Income:** $14,662
**Area (rank):** 56,275 sq. mi. (25th)
**Highest Point:** 1,670 feet
**Lowest Point:** 480 feet

## KANSAS

**Capital:** Topeka (118,690)
**Governor:** Joan Finney (to Jan. 1995)
**Entered Union (rank):** Jan. 29, 1861 (34th)
**Motto:** *Ad astra per aspera* (To the stars through difficulties)
**State Song:** "Home on the Range"
**State Flower:** Wild Sunflower
**State Bird:** Western Meadowlark
**State Tree:** Cottonwood
**Nicknames:** Sunflower State, Jayhawk State
**Origin of Name:** From Siouan meaning "people of the south wind"
**Population (rank):** 2,485,600 (32)
**Population Density:** 30 per sq. mi.
**Per Capita Income:** $15,759
**Area (rank):** 82,277 sq. mi. (14th)
**Highest Point:** 4,039 feet
**Lowest Point:** 679 feet

## KENTUCKY

**Capital:** Frankfort (25,973)
**Governor:** Wallace J. Wilkinson (to Dec. 1991)
**Entered Union (rank):** June 1, 1792 (15th)
**Motto:** United we stand, divided we fall
**State Song:** "My Old Kentucky Home"
**State Flower:** Goldenrod
**State Bird:** Kentucky Cardinal
**State Tree:** Kentucky Coffee Tree
**Nickname:** Bluegrass State
**Origin of Name:** From Iroquois word meaning "land of tomorrow"
**Population (rank):** 3,698,969 (23rd)
**Population Density:** 92 per sq. mi.
**Per Capita Income:** $12,822
**Area (rank):** 40,410 sq. mi. (37th)
**Highest Point:** 4,139 feet
**Lowest Point:** 257 feet

## LOUISIANA

**Capital:** Baton Rouge (220,394)
**Governor:** Buddy Roemer (to March 1992)
**Entered Union (rank):** April 30, 1812 (18th)
**Motto:** Union, Justice, and Confidence
**State Song:** "Give Me Louisiana" and "You Are My Sunshine"
**State Flower:** Magnolia
**State Bird:** Eastern Brown Pelican
**State Tree:** Bald Cypress
**Nicknames:** Pelican State, Sportsman's Paradise, Creole State, Sugar State
**Origin of Name:** In honor of Louis XIV of France
**Population (rank):** 4,238,216 (21st)
**Population Density:** 89 per sq. mi.
**Per Capita Income:** $12,292
**Area (rank):** 47,752 sq. mi. (31st)
**Highest Point:** 535 feet
**Lowest Point:** -8 feet

## MAINE

**Capital:** Augusta (21,819)
**Governor:** John R. McKernan, Jr., (to Jan. 1995)
**Entered Union (rank):** March 15, 1820 (23rd)
**Motto:** *Dirigo* (I direct)
**State Song:** "State of Maine Song"
**State Flower:** White Pine Cone and Tassel
**State Bird:** Chickadee
**State Tree:** White Pine
**Nickname:** Pine Tree State
**Origin of Name:** Name first used to distinguish the mainland from offshore islands
**Population (rank):** 1,233,223 (38th)
**Population Density:** 37 per sq. mi.
**Per Capita Income:** $15,106
**Area (rank):** 33,265 sq. mi. (39th)
**Highest Point:** 5,267 feet
**Lowest Point:** Sea level

## MARYLAND

**Capital:** Annapolis (31,740)
**Governor:** William Donald Schaefer (to Jan. 1995)
**Entered Union (rank):** April 28, 1788 (7th)
**Motto:** *Fatti maschii, parole femine* (Manly deeds, womanly words)
**State Song:** "Maryland! My Maryland!"
**State Flower:** Black-Eyed Susan
**State Bird:** Baltimore Oriole
**State Tree:** White Oak
**Nicknames:** Old Line State, Free State
**Origin of Name:** In honor of Henrietta Maria, Queen of England
**Population (rank):** 4,798,622 (19th)
**Population Density:** 459 per sq. mi.
**Per Capita Income:** $19,487
**Area (rank):** 10,460 sq. mi. (42nd)
**Highest Point:** 3,360 feet
**Lowest Point:** Sea level

## MASSACHUSETTS

**Capital:** Boston (562,994)
**Governor:** William F. Weld (to Jan. 1995)
**Entered Union (rank):** Feb. 6, 1788 (6th)
**Motto:** *Ense petit placidam sub libertate quietem* (By the sword we seek peace, but peace only under liberty)
**State Song:** "All Hail to Massachusetts"

State Flower: Mayflower
State Bird: Chickadee
State Tree: American Elm
Nicknames: Bay State, Old Colony State
Origin of Name: From Indian words meaning "great mountain place"
Population (rank): 6,029,051 (13th)
Population Density: 728 per sq. mi.
Per Capita Income: $20,816
Area (rank): 8,284 sq. mi. (45th)
Highest Point: 3,487 feet
Lowest Point: Sea level

## MICHIGAN
Capital: Lansing (130,414)
Governor: John Engler (to Jan. 1995)
Entered Union (rank): Jan. 26, 1837 (26th)
Motto: *Si quaeris peninsulam amoenam circumspice* (If you seek a pleasant peninsula, look about you)
State Song: "Michigan, My Michigan"
State Flower: Apple Blossom
State Bird: Robin
State Tree: White Pine
Nickname: Wolverine State, Great Lake State
Origin of Name: From Indian words meaning "great lake"
Population (rank): 9,328,784 (8th)
Population Density: 159 per sq. mi.
Per Capita Income: $16,552
Area (rank): 58,527 sq. mi. (23rd)
Highest Point: 1,979 feet
Lowest Point: 572 feet

## MINNESOTA
Capital: St. Paul (270,230)
Governor: Arne Carlson (to Jan. 1995)
Entered Union (rank): May 11, 1858 (32nd)
Motto: *L'Etoile du Nord* (The Star of the North)
State Song: "Hail! Minnesota"
State Flower: Pink and White Lady's Slipper
State Bird: Common Loon
State Tree: Red Pine

Nicknames: North Star State, Gopher State, Land of 10,000 Lakes
Origin of Name: From Dakota Indian word meaning "sky-tinted water"
Population (rank): 4,387,029 (20th)
Population Density: 52 per sq. mi.
Per Capita Income: $16,674
Area (rank): 84,402 sq. mi. (12th)
Highest Point: 2,301 feet
Lowest Point: 602 feet

## MISSISSIPPI
Capital: Jackson (202,895)
Governor: Ray Mabus (to Jan. 1992)
Entered Union (rank): Dec. 10, 1817 (20th)
Motto: *Virtute et armis* (By valor and arms)
State Song: "Go, Mississippi"
State Flower: Magnolia
State Bird: Mockingbird
State Tree: Magnolia
Nickname: Magnolia State
Origin of Name: From Indian word meaning "Father of Waters"
Population (rank): 2,586,443 (31st)
Population Density: 54 per sq. mi.
Per Capita Income: $11,116
Area (rank): 47,689 sq. mi. (32nd)
Highest Point: 806 feet
Lowest Point: Sea level

## MISSOURI
Capital: Jefferson City (33,619)
Governor: John D. Ashcroft (to Jan. 1993)
Entered Union (rank): Aug. 10, 1821 (24th)
Motto: *Salus populi suprema lex esto* (The welfare of the people shall be the supreme law)
State Song: "Missouri Waltz"
State Flower: White Hawthorn
State Bird: Bluebird
State Tree: Flowering Dogwood
Nickname: Show-Me State
Origin of Name: Named after Missouri Indian tribe. "Missouri" means "town of the large canoes."
Population (rank): 5,137,804 (15th)

Population Density: 74 per sq. mi.
Per Capita Income: $15,452
Area (rank): 69,697 sq. mi. (19th)
Highest Point: 1,772 feet
Lowest Point: 230 feet

## MONTANA
Capital: Helena (23,938)
Governor: Stan Stephens (to Jan. 1993)
Entered Union (rank): Nov. 8, 1889 (41st)
Motto: *Oro y plata* (Gold and silver)
State Song: "Montana"
State Flower: Bitterroot
State Bird: Western Meadowlark
State Tree: Ponderosa Pine
Nickname: Treasure State
Origin of Name: Chosen from Latin dictionary
Population (rank): 803,655 (44th)
Population Density: 5 per sq. mi.
Per Capita Income: $12,866
Area (rank): 147,046 sq. mi. (4th)
Highest Point: 12,799 feet
Lowest Point: 1,800 feet

## NEBRASKA
Capital: Lincoln (171,932)
Governor: Ben Nelson (to Jan. 1995)
Entered Union (rank): March 1, 1867 (37th)
Motto: Equality before the law
State Song: "Beautiful Nebraska"
State Flower: Goldenrod
State Bird: Western Meadowlark
State Tree: Western Cottonwood
Nicknames: Cornhusker State, Beef State, Tree Planters State
Origin of Name: From Oto Indian meaning "flat water"
Population (rank): 1,584,617 (36th)
Population Density: 20 per sq. mi.
Per Capita Income: $14,774
Area (rank): 77,355 sq. mi. (15th)
Highest Point: 5,426 feet
Lowest Point: 840 feet

## NEVADA
Capital: Carson City (32,022)
Governor: Bob Miller (to Jan. 1995)

Entered Union (rank): Oct. 31, 1864 (36th)
Motto: All for Our Country
State Song: "Home Means Nevada"
State Flower: Sagebrush
State Bird: Mountain Bluebird
State Trees: Bristlecone Pine and Single-Leaf Piñon
Nicknames: Silver State, Sagebrush State, Battle-born State
Origin of Name: Spanish meaning "snowcapped"
Population (rank): 1,206,152 (39th)
Population Density: 11 per sq. mi.
Per Capita Income: $17,511
Area (rank): 110,561 sq. mi. (7th)
Highest Point: 13,140 feet
Lowest Point: 470 feet

## NEW HAMPSHIRE

Capital: Concord (30,400)
Governor: Judd Gregg (to Jan. 1993)
Entered Union (rank): June 21, 1788 (9th)
Motto: Live free or die
State Songs: "Old New Hampshire"
State Flower: Purple Lilac
State Bird: Purple Finch
State Tree: White Birch
Nickname: Granite State
Origin of Name: From the English county of Hampshire
Population (rank): 1,113,915 (41st)
Population Density: 120 per sq. mi.
Per Capita Income: $19,434
Area (rank): 9,279 sq. mi. (44th)
Highest Point: 6,288 feet
Lowest Point: Sea level

## NEW JERSEY

Capital: Trenton (92,124)
Governor: James Florio (to Jan. 1994)
Entered Union (rank): Dec. 18, 1787 (3rd)
Motto: Liberty and Prosperity
State Song: None
State Flower: Purple Violet
State Bird: Eastern Goldfinch
State Tree: Red Oak
Nickname: Garden State
Origin of Name: From the Channel Isle of Jersey
Population (rank): 7,748,634 (9th)

Population Density: 995 per sq. mi.
Per Capita Income: $21,994
Area (rank): 7,787 sq. mi. (46th)
Highest Point: 1,803 feet
Lowest Point: Sea level

## NEW MEXICO

Capital: Santa Fe (49,160)
Governor: Bruce King (to Jan. 1995)
Entered Union (rank): Jan. 6, 1912 (47th)
Motto: *Crescit eundo* (It grows as it goes)
State Song: "O Fair New Mexico"
State Flower: Yucca
State Bird: Chaparral Bird (Roadrunner)
State Tree: Piñon
Nicknames: Land of Enchantment, Sunshine State
Origin of Name: From the country of Mexico
Population (rank): 1,521,779 (37th)
Population Density: 13 per sq. mi.
Per Capita Income: $12,488
Area (rank): 121,593 sq. mi. (5th)
Highest Point: 13,161 feet
Lowest Point: 2,842 feet

## NEW YORK

Capital: Albany (101,727)
Governor: Mario M. Cuomo (to Jan. 1995)
Entered Union (rank): July 26, 1788 (11th)
Motto: *Excelsior* (Ever upward)
State Song: "I Love New York"
State Flower: Rose
State Bird: Bluebird
State Tree: Sugar Maple
Nickname: Empire State
Origin of Name: In honor of the English Duke of York
Population (rank): 18,044,505 (2nd)
Population Density: 367 per sq. mi.
Per Capita Income: $19,305
Area (rank): 49,108 sq. mi. (30th)
Highest Point: 5,344 feet
Lowest Point: Sea level

## NORTH CAROLINA

Capital: Raleigh (149,771)

Governor: James G. Martin (to Jan. 1993)
Entered Union (rank): Nov. 21, 1789 (12th)
Motto: *Esse quam videri* (To be rather than to seem)
State Song: "The Old North State"
State Flower: Dogwood
State Bird: Cardinal
State Tree: Pine
Nickname: Tar Heel State, Old North State
Origin of Name: In honor of Charles I of England
Population (rank): 6,657,630 (10th)
Population Density: 126 per sq. mi.
Per Capita Income: $14,304
Area (rank): 52,669 sq. mi. (28th)
Highest Point: 6,684 feet
Lowest Point: Sea level

## NORTH DAKOTA

Capital: Bismarck (44,485)
Governor: George A. Sinner (to Jan. 1993)
Entered Union (rank): Nov. 2, 1889 (39th)
Motto: Liberty and union, now and forever, one and inseparable
State Song: "North Dakota Hymn"
State Flower: Wild Prairie Rose
State Bird: Western Meadowlark
State Tree: American Elm
Nicknames: Peace Garden State, Sioux State, Flickertail State
Origin of Name: From the Dakotah tribe, meaning "allies"
Population (rank): 641,364 (47th)
Population Density: 9 per sq. mi.
Per Capita Income: $12,833
Area (rank): 70,702 sq. mi. (17th)
Highest Point: 3,506 feet
Lowest Point: 750 feet

## OHIO

Capital: Columbus (565,032)
Governor: George G. Voinovich (to Jan. 1995)
Entered Union (rank): March 1, 1803 (17th)
Motto: With God, all things are possible
State Song: "Beautiful Ohio"
State Flower: Scarlet Carnation

**State Bird:** Cardinal
**State Tree:** Buckeye
**Nickname:** Buckeye State
**Origin of Name:** From Iroquois word meaning "great river"
**Population (rank):** 10,887,325 (7th)
**Population Density:** 263 per sq. mi.
**Per Capita Income:** $15,536
**Area (rank):** 41,330 sq. mi. (35th)
**Highest Point:** 1,549 feet
**Lowest Point:** 455 feet

## OKLAHOMA

**Capital:** Oklahoma City (404,014)
**Governor:** David Walters (to Jan. 1995)
**Entered Union (rank):** Nov. 16, 1907 (46th)
**Motto:** *Labor omnia vincit* (Labor conquers all things)
**State Song:** "Oklahoma"
**State Flower:** Mistletoe
**State Bird:** Scissor-Tailed Flycatcher
**State Tree:** Redbud
**Nickname:** Sooner State
**Origin of Name:** From Choctaw Indian words meaning "red people"
**Population (rank):** 3,157,604 (28th)
**Population Density:** 45 per sq. mi.
**Per Capita Income:** $13,323
**Area (rank):** 69,956 sq. mi. (18th)
**Highest Point:** 4,973 feet
**Lowest Point:** 289 feet

## OREGON

**Capital:** Salem (89,091)
**Governor:** Barbara Roberts (to Jan. 1995)
**Entered Union (rank):** Feb. 14, 1859 (33rd)
**Motto:** *Alis volat Propriis* (She flies with her own wings)
**State Song:** "Oregon, My Oregon"
**State Flower:** Oregon Grape
**State Bird:** Western Meadowlark
**State Tree:** Douglas Fir
**Nickname:** Beaver State
**Origin of Name:** Unknown, possibly taken from the writings of Major Robert Rogers, an English army officer
**Population (rank):** 2,853,733 (29th)

**Population Density:** 29 per sq. mi.
**Per Capita Income:** $14,885
**Area (rank):** 97,073 sq. mi. (10th)
**Highest Point:** 11,239 feet
**Lowest Point:** Sea level

## PENNSYLVANIA

**Capital:** Harrisburg (53,264)
**Governor:** Robert P. Casey (to Jan. 1995)
**Entered Union (rank):** Dec. 12, 1787 (2nd)
**Motto:** Virtue, Liberty, and Independence
**State Song:** None
**State Flower:** Mountain Laurel
**State Bird:** Ruffed Grouse
**State Tree:** Hemlock
**Nickname:** Keystone State
**Origin of Name:** In honor of Sir William Penn, William Penn's father. It means "Penn's Woodland"
**Population (rank):** 11,924,710 (5th)
**Population Density:** 263 per sq. mi.
**Per Capita Income:** $16,233
**Area (rank):** 45,308 sq. mi. (33rd)
**Highest Point:** 3,213 feet
**Lowest Point:** Sea level

## RHODE ISLAND

**Capital:** Providence (156,804)
**Governor:** Bruce Sundlun (to Jan. 1993)
**Entered Union (rank):** May 29, 1790 (13th)
**Motto:** Hope
**State Song:** "Rhode Island"
**State Flower:** Violet
**State Bird:** Rhode Island Red
**State Tree:** Red Maple
**Nickname:** Little Rhody, Ocean State
**Origin of Name:** From the Greek Island of Rhodes
**Population (rank):** 1,005,984 (43rd)
**Population Density:** 830 per sq. mi.
**Per Capita Income:** $16,892
**Area (rank):** 1,212 sq. mi. (50th)
**Highest Point:** 812 feet
**Lowest Point:** Sea level

## SOUTH CAROLINA

**Capital:** Columbia (101,229)

**Governor:** Carroll A. Campbell, Jr. (to Jan. 1995)
**Entered Union (rank):** May 23, 1788 (8th)
**Mottos:** *Animis opibusque parati* (Prepared in mind and resources) and *Dum spiro spero* (While I breathe, I hope)
**State Songs:** "Carolina" and "South Carolina on My Mind"
**State Flower:** Yellow Jessamine
**State Bird:** Carolina Wren
**State Tree:** Palmetto Tree
**Nickname:** Palmetto State
**Origin of Name:** In honor of Charles I of England
**Population (rank):** 3,505,707 (25th)
**Population Density:** 113 per sq. mi.
**Per Capita Income:** $12,926
**Area (rank):** 31,113 sq. mi. (40th)
**Highest Point:** 3,560 feet
**Lowest Point:** Sea level

## SOUTH DAKOTA

**Capital:** Pierre (11,973)
**Governor:** George S. Mickelson (to Jan. 1995)
**Entered Union (rank):** Nov. 2, 1889 (40th)
**Motto:** Under God the People Rule
**State Song:** "Hail! South Dakota"
**State Flower:** American Pasque Flower
**State Bird:** Ring-Necked Pheasant
**State Tree:** Black Hills Spruce
**Nicknames:** Coyote State, Sunshine State
**Origin of Name:** From the Dakotah tribe, meaning "allies"
**Population (rank):** 699,999 (45th)
**Population Density:** 9 per sq. mi.
**Per Capita Income:** $12,755
**Area (rank):** 77,116 sq. mi. (16th)
**Highest Point:** 7,242 feet
**Lowest Point:** 966 feet

## TENNESSEE

**Capital:** Nashville (455,651)
**Governor:** Ned Ray McWherter (to Jan. 1995)
**Entered Union (rank):** June 1, 1796 (16th)
**Motto:** Agriculture and Commerce
**State Song:** "Tennessee Waltz"

State Flower: Iris
State Bird: Mockingbird
State Tree: Tulip Poplar
Nickname: Volunteer State
Origin of Name: From Cherokee, meaning unknown
Population (rank): 4,896,641 (17th)
Population Density: 116 per sq. mi.
Per Capita Income: $13,873
Area (rank): 42,144 sq. mi. (34th)
Highest Point: 6,643 feet
Lowest Point: 178 feet

## TEXAS
Capital: Austin (345,890)
Governor: Ann Richards (to Jan. 1995)
Entered Union (rank): Dec. 29, 1845 (28th)
Motto: Friendship
State Song: "Texas, Our Texas"
State Flower: Bluebonnet
State Bird: Mockingbird
State Tree: Pecan
Nickname: Lone Star State
Origin of Name: From an Indian word meaning "friends"
Population (rank): 17,059,805 (3rd)
Population Density: 64 per sq. mi.
Per Capita Income: $14,586
Area (rank): 266,807 sq. mi. (2nd)
Highest Point: 8,749 feet
Lowest Point: Sea level

## UTAH
Capital: Salt Lake City (163,034)
Governor: Norman H. Bangerter (to Jan. 1993)
Entered Union (rank): Jan. 4, 1896 (45th)
Motto: Industry
State Song: "Utah, We Love Thee"
State Flower: Sego Lily
State Bird: Seagull
State Tree: Blue Spruce
Nickname: Beehive State
Origin of Name: From Ute, meaning "people of the mountains"
Population (rank): 1,727,784 (35th)
Population Density: 20 per sq. mi.
Per Capita Income: $12,193
Area (rank): 84,899 sq. mi. (11th)
Highest Point: 13,528 feet
Lowest Point: 2,000 feet

## VERMONT
Capital: Montpelier (8,241)
Governor: Dick Snelling (to Jan. 1993)
Entered Union (rank): March 4, 1791 (14th)
Motto: Freedom and Unity
State Song: "Hail, Vermont!"
State Flower: Red Clover
State Bird: Hermit Thrush
State Tree: Sugar Maple
Nickname: Green Mountain State
Origin of Name: From French "vert mont," meaning "green mountain"
Population (rank): 564,964 (48th)
Population Density: 59 per sq. mi.
Per Capita Income: $15,302
Area (rank): 9,614 sq. mi. (43rd)
Highest Point: 4,393 feet
Lowest Point: 95 feet

## VIRGINIA
Capital: Richmond (219,214)
Governor: Douglas Wilder (to Jan. 1994)
Entered Union (rank): June 25, 1788 (10th)
Motto: *Sic semper tyrannis* (Thus always to tyrants)
State Song: "Carry Me Back to Old Virginia"
State Flower: American Dogwood
State Bird: Cardinal
State Tree: Flowering Dogwood
Nicknames: The Old Dominion, Mother of Presidents
Origin of Name: In honor of Elizabeth "Virgin Queen" of England
Population (rank): 6,216,568 (12th)
Population Density: 152 per sq. mi.
Per Capita Income: $17,675
Area (rank): 40,767 sq. mi. (36th)
Highest Point: 5,729 feet
Lowest Point: Sea level

## WASHINGTON
Capital: Olympia (27,447)
Governor: Booth Gardner (to 1993)
Entered Union (rank): Nov. 11, 1889 (42nd)
Motto: *Alki* (Chinook Indian word meaning "by and by")
State Song: "Washington, My Home"
State Flower: Coast Rhododendron
State Bird: Willow Goldfinch
State Tree: Western Hemlock
Nicknames: Evergreen State, Chinook State
Origin of Name: In honor of George Washington
Population (rank): 4,887,941 (18th)
Population Density: 72 per sq. mi.
Per Capita Income: $16,473
Area (rank): 68,139 sq. mi. (20th)
Highest Point: 14,410 feet
Lowest Point: Sea level

## WEST VIRGINIA
Capital: Charleston (63,968)
Governor: Gaston Caperton (to Jan. 1993)
Entered Union (rank): June 20, 1863 (35th)
Motto: *Montani semper liberi* (Mountaineers are always free)
State Songs: "West Virginia, My Home Sweet Home," "The West Virginia Hills," and "This Is My West Virginia"
State Flower: Big Rhododendron
State Bird: Cardinal
State Tree: Sugar Maple
Nickname: Mountain State
Origin of Name: In honor of Elizabeth "Virgin Queen" of England
Population (rank): 1,801,625 (34th)
Population Density: 74 per sq. mi.
Per Capita Income: $11,735
Area (rank): 24,232 sq. mi. (41st)
Highest Point: 4,861 feet
Lowest Point: 240 feet

## WISCONSIN
Capital: Madison (170,616)
Governor: Tommy G. Thompson (to Jan. 1995)
Entered Union (rank): May 29, 1848 (30th)
Motto: Forward
State Song: "On, Wisconsin!"
State Flower: Wood Violet
State Bird: Robin
State Tree: Sugar Maple
Nickname: Badger State

**Origin of Name:** French version of Indian word, meaning uncertain
**Population (rank):** 4,906,745 (16th)
**Population Density:** 87 per sq. mi.
**Per Capita Income:** $15,524
**Area (rank):** 56,153 sq. mi. (26th)
**Highest Point:** 1,951 feet
**Lowest Point:** 581 feet

## WYOMING

**Capital:** Cheyenne (47,283)
**Governor:** Michael J. Sullivan (to Jan. 1995)
**Entered Union (rank):** July 10, 1890 (44th)
**Motto:** Equal rights
**State Song:** "Wyoming"
**State Flower:** Indian Paintbrush
**State Bird:** Western Meadowlark
**State Tree:** Cottonwood
**Nickname:** Equality State, Cowboy State
**Origin of Name:** From Delaware Indian word meaning "mountains and valleys alternating"
**Population (rank):** 455,975 (50th)
**Population Density:** 5 per sq. mi.
**Per Capita Income:** $13,609
**Area (rank):** 97,809 sq. mi. (9th)
**Highest Point:** 13,804 feet
**Lowest Point:** 3,009 feet

### CONFEDERATE STATES OF AMERICA

These states seceded from the United States during the Civil War of 1861-1865.
1. South Carolina
2. Mississippi
3. Florida
4. Alabama
5. Georgia
6. Louisiana
7. Texas
8. Virginia
9. Arkansas
10. North Carolina
11. Tennessee

## CHART OF STATES AND THEIR ABBREVIATIONS

P.O. means Post Office abbreviation. Trad. means traditional abbreviation.

| STATE | P.O. | Trad. | STATE | P.O. | Trad. |
|-------|------|-------|-------|------|-------|
| Alabama | AL | Ala. | New Mexico | NM | N.M. |
| Alaska | AK | Alas. | New York | NY | N.Y. |
| Arizona | AZ | Ariz. | North Carolina | NC | N.C. |
| Arkansas | AR | Ark. | North Dakota | ND | N. Dak. |
| California | CA | Calif. | Ohio | OH | O. |
| Colorado | CO | Colo. | Oklahoma | OK | Okla. |
| Connecticut | CT | Conn. | Oregon | OR | Oreg. |
| Delaware | DE | Del. | Pennsylvania | PA | Penn. |
| Florida | FL | Fla. | Rhode Island | RI | R.I. |
| Georgia | GA | Ga. | South Carolina | SC | S.C. |
| Hawaii | HI | | South Dakota | SD | S. Dak. |
| Idaho | ID | Ida. | Tennessee | TN | Tenn. |
| Illinois | IL | Ill. | Texas | TX | Tex. |
| Indiana | IN | Ind. | Utah | UT | Ut. |
| Iowa | IA | Ia. | Vermont | VT | Vt. |
| Kansas | KS | Kan. | Virginia | VA | Va. |
| Kentucky | KY | Ky. | Washington | WA | Wash. |
| Louisiana | LA | La. | West Virginia | WV | W. Va. |
| Maine | ME | Me. | Wisconsin | WI | Wisc. |
| Maryland | MD | Md. | Wyoming | WY | Wyo. |
| Massachusetts | MA | Mass. | | | |
| Michigan | MI | Mich. | | | |
| Minnesota | MN | Minn. | **Districts and Territories** | | |
| Mississippi | MS | Miss. | | | |
| Missouri | MO | Mo. | Canal Zone | CZ | |
| Montana | MT | Mont. | District of | DC | D.C. |
| Nebraska | NE | Neb. | Columbia | | |
| Nevada | NV | Nev. | Guam | GU | |
| New Hampshire | NH | N.H. | Puerto Rico | PR | |
| New Jersey | NJ | N.J. | Virgin Islands | VI | |

**Largest state:** Alaska
**Smallest state:** Rhode Island

**Largest population:** California
**Smallest population:** Wyoming

**Northernmost point in U.S.:** Point Barrow, Alaska—71°23'N, 156°29'W
**Easternmost point:** West Quoddy Head, Maine—44°49'N, 66°57'W

**Southernmost point:** Ka Lae (South Cape), Hawaii—18°55'N, 155°41'W
**Westernmost point:** Pochnoi Point, Alaska—51°17'N, 172°09'E

# STATE TOURISM OFFICES

**Alabama**—Bureau of Tourism & Travel, 532 S. Perry Street, Montgomery, AL 36104

**Alaska**—Division of Tourism, Commerce & Economic Development Department, P.O. Box E, Juneau, AK 99811

**Arizona**—Governor's Office of Tourism, 1100 West Washington, Phoenix, AZ 85007

**Arkansas**—Tourism Division, Department of Parks & Tourism, #1 Capitol Mall, Little Rock, AR 72201

**California**—Office of Tourism, 1121 L Street, #103, Sacramento, CA 95814-3908

**Colorado**—Colorado Tourism Board, Department of Local Affairs, 1625 Broadway, Room 1700, Denver, CO 80202

**Connecticut**—Tourism Division, Department of Economic Development, 865 Brook Street, Rocky Hill, CT 06067

**Delaware**—State Travel Service, Development Office, Townsend Building, Dover, DE 19901

**District of Columbia**—Washington Visitor's & Convention Assn., 1575 I Street, NW, Suite 250, Washington, DC 20005

**Florida**—Division of Tourism, Dept. of Commerce, 505 Collins Bldg., 107 W. Gaines St., Tallahassee, FL 32399-2000

**Georgia**—Tourist Division, Dept. of Industry & Trade, 230 Peachtree Street, NW, Atlanta, GA 30301

**Hawaii**—Department of Business & Economic Development, 250 S. King Street, Honolulu, HI 96813

**Idaho**—Department of Commerce, Statehouse, Boise, ID 83720

**Illinois**—Department of Commerce & Community Affairs, 620 E. Adams Street, 3rd Floor, Springfield, IL 62701

**Indiana**—Tourism Development, Department of Commerce, 1 North Capitol, Indianapolis, IN 46204

**Iowa**—Bureau of Tourism & Visitors, Dept. of Economic Development, 200 E. Grand, Des Moines, IA 50319

**Kansas**—Division of Travel & Tourism, Dept. of Commerce, 400 SW Eighth Street, 5th Floor, Topeka, KS 66603

**Kentucky**—Tourism Cabinet, Capital Plaza Tower, Frankfort, KY 40601

**Louisiana**—Louisiana Office of Tourism, P.O. Box 94291, Baton Rouge, LA 70804-9291

**Maine**—Division of Tourism, Dept. of Economic & Community Dev., State House Station #59, Augusta, ME 04333

**Maryland**—Office of Tourism, Dept. of Economic & Employment, 217 E. Redwood Street, Baltimore, MD 21201

**Massachusetts**—Div. of Tourism, Commerce & Development Dept., 100 Cambridge St., 13th Floor, Boston, MA 02202

**Michigan**—Travel Bureau, Department of Commerce, P.O. Box 30226, Lansing, MI 48909

**Minnesota**—Office of Tourism, Room 250, Farm Center Building, 375 Jackson Street, St. Paul, MN 55101

**Mississippi**—Div. of Tourism Services, Economic & Community Development, 1200 Sillers Bldg., Jackson, MS 39201

**Missouri**—Division of Tourism, Truman Building, Box 1055, Jefferson City, MO 65102

**Montana**—Promotion Bureau, Department of Commerce, 1424 Ninth Avenue, Helena, MT 59620

**Nebraska**—Div. of Travel & Tourism, Dept. of Economic Development, P.O. Box 94666, Lincoln, NE 68509-4666

**Nevada**—Commission on Tourism, 600 E. Williams, Carson City, NV 89710

**New Hampshire**—Vacation Travel Promotion Office, 6 Loudon Road, Concord, NH 03301

**New Jersey**—Division of Travel and Tourism, 1 West State Street, CN 826, Trenton, NJ 08625

**New Mexico**—Tourism & Travel Div., Economic Dev. & Tourism Dept., 1100 St. Francis Dr., Santa Fe, NM 87503

**New York**—Department of Commerce, 1 Commerce Plaza, Albany, NY 12245

**North Carolina**—Travel Development Div., Dept. of Commerce, 430 North Salisbury St., Raleigh, NC 27603-5900

**North Dakota**—Tourism Division, Economic Development Commission, 604 East Boulevard, Bismarck, ND 58505

**Ohio**—Office of Travel & Tourism, Dept. of Development, 30 E. Broad Street, 25th Floor, Columbus, OH 43266-0101

**Oklahoma**—Natural Resources, 500 Will Rogers Building, Oklahoma City, OK 73105

**Oregon**—Tourism Division, Dept. of Economic Development, 595 Cottage Street, NE, Salem, OR 97310

**Pennsylvania**—Department of Commerce, 433 Forum Building, Harrisburg, PA 17120

**Rhode Island**—Division of Tourism, Dept. of Economic Development, 7 Jackson Walkway, Providence, RI 02903

**South Carolina**—Division of Tourism, Parks, Recreation & Tourism, 1205 Pendleton Street, Columbia, SC 29201

**South Dakota**—Department of Tourism, Capitol Lake Plaza, Pierre, SD 57501

**Tennessee**—Department of Tourist Development, 320 Sixth Avenue North, Nashville, TN 37202

**Texas**—Tourist Development Agency, Box 12008, Capitol Station, Austin, TX 78711

**Utah**—Division of Travel Development, Council Hall & Capitol Hill, Salt Lake City, UT 84114

**Vermont**—Travel Division, Agency of Development & Community Affairs, 134 State St., Montpelier, VT 05602

**Virginia**—Division of Tourism, Dept. of Economic Dev., Ninth Street Office Bldg., 5th Floor, Richmond, VA 23219

**Washington**—Tourism Development Div., Trade & Economic Development Dept., 101 General Administration Bldg. M/S: AX-13, Olympia, WA 98504-0613

**West Virginia**—Tourism Marketing Div., Div. of Commerce, State Capitol Complex, Bldg. 6, Charleston, WV 25305

**Wisconsin**—Division of Tourism Development, Dept. of Development, P.O. Box 7970, Madison, WI 53707

**Wyoming**—Wyoming Travel Commission, Dept. of Commerce, I-25 at College Drive, Cheyenne, WY 82002

# LARGEST CITIES OF THE UNITED STATES

## ALBUQUERQUE
**State:** New Mexico
**Population (rank):** 366,750 (40)
**Area:** 95 sq. mi.
**Altitude:** 4,958 feet
**Latitude:** 35°05'N
**Longitude:** 106°40'W

## ATLANTA
**State:** Georgia
**Population (rank):** 421,910 (32)
**Area:** 136 sq. mi.
**Altitude:** 940 to 1,050 feet
**Latitude:** 33°45'N
**Longitude:** 84°23'W

## AUSTIN
**State:** Texas
**Population (rank):** 466,550 (27)
**Area:** 116 sq. mi.
**Altitude:** 425 to 1000 feet
**Latitude:** 30°16'N
**Longitude:** 97°45'W

## BALTIMORE
**State:** Maryland
**Population (rank):** 752,800 (11)
**Area:** 80.3 sq. mi.
**Altitude:** Sea level to 490 feet
**Latitude:** 39°17'N
**Longitude:** 76°37'W

## BOSTON
**State:** Massachusetts
**Population (rank):** 573,600 (19)
**Area:** 47.2 sq. mi.
**Altitude:** Sea level to 330 feet
**Latitude:** 42°21'N
**Longitude:** 71°04'W

## BUFFALO
**State:** New York
**Population (rank):** 324,820 (48)
**Area:** 42.67 sq. mi.
**Altitude:** 572 to 705 feet
**Latitude:** 42°54'N
**Longitude:** 78°53'W

## CHARLOTTE
**State:** North Carolina
**Population (rank):** 352,070 (44)
**Area:** 162.3 sq. mi.
**Altitude:** 765 feet
**Latitude:** 35°14'N
**Longitude:** 80°50'W

## CHICAGO
**State:** Illinois
**Population (rank):** 3,009,530 (3)
**Area:** 228.1 sq. mi.
**Altitude:** 579 to 672 feet
**Latitude:** 41°53'N
**Longitude:** 87°38'W

## CINCINNATI
**State:** Ohio
**Population (rank):** 369,750 (39)
**Area:** 78.1 sq. mi.
**Altitude:** 441 to 960 feet
**Latitude:** 39°06'N
**Longitude:** 84°31'W

## CLEVELAND
**State:** Ohio
**Population (rank):** 535,830 (22)
**Area:** 79 sq. mi
**Altitude:** 573 to 1048 feet
**Latitude:** 41°30'N
**Longitude:** 81°41'W

## COLUMBUS
**State:** Ohio
**Population (rank):** 566,030 (20)
**Area:** 190.297 sq. mi.
**Altitude:** 702 to 902 feet
**Latitude:** 39°57'N
**Longitude:** 83°00'W

## DALLAS
**State:** Texas
**Population (rank):** 1,003,520 (8)
**Area:** 378 sq. mi.
**Altitude:** 375 to 750 feet
**Latitude:** 32°47'N
**Longitude:** 96°48'W

## DENVER
**State:** Colorado
**Population (rank):** 505,000 (23)
**Area:** 110.6 sq. mi.
**Altitude:** 5,130 to 5,470 feet
**Latitude:** 39°43'N
**Longitude:** 105°01'W

## DETROIT
**State:** Michigan
**Population (rank):** 1,086,220 (6)
**Area:** 143 sq. mi.
**Altitude:** 574 to 685 feet
**Latitude:** 42°20'N
**Longitude:** 83°03'W

## EL PASO
**State:** Texas
**Population (rank):** 491,800 (24)
**Area:** 247.4 sq. mi.
**Altitude:** 4,000 feet
**Latitude:** 31°45'N
**Longitude:** 106°29'W

## FORT WORTH
**State:** Texas
**Population (rank):** 429,550 (30)
**Area:** 286 sq. mi.
**Altitude:** 520 to 780 feet
**Latitude:** 32°45'N
**Longitude:** 97°20'W

## HONOLULU
**State:** Hawaii
**Population (rank):** 372,330 (38)
**Area:** 600 sq. mi.
**Altitude:** Sea level to 4,025 feet
**Latitude:** 21°19'N
**Longitude:** 157°52'W

## HOUSTON
**State:** Texas
**Population (rank):** 1,728,910 (4)
**Area:** 579.58 sq. mi.
**Altitude:** Sea level to 120 feet
**Latitude:** 29°46'N
**Longitude:** 95°22'W

## INDIANAPOLIS
**State:** Indiana
**Population (rank):** 719,820 (13)
**Area:** 352 sq. mi.
**Altitude:** 700 to 840 feet
**Latitude:** 39°46'N
**Longitude:** 86°09'W

## JACKSONVILLE
State: Florida
Population (rank): 609,860 (17)
Area: 759.6 sq. mi.
Altitude: Sea level to 71 feet
Latitude: 30°20'N
Longitude: 81°40'W

## KANSAS CITY
State: Missouri
Population (rank): 441,170 (29)
Area: 316.3 sq. mi.
Altitude: 722 to 1,014 feet
Latitude: 39°05'N,
Longitude: 94°35'W

## LONG BEACH
State: California
Population (rank): 396,280 (33)
Area: 49.8 sq. mi.
Altitude: Sea level to 170 feet
Latitude: 33°46'N
Longitude: 118°11'W

## LOS ANGELES
State: California
Population (rank): 3,259,340 (2)
Area: 470 sq. mi.
Altitude: Sea level to 5,081 feet
Latitude: 34°03'N
Longitude: 118°15'W

## MEMPHIS
State: Tennessee
Population (rank): 652,640 (15)
Area: 290 sq. mi.
Altitude: 331 feet
Latitude: 35°08'N
Longitude: 90°03'W

## MIAMI
State: Florida
Population (rank): 373,940 (36)
Area: 34.3 sq. mi.
Altitude: 12 feet
Latitude: 25°46'N,
Longitude: 80°12'W

## MILWAUKEE
State: Wisconsin
Population (rank): 605,090 (18)
Area: 95.8 sq. mi.
Altitude: 581 feet

Latitude: 43°02'N
Lngitude: 87°54'W

## MINNEAPOLIS
State: Minnesota
Population (rank): 356,840 (43)
Area: 55.1 sq. mi.
Altitude: 695 to 945 feet
Latitude: 44°59'N
Longitude: 93°13'W

## NASHVILLE-DAVIDSON
State: Tennessee
Population (rank): 473,670 (26)
Area: 533 sq. mi.
Altitude: 400 to 1,100 feet
Latitude: 36°09'N
Longitude: 86°48'W

## NEW ORLEANS
State: Louisiana
Population (rank): 554,500 (21)
Area: 199.4 sq. mi.
Altitude: -4 to 15 feet
Latitude: 29°58'N
Longitude: 90°07'W

## NEW YORK
State: New York
Population (rank): 7,262,700 (1)
Area: 314.7 sq. mi.
Altitude: Sea level to 410 feet
Latitude: 40°43'N
Longitude: 74°01'W

## NEWARK
State: New Jersey
Population (rank): 316,240 (50)
Area: 24.1 sq. mi.
Altitude: Sea level to 273 feet
Latitude: 40°44'N
Longitude: 74°11'W

## OAKLAND
State: California
Population (rank): 356,960 (42)
Area: 53.9 sq. mi.
Altitude: Sea level to 1,700 feet
Latitude: 37°47'N
Longitude: 122°13'W

## OKLAHOMA CITY
State: Oklahoma

Population (rank): 446,120 (28)
Area: 648.3 sq. mi.
Altitude: 1,140 to 1,320 feet
Latitude: 35°28'N
Longitude: 97°32'W

## OMAHA
State: Nebraska
Population (rank): 349,270 (45)
Area: 90.9 sq. mi.
Altitude: 1,270 feet
Latitude: 41°16'N
Longitude: 95°57'W

## PHILADELPHIA
State: Pennsylvania
Population (rank): 1,642,900 (5)
Area: 136 sq. mi.
Altitude: Sea level to 440 feet
Latitude: 39°57'N
Longitude: 75°07'W

## PHOENIX
State: Arizona
Population (rank): 894,070 (10)
Area: 403.4 sq. mi.
Altitude: 1,017 to 2,740 feet
Latitude: 33°27'N
Longitude: 112°05'W

## PITTSBURGH
State: Pennsylvania
Population (rank): 387,490 (35)
Area: 55.5 sq. mi.
Altitude: 715 to 1,240 feet
Latitude: 40°26'N
Longitude: 80°00'W

## PORTLAND
State: Oregon
Population (rank): 387,870 (34)
Area: 135 sq. mi.
Altitude: Sea level to 1,073 feet
Latitude: 45°33'N
Longitude: 122°36'W

## SACRAMENTO
State: California
Population (rank): 323,550 (49)
Area: 96 sq. mi.
Altitude:
Latitude: 38°35'N
Longitude: 121°30' W

## ST. LOUIS
**State:** Missouri
**Population (rank):** 426,300 (31)
**Area:** 61.4 sq. mi.
**Altitude:** 413 to 616 feet
**Latitude:** 38°38'N
**Longitude:** 90°11'W

## SAN ANTONIO
**State:** Texas
**Population (rank):** 914,350 (9)
**Area:** 309.1 sq. mi.
**Altitude:** 700 feet
**Latitude:** 29°28'N
**Longitude:** 98°31'W

## SAN DIEGO
**State:** California
**Population (rank):** 1,050,400 (7)
**Area:** 403.4 sq. mi.
**Altitude:** Sea level to 1,591 feet
**Latitude:** 32°43'N
**Longitude:** 117°09'W

## SAN FRANCISCO
**State:** California
**Population (rank):** 749,000 (12)
**Area:** 46.1 sq. mi.
**Altitude:** Sea level to 925 feet

**Latitude:** 37°48'N
**Longitude:** 122°24'W

## SAN JOSE
**State:** California
**Population (rank):** 712,080 (14)
**Area:** 171.6 sq. mi.
**Altitude:** Sea level to 4,372 feet
**Latitude:** 37°20'N
**Longitude:** 121°53'W

## SEATTLE
**State:** Washington
**Population (rank):** 486,200 (25)
**Area:** 144.6 sq. mi.
**Altitude:** Sea level to 540 feet
**Latitude:** 47°36'N
**Longitude:** 122°20'W

## TOLEDO
**State:** Ohio
**Population (rank):** 340,680 (46)
**Area:** 84.2 sq. mi.
**Altitude:** 630 feet
**Latitude:** 41°39'N
**Longitude:** 83°32'W

## TUCSON
**State:** Arizona

**Population (rank):** 358,850 (41)
**Area:** 130 sq. mi.
**Altitude:** 2,500 feet
**Latitude:** 32°13'N
**Longitude:** 110°58'W

## TULSA
**State:** Oklahoma
**Population (rank):** 373,750 (37)
**Area:** 192.459 sq. mi.
**Altitude:** 674 feet
**Latitude:** 36°09'N
**Longitude:** 95°58'W

## VIRGINIA BEACH
**State:** Virginia
**Population (rank):** 333,400 (47)
**Area:** 258.7 sq. mi.
**Altitude:** 12 feet
**Latitude:** 36°51'N
**Longitude:** 75°59'W

## WASHINGTON, D.C.
**State:** District of Columbia
**Population (rank):** 626,000 (16)
**Area:** 68.25 sq. mi.
**Altitude:** Sea level to 420 feet
**Latitude:** 38°54'N
**Longitude:** 77°01'W

# LARGEST URBAN AREAS OF THE WORLD

**Tokyo-Yokohama, Japan**
**Population (rank):** 27 million (1)
**Location:** 35°40'N, 139°46'E

**Mexico City, Mexico**
**Population (rank):** 20.2 million (2)
**Location:** 19°24'N, 99°09'W

**Sao Paulo, Brazil**
**Population (rank):** 18 million (3)
**Location:** 23°32'S, 46°37'W

**Seoul, South Korea**
**Population (rank):** 16.3 million (4)
**Location:** 37°34'N, 127°00'E

**New York, United States**
**Population (rank):** 14.6 million in metropolitan area (5)
**Location:** 40°43'N, 74°01'W

**Osaka/Kobe, Japan**
**Population (rank):** 13.8 million (6)
**Location:** 34°40'N, 135°30'E

**Bombay, India**
**Population (rank):** 21.8 million (7)
**Location:** 18°58'N, 72°50'E

**Calcutta, India**
**Population (rank):** 11.7 million (8)
**Location:** 22°30'N, 88°22'E

**Buenos Aires, Argentina**
**Population (rank):** 11.5 million (9)
**Location:** 34°36'S, 58°27'W

**Rio de Janeiro, Brazil**
**Population (rank):** 11.4 million (10)
**Location:** 22°54'S, 43°15'W

**Moscow, Soviet Union**
**Population (rank):** 10.4 million (11)
**Location:** 55°45'N, 37°35'E

**Los Angeles, United States**
**Population (rank):** 10.1 million (12)
**Location:** 34°03'N, 118°15'W

**Manila, Philippines**
**Population (rank):** 9.9 million (13)
**Location:** 14°35'N, 121°00'E

**Cairo, Egypt**
**Population (rank):** 9.9 million (14)
**Location:** 30°03'N, 31°15'E

**Jakarta, Indonesia**
**Population (rank):** 9.6 million (15)
**Location:** 6°10'S, 106°46'E

# NATIONAL PARKS

On March 1, 1872, the United States Congress established Yellowstone National Park "as a public park or pleasuring ground for the benefit and enjoyment of the people." This began a worldwide national park movement. Today, more than 100 nations of the world has some 1,200 national parks or preserves. The United States contains 50 national parks, as well as many national monuments, preserves, lakeshores, scenic trails and historic sites.

| NATIONAL PARK | Date Established and Acreage | OUTSTANDING FEATURES |
|---|---|---|
| **Acadia National Park** <br> P.O. Box 177 <br> Bar Harbor, Maine 04609 | February 26, 1919 <br> 41,408.63 acres | Rugged coastal area, highest land on the eastern seaboard |
| **Arches National Park** <br> P.O. Box 907 <br> Moab, Utah 84532 | November 12, 1971 <br> 73,378.98 acres | Giant eroded arches, windows, and towers. |
| **Badlands National Park** <br> P.O. Box 6 <br> Interior, South Dakota 57750 | November 10, 1978 <br> 243,244.48 acres | Eroded landscape, animal fossils 40 million years old. |
| **Big Bend National Park** <br> Texas 79834 | June 20, 1935 <br> 802,541.3 acres | The big bend of the Rio Grande River, mountains and desert. |
| **Biscayne National Park** <br> P.O. Box 1369 <br> Homestead, Florida 33090 | June 28, 1980 <br> 173,039.39 acres | Coral reef and islands. |
| **Bryce Canyon National Park** <br> Bryce Canyon, Utah 84717 | June 7, 1924 <br> 35,835.08 acres | Some of the most colorful and unusual eroded forms in the world. |
| **Canyonlands National Park** <br> 125 West 200 South <br> Moab, Utah 84532 | September 12, 1964 <br> 337,570.43 acres | Geological wonderland of rocks, spires and mesas. |
| **Capitol Reef National Park** <br> Torrey, Utah 84775 | December 18, 1971 <br> 241,904.26 acres | Narrow high-walled gorges, white dome-shaped rock. |
| **Carlsbad Caverns National Park** <br> 3225 National Parks Highway <br> Carlsbad, New Mexico 88220 | May 14, 1930 <br> 46,755.33 acres | Large underground caverns with magnificent limestone formations. |
| **Channel Islands National Park** <br> 1901 Spinnaker Drive <br> Ventura, California 93001 | March 5, 1980 <br> 249,353.77 acres | Five islands with nesting sea birds, sea lion rookeries and unique plants. |
| **Crater Lake National Park** <br> P.O. Box 7 <br> Crater Lake, Oregon 97604 | May 22, 1902 <br> 183,224.05 acres | Deep lake in ancient volcano crater. Colorful lava walls 500-2000 feet above water. |
| **Denali National Park & Preserve** <br> P.O. Box 9 <br> McKinley Park, Alaska 99755 | February 26, 1917 <br> 4,716,726 acres | Mt. McKinley, North America's highest mountain (20,320 feet), large glaciers, wildlife. |

| NATIONAL PARK | Date Established and Acreage | OUTSTANDING FEATURES |
|---|---|---|
| **Everglades National Park**<br>P.O. Box 279<br>Homestead, Florida 33030 | December 6, 1947<br>1,398,938.4 acres | Subtropical wilderness with abundant wildlife. |
| **Gates of the Arctic National Park and Preserve**<br>P.O. Box 74680<br>Fairbanks, Alaska 99707 | December 2, 1980<br>7,523,888 acres | Often called the greatest remaining wilderness in North America. Jagged peaks, arctic valleys, wild rivers and many lakes. |
| **Glacier Bay National Park and Preserve**<br>Bartlett Cove<br>Gustavus, Alaska 99826 | December 2, 1980<br>3,225,284 acres | Huge glaciers that break up into the sea, whales and other wild animals. |
| **Glacier National Park**<br>West Glacier, Montana 59936 | May 11, 1910<br>1,013,572.43 acres | Ruggedly beautiful land, towering peaks, many glaciers. |
| **Grand Canyon National Park**<br>P.O. Box 129<br>Grand Canyon, Arizona 86023 | February 26, 1919<br>1,218,375.24 acres | The one-mile deep Grand Canyon of the Colorado River. |
| **Grand Teton National Park**<br>P.O. Drawer 170<br>Moose, Wyoming 83012 | February 26, 1929<br>309,993.93 acres | Blue-gray mountain peaks rising more than a mile above the flats, winter feeding ground for elk. |
| **Great Basin National Park**<br>Baker, Nevada 89311 | October 27, 1986<br>77,109.15 | Peaks, ancient bristlecone pine forest, Lehman Caves. |
| **Great Smoky Mountains National Park**<br>Gatlinburg, Tennessee 37738 | June 15, 1934<br>520,269.44 acres | One of the oldest mountain ranges on earth, extraordinary plant life. |
| **Guadalupe Mountains National Park**<br>H. C. 60, Box 400<br>Salt Flat, Texas 79847-9400 | September 30, 1972<br>86,416.01 acres | Limestone fossil reef, geological fault. |
| **Haleakala National Park**<br>P.O. Box 369<br>Makawao, Hawaii 96768 | August 1, 1916<br>28,655.25 acres | Inactive volcano on the island of Maui. Originally part of Hawaii Volcanoes National Park. |
| **Hawaii Volcanoes National Park**<br>Hawaii 96718 | August 1, 1916<br>229,117.03 acres | Active volcanoes on the island of Hawaii |
| **Hot Springs National Park**<br>P.O. Box 1860<br>Hot Springs, Arkansas 71902 | March 4, 1921<br>5,839.24 acres | 47 thermal hot springs. |
| **Isle Royale National Park**<br>87 North Ripley Street<br>Houghton, Michigan 49931 | March 3, 1931<br>571,790.11 acres | Largest island in Lake Superior, wilderness forest with much wildlife. |
| **Katmai National Park & Preserve**<br>P.O. Box 7<br>King Salmon, Alaska 99613 | December 2, 1980<br>3,716,000 acres | Valley of Ten Thousand Smokes, Alaska brown bear feeding on spawning salmon. |

| NATIONAL PARK | Date Established and Acreage | OUTSTANDING FEATURES |
|---|---|---|
| **Kenai Fjords National Park**<br>P.O. Box 1727<br>Seward, Alaska 99664 | December 2, 1980<br>669,541 acres | One of the major icecaps in the United States, coastal fjords, breeding birds and sea mammals. |
| **Kings Canyon National Park**<br>Three Rivers, California 93271 | October 1, 1890<br>461,901.2 acres | Two enormous canyons, summit peaks of High Sierra, giant sequoia trees. |
| **Kobuk Valley National Park**<br>P.O. Box 1029<br>Kotzebue, Alaska 99752 | December 2, 1980<br>1,750,421 acres | Arctic wildlife, Great Kobuk Sand Dunes, archeological sites, arctic wildlife. |
| **Lake Clark National Park and Preserve**<br>222 West 7th Avenue, Box 61<br>Anchorage, Alaska 99513 | December 2, 1980<br>2,636,839 acres | Jagged peaks, granite spires, two active volcanoes, glaciers, lakes, spawning salmon. |
| **Lassen Volcanic National Park**<br>Mineral, California 96063 | August 9, 1916<br>106,372.36 acres | Volcano which last erupted in 1921. Hot springs, fumaroles, mud pots, sulfur vents. |
| **Mammoth Cave National Park**<br>Mammoth Cave<br>Kentucky 42259 | July 1, 1941<br>52,419 acres | Longest recorded cave system in the world. Underground river, beautiful limestone formations. |
| **Mesa Verde National Park**<br>Colorado 81330 | June 29, 1906<br>52,085.14 acres | Well-preserved prehistoric Indian cliff dwelling. |
| **Mount Rainier National Park**<br>Tahoma Woods, Star Route<br>Ashford, Washington 98304 | March 2, 1899<br>235,404 acres | Greatest single-peak glacial system in the United States. |
| **North Cascades National Park**<br>2105 Highway 20<br>Sedro Woolley, WA 98284 | October 2, 1968<br>504,780.94 acres | High jagged peaks, glaciers, lakes, waterfalls. |
| **Olympic National Park**<br>600 East Park Avenue<br>Port Angeles, Washington 98362 | June 29, 1938<br>921,942.14 acres | Mountain wilderness with Pacific Northwest rain forest, active glaciers, wild ocean coastline. |
| **Petrified Forest National Park**<br>Arizona 86028 | December 9, 1962<br>93,532.57 acres | Petrified trees, Indian ruins and rock carvings, portions of the Painted Desert. |
| **Redwood National Park**<br>1111 Second Street<br>Crescent City, California 95531 | October 2, 1968<br>110,132.4 acres | Coastal redwood forest containing the world's tallest trees, scenic Pacific coastline. |
| **Rocky Mountain National Park**<br>Estes Park, Colorado 80517 | January 26, 1915<br>265,200.07 acres | High Rocky Mountain peaks, wildlife and wildflowers, 14,000 foot peaks. |
| **Sequoia National Park**<br>Three Rivers, California 93271 | September 25, 1890<br>402,482.38 acres | Great groves of giant sequoias, Mount Whitney. |
| **Shenandoah National Park**<br>Route 4, Box 348<br>Luray, Virginia 22835 | December 26, 1935<br>195,382.13 acres | Hardwood forests, Blue Ridge Mountains, Shenandoah Valley |

| NATIONAL PARK | Date Established and Acreage | OUTSTANDING FEATURES |
| --- | --- | --- |
| **Theodore Roosevelt National Park** P.O. Box 7 Medora, North Dakota 58645 | November 10, 1978 70,416.39 acres | Scenic badlands and part of Theodore Roosevelt's Elkhorn Ranch. |
| **Virgin Islands National Park** P.O. Box 7789, Charlotte Amalie St. Thomas, Virgin Islands 00801 | August 2, 1956 14,688.87 acres | Quiet coves, blue-green waters and white sandy beaches. |
| **Voyageurs National Park** P.O. Box 50 Intl. Falls, Minnesota 56649 | April 8, 1975 218,035.93 acres | Numerous interconnected lakes surrounded by northern forest. |
| **Wind Cave National Park** Hot Springs South Dakota 57747 | January 9, 1903 28,292.08 acres | Limestone caverns in the scenic Black Hills, wildlife. |
| **Wrangell-St. Elias National Park and Preserve** P.O. Box 29 Glennallen, Alaska 99588 | December 2, 1980 8,331,604 acres | The continent's greatest collection of peaks over 16,000 feet. Numerous glaciers. Remote mountains, valleys, wild rivers. Much wildlife. |
| **Yellowstone National Park** P.O. Box 168 Yellowstone National Park Wyoming 82190 | March 1, 1872 2,219,790.71 acres | Earth's greatest geyser area, with some 10,000 geysers and hot springs including Old Faithful. Lakes, waterfalls and canyons. |
| **Yosemite National Park** P.O. Box 577 Yosemite National Park California 95389 | October 1, 1890 761,170.2 acres | Nation's highest waterfalls. Granite peaks and domes, mountains, giant sequoias trees. |
| **Zion National Park** Springdale, Utah 84767-1099 | November 19, 1919 146,597.64 acres | Colorful canyon and mesa scenery. |

In addition to the 50 National Parks, the National Park System includes the the Statue of Liberty and the U.S. Capitol Building, as well as the areas listed below with their respective acreages. Altogether, the National Park System manages about 125,000 square miles, an area nearly as large as Texas!

| | | |
| --- | --- | --- |
| 1 International Historic Site | 35.39 | |
| 11 National Battlefields | 12,771.90 | |
| 3 National Battlefield Parks | 8,767.39 | |
| 1 National Battlefield Site | 1.00 | |
| 1 National Capitol Park | 6,468.88 | |
| 69 National Historic Sites | 18,467.71 | |
| 29 National Historical Parks | 151,632.86 | |
| 4 National Lakeshores | 227,244.37 | |
| 1 National Mall | 146.35 | |
| 23 National Memorials | 7,949.16 | |
| 9 National Military Parks | 34,046.72 | |
| 79 National Monuments | 4,844,610.12 | |
| 4 National Parkways | 168,618.32 | |
| 14 National Preserves | 22,155,497.84 | |
| 18 National Recreation Areas | 3,686,923.39 | |
| 5 National Rivers | 360,629.91 | |
| 3 National Scenic Trails | 172,202.61 | |
| 10 National Seashores | 597,096.47 | |
| 9 National Wild & Scenic Rivers and Riverways | 292,596.82 | |
| 10 Parks (other than Natl. Parks) | 40,120.70 | |
| 1 White House | 18.07 | |

# INDIANS OF THE UNITED STATES AND CANADA

## ESKIMOS

**Location:** arctic coastlines, eastern Soviet Union, Alaska, Canada and Greenland

**Staple foods:** sea mammals such as whale and seal, caribou, fish

**Clothing:** caribou skins, fur, seal skins

**Shelter:** tents of caribou or sealskin, sod houses, snowhouses or igloos (seldom used)

**Transportation:** dogsleds, kayaks, umiaks

**Tools:** soapstone, wood, bones, ulu (knife)

**Art:** carved and decorated bone, ivory, antler and stone

## INDIANS OF THE FAR NORTH

**Location:** most of Canada from Rocky Mountains to Hudson Bay

**Major tribes:** Algonquin, Beothuk, Cree, Micmac, Montagnais, Naskapi

**Staple foods:** caribou, moose, wild plants, fish

**Clothing:** caribou or moose skin

**Shelter:** caribou-skin tents, bark lodges, teepees

**Transportation:** canoes, toboggans, snowshoes

**Tools:** containers of bark or spruce roots, utensils of wood

**Art:** quill work, embroidery

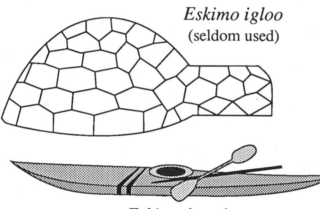

*Eskimo igloo*
(seldom used)

*Eskimo kayak*

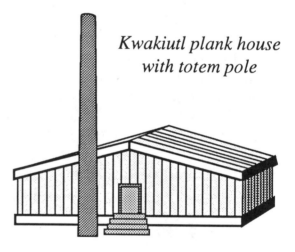

*Kwakiutl plank house with totem pole*

## INDIANS OF THE NORTHWEST

**Location:** along the Pacific Ocean from southern Alaska to northern California

**Major tribes:** Bella Coola, Chinook, Haida, Kwakiutl, Nootka, Tlingit, Tsimshian

**Staple foods:** primarily salmon, but also seals, whales, elk and other game, bulbs, berries

**Clothing:** varied, some woven blankets of wool or dog hair

**Shelter:** plank houses, often with totem poles

**Transportation:** dugout canoes, cedar planked canoes

**Art:** copper shields, weaving, wooden boxes, rattles and masks

**Customs:** potlatch, slaves

## INDIANS OF THE PLATEAU AREA
### (CALIFORNIA-INTERMOUNTAIN)

**Location:** California and the Great Basin area west of the Rocky Mountains and east of the coastal ranges, from north of the Canadian border to the Southwest.

**Major tribes:** Bannock, Klamath, Kutenai, Maidu, Nez Percé, Paiute, Pomo, Shoshone, Ute

**Staple foods:** wild plants, seeds, nuts, acorns, roots, fruit, small game, insects

**Clothing:** skins

**Shelter:** wickiup, brush shelters, lean-tos

**Transportation:** foot

**Art:** baskets

## INDIANS OF THE SOUTHWEST

**Location:** Arizona, New Mexico, parts of Colorado and Utah
**Major tribes:** Apache, Navajo, Pima, Yaqui. Pueblo Indians: Hopi, Zuni
**Staple foods of the Pueblo Indians:** corn, beans, squash
**Staple foods of the Apache and Navajo:** antelope, rabbit, cactus fruit, piñon nuts, roots
**Clothing of the Pueblo Indians:** cotton
**Clothing of the Apache and Navajo:** skins
**Shelter of the Pueblo Indians:** adobe
**Shelter of the Navajo:** hogans or teepees
**Transportation:** foot, horses
**Tools:** atlatl (spear thrower)
**Art:** pottery, Navajo sand paintings
**Customs:** rain dances

*Navajo hogan*

## INDIANS OF THE PLAINS

**Location:** from just north of the Canadian border south to Texas between the Mississippi River and the Rocky Mountains
**Major tribes:** Arapahoe, Arikana, Assiniboine, Blackfeet, Caddo, Cheyenne, Comanche, Crow, Gros Ventre, Iowa, Kansa, Kiowa, Mandan, Osage, Pawnee, Sioux
**Staple food:** buffalo (jerky, pemmican)
**Clothing:** buffalo hides and deerskins
**Shelter:** teepees made with buffalo hides
**Transportation:** before 1700 A.D., foot and dog-drawn travois; after white man, horses
**Tools:** travois, tools from buffalo horns and bone
**Art:** bead and feather work, decorated hides
**Customs:** sign language, counting coup, sun dance

*Sioux Teepee*

## INDIANS OF THE EASTERN WOODLANDS

**Location:** eastern U.S. from the Atlantic Ocean to the Mississippi River, including the Great Lakes
**Major tribes of the Northeast:** Cayuga, Chippewa, Delaware, Illinois, Iroquois, Kickapoo, Sauk, Mahican, Menominee, Miami, Mohawk, Mohegan, Munsee, Narraganset, Potawatomi, Seneca
**Major tribes of the Southeast:** Cherokee, Chickasaw, Choctaw, Creek, Lumbee, Natchez, Powhatan, Seminole, Shawnee
**Staple foods:** corn, beans, squash, deer, wild rice, maple sugar
**Clothing:** deerskin, feather robes
**Shelter:** wigwams, Iroquois longhouses
**Transportation:** foot, birchbark canoes
**Art:** wicker baskets, pottery and wooden bowls
**Customs:** peace pipe, wampum belts

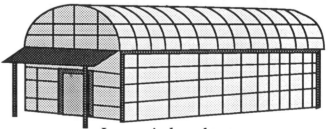

*Iroquois longhouse*

# THE DECLARATION OF INDEPENDENCE

The Declaration of Independence was adopted in Philadelphia by the Second Continental Congress, a meeting of delegates from the original thirteen colonies. It lists the complaints of the American colonists against the British government, and proclaims a new nation, the United States of America. The date it was signed, July 4, 1776, is considered the birthdate of the nation, and is celebrated yearly as the "Fourth of July" or "Independence Day."

## THE DECLARATION OF INDEPENDENCE

## IN CONGRESS, JULY 4, 1776

The unanimous Declaration of the thirteen united States of America.

When in the Course of human events it becomes necessary for one people to dissolve the political bands which have connected them with another, and to assume among the powers of the earth, the separate and equal station to which the Laws of Nature and of Nature's God entitle them, a decent respect to the opinions of mankind requires that they should declare the causes which impel them to the separation.

We hold these truths to be self-evident, that all men are created equal, that they are endowed by their Creator with certain unalienable Rights, that among these are Life, Liberty and the pursuit of Happiness.—That to secure these rights, Governments are instituted among Men, deriving their just powers from the consent of the governed,—That whenever any Form of Government becomes destructive of these ends, it is the Right of the People to alter or to abolish it, and to institute new Government, laying its foundation on such principles and organizing its powers in such form, as to them shall seem most likely to effect their Safety and Happiness. Prudence, indeed, will dictate that Governments long established should not be changed for light and transient causes; and accordingly all experience hath shewn that mankind are more disposed to suffer, while evils are sufferable, than to right themselves by abolishing the forms to which they are accustomed. But when a long train of abuses and usurpations, pursuing invariably the same Object evinces a design to reduce them under absolute Despotism, it is their right, it is their duty, to throw off such Government, and to provide new Guards for their future security.—Such has been the patient sufferance of these Colonies; and such is now the necessity which constrains them to alter their former Systems of Government. The history of the present King of Great Britain is a history of repeated injuries and usurpations, all having in direct object the establishment of an absolute Tyranny over these States. To prove this, let Facts be submitted to a candid world.

He has refused his Assent to Laws, the most wholesome and necessary for the public good.

He has forbidden his Governors to pass Laws of immediate and pressing importance, unless suspended in their operation till his Assent should be obtained; and when so suspended, he has utterly neglected to attend to them.

He has refused to pass other Laws for the accommodation of large districts of people, unless those people would relinquish the right of Representation in the Legislature, a right inestimable to them and formidable to tyrants only.

He has called together legislative bodies at places unusual, uncomfortable, and distant from the depository of their Public Records, for the sole purposes of fatiguing them into compliance with his measures.

He has dissolved Representative Houses repeatedly, for opposing with manly firmness his invasions on the rights of the people.

He has refused for a long time, after such dissolutions, to cause others to be elected; whereby the Legislative Powers, incapable of Annihilation, have returned to the People at large for their exercise; the State remaining in the mean time exposed to all the dangers of invasion from without, and convulsions within.

He has endeavored to prevent the population of these States; for that purpose obstructing the Laws for Naturalization of Foreigners; refusing to pass others to encourage their migrations hither, and raising the conditions of new Appropriations of Lands.

He has obstructed the Administration of Justice, by refusing his Assent to Laws for establishing Judiciary Powers.

He has made Judges dependent on his Will alone, for the tenure of their offices, and the amount and payment of their salaries.

He has erected a multitude of New Offices, and sent hither swarms of Officers to harass our people, and eat out their substance.

He has kept among us, in times of peace, Standing Armies without the Consent of our legislatures.

He has affected to render the Military independent of and superior to the Civil Power.

He has combined with others to subject us to a jurisdiction foreign to our constitution, and unacknowledged by our laws; giving his Assent to their Acts of pretended Legislation:

For quartering large bodies of armed troops among us:

For protecting them, by a mock Trial, from punishment for any Murders which they should commit on the Inhabitants of these States:

For cutting off our Trade with all parts of the world:

For imposing Taxes on us without our Consent:

For depriving us in many cases, of the benefits of Trial by Jury:

For transporting us beyond Seas to be tried for pretended offences:

For abolishing the free System of English Laws in a neighbouring Province, establishing therein an Arbitrary government, and enlarging its Boundaries so as to render it at once an example and fit instrument for introducing the same absolute rule into these Colonies:

For taking away our Charters, abolishing our most valuable Laws and altering fundamentally the Forms of our Governments:

For suspending our own Legislatures, and declaring themselves invested with power to legislate for us in all cases whatsoever.

He has abdicated Government here, by declaring us out of his Protection and waging War against us.

He has plundered our seas, ravaged our Coasts, burnt our towns, and destroyed the lives of our people.

He is at this time transporting large Armies of foreign Mercenaries to compleat the works of death, desolation, and tyranny, already begun with circumstances of Cruelty & Perfidy scarcely paralleled in the most barbarous ages, and totally unworthy the Head of a civilized nation.

He has constrained our fellow Citizens taken Captive on the high Seas to bear Arms against their Country, to become the executioners of their friends and Brethren, or to fall themselves by their Hands.

He has excited domestic insurrections amongst us, and has endeavoured to bring on the inhabitants of our frontiers, the merciless Indian Savages, whose known rule of warfare, is an undistinguished destruction of all ages, sexes and conditions.

In every stage of these Oppressions We have Petitioned for Redress in the most humble terms:  Our repeated Petitions have been answered only by repeated injury.  A Prince, whose character is thus marked by every act which may define a Tyrant, is unfit to be the ruler of a free people.

Nor have We been wanting in attentions to our Brittish brethren. We have warned them from time to time of attempts by their legislature to extend an unwarrantable jurisdiction over us.  We have reminded them of the circumstances of our emigration and settlement here.  We have appealed to their native justice and magnanimity, and we have conjured them by the ties of our common kindred to disavow these usurpations, which would inevitably interrupt our connections and correspondence.  They too have been deaf to the voice of justice and of consanguinity. We must, therefore, acquiesce in the necessity, which denounces our Separation, and hold them, as we hold the rest of mankind, Enemies in War, in Peace Friends.

We, therefore, the Representatives of the United States of America, in General Congress, Assembled, appealing to the Supreme Judge of the world for the rectitude of our intentions, do, in the Name, and by Authority of the good People of these Colonies, solemnly publish and declare, That these United Colonies are, and of Right ought to be Free and Independent States; that they are Absolved from all Allegiance to the British Crown, and that all political connection between them and the State of Great Britain, is and ought to be totally dissolved; and that as Free and Independent States, they have full Power to levy War, conclude Peace, contract Alliances, establish Commerce, and to do all other Acts and Things which Independent States may of right do.—And for the support of this Declaration, with a firm reliance on the protection of Divine Providence, we mutually pledge to each other our Lives, our Fortunes and our sacred Honor.

—John Hancock

| *New Hampshire* | *New York* | *Pennsylvania* | John Adams | Charles Carroll of | Joseph Hewes |
|---|---|---|---|---|---|
| Josiah Bartlett | Wm. Floyd | Robt. Morris | Robt. Treat Paine | Carrollton | John Penn |
| Wm. Whipple | Phil. Livingston | Benjamin Rush | Elbridge Gerry | *Virginia* | *South Carolina* |
| Matthew Thornton | Frans. Lewis | Benj. Franklin | *Delaware* | George Wythe | Edward Rutledge |
| *Rhode Island* | Lewis Morris | John Morton | Caesar Rodney | Richard Henry Lee | Thos. Heyward, Junr. |
| Step. Hopkins | *New Jersey* | Geo. Clymer | Geo. Read | Th. Jefferson | Thomas Lynch, Junr. |
| William Ellery | Richd. Stockton | Jas. Smith | Tho. M'Kean | Benj. Harrison | Arthur Middleton |
| *Connecticut* | Jno. Witherspoon | Geo. Taylor | *Maryland* | Ths. Nelson, Jr. | *Georgia* |
| Roger Sherman | Fras. Hopkinson | James Wilson | Samuel Chase | Francis Lightfoot Lee | Button Gwinnett |
| Sam'el Huntington | John Hart | Geo. Ross | Wm. Paca | Carter Braxton | Lyman Hall |
| Wm. Williams | Abra. Clark | *Massachusetts-Bay* | Thos. Stone | *North Carolina* | Geo. Walton |
| Oliver Wolcott | | Saml. Adams | | Wm. Hooper | |

# THE UNITED STATES CONSTITUTION

The Constitution of the United States outlines the organization of the national government, defines the process of making and enforcing rules (laws), and describes the rights of the people. It was signed on September 17, 1787, at Independence Hall in Philadelphia and is currently the oldest written national constitution still in force. The first ten amendments are called the Bill of Rights and were added by the First Congress in 1791 to safeguard individual rights. The additional amendments were added since that time. Sections in parentheses have been amended.

## CONSTITUTION OF THE UNITED STATES OF AMERICA

### (Preamble)

We the people of the United States, in order to form a more perfect Union, establish justice, insure domestic tranquility, provide for the common defence, promote the general welfare, and secure the blessings of liberty to ourselves and our posterity, do ordain and establish this Constitution for the United States of America.

### ARTICLE 1

**Section 1.** All legislative powers herein granted shall be vested in a Congress of the United States, which shall consist of a Senate and House of Representatives.

**Section 2.** The House of Representatives shall be composed of members chosen every second year by the people of the several States, and the electors in each State shall have the qualifications requisite for electors of the most numerous branch of the State Legislature.

No Person shall be a Representative who shall not have attained to the age of twenty-five years, and been seven years a citizen of the United States, and who shall not, when elected, be an inhabitant of that State in which he shall be chosen.

(Representatives and direct taxes shall be apportioned among the several States which may be included within this Union, according to their respective numbers, which shall be determined by adding to the whole number of free persons, including those bound to service for a term of years, and excluding Indians not taxed, three fifths of all other persons.) The actual enumeration shall be made within three years after the first meeting of the Congress of the United States, and within every subsequent term of ten years, in such manner as they shall by law direct. The number of Representatives shall not exceed one for every thirty thousand, but each State shall have at least one Representative; and until such enumeration shall be made, the State of New Hampshire shall be entitled to choose three, Massachusetts eight, Rhode-Island and Providence Plantations one, Connecticut five, New York six, New Jersey four, Pennsylvania eight, Delaware one, Maryland six, Virginia ten, North Carolina five, South Carolina five, and Georgia three.

When vacancies happen in the representation from any State, the Executive Authority thereof shall issue writs of election to fill such vacancies.

The House of Representatives shall choose their Speaker and other officers and shall have the sole power of impeachment.

**Section 3.** The Senate of the United States shall be composed of two Senators from each State, chosen by the Legislature thereof, for six years; and each Senator shall have one vote

Immediately after they shall be assembled in consequence of the first election, they shall be divided as equally as may be into three classes. The seats of the Senators of the first class shall be vacated at the expiration of the second year, of the second class at the expiration of the fourth year, and of the third class at the expiration of the sixth year, so that one-third may be chosen every second year; and if vacancies happen by resignation, or otherwise, during the recess of the Legislature of any State, the Executive thereof may make temporary appointments (until the next meeting of the Legislature, which shall then fill such vacancies).

No person shall be a Senator who shall not have attained to the age of thirty years, and been nine years a citizen of the United States, and who shall not, when elected, be an inhabitant of that State for which he shall be chosen.

The Vice President of the United States shall be President of the Senate, but shall have no vote, unless they be equally divided.

The Senate shall choose their other officers, and also a President pro tempore, in the absence of the Vice President, or when he shall exercise the office of President of the United States.

The Senate shall have the sole power to try all impeachments. When sitting for that purpose, they shall be on oath or affirmation. When the President of the United States is tried, the Chief Justice shall preside: and no person shall be convicted without the concurrence of two thirds of the members present.

Judgment in cases of impeachment shall not extend further than to removal from office, and disqualification to hold and enjoy any office of honor, trust, or profit under the United States: but the party convicted shall nevertheless be liable and subject to indictment, trial, judgment and punishment, according to Law.

**Section 4.** The times, places, and manner of holding elections for Senators and Representatives, shall be prescribed in each

State by the Legislature thereof; but the Congress may at any time by law make or alter such regulations, except as to the places of choosing Senators.

The Congress shall assemble at least once in every year, and such meeting shall be on the first Monday in December, unless they shall by law appoint a different day.

**Section 5.** Each House shall be the judge of the elections, returns, and qualifications of its own members, and a majority of each shall constitute a quorum to do business; but a smaller number may adjourn from day to day, and may be authorized to compel the attendance of absent members, in such manner, and under such penalties as each House may provide.

Each House may determine the rules of its proceedings, punish its members for disorderly behavior, and, with the concurrence of two thirds, expel a member.

Each House shall keep a journal of its proceedings, and from time to time publish the same, excepting such parts as may in their judgment require secrecy; and the yeas and nays of the members of either House on any question shall, at the desire of one fifth of those present, be entered on the journal.

Neither House, during the session of Congress, shall, without the consent of the other, adjourn for more than three days, nor to any other place than that in which the two Houses shall be sitting.

**Section 6.** The Senators and Representatives shall receive a compensation for their services, to be ascertained by law, and paid out of the Treasury of the United States. They shall in all cases, except treason, felony, and breach of the peace, be privileged from arrest during their attendance at the session of their respective Houses, and in going to and returning from the same; and for any speech or debate in either House, they shall not be questioned in any other place.

No Senator or Representative shall, during the time for which he was elected, be appointed to any civil office under the authority of the United States, which shall have been created, or the emoluments whereof shall have been increased during such time; and no person holding any office under the United States shall be a member of either House during his continuance in office.

**Section 7.** All bills for raising revenue shall originate in the House of Representatives; but the Senate may propose or concur with amendments as on other bills.

Every bill which shall have passed the House of Representatives and the Senate, shall, before it becomes a law, be presented to the President of the United States; if he approve he shall sign it, but if not he shall return it, with his objections to that House in which it shall have originated, who shall enter the objections at large on their journal, and proceed to reconsider it. If after such reconsideration two thirds of that House shall agree to pass the bill, it shall be sent, together with the objections, to the other

House, by which it shall likewise be reconsidered, and if approved by two thirds of that House, it shall become a law. But in all such cases the votes of both Houses shall be determined by yeas and nays, and the names of the persons voting for and against the bill shall be entered on the journal of each house, respectively. If any bill shall not be returned by the President within ten days (Sundays excepted) after it shall have been presented to him, the same shall be a law, in like manner as if he had signed it, unless the Congress by their adjournment prevent its return, in which case it shall not be a law.

Every order, resolution, or vote to which the concurrence of the Senate and House of Representatives may be necessary (except on a question of adjournment) shall be presented to the President of the United States; and before the same shall take effect, shall be approved by him, or being disapproved by him, shall be repassed by two thirds of the Senate and House of Representatives, according to the rules and limitations prescribed in the case of a bill.

**Section 8.** The Congress shall have power to lay and collect taxes, duties, imposts and excises, to pay the debts and provide for the common defense and general welfare of the United States; but all duties, imposts and excises shall be uniform throughout the United States;

To borrow money on the credit of the United States;

To regulate commerce with foreign nations, and among the several States, and with the Indian tribes;

To establish a uniform rule of naturalization, and uniform laws on the subject of bankruptcies throughout the United States;

To coin money, regulate the value thereof, and of foreign coin, and fix the standard of weights and measures;

To provide for the punishment of counterfeiting the securities and current coin of the United States;

To establish post offices and post roads;

To promote the progress of science and useful arts, by securing for limited times to authors and inventors the exclusive right to their respective writings and discoveries;

To constitute tribunals inferior to the Supreme Court;

To define and punish piracies and felonies committed on the high seas, and offences against the law of nations;

To declare war, grant letters of marque and reprisal, and make rules concerning captures on land and water;

To raise and support armies, but no appropriation of money to that use shall be for a longer term than two years;

To provide and maintain a navy;

To make rules for the government and regulation of the land and naval forces;

To provide for calling forth the militia to execute the laws of the Union, suppress insurrections, and repel invasions.

To provide for organizing, arming, and disciplining, the militia, and for governing such part of them as may be employed in the service of the United States, reserving to the States, respectively, the appointment of the officers, and the authority of training the militia according to the discipline prescribed by Congress;

To exercise exclusive legislation in all cases whatsoever, over such district (not exceeding ten miles square) as may, by cession of particular States, and the acceptance of Congress, become the seat of the Government of the United States, and to exercise like authority over all places purchased by the consent of the Legislature of the State in which the same shall be, for the erection of forts, magazines, arsenals, dock-yards, and other needful buildings;—And

To make all laws which shall be necessary and proper for carrying into execution the foregoing powers, and all other powers vested by this Constitution in the Government of the United States, or in any department or officer thereof.

**Section 9.** The migration or importation of such persons as any of the States now existing shall think proper to admit, shall not be prohibited by the Congress prior to the year one thousand eight hundred and eight, but a tax or duty may be imposed on such importation, not exceeding ten dollars for each person.

The privilege of the writ of habeas corpus shall not be suspended, unless when in cases of rebellion or invasion the public safety may require it.

No bill of attainder or ex post facto law shall be passed.

No capitation, or other direct, tax shall be laid, unless in proportion to the census or enumeration herein before directed to be taken.

No tax or duty shall be laid on articles exported from any State.

No preference shall be given by any regulation of commerce or revenue to the ports of one State over those of another: nor shall vessels bound to, or from, one State, be obliged to enter, clear, or pay duties in another.

No money shall be drawn from the Treasury, but in consequence of appropriations made by law; and a regular statement and account of the receipts and expenditures of all public money shall be published from time to time.

No title of nobility shall be granted by the United States: and no person holding any office of profit or trust under them, shall, without the consent of the Congress, accept of any present, emolument, office, or title, of any kind whatever, from any king, prince, or foreign state.

**Section 10.** No State shall enter into any treaty, alliance, or confederation; grant letters of marque and reprisal; coin money; emit bills of credit; make any thing but gold and silver coin a tender in payment of debts; pass any bill of attainder, ex post facto law, or law impairing the obligation of contracts, or grant any title of nobility.

No State shall, without the consent of the Congress, lay any imposts or duties on imports or exports, except what may be absolutely necessary for executing its inspection laws; and the net produce of all duties and imposts, laid by any State on imports or exports, shall be for the use of the Treasury of the United States; and all such laws shall be subject to the revision and control of the Congress.

No State shall, without the consent of Congress, lay any duty of tonnage, keep troops, or ships of war in time of peace, enter into any agreement or compact with another state, or with a foreign power, or engage in war, unless actually invaded, or in such imminent danger as will not admit of delay.

## ARTICLE 2

**Section 1.** The executive power shall be vested in a President of the United States of America. He shall hold his office during the term of four years, and, together with the Vice President, chosen for the same term, be elected, as follows:

Each State shall appoint, in such manner as the Legislature thereof may direct, a number of electors, equal to the whole number of Senators and Representatives to which the State may be entitled in the Congress: but no Senator or Representative, or person holding an office of trust or profit under the United States, shall be appointed an elector.

(The electors shall meet in their respective States, and vote by ballot for two persons, of whom one at least shall not be an inhabitant of the same State with themselves. And they shall make a list of all the persons voted for, and of the number of votes for each; which list they shall sign and certify, and transmit sealed to the seat of the Government of the United States, directed to the President of the Senate. The President of the Senate shall, in the presence of the Senate and House of Representatives, open all the certificates, and the votes shall then be counted. The person having the greatest number of votes shall be the President, if such number be a majority of the whole number of electors appointed; and if there be more than one who have such majority, and have an equal number of votes, then the House of Representatives shall immediately choose by ballot one of them for President; and if no person have a majority, then from the five highest on the list the said House shall in like manner choose the President. But in choosing the President, the votes shall be taken by States, the representative from each State having one vote; A quorum for this purpose shall consist of a member or members from two thirds of the States, and a majority of all the states shall be necessary to a choice. In every case, after the choice of the President, the person having the greatest number of votes of the electors shall be the Vice President. But if there should remain two or more who have equal votes, the Senate should choose from them by ballot the Vice President.)

The Congress may determine the time of choosing the electors, and the day on which they shall give their votes; which day shall be the same throughout the United States.

No person except a natural born citizen, or a citizen of the United States, at the time of the adoption of this Constitution, shall be eligible to the office of President; neither shall any person be eligible to that office who shall not have attained to the age of thirty-five years, and been fourteen years a resident within the United States.

In case of the removal of the President from office, or of his death, resignation, or inability to discharge the powers and duties of the said office, the same shall devolve on the Vice President, and the Congress may by law provide for the case of removal, death, resignation or inability, both of the President and Vice President, declaring what officer shall then act as President, and such officer shall act accordingly, until the disability be removed, or a President shall be elected.

The President shall, at stated times, receive for his services, a compensation, which shall neither be increased nor diminished during the period for which he shall have been elected, and he shall not receive within that period any other emolument from the United States, or any of them.

Before he enter on the execution of his office, he shall take the following oath or affirmation—"I do solemnly swear (or affirm) that I will faithfully execute the office of President of the United States, and will to the best of my ability, preserve, protect, and defend the Constitution of the United States."

**Section 2.** The President shall be Commander in Chief of the Army and Navy of the United States, and of the militia of the several States, when called into the actual service of the United States; he may require the opinion, in writing, of the principal officer in each of the executive departments, upon any subject relating to the duties of their respective offices, and he shall have power to grant reprieves and pardons for offences against the United States, except in cases of impeachment.

He shall have power, by and with the advice and consent of the Senate, to make treaties, provided two thirds of the Senators present concur; and he shall nominate, and by and with the advice and consent of the Senate, shall appoint ambassadors, other public ministers and consuls, judges of the Supreme Court, and all other officers of the United States, whose appointments are not herein otherwise provided for, and which shall be established by law: but the Congress may by law vest the appointment of such inferior officers, as they think proper, in the President alone, in the courts of law, or in the heads of departments.

The President shall have power to fill up all vacancies that may happen during the recess of the Senate, by granting commissions which shall expire at the end of their session.

**Section 3.** He shall from time to time give to the Congress information of the state of the Union, and recommend to their consideration such measures as he shall judge necessary and expedient; he may, on extraordinary occasions, convene both Houses, or either of them, and in case of disagreement between them, with respect to the time of adjournment, he may adjourn them to such time as he shall think proper; he shall receive ambassadors and other public ministers: he shall take care that the laws be faithfully executed, and shall commission all the officers of the United States.

**Section 4.** The President, Vice President, and all civil officers of the United States shall be removed from office on impeachment for, and conviction of, treason, bribery, or other high crimes and misdemeanors.

## ARTICLE 3

**Section 1.** The judicial Power of the United States, shall be vested in one Supreme Court, and in such inferior courts as the Congress may from time to time ordain and establish. The judges, both of the supreme and inferior courts, shall hold their offices during good behavior, and shall, at stated times, receive for their services, a compensation, which shall not be diminished during their continuance in office.

**Section 2.** The judicial power shall extend to all cases, in law and equity, arising under this Constitution, the laws of the United States, and treaties made, or which shall be made, under their authority; to all cases affecting ambassadors, other public ministers and consuls; to all cases of admiralty and maritime jurisdiction; to controversies to which the United States, shall be a party; to controversies between two or more States; between a State and citizens of another State; between citizens of different States; between citizens of the same State claiming lands under grants of different states, and between a State, or the citizens thereof, and foreign states, citizens, or subjects.

In all cases affecting ambassadors, other public ministers and consuls, and those in which a State shall be party, the Supreme Court shall have original jurisdiction. In all the other cases before mentioned, the Supreme Court shall have appellate jurisdiction, both as to law and fact, with such exceptions, and under such regulations, as the Congress shall make.

The trial of all crimes, except in cases of impeachment, shall be by jury; and such trial shall be held in the State where the said crimes shall have been committed; but when not committed within any State, the trial shall be at such place or places as the Congress may by law have directed.

**Section 3.** Treason against the United States, shall consist only in levying war against them, or, in adhering to their enemies, giving them aid and comfort. No person shall be convicted of treason unless on the testimony of two witnesses to the same overt act, or on confession in open court.

The Congress shall have power to declare the punishment of treason, but no attainder of treason shall work corruption of blood, or forfeiture except during the life of the person attained.

## ARTICLE 4

**Section 1.** Full faith and credit shall be given in each State to the public acts, records, and judicial proceedings of every other State. And the Congress may by general laws prescribe the manner in which such acts, records, and proceedings shall be proved, and the effect thereof.

**Section 2.** The citizens of each State shall be entitled to all privileges and immunities of citizens in the several States.

A person charged in any State with treason, felony, or other crime, who shall flee from justice, and be found in another State, shall on demand of the Executive authority of the State from which he fled, be delivered up, to be removed to the State having jurisdiction of the crime.

No person held to service or labor in one State, under the laws thereof, escaping into another, shall, in consequence of any law or regulation therein, be discharged from such service or labor, but shall be delivered up on claim of the party to whom such service or labor may be due.

**Section 3.** New States may be admitted by the Congress into this Union; but no new State shall be formed or erected within the jurisdiction of any other State; nor any State be formed by the junction of two or more States, or parts of States, without the consent of the Legislatures of the States concerned as well as of the Congress.

The Congress shall have power to dispose of and make all needful rules and regulations respecting the territory or other property belonging to the United States; and nothing in this Constitution shall be so construed as to prejudice any claims of the United States, or of any particular State.

**Section 4.** The United States shall guarantee to every State in this Union a Republican form of government, and shall protect each of them against invasion; and on application of the Legislature, or of the Executive (when the Legislature cannot be convened) against domestic violence.

## ARTICLE 5

The Congress, whenever two-thirds of both houses shall deem it necessary, shall propose amendments to this Constitution, or, on the application of the legislatures of two-thirds of the several states, shall call a convention for proposing amendments, which, in either case, shall be valid to all intents and purposes, as part of this Constitution, when ratified by the legislatures of three-fourths of the several states, or by conventions in three-fourths thereof, as the one or the other mode of ratification may be proposed by the Congress; provided (that no amendment which may be made prior to the year one thousand eight hundred and eight shall in any manner affect the first and fourth clauses in the ninth section of the first article; and) that no state, without its consent, shall be deprived of its equal suffrage in the Senate.

## ARTICLE 6

All debts contracted and engagements entered into, before the adoption of this Constitution, shall be as valid against the United States under this Constitution, as under the Confederation.

This Constitution, and the laws of the United States which shall be made in pursuance thereof; and all treaties made, or which shall be made, under the authority of the United States, shall be the supreme law of the land; and the judges in every State shall be bound thereby, any thing in the Constitution or laws of any State to the contrary notwithstanding.

The Senators and Representatives before mentioned, and the members of the several State Legislatures, and all executive and judicial officers, both of the United States and of the several States, shall be bound by oath or affirmation, to support this Constitution; but no religious test shall ever be required as a qualification to any office or public trust under the United States.

## ARTICLE 7

The ratification of the conventions of nine States shall be sufficient for the establishment of this Constitution between the States so ratifying the same.

Done in convention by the unanimous consent of the States present the seventeenth day of September in the year of our Lord one thousand seven hundred and eighty seven and of the independence of the United States of America the Twelfth. In witness whereof we have hereunto subscribed our names

George Washington, President and Deputy from Virginia

*New Hampshire*
John Langdon
Nicholas Gilman

*Massachusetts*
Nathaniel Gorham
Rufus King

*Connecticut*
Wm. Saml. Johnson
Roger Sherman

*New York*
Alexander Hamilton

*New Jersey*
Wil. Livingston
David Brearley
Wm. Paterson
Jona. Dayton

*Pennsylvania*
B. Franklin
Robt. Morris
Thos. FitzSimons
James Wilson
Thomas Mifflin
Geo. Clymer

Jared Ingersoll
Gouv. Morris

*Delaware*
Geo. Read
John Dickinson
Jaco. Broom
Gunning Bedford
   Jun.
Richard Bassett

*Maryland*
James McHenry
Danl. Carrol
Dan. of St. Thos.
   Jenifer

*Virginia*
John Blair
James Madison, Jr.

*North Carolina*
Wm. Blount
Hu. Williamson
Richd Dobbs Spaight

*South Carolina*
J. Rutledge
Charles Pinckney
Charles Cotesworth
   Pinckney
Pierce Butler

*Georgia*
William Few
Abr. Baldwin
Attest:
   William Jackson,
   Secretary

# AMENDMENTS TO THE CONSTITUTION OF THE UNITED STATES

*The first 10 amendments were ratified December 15, 1791, and form what is known as the Bill of Rights.*

### ARTICLE 1

Congress shall make no law respecting an establishment of religion, or prohibiting the free exercise thereof; or abridging the freedom of speech, or of the press; or the right of the people peaceably to assemble, and to petition the Government for a redress of grievances.

### ARTICLE 2

A well regulated militia, being necessary to the security of a free State, the right of the people to keep and bear arms, shall not be infringed.

### ARTICLE 3

No soldier shall, in time of peace be quartered in any house, without the consent of the owner, nor in time of war, but in a manner to be prescribed by law.

### ARTICLE 4

The right of the people to be secure in their persons, houses, papers, and effects, against unreasonable searches and seizures, shall not be violated, and no warrants shall issue, but upon probable cause, supported by oath or affirmation, and particularly describing the place to be searched, and the persons or things to be seized.

### ARTICLE 5

No person shall be held to answer for a capital, or otherwise infamous crime, unless on a presentment or indictment of a Grand Jury, except in cases arising in the land or naval forces, or in the militia, when in actual service in time of war or public danger; nor shall any person be subject for the same offence to be twice put in jeopardy of life or limb; nor shall be compelled in any criminal case to be a witness, against himself, nor be deprived of life, liberty, or property, without due process of law; nor shall private property be taken for public use, without just compensation.

### ARTICLE 6

In all criminal prosecutions, the accused shall enjoy the right to a speedy and public trial, by an impartial jury of the State and district wherein the crime shall have been committed, which district shall have been previously ascertained by law, and to be informed of the nature and cause of the accusation; to be confronted with the witnesses against him; to have compulsory process for obtaining witnesses in his favor, and to have the assistance of counsel for his defense.

### ARTICLE 7

In suits at common law, where the value in controversy shall exceed twenty dollars, the right of trial by jury shall be preserved, and no fact tried by a jury, shall be otherwise re-examined in any court of the United States, than according to the rules of the common law.

### ARTICLE 8

Excessive bail shall not be required, nor excessive fines imposed, nor cruel and unusual punishments inflicted.

### ARTICLE 9

The enumeration in the Constitution, of certain rights, shall not be construed to deny or disparage others retained by the people.

### ARTICLE 10

The powers not delegated to the United States by the Constitution, nor prohibited by it to the States, are reserved to the States, respectively, or to the people.

### ARTICLE 11
*(Ratified February 7, 1795)*

The judicial power of the United States shall not be construed to extend to any suit in law or equity, commenced or prosecuted against one of the United States by citizens of another State, or by citizens or subjects of any foreign state.

### ARTICLE 12
*(Ratified July 27, 1804)*

The electors shall meet in their respective states, and vote by ballot for President and Vice President, one of whom, at least, shall not be an inhabitant of the same state with themselves; they shall name in their ballots the person voted for as President, and in distinct ballots the person voted for as Vice President, and they shall make distinct lists of all persons voted for as President, and of all persons voted for as Vice President, and of the number of votes for each, which lists they shall sign and certify, and transmit sealed to the seat of the government of the United States, directed to the President of the Senate; the President of the Senate shall, in the presence of the Senate and House of Representatives, open all the certificates and the votes shall then be counted; the person having the greatest number of votes for President, shall be the President, if such number be a majority of the whole number of electors appointed; and if no person have such majority, then from the persons having the highest numbers not exceeding three on the list of those voted for as President, the House of Representatives shall choose immediately, by ballot, the President. But in choosing the President, the votes shall be taken by states, the representation from each State having one vote; a quorum for this purpose shall consist of a member or members from two thirds of the states, and a majority of all the states shall be necessary to a choice. And if the House of Representatives shall not choose a President whenever the right of choice shall devolve upon them, before the fourth day of March next following, then the Vice President shall act as President, as in the case of the death or other constitutional disability of the President. The person having the greatest number of votes as Vice President, shall be the Vice President, if such number be a majority of the whole number of electors appointed, and if no person have a majority, then from the two highest numbers on the list, the Senate shall choose the Vice President; a quorum for the purpose shall consist of two thirds of the whole number of Senators, and a majority of the whole number shall be necessary to a choice. But no person constitutionally ineligible to the office of President shall be eligible to that of Vice President of the United States.

## ARTICLE 13
*(Ratified December 6, 1865)*

**Section 1.** Neither slavery nor involuntary servitude, except as a punishment for crime whereof the party shall have been duly convicted, shall exist within the United States, or any place subject to their jurisdiction.

**Section 2.** Congress shall have power to enforce this article by appropriate legislation.

## ARTICLE 14
*(Ratified July 9, 1868)*

**Section 1.** All persons born or naturalized in the United States, and subject to the jurisdiction thereof, are citizens of the United States and of the State wherein they reside. No State shall make or enforce any law which shall abridge the privileges or immunities of citizens of the United States; nor shall any State deprive any person of life, liberty, or property, without due process of law; nor deny to any person within its jurisdiction the equal protection of the laws.

**Section 2.** Representatives shall be apportioned among the several States according to their respective numbers, counting the whole number of persons in each State, excluding Indians not taxed. But when the right to vote at any election for the choice of electors for President and Vice President of the United States, Representatives in Congress, the executive and judicial officers of a State, or the members of the Legislature thereof, is denied to any of the male inhabitants of such State, being twenty-one years of age, and citizens of the United States, or in any way abridged, except for participation in rebellion, or other crime, the basis of representation therein shall be reduced in the proportion which the number of such male citizens shall bear to the whole number of male citizens twenty-one years of age in such State.

**Section 3.** No person shall be a Senator or Representative in Congress, or elector of President and Vice President, or hold any office, civil or military, under the United States, or under any State, who, having previously taken an oath, as a member of Congress, or as an officer of the United States, or as a member of any State Legislature, or as an executive or judicial officer of any State, to support the Constitution of the United States, shall have engaged in insurrection or rebellion against the same, or given aid or comfort to the enemies thereof. But Congress may by a vote of two thirds of each House, remove such disability.

**Section 4.** The validity of the public debt of the United States, authorized by law, including debts incurred for payment of pensions and bounties for services in suppressing insurrection or rebellion, shall not be questioned. But neither the United States nor any State shall assume or pay any debt or obligation incurred in aid of insurrection or rebellion against the United States, or any claim for the loss or emancipation of any slave; but all such debts, obligations, and claims shall be held illegal and void.

**Section 5.** The Congress shall have power to enforce, by appropriate legislation, the provisions of this article.

## ARTICLE 15
*(Ratified February 3, 1870)*

**Section 1.** The right of citizens of the United States to vote shall not be denied or abridged by the United States or by any State on account of race, color, or previous condition of servitude.

**Section 2.** The Congress shall have power to enforce this article by appropriate legislation.

## ARTICLE 16
*(Ratified February 3, 1913)*

The Congress shall have power to lay and collect taxes on incomes, from whatever source derived, without apportionment among the several States, and without regard to any census or enumeration.

## ARTICLE 17
*(Ratified April 8, 1913)*

The Senate of the United States shall be composed of two Senators from each State, elected by the people thereof, for six years; and each Senator shall have one vote. The electors in each State shall have the qualifications requisite for electors of the most numerous branch of the State Legislatures.

When vacancies happen in the representation of any State in the Senate, the executive authority of such State shall issue writs of election to fill such vacancies: Provided, that the legislature of any State may empower the executive thereof to make temporary appointment until the people fill the vacancies by election as the legislature may direct.

This amendment shall not be so construed as to affect the election or term of any Senator chosen before it becomes valid as part of the Constitution.

## ARTICLE 18
*(Ratified January 16, 1919. Repealed December 5, 1933 by Amendment 21)*

**Section 1.** After one year from the ratification of this article the manufacture, sale, or transportation of intoxicating liquors within, the importation thereof into, or the exportation thereof from the United States and all territory subject to the jurisdiction thereof for beverage purposes is hereby prohibited.

**Section 2.** The Congress and the several States shall have concurrent power to enforce this article by appropriate legislation.

**Section 3.** This article shall be inoperative unless it shall have been ratified as an amendment to the Constitution by the legislatures of the several States, as provided in the Constitution, within seven years from the date of the submission hereof to the States by Congress.

## ARTICLE 19
*(Ratified August 18, 1920)*

The right of citizens of the United States to vote shall not be denied or abridged by the United States or by any State on account of sex.

Congress shall have power to enforce this article by appropriate legislation.

## ARTICLE 20
*(Ratified January 23, 1933)*

**Section 1.** The terms of the President and Vice President shall end at noon on the twentieth day of January, and the terms of Senators and Representatives at noon on the third day of January, of the years in which such terms would have ended if this article had not been ratified; and the terms of their successors shall then begin.

**Section 2.** The Congress shall assemble at least once in every year, and such meetings shall begin at noon on the third day of January, unless they shall by law appoint a different day.

**Section 3.** If, at the time fixed for the beginning of the term of the President, the President-elect shall have died, the Vice President-elect shall become President. If a President shall not have been chosen before the time fixed for the beginning of his term, or if the President-elect shall have failed to qualify, then the Vice President shall have qualified; and the Congress may by law provide for the case wherein neither a President-elect nor a Vice President-elect shall have qualified, declaring who shall then act as President, or the manner in which one who is to act shall be selected, and such person shall act accordingly until a President or Vice President shall have qualified.

**Section 4.** The Congress may by law provide for the case of the death of any of the persons from whom the House of Representatives may choose a President whenever the right of choice shall have devolved upon them, and for the case of the death of any of the persons from whom the Senate may choose a Vice President whenever the right of choice shall have devolved upon them.

**Section 5.** Sections 1 and 2 shall take effect on the 15th day of October following the ratification of this article.

**Section 6.** This article shall be inoperative unless it shall have been ratified as an amendment to the Constitution by the legislatures of three fourths of the several States within seven years from the date of its submission.

## ARTICLE 21
*(Ratified December 5, 1933)*

**Section 1.** The eighteenth article of amendment to the Constitution of the United States is hereby repealed.

**Section 2.** The transportation or importation into any State, territory, or possession of the United States for delivery or use therein of intoxicating liquors, in violation of the laws thereof, is hereby prohibited.

**Section 3.** This article shall be inoperative unless it shall have been ratified as an amendment to the Constitution, within seven years from the date of the submission thereof to the States by the Congress.

## ARTICLE 22
*(Ratified February 27, 1951)*

**Section 1.** No person shall be elected to the office of the President more than twice, and no person who has held the office of President, or acted as President, for more than two years of a term to which some other person was elected President shall be elected to the office of the President more than once. But this article shall not apply to any person holding the office of President when this article was proposed by the Congress, and shall not prevent any person who may be holding the office of President, or acting as President, during the term within which this article becomes operative from holding the office of President or acting as President during the remainder of such term.

**Section 2.** This article shall be inoperative unless it shall have been ratified as an amendment to the Constitution by the legislatures of three fourths of the several States within seven years from the date of its submission to the States by the Congress.

## ARTICLE 23
*(Ratified March 29, 1961)*

**Section 1.** The District constituting the seat of Government of the United States shall appoint in such manner as the Congress may direct:

A number of electors of President and Vice President equal to the whole number of Senators and Representatives in Congress to which the District would be entitled if it were a State, but in no event more than the least populous State; they shall be in addition to those appointed by the States, but they shall be considered, for the purposes of the election of President and Vice President, to be electors appointed by a State; and they shall meet in the District and perform such duties as provided by the twelfth article of amendment.

**Section 2.** The Congress shall have the power to enforce this article by appropriate legislation.

## ARTICLE 24
*(Ratified January 23, 1964)*

**Section 1.** The right of citizens of the United States to vote in any primary or other election for President or Vice President, or for Senator or Representative in Congress, shall not be denied or abridged by the United States or any State by reasons of failure to pay any poll tax or other tax.

**Section 2.** The Congress shall have the power to enforce this article by appropriate legislation.

## ARTICLE 25
*(Ratified February 10, 1967)*

**Section 1.** In case of the removal of the President from office or of his death or resignation, the Vice President shall become President.

**Section 2.** Whenever there is a vacancy in the office of the Vice President, the President shall nominate a Vice President who shall take office upon confirmation by a majority vote of both Houses of Congress.

**Section 3.** Whenever the President transmits to the President pro tempore of the Senate and the Speaker of the House of Representatives his written declaration that he is unable to discharge the powers and duties of his office, and until he transmits to them a written declaration to the contrary, such powers and duties shall be discharged by the Vice President as Acting President.

**Section 4.** Whenever the Vice President and a majority of either the principal officers of the executive departments or of such other body as Congress may by law provide, transmit to the President pro tempore of the Senate and the Speaker of the House of Representatives their written declaration that the President is unable to discharge the powers and duties of his office, the Vice President shall immediately assume the powers and duties of the office as Acting President.

Thereafter, when the President transmits to the President pro tempore of the Senate and the Speaker of the House of Representatives his written declaration that no inability exists, he shall resume the powers and duties of his office unless the Vice President and a majority of either the principal officers of

the executive department or of such other body as Congress may by law provide, transmit within four days to the President pro tempore of the Senate and the Speaker of the House of Representatives their written declaration that the President is unable to discharge the powers and duties of his office. Thereupon Congress shall decide the issue, assembling within forty-eight hours for that purpose if not in session. If the Congress, within twenty-one days after receipt of the latter written declaration, or, if Congress is not in session, within twenty-one days after Congress is required to assemble, determines by two thirds vote of both Houses that the President is unable to discharge the powers and duties of his office, the Vice President shall continue to discharge the same as Acting President; otherwise, the President shall resume the powers and duties of his office.

## ARTICLE 26
*(Ratified July 1, 1971)*

**Section 1.** The right of citizens of the United States, who are 18 years of age or older, to vote shall not be denied or abridged by the United States or by any state on account of age.

**Section 2.** The Congress shall have power to enforce this article by appropriate legislation.

# INTERESTING FACTS ABOUT THE CONSTITUTION

* The United States has the world's oldest written Constitution still in effect. All countries in the world now have one, except Israel, Libya, New Zealand, Oman and the United Kingdom.

* For thirteen years, the United States did not have a Constitution or a President.

* The Constitutional Convention was supposed to begin May 14, 1787, but almost no one showed up! It finally began 11 days late, on May 25.

* Rhode Island did not send anyone to the convention and no one from Rhode Island signed the Constitution because it did not want a national government interfering with Rhode Island's affairs. Rhode Island and North Carolina would not sign without a Bill of Rights.

# FORMS OF GOVERNMENT

When people live together in groups, they must share resources such as food and space. To keep things running smoothly, rules must be made to govern the members. If there were no rules, life would be unsafe and nothing much would be accomplished. Because not everyone follows the rules willingly, there must be a "power structure"—people with the power to make and enforce the rules.

"Government" is the process of making and enforcing rules. People have many different ideas and so there are many kinds of governments. The success of any form of government depends on how good the rules are and how well people follow them. Some governments allow people freedom and depend on them to be responsible citizens; others use force to make people follow the rules.

## FORMS OF GOVERNMENT

A. **Rule by one person—autocracy**
   1. **Monarchy.** The leader usually inherits the throne and holds power for life. Kings and emperors are monarchs.
   2. **Dictatorship.** The leader generally comes to power when a country is having many problems, and may seize power by force. The dictator has complete authority. Famous dictators are Adolf Hitler, Joseph Stalin, and Benito Mussolini.

B. **Rule by a few persons**
   1. **Aristocracy.** Leaders may be members of a royal family or wealthy landowners. They are generally the powerful upper-class citizens.
   2. **Oligarchy.** A small group of people holds power and rules as in a dictatorship.

C. **Rule by many**
   1. **Democracy.** All the people meet and decide on every issue.
   2. **Representative Democracy (Republic).** People elect representatives to rule because it is not possible for everyone to get together. The United States is a republic.

## THEORIES OF HOW GOVERNMENTS SHOULD RUN

A. **Anarchism.** Private individuals govern themselves. There is little or no public government.
B. **Socialism.** The government works to own the country's main resources, factories, etc., generally in a peaceful way.
C. **Communism.** The government takes control of factories, land, and other means of production. The government may rule strictly and allow little or no criticism. The stated goal of communism is common ownership of means of production and common sharing of labor and products.

## GOVERNMENTAL SYSTEMS

A. **Authoritarianism.** Power of government is used without the consent of the people. People are expected to obey without question. There is little individual freedom.
B. **Capitalism.** An economic system in which individual people and private businesses own most of a country's resources and industries. Capitalism is often called a *free-enterprise system*.
C. **Fascism.** A system of government with a rigid, one-party dictatorship.
D. **Totalitarianism.** The government controls all of the activities of the people.

# SPEECHES AND QUOTES

I know not what course others may take, but as for me, give me liberty or give me death!

> —Patrick Henry, 1775, urging the colonies to revolt against England.

These are the times that try men's souls.

> —Thomas Paine, 1776, in pamphlets trying to stir up the revolutionary spirit of Americans against the British.

We must indeed all hang together, or most assuredly, we shall all hang separately.

> —Benjamin Franklin, 1776, at the signing of the Declaration of Independence.

I only regret that I have but one life to lose for my country.

> —Nathan Hale, 1776, in a speech just before he was hanged by the British for spying during the American Revolution.

I have not yet begun to fight!

> —John Paul Jones, 1779. Jones' ship was badly damaged. The British commander asked if he would surrender. He answered, "I have not yet begun to fight!" As Jones' ship sank, his crew captured the British ship.

Go west, young man!

> —John Soule, later Horace Greeley, 1851, urging young people to take advantage of the opportunities on the American frontier.

Speak softly and carry a big stick.

> —Proverb quoted in 1902 by President Theodore Roosevelt. He believed the United States should negotiate with other countries carefully, but backed by the threat of force.

The world must be made safe for democracy.

> —President Woodrow Wilson, 1917, to justify his call for a declaration of war on Germany during World War I.

The business of America is business.

> —President Calvin Coolidge, 1925.

The only thing we have to fear is fear itself.

> — President Franklin D. Roosevelt, 1933, at first inaugural address. It was the worst point of the Great Depression.

I shall return.

> —General Douglas MacArthur, 1942, commander of the U.S. forces in the Far East during World War II. He was promising to return to his men in the Philippines after he was ordered to leave.

The buck stops here.

> —On President Harry Truman's desk.

Ask not what your country can do for you; ask what you can do for your country.

> —President John F. Kennedy, 1961, from his Inaugural Address

# GETTYSBURG ADDRESS

The **Gettysburg Address** is a short speech delivered by President Abraham Lincoln on November 19, 1863 during the Civil War. Its purpose was to dedicate a part of the battlefield of the Battle of Gettysburg as a cemetery for people who had lost their lives in the battle. The Gettysburg Address is engraved on a tablet in the Lincoln Memorial in Washington, D.C.

Four score and seven years ago our fathers brought forth on this continent, a new nation, conceived in Liberty, and dedicated to the proposition that all men are created equal.

Now we are engaged in a great civil war, testing whether that nation, or any nation so conceived and so dedicated, can long endure. We are met on a great battlefield of that war. We have come to dedicate a portion of that field, as a final resting place for those who here gave their lives that that nation might live. It is altogether fitting and proper that we should do this.

But in a larger sense, we can not dedicate—we can not consecrate—we can not hallow—this ground. The brave men, living and dead, who struggled here, have consecrated it, far above our poor power to add or detract. The world will little note, nor long remember what we say here, but it can never forget what they did here. It is for us the living, rather, to be dedicated here to the unfinished work which they who fought here have thus far so nobly advanced. It is rather for us to be here dedicated to the great task remaining before us—that from these honored dead we take increased devotion to that cause for which they gave the last full measure of devotion—that we here highly resolve that these dead shall not have died in vain—that this nation, under God, shall have a new birth of freedom—and that government of the people, by the people, for the people, shall not perish from the earth.

# I HAVE A DREAM

Martin Luther King, Jr. delivered a speech which included the following words on August 28, 1963, when more than 200,000 people marched from the Washington Monument to the Lincoln Memorial in Washington, D.C. to protest racial discrimination. Martin Luther King, Jr. won the Nobel peace prize in 1964 for leading the black struggle for equality through nonviolent means.

I say to you today, my friends, so even though we face the difficulties of today and tomorrow, I still have a dream. It is a dream deeply rooted in the American dream.

I have a dream that one day this nation will rise up and live out the true meaning of its creed: "We hold these truths to be self-evident; that all men are created equal."

I have a dream that one day, on the red hills of Georgia, sons of former slaves and the sons of former slaveowners will be able to sit down together at the table of brotherhood.

I have a dream that one day even the state of Mississippi, a state sweltering with the heat of oppression, will be transformed into an oasis of freedom and justice.

I have a dream that my four little children will one day live in a nation where they will not be judged by the color of their skin but by the content of their character.

I have a dream today...

# SYMBOLS OF AMERICA

The **United States Flag** is a symbol of the land, the people, the ideals and the government of the  United States. It was adopted on June 14, 1777. The flag is also known as the Stars & Stripes, the Star-Spangled Banner, and Old Glory.

The stripes stand for the original 13 colonies. The stars stand for the states. There is one for each of the 50 states.
Red stands for hardiness and courage.
White stands for innocence and purity.
Blue stands for vigilance, perseverance and justice.

The **Pledge of Allegiance** is a pledge of loyalty to the United States. It was first said by public school children in 1892.

I pledge allegiance to the flag of the United States of America and to the Republic for which it stands, one Nation under God, indivisible, with liberty and justice for all.

The **Star-Spangled Banner** is our national anthem. It was written by Francis Scott Key while on a British warship in Chesapeake Bay, Maryland, during the War of 1812. He watched a night-long battle and wrote the song to express his joy at seeing the American flag still flying in the morning. The music was borrowed from an English song composed by John Stafford Smith. The Star-Spangled Banner was officially adopted as the national anthem in March 1931.

Oh! say, can you see, by the dawn's early light,
What so proudly we hailed at the twilight's last gleaming?
Whose broad stripes and bright stars, thro' the perilous fight,
O'er the ramparts we watched were so gallantly streaming?
And the rockets' red glare, the bombs bursting in air,
Gave proof thro' the night that our flag was still there.
Oh! say, does that star-spangled banner yet wave
O'er the land of the free and the home of the brave?

The **Liberty Bell** is a symbol of American 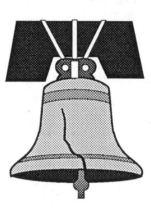 independence. It rang on July 8, 1776, to celebrate the adoption of the Declaration of Independence. It was rung every year on the Fourth of July until 1835 when it cracked. It is in Philadelphia, Pennsylvania. The inscription reads: "Proclaim Liberty throughout all the land unto all the inhabitants thereof." (from the Bible—Leviticus 25:10) It weighs over 2,080 pounds.

The **Motto** of the United States is "In God We Trust." It was officially adopted on July 30, 1956, and is printed on money.

The **Statue of Liberty** is a symbol of American democracy. It stands on Liberty Island in New York Harbor and is the first thing many immigrants saw as they came to America. The Statue of Liberty was given to the United States by France on July 4, 1884 as a gift of friendship. It is 151 feet 1 inch high, weighs 450,000 pounds and has 142 steps inside.

A woman named Emma Lazarus wrote a poem for the Statue of Liberty, which was inscribed on a tablet in the pedestal in 1903. It is called "The New Colossus."

Not like the brazen giant of Greek fame,
 With conquering limbs astride from land to land;
 Here at our sea-washed, sunset gates shall stand
A mighty woman with a torch, whose flame
Is the imprisoned lightning, and her name
 Mother of Exiles. From her beacon-hand
 Glows world-wide welcome; her mild eyes
 command
The air-bridged harbor that twin cities frame.
"Keep ancient lands, your storied pomp!" cries she
 With silent lips. "Give me your tired, your poor,
Your huddled masses yearning to breathe free,
 The wretched refuse of your teeming shore.
Send these, the homeless, tempest-tost to me,
 I lift my lamp beside the golden door!"

**Uncle Sam** is a symbol for the United States. The name came from the initials U.S. It was first used during the War of 1812 as an unfriendly nickname for the United States government. In 1961, Congress recognized Uncle Sam as a national symbol.

The two major **political parties**, or organized political groups, in the United States are the Democratic and Republican Parties.

The **Great Seal of the United States** is a symbol of the sovereignty of the United States. It was adopted on June 20, 1782.

The American eagle symbolizes self-reliance.
The vertical stripes represent the 13 stripes of the flag.
The blue above the stripes symbolizes the U.S. government.
The olive branch stands for peace and the arrows for war.
The motto, *E pluribus unum*, stands for one (nation) out of many (states).

The **donkey** has been a symbol of the Democratic Party since Andrew Jackson's presidential campaign in 1828, and was used mainly in political cartoons. The Democratic Party is the oldest existing party in the United States. Most historians date its origin from Andrew Jackson's campaign.

The **Bald Eagle** is a symbol of American freedom and power. It was adopted as the national bird on June 20, 1782.

The **elephant** was first used as a symbol of the Republican Party in political cartoons in 1874. The party formed in 1854 in opposition to slavery, and Abraham Lincoln was the first Republican president. The Republican Party was nicknamed the G.O.P., or *Grand Old Party,* in the 1880's.

# BRANCHES OF THE

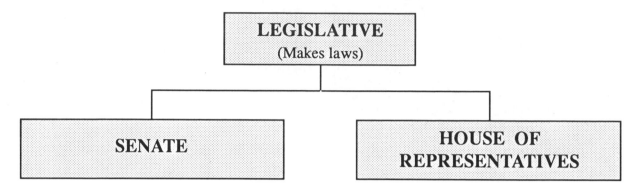

**LEGISLATIVE**
(Makes laws)

**SENATE**

**HOUSE OF REPRESENTATIVES**

The Senate and the House of Representatives are jointly known as the **United States Congress.**

*Membership:* 100 members, two from each of the 50 states.

*Term:* Six years. About one-third of the members are up for re-election every two years. Terms expire in January.

*Qualifications:*
1. At least 30 years old.
2. U.S. citizen for at least 9 years.
3. Legal resident of the state from which elected.

*Salary :* $89,500

*Address:* The Senate
Washington, D.C. 20510

*Phone number:* (202) 224-3121

*Membership:* 435 members—one or more from each state based on population. California, the most populous state, has 45 representatives. Six states have only one representative.

*Term:* Two years. Elections are held in even numbered years. Terms expire in January.

*Qualifications:*
1. At least 25 years old.
2. U.S. citizen for at least 7 years.
3. Legal resident of the state from which elected.

*Salary :* $89,500

*Address:* House of Representatives
Washington, D.C. 20515

*The Senate and House of Representatives meet in the United States Capitol Building.*

# UNITED STATES GOVERNMENT

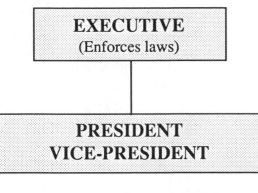

## EXECUTIVE
(Enforces laws)

### PRESIDENT
### VICE-PRESIDENT

*President:*  George H. W. Bush
*Vice-President:*  J. Danforth Quayle

*Term:*  Four years.  Limited to two terms.

*Qualifications:*
1. At least 35 years old.
2. Natural born U.S. citizen.
3. Has lived in the U.S. at least 14 years.

*Salary :*  President: $200,000
Vice-President: $115,000

*Address:*  The White House
1600 Pennsylvania Avenue NW
Washington, D.C.  20500

## THE CABINET

Secretary of Agriculture
Secretary of Commerce
Secretary of Defense
Secretary of Education
Secretary of Energy
Secretary of Health and Human Services
Secretary of Housing and Urban Development
Secretary of the Interior
Secretary of Labor
Secretary of State
Secretary of Transportation
Secretary of the Treasury
Secretary of Veterans Affairs
Attorney General

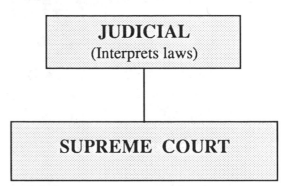

## JUDICIAL
(Interprets laws)

### SUPREME COURT

*Membership:*  Nine members, appointed by the President, with the advice and consent of the Senate.

*Term:*  Life.

*Qualifications:*  None set in the Constitution.

*Salary :*  Chief Justice: $115,000
Associate Justices:  $110,000

*Address:*  United States Supreme Court
1 First Street NE
Washington, D.C.  20543

**SUPREME COURT JUSTICES**
Chief Justice William H. Rehnquist
Harry A. Blackmun
Thurgood Marshall
Sandra Day O'Connor
David Souter
John Paul Stevens
Byron R. White
Antonin Scalia
Anthony M. Kennedy

*The President lives and works in the White House.*

| | | | | |
|---|---|---|---|---|
| **UNITED STATES PRESIDENTS** | | | | |
| **NAME** | **DATE OF BIRTH** | **STATE OF BIRTH** | **TERM** | **DATE OF DEATH** |
| 1. George Washington | Feb. 22, 1732 | Virginia | 1789-1797 | Dec. 14, 1799 |
| 2. John Adams | Oct. 30, 1735 | Massachusetts | 1797-1801 | July 4, 1826 |
| 3. Thomas Jefferson | Apr. 13, 1743 | Virginia | 1801-1809 | July 4, 1826 |
| 4. James Madison | Mar. 16, 1751 | Virginia | 1809-1817 | June 28, 1836 |
| 5. James Monroe | Apr. 28, 1758 | Virginia | 1817-1825 | July 4, 1831 |
| 6. John Quincy Adams | July 11, 1767 | Massachusetts | 1825-1829 | Feb. 23, 1848 |
| 7. Andrew Jackson | Mar. 15, 1767 | South Carolina | 1829-1837 | June 8, 1845 |
| 8. Martin Van Buren | Dec. 5, 1782 | New York | 1837-1841 | July 24, 1862 |
| 9. William H. Harrison | Feb. 9, 1773 | Virginia | 1841 | Apr. 4, 1841 |
| 10. John Tyler | Mar. 29, 1790 | Virginia | 1841-1845 | Jan. 18, 1862 |
| 11. James K. Polk | Nov. 2, 1795 | North Carolina | 1845-1849 | June 15, 1849 |
| 12. Zachary Taylor | Nov. 24, 1784 | Virginia | 1849-1850 | July 9, 1850 |
| 13. Millard Fillmore | Jan. 7, 1800 | New York | 1850-1853 | Mar. 8, 1874 |
| 14. Franklin Pierce | Nov. 23, 1804 | New Hampshire | 1853-1857 | Oct. 8, 1869 |
| 15. James Buchanan | Apr. 23, 1791 | Pennsylvania | 1857-1861 | June 1, 1868 |
| 16. Abraham Lincoln | Feb. 12, 1809 | Kentucky | 1861-1865 | Apr. 15, 1865 |
| 17. Andrew Johnson | Dec. 29, 1808 | North Carolina | 1865-1869 | July 31, 1875 |
| 18. Ulysses S. Grant | Apr. 27, 1822 | Ohio | 1869-1877 | July 23, 1885 |
| 19. Rutherford B. Hayes | Oct. 4, 1822 | Ohio | 1877-1881 | Jan. 17, 1893 |
| 20. James A. Garfield | Nov. 19, 1831 | Ohio | 1881 | Sept. 19, 1881 |
| 21. Chester A. Arthur | Oct. 5, 1829 | Vermont | 1881-1885 | Nov. 18, 1886 |
| 22. Grover Cleveland | Mar. 18, 1837 | New Jersey | 1885-1889 | June 24, 1908 |
| 23. Benjamin Harrison | Aug. 20, 1833 | Ohio | 1889-1893 | Mar. 13, 1901 |
| 24. Grover Cleveland | Mar. 18, 1837 | New Jersey | 1893-1897 | June 24, 1908 |
| 25. William McKinley | Jan. 29, 1843 | Ohio | 1897-1901 | Sept. 14, 1901 |
| 26. Theodore Roosevelt | Oct. 27, 1858 | New York | 1901-1909 | Jan. 6, 1919 |
| 27. William H. Taft | Sept. 15, 1857 | Ohio | 1909-1913 | Mar. 8, 1930 |
| 28. Woodrow Wilson | Dec. 29, 1856 | Virginia | 1913-1921 | Feb. 3, 1924 |
| 29. Warren G. Harding | Nov. 2, 1865 | Ohio | 1921-1923 | Aug. 2, 1923 |
| 30. Calvin Coolidge | July 4, 1872 | Vermont | 1923-1929 | Jan. 5, 1933 |
| 31. Herbert C. Hoover | Aug. 10, 1874 | Iowa | 1929-1933 | Oct. 10, 1964 |
| 32. Franklin D. Roosevelt | Jan. 30, 1882 | New York | 1933-1945 | Apr. 12, 1945 |
| 33. Harry S. Truman | May 8, 1884 | Missouri | 1945-1953 | Dec. 26, 1972 |
| 34. Dwight D. Eisenhower | Oct. 14, 1890 | Texas | 1953-1961 | Mar. 28, 1969 |
| 35. John F. Kennedy | May 29, 1917 | Massachusetts | 1961-1963 | Nov. 22, 1963 |
| 36. Lyndon B. Johnson | Aug. 27, 1908 | Texas | 1963-1969 | Jan. 22, 1973 |
| 37. Richard M. Nixon | Jan. 9, 1913 | California | 1969-1974 | |
| 38. Gerald R. Ford | July 14, 1913 | Nebraska | 1974-1977 | |
| 39. James E. Carter, Jr. | Oct. 1, 1924 | Georgia | 1977-1981 | |
| 40. Ronald W. Reagan | Feb. 6, 1911 | Illinois | 1981-1989 | |
| 41. George H. W. Bush | June 12, 1924 | Massachusetts | 1989- | |

# NORTH AMERICA

SOVIET UNION

*Arctic Ocean*

*Chukchi Sea*

*Ellesmere Island*

*Greenland Sea*

*Greenland (DEN.)*

ICELAND

*Reykjavik*

*Bering Strait*

*Beaufort Sea*

*Baffin Bay*

*Denmark Strait*

*Bering Sea*

UNITED STATES (Alaska)

Fairbanks

Anchorage

*Baffin Island*

*Victoria Island*

Godthab (Nuuk)

*Davis Strait*

*Labrador Sea*

*Gulf of Alaska*

Whitehorse

*Hudson Bay*

Goose Bay

Churchill

Newfoundland

C A N A D A

Edmonton

*North Pacific Ocean*

Vancouver

Seattle

Winnipeg

Quebec

Halifax

Montreal

Ottawa ★

Boston

Detroit

Chicago

Pittsburgh

New York

Salt Lake City

UNITED STATES

Washington D.C.

*North Atlantic Ocean*

San Francisco

Denver

St. Louis

Los Angeles

Atlanta

El Faso

Houston

New Orleans

Miami

THE BAHAMAS

Nassau

*Gulf of Mexico*

Havana

Santo Domingo

CUBA

HAITI

DOM. REP.

Port-au-Prince

MEXICO

JAMAICA

Kingston

Mexico

Belmopan

BELIZE

*Caribbean Sea*

GUATEMALA

HONDURAS

Tegucigalpa

Guatemala

San Salvador

NICARAGUA

EL SALVADOR

Managua

San José

Panama

COSTA RICA

PANAMA

COLOMBIA

Bogota ★

0    1000 Kilometers

0    1000 Miles

MAINE

Augusta

Montpelier

VT. N. H.
Concord

MINNESOTA

Duluth

Lake
Superior

MICHIGAN

St. Paul
Minneapolis

WISCONSIN

Lake
Huron

Lake
Michigan

Albany

NEW YORK

Boston
MASS.
Providence
Hartford
CONN. R.I.

New York

Madison

MICHIGAN
Lansing

Milwaukee

Detroit

Buffalo

Lake Ontario

Lake Erie

Cleveland

PENNSYLVANIA

Philadelphia
Pittsburgh
Harrisburg

Trenton

NEW JERSEY

IOWA

Chicago

Toledo

OHIO

Columbus

Dover

DELAWARE

Des Moines

ILLINOIS

INDIANA

Indianapolis

Cincinnati

WEST
VIRGINIA
Charleston

MARYLAND

Washington,
D.C.

Annapolis

Kansas City
Jefferson City

Springfield

St. Louis

Frankfort

KENTUCKY

Richmond

VIRGINIA

Norfolk

MISSOURI

Nashville

Raleigh

NORTH CAROLINA

Charlotte

Atlantic

ARKANSAS

Little Rock

Memphis

TENNESSEE

SOUTH CAROLINA
Columbia

Ocean

Birmingham

Atlanta

Charleston

ALABAMA

GEORGIA

Jackson

Montgomery

LOUISIANA

Baton
Rouge

MISSISSIPPI

Jacksonville

Tallahassee

New Orleans

FLORIDA

Tampa

Gulf of Mexico

Miami

THE BAHAMAS

500 Miles

0

500 Kilometers

0

Key West

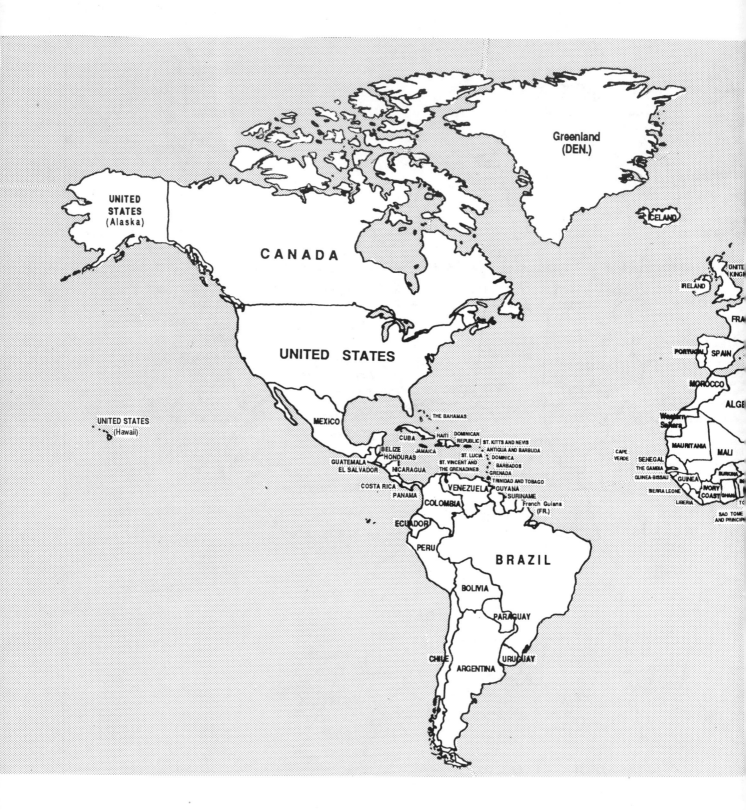

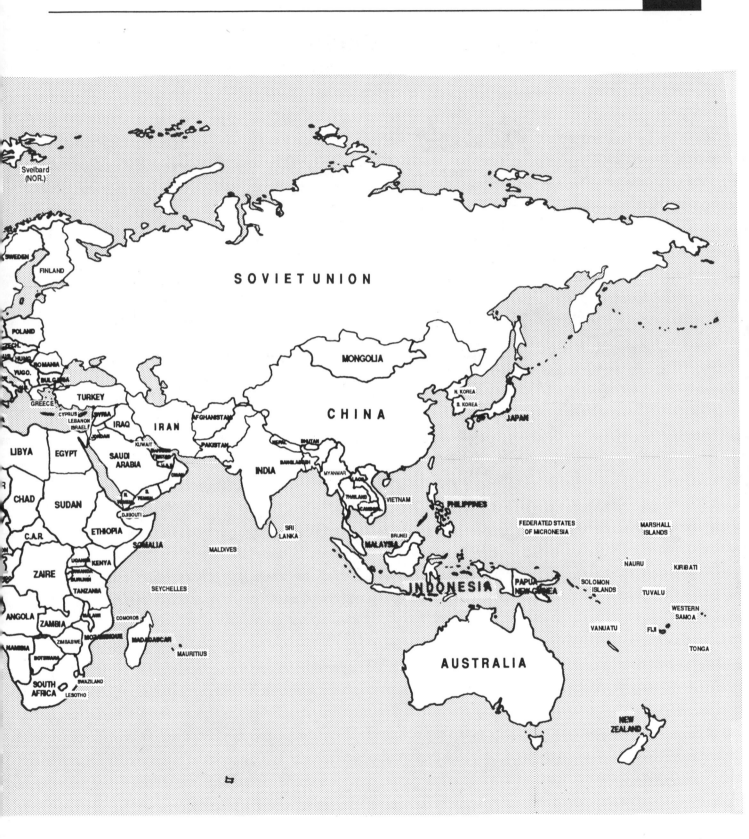

# SOUTH AMERICA

North
Atlantic
Ocean

Caribbean Sea

Barranquilla

Maracaibo ★ Caracas

**VENEZUELA**

Medellin

Bogotá

**COLOMBIA**

Cali

Mitu

Boa Vista

Georgetown
Paramaribo
**GUYANA**
French Guiana
(FR.)
**SURINAME**
Cayenne

Macapá

★ Quito
**ECUADOR**

Guayaquil

Iquitos

Fonte Boa

Manaus

Santarem

Belém

São Luís

Fortaleza

Piura

Rio
Branco

Porto Velho

**B R A Z I L**

Teresina

Natal

Trujillo

Huánuco

**PERU**

Porto Nacional

Recife

*South
Pacific
Ocean*

Lima

Cusco

Ica

Trinidad

Cuiabá

Aracaju

Salvador

Arequipa

Lake
Titicaca

**BOLIVIA**

★
La Paz

Sucre

Santa
Cruz

Goiania

★ Brasilia

Belo
Horizonte

Vitória

Arica

**PARAGUAY**

Asunción
★

Rio de Janeiro

São Paulo

Antofagasta

San Miguel
de Tucumán

Resistencia

Curitiba

Florianópolis

Porto Alegre

*South
Atlantic
Ocean*

**CHILE**

Córdoba

Rosario

Salto
**URUGUAY**

Valparaiso

Mendoza

Santiago ★

Buenos Aires

Montevideo

**ARGENTINA**

Concepción

Bahia Blanca

Mar del Plata

Puerto Montt

San Carlos
de Bariloche

500 Kilometers

500 Nautical Miles

Comodoro Rivadavia

Strait of
Magellan

Stanley
**Falkland Islands**

Ushuaia

South Georgia

# AFRICA

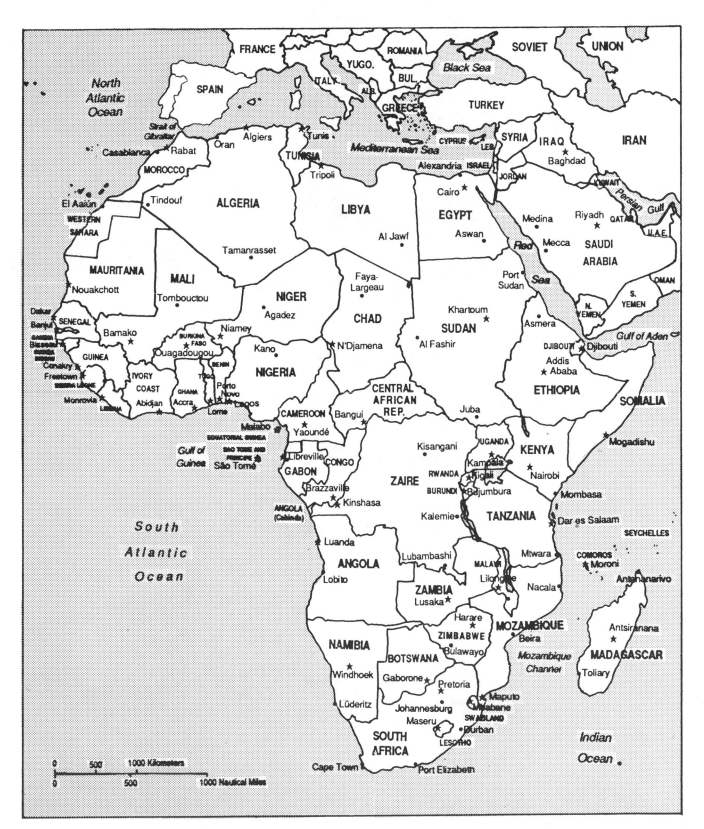

# EUROPE

# ASIA

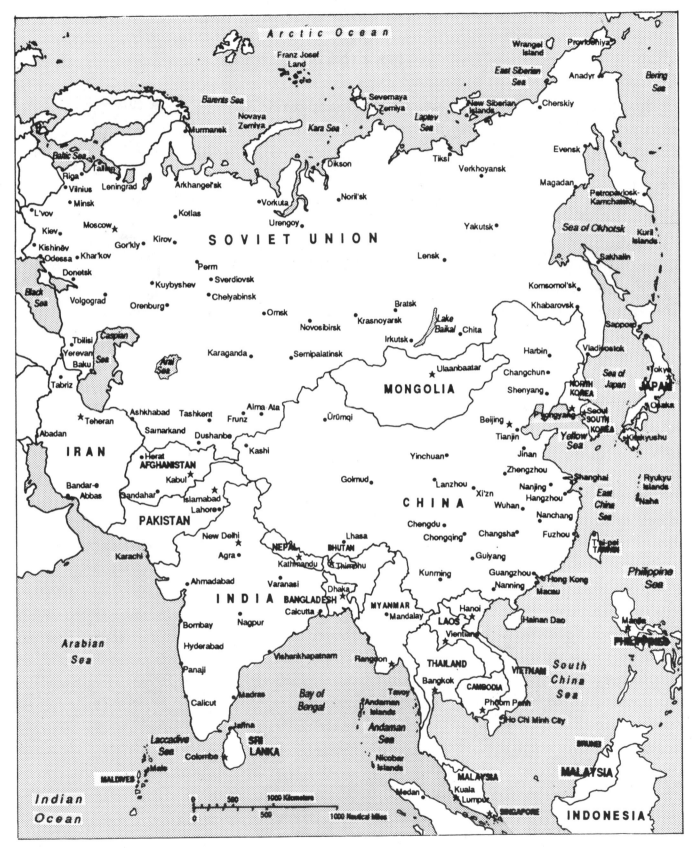

# AUSTRALIA

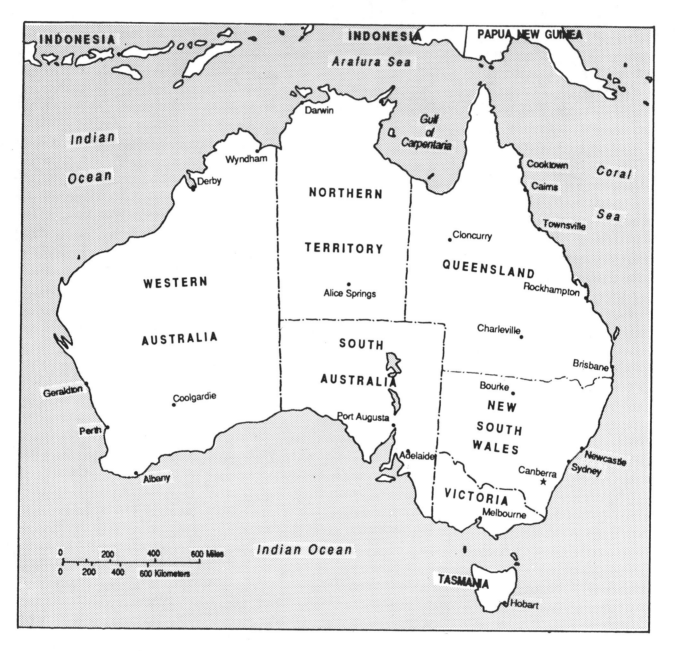

# LIBRARIES AND BOOKS

# THE GLOBE

The **globe** is a model of the earth.

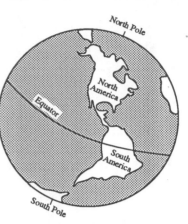

The **North Pole** and **South Pole** are imaginary points. An imaginary line from the North Pole to the South Pole through the center of the earth is the **axis** on which the earth rotates, or spins.

The **equator** is an imaginary line that circles the globe halfway between the North and South Poles. It divides the earth into two halves, called **hemispheres**.

The **northern hemisphere** is the half with the North Pole.

The **southern hemisphere** is the half with the South Pole.

The earth is also divided into Eastern and Western Hemispheres. The imaginary dividing lines are the **Prime Meridian**, which runs through Greenwich, England, and the **International Date Line**, which is exactly halfway around the world from Greenwich.

The **western hemisphere** contains North and South America.

The **eastern hemisphere** contains most of Africa, Asia, Europe and Australia.

Imaginary lines of **latitude** and **longitude** can be used to locate places on the globe.

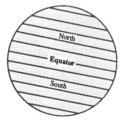

Lines of latitude, or parallels, tell how far north or south of the equator a place is. The equator is 0° latitude. The North Pole is 90° north latitude (90° N) and the South Pole is 90° south latitude (90° S).

Lines of longitude, or meridians, go around the globe through the North and South Poles. They measure distance east and west of the Prime Meridian. The Prime Meridian is 0° longitude. The International Date Line is 180° longitude.

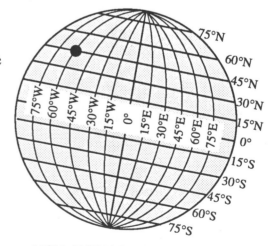

45°N 60°W identifies an exact place on the earth.

# READING MAPS

**Maps** are drawings of the earth's surface that use lines, color and symbols to give information about the location of things. They are more useful than globes because they are easier to carry and store, and because they can show more detail about small areas of the earth than a globe.

Since the earth is round and a map is flat, a map of the world will have distortions. Map makers use different **projections** to "flatten" the earth's surface.

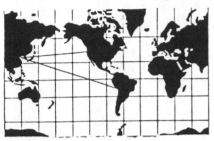

Mercator projection

Robinson projection

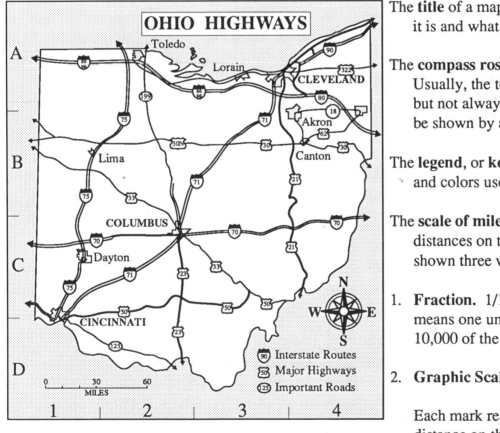

Azimuthal Equidistant

## FEATURES OF A MAP

The **title** of a map tells what kind of map it is and what area it covers.

The **compass rose** shows direction. Usually, the top of the map is north, but not always. Direction may also be shown by an arrow pointing north.

The **legend**, or **key** explains the symbols and colors used on a map.

The **scale of miles** is used to figure the distances on the map. It can be shown three ways:

1. **Fraction.** 1/10,000 or 1:10,000 means one unit on the map equals 10,000 of the same units on the earth.

2. **Graphic Scale.** 0    5    10    15    MILES

   Each mark represents a certain distance on the earth.

An **index** and **map grid** is used to find specific places on the map. For example, if the index says Lorain is at A3, locate A on the left and 3 at the bottom. Find where the imaginary lines meet and look for Lorain in that area.

3. **Words and Figures**, such as 1 inch = 20 miles.

# ATLASES AND TYPES OF MAPS

An **atlas** is a book of maps. Atlases may also contain a variety of other reference information in the front or back. The following kinds of maps may be included in an atlas.

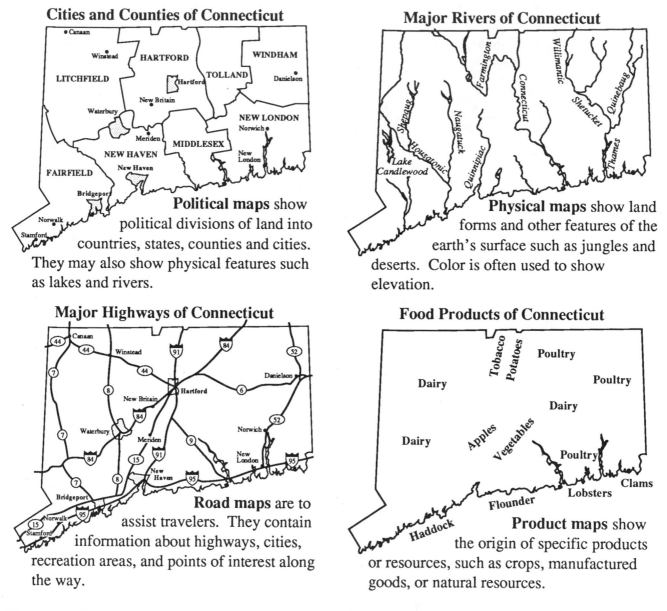

### Cities and Counties of Connecticut

**Political maps** show political divisions of land into countries, states, counties and cities. They may also show physical features such as lakes and rivers.

### Major Rivers of Connecticut

**Physical maps** show land forms and other features of the earth's surface such as jungles and deserts. Color is often used to show elevation.

### Major Highways of Connecticut

**Road maps** are to assist travelers. They contain information about highways, cities, recreation areas, and points of interest along the way.

### Food Products of Connecticut

**Product maps** show the origin of specific products or resources, such as crops, manufactured goods, or natural resources.

**Topographical maps** are very detailed physical maps which use contour lines to show both elevation and steepness of the land. They are often used by hikers.

**Historical maps** give specific information about something in history, such as the routes of explorers, the locations of battles, or the changes in political boundaries over time.

**Population maps** show population density, or people per square mile. **Rainfall maps** use color or shading to show average yearly rainfall of areas on the map. **Temperature maps** use the same techniques to show temperatures. **Weather maps** show weather patterns.

# GRAPHIC AIDS

## GRAPHS

**FAVORITE FRUITS IN ROOM 12**

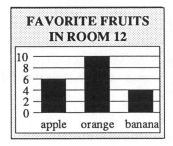

**Pictographs** use symbols or pictures of objects and have keys.

**FAVORITE FRUITS IN ROOM 12**

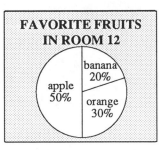

**Circle graphs**, or **pie graphs**, show how parts are related to the whole by percent.

**FAVORITE FRUITS IN ROOM 12**

Bar graph with apple, orange, banana.

**Bar graphs** compare items directly.

**FAVORITE FRUITS IN ROOM 12**

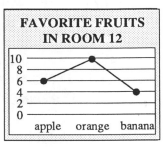

**Line graphs** are best used to show changes over time.

## TIME LINE

**The American Revolution**

Stamp Act March 1765

Boston Massacre March 5, 1770

Boston Tea Party Dec. 16, 1773

Paul Revere's Ride April 1775

Declaration of Independence July 4, 1776

Victory at Saratoga Oct. 17, 1777

Washington's Winter at Valley Forge 1777-78

British surrender Oct. 9, 1781

1766  1767  1768  1769  1770  1771  1772  1773  1774  1775  1776  1777  1778  1779  1780  1781  1782

A **time line** shows time spans between historical events. It shows what happened, when it happened, the time between events, and other important things that happened at about the same time.

## DIAGRAM

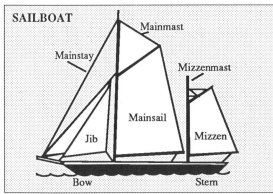

SAILBOAT — Mainmast, Mainstay, Mizzenmast, Mainsail, Jib, Mizzen, Bow, Stern

A **diagram** is a drawing that shows how something works or shows the relationship between its parts. Often, there are labels that name the parts and/or arrows to show the direction or movement of the parts.

## TABLE

| Most Populous Countries | |
|---|---|
| Country | Population |
| 1. China | 1,119,877,000 |
| 2. India | 853,373,000 |
| 3. USSR | 290,938,000 |
| 4. United States | 251,398,000 |
| 5. Indonesia | 189,399,000 |
| 6. Brazil | 150,368,000 |
| 7. Japan | 123,638,000 |
| 8. Nigeria | 118,819,000 |
| 9. Bangladesh | 114,783,000 |
| 10. Pakistan | 114,649,000 |

A **table** presents information in columns and rows.

## SCHEDULE

| DAILY SCHEDULE | |
|---|---|
| 7:45 - 8:00 | Homeroom |
| 8:00 - 8:50 | Math |
| 9:00 - 9:50 | Physical Ed. |
| 10:00 - 10:50 | Geography |
| 11:00 - 11:50 | Science |
| 12:00 - 12:50 | Lunch |
| 1:00 - 1:50 | Band |
| 2:00 - 2:50 | English |
| 3:00 - 4:00 | Track |

A **schedule**, or **timetable**, shows when events are going to occur.

**Photographs, cartoons, illustrations,** and **charts** are also graphic aids.

# THE LIBRARY

A **library** is a place where books, magazines, records and other information resources are kept. People may use these materials in the library and/or check them out. Many people share the library, and it is important for everyone to be considerate of others by being quiet and by taking good care of books and materials. The most important library in the United States is the Library of Congress in Washington, D.C. It has over 84 million items in 470 languages. Since 1870, the Library of Congress has received 2 free copies of every book copyrighted in the United States.

## LIBRARY ORGANIZATION

Most libraries have a catalog, stacks of books, a reference section, a periodical section and a vertical file. Libraries also have other collections of information in many formats, such as maps, films, audio and videotapes, microfiche and microfilm.

The **catalog** is the key to locating books in a library. It contains an alphabetical arrangement of **author entries**, **title entries** and **subject entries**. Letters on the front of each drawer in a **card catalog** indicate which alphabetical group of cards are in that drawer. Modern libraries often have **microfilm readers** or **computers** as the catalog. When using the catalog, note on a piece of paper the call numbers for any resources you wish to find.

The **author entry** is the main entry. **Title entries** and **subject entries** are copies of the

## CARD CATALOG

Modern libraries have computers or microfilm readers in place of the card catalog.

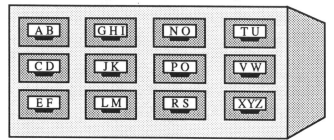

author entry. The title entry may be used whenever the name of the book is known. Subject entries are useful for finding the materials a library contains on any subject. Never look up a title or subject under the words "a", "an" or "the." Look under the next word in the title or subject.

**Cross-reference entries** refer the user to another place in the catalog for further information.

## EXAMPLE OF AN AUTHOR ENTRY

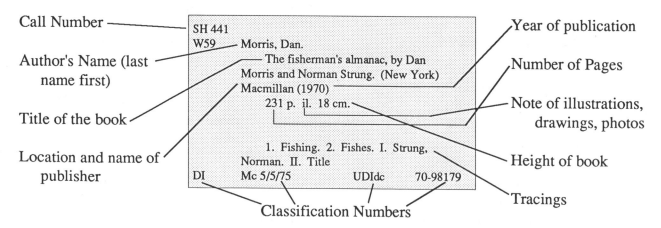

Call Number

Author's Name (last name first)

Title of the book

Location and name of publisher

SH 441
W59 — Morris, Dan.
— The fisherman's almanac, by Dan
Morris and Norman Strung. (New York)
Macmillan (1970)
231 p. il. 18 cm.

1. Fishing. 2. Fishes. I. Strung, Norman. II. Title
DI      Mc 5/5/75          UDIdc          70-98179

Year of publication

Number of Pages

Note of illustrations, drawings, photos

Height of book

Tracings

Classification Numbers

The **stacks** are the shelves of books. Call numbers on the ends of the stacks aid in quickly finding the section with the book you are seeking. Books are shelved from left to right in order by call number. Most libraries have two main sections in the stacks.

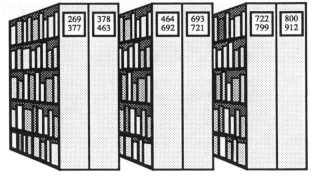

**STACKS**

a. **Fiction books,** or books about imaginary characters and happenings, are shelved in alphabetical order by the author's last name.

b. **Nonfiction books,** or books about real events or factual information, are classified by general subject using the Dewey Decimal System or the Library of Congress classification system.

The **reference section** consists of encyclopedias, atlases, almanacs, dictionaries and other reference sources. Many libraries do not allow reference books to be checked out.

**Periodicals** such as magazines and newspapers are generally kept together in a special section. Periodical indexes are often kept in the reference section.

The **vertical file** consists of filing cabinets with folders on various subjects. Pamphlets, newspaper articles, brochures, photographs and other materials not sturdy enough for the regular shelf may be filed by subject in the vertical file.

## DEWEY DECIMAL SYSTEM

| | |
|---|---|
| 000-099 | General works (encyclopedias, bibliographies, periodicals) |
| 100-199 | Philosophy and Related Disciplines (psychology, logic) |
| 200-299 | Religion |
| 300-399 | Social Sciences (economics, sociology, civics, law, education, vocations, customs) |
| 400-499 | Language (language, dictionaries, grammar) |
| 500-599 | Pure Sciences (mathematics, astronomy, physics, chemistry, geology, biology) |
| 600-699 | Technology (medicine, engineering, agriculture, home economics, business, radio, television, aviation) |
| 700-799 | The Arts (architecture, sculpture, painting, music, photography, recreation) |
| 800-899 | Literature (novels, poetry, plays, criticism) |
| 900-999 | General Geography and History |

## LIBRARY OF CONGRESS CLASSIFICATION SYSTEM

| | |
|---|---|
| A | General Works |
| B | Philosophy, Psychology, Religion |
| C–F | History |
| G | Geography, Anthropology, Recreation |
| H | Social Science |
| J | Political Science |
| K | Law |
| L | Education |
| M | Music |
| N | Fine Arts |
| P | Language and Literature |
| Q | Science |
| R | Medicine |
| S | Agriculture |
| T | Technology |
| U | Military Science |
| V | Naval Science |
| Z | Bibliography and Library Science |

# PARTS OF A BOOK

The main parts of a book are the front matter, the text, and the back matter.

The **front matter** includes the title page, copyright page, dedication, acknowledgements, preface, foreword or introduction, and the table of contents.

## TITLE PAGE

The **title** is the name of the book.

The **author** is the person who wrote the book. Some books do not have an author, but instead have an **editor,** who is the person who put the book together.

The **publisher** is the company which printed the book.

The **place of publication** is where the book was printed. Sometimes several places are listed. The first place listed is generally where the book was published.

## COPYRIGHT PAGE

The **copyright notice** tells when the book was published and who owns the rights to the book. If there is more than one date, the most recent one is the most important. A copyright keeps people from legally copying books instead of buying them. It also keeps people from copying and selling the work of another person. In some cases, it is very important to use books with a recent copyright date in order to get the most accurate facts and information possible.

Copyright © 1987 by Travel Time, Inc.

All rights reserved. No part of this work may be reproduced or transmitted in any form or by any means, electronic or mechanical, including photocopying and recording, or by any information storage or retrieval system, except as may be expressly permitted by the 1976 Copyright Act or in writing from the publisher. Requests for permission should be addressed in writing to Travel Time, Inc., 5826 First Street, New York, New York 02183.

**Dedication.** Some authors dedicate their books to someone special in their lives, usually the person who inspired them to write the book or someone in their family. Some books do not have a dedication.

**Acknowledgements.** This is a section to thank people who helped with the book.

**Preface/Foreword/Introduction.** This is generally a message from the author to the reader, telling the background of the book or the reason it was written.

# TABLE OF CONTENTS

The **table of contents** lists chapters or sections of the book in order and tells the page number of each. Scanning the table of contents can give a reader a good general sense of what is in the book.

# TEXT

The **text** is the main part of the book, the written words with the author's message. The text may contain graphic aids, such as pictures, graphs, etc. as well as words. Some books have chapter titles, headings and subheadings which are part of the text.

CHAPTER 5

*The Steaming Jungle*

We waited in Bumba, Zaire, for several days for the ferry to Kisingani. It would cut off miles of very bad road, and was supposed to be a highlight of the trip, three days on the Zaire River, formerly known as the Congo, traveling with the local people.

The ferry has no time schedule. It goes up and down the river, arriving when it arrives and not before. Prospects didn't look good. So we arranged an alternative, a two-day excursion out on the Zaire River in the only boat in town available for hire. We could camp on an island and return by a different route. For $6.00 a person, it sounded great!

The **back matter** may contain an appendix, glossary, bibliography, and/or index.

The **appendix** contains any charts, notes, lists, diagrams, maps or tables that the author did not include in the main text.

> **Appendix:** List of Important Gear
>
> | | |
> |---|---|
> | Backpack | Small pouch |
> | Daypack | Small towel and washcloth |
> | Small camp stove | Razors |
> | Lighter or matches | Soap and shampoo |
> | Frying pan | Toothbrush |

The **glossary** is a list of the special words used in the book and their definitions. It is like a mini-dictionary.

> **Glossary**
>
> **baksheesh**—a tip, gratuity, or alms. It is from an Arab word meaning "share the wealth."
> **hajj**—a pilgrimage to Mecca, the Moslem holy city. Every Moslem is supposed to make this journey once in a lifetime.

The **bibliography** is a list of books with their authors, publishers, and dates of publication. A bibliography may list the books an author referred to while writing the book, or it could list books recommended for further reading.

> **Bibliography**
>
> Ellis, William S. "Africa's Stricken Sahel," *National Geographic,* Vol. 172, No. 2 (August 1987), p. 140.
> Grove, A.T. *Africa.* Oxford, N.Y.: Oxford University Press, 1978.

# INDEX

The **index** is a detailed list of information in a book, arranged in alphabetical order with page numbers. To find specific information in a book, think of the key words which describe your subject and look for them in the index.

> **Index**
>
> | | |
> |---|---|
> | Beggars, 62-63, 98. | Markets, 61, 77-79. |
> | Camels, desert adaptations, 79, riding, 83-84. | Photography, tips for good photos, 7, 10, 63-68, permits, 82. See also FILM. |
> | Cave paintings, 80, 83. | Poaching, 91. |
> | Cooking, 64-65, 98. | Pygmies, 105-108. |
> | Customs, regulations and | |
> | 48, | |
> | Deser | |
> | Disea | |
> | 38, | |
> | ag | |
> | me | |
> | See also MALARIA. | snake charmers, 63-65, safety precautions, 58, 94. See also REPTILES. |
> | Film, availability, 42, 86. | |
> | Languages, phrases, 30, difficulties, 69, 94. | Tamanrasset, 87-90. |
> | Malaria, 98-100. | Theft, 67, 95-98, |
>
> **Photography**, 25-28, tips for good photos, 7, 10, 63-68, permits, 82. See also FILM.

The **topic,** "**Photography,**" is the main heading.

**Subtopics** break topics into smaller divisions and are to help the reader more quickly find specific information. The subtopics in this entry are "tips for good photos" and "permits."

A **dash** between page numbers means "through." "25-33" means page 25 through page 28.

A **comma** between page numbers means "and." "7, 10" means page 7 and page 10.

A **cross-reference** refers the reader to another topic.

# ENCYCLOPEDIA

An **encyclopedia** is a book or set of books which contains articles on many subjects in alphabetical order. It is useful for brief, general information on many subjects. Encyclopedias often list books or other resources for more in-depth information.

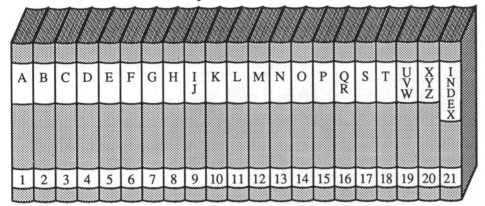

**Volume numbers** help keep the books shelved in order.

**Guide letters** help in quickly finding the correct volume for any subject.

The **index** lists all encyclopedia articles that contain information about a subject. It tells the volume and page number for each article, and helps in locating articles besides the main entry which have information on a subject.

## ADAMS

**ADAMS, JOHN QUINCY** (1767-1848), was the sixth president of the United States. He also served as secretary of state from 1817-25 and was an eight-term member of the U.S. House of Representatives.

**Early Career.** John Quincy Adams was born in Massachusetts, the son of John Adams, the second U.S. president. He was very bright, and at the age of only 14, he was working as a French translator for the U.S. minister to Russia. He was his father's secretary in 1783, during the peace negotiations which ended the American Revolution. He graduated from Harvard College in 1787 and opened a law office in Boston.

He married Louisa Catherine Johnson in 1797, and was elected to the Massachusetts Senate in 1801. Two years later, he was elected to the U.S. Senate.

**Secretary of State.** In 1817, President James Monroe appointed Adams secretary of state. Adams worked with Monroe to force Spain to cede Florida and to make a favorable settlement with France on the Louisiana boundary.

**President.** Adams ran against three other men for president in 1824. None of the candidates won a majority in the electoral college, so the race was decided by the House of

15

Representatives. Although Adams was chosen, the supporters of the other candidates made it difficult for Adams to get the support he

*John Quincy Adams*

needed from Congress to carry out many of his plans as President. In the 1828 elections, he was overwhelmingly defeated by Andrew Jackson.

**Later Congressional Service.** Two years after his term as president ended, Adams was elected to the House of Representatives, where he served eight terms. He was an eloquent speaker. On February 21, 1848, he suffered a stroke on the floor of the House, and died two days later.

**Related articles:** Presidents of the U.S.

**Additional Resources**

Hecht, Marie B. *John Quincy Adams: A Personal History of an Independent Man.* Macmillan, 1972.
Lipsky, George A. *John Quincy Adams: His Theory and Ideas.* Harper, 1965.

**ADDIS ABABA,** is the capital and largest city of Ethiopia. It is located on a plateau in central Ethiopia and is about 8000 feet above sea level. Its population is approximately 1,500,000.

See also ETHIOPIA.

**ADDITION.** See ARITHMETIC.

**Guide words** show the first and last article listed on each set of facing pages. They help in quickly locating articles.

**Illustrations** are graphic aids.

**Sections** and **headings** divide longer articles into shorter segments. They may be quickly scanned to locate answers to questions.

**Related articles** refer the reader to additional articles.

**Additional resources** are listed at the end of some articles, and refer the reader to other books.

**Cross references** refer the reader to an article of a different title.

A **yearbook** may be issued each year to update old encyclopedias. It has information from the past year.

# DICTIONARY

A **dictionary** is a book alphabetically listing words and giving information about each word. An **unabridged dictionary** lists all or nearly all English words. There are more than 600,000 words in English, and such a book is very large. Most dictionaries are **abridged**, and list only words which occur fairly frequently.

**Guide words** tell the first and last words on the page. They are useful for quickly finding the page on which a word will be listed.

The **entry** is in bold face type. It shows the correct spelling and syllabication of the word.

The **phonetic spelling**, in parentheses, uses letters and symbols from the pronunciation key to show how the word is pronounced. The accent mark shows which syllable(s) to stress when saying the word.

ra·tion·al·ize (rash′ə nᵊliz′), v., ra·tion·al·ized, ra·tion·al·iz·ing. 1. to explain (an act, behavior, etc.) in a favorable and seemingly reasonable way while avoiding the true reason, which one is unwilling to admit: *to rationalize stinginess by calling it thrift.* 2. to explain (something supernatural or the like) according to reason or natural laws: *to rationalize a miracle.* —ra′tion·al·i·za′tion, n. —ra′tion·al·iz′er, n.

Reprinted by permission from the Random House Dictionary of the English Language, School Edition. ©1984 by Random House, Inc.

**Illustrations** are pictures.

An abbreviation shows **part of speech**. Many words have more than one part of speech, depending on how they are used.

| | |
|---|---|
| *n.* | noun |
| *pron.* | pronoun |
| *adj.* | adjective |
| *v.* | verb |
| *adv.* | adverb |
| *prep.* | preposition |
| *conj.* | conjunction |
| *interj.* | interjection |

**Inflected forms** are other words made from the same root word (such as run, ran, running).

The **pronunciation key** tells what sounds are represented by the symbols used in phonetic spellings. This page has a short version of a complete pronunciation key, which would be found at the beginning of the dictionary.

**Definitions** are explanations of what the word means. Words may have more than one definition and the user must choose the correct one based on how the word was used.

**Examples** such as sentences or phrases illustrate correct usage of the word.

Some dictionaries also show etymology, or the history of the word, as well as synonyms and antonyms. Besides information on words, a dictionary may have useful general information, such as tables of weights and measures, lists of colleges, maps, and lists of famous people. This information is generally in the front or the back of a dictionary.

# ALMANAC AND THESAURUS

An **almanac** is a collection of facts and information such as calendars, statistics, movements of heavenly bodies, and outstanding dates and events. Many almanacs are published once a year with current information. Tables and charts are often used to save space. Specific information in an almanac can be found by using the index.

> Poor Richard's Almanac was written and published by Benjamin Franklin yearly from 1733-1758. In each almanac, there were proverbs, many of which are well known today:
> *Haste makes waste.*
> *A penny saved is a penny earned.*
> *God helps them that help themselves.*

A **thesaurus** is a book of synonyms and antonyms. It is helpful to a writer who wants to find exactly the right word or who wants to vary words instead of using the same ones over and over.

## MINI THESAURUS

**big -** large, huge, gigantic, bulky, great, vast, extensive, enormous, immense, colossal

**fast -** quick, swift, speedy, rapid, hasty, snappy

**fly -** soar, hover, flit, waft, glide, wing

**funny -** humorous, amusing, comical, silly, laughable

**get -** acquire, obtain, secure, procure, fetch, find, win, earn, collect, gather

**good -** excellent, fine, superior, wonderful, marvelous, splendid, great, grand, superb

**happy -** pleased, contented, satisfied, delighted, elated, overjoyed, tickled, glad

**hate -** despise, loathe, detest, abhor, dislike

**have -** possess, own

**hide -** conceal, cover, mask, camouflage, screen, shroud, veil

**hurry -** rush, speed, hasten, bustle

**hurt -** damage, harm, injure, wound

**interesting -** fascinating, intriguing, thought-provoking, inspiring, moving, exciting, entertaining, appealing

**little -** tiny, small, miniature, puny, dinky, microscopic, minute, petite

**look -** gaze, glance, watch, survey, study, seek, peek, glimpse, stare, contemplate, examine, gape, scrutinize, inspect, behold, observe, view, witness, peer, gawk

**place -** space, area, spot, region, location, site

**quiet -** silent, still, soundless, mute, tranquil, peaceful, calm, restful

**said -** asked, answered, exclaimed, replied, repeated, insisted, roared, protested, remarked, stammered, announced, drawled, stated, echoed, sighed, whispered, murmured, commanded, ordered, demanded, grumbled, muttered, snarled, hissed, growled, snapped, moaned, mumbled, pleaded, whimpered, whined, yelled, screamed, howled, shouted, squeaked, squealed, laughed, chuckled, giggled

**scared -** afraid, frightened, alarmed, terrified, petrified, paralyzed

**slow -** unhurried, leisurely, gradual

**stop -** cease, halt, discontinue, end, finish, quit

**walk -** plod, creep, crawl, inch, drag, toddle, shuffle, trot, dawdle, jog, plug, trudge, stump, lumber, trail, run, sprint, bound, streak, stride, breeze, rush, dash, dart, bolt, scamper, scurry, scoot, scuttle, scramble, race, hasten, hurry, gallop, lope, wander, roam, trek, slip, glide, slither, saunter, hobble, amble, stagger, slouch, prance, straggle, meander, waddle, wobble, stroll, swagger, lunge, race, spring, dash, flee

# NEWSPAPER

A **newspaper** is a daily or weekly publication which is made up of loose pieces of paper folded together. It contains up-to-date news and information on a large variety of subjects of interest. In fact, newspapers contain the most up-to-date information on the widest variety of subjects. Although some newspapers are saved on microfiche for later reference, most are not indexed. The **New York Times Index** can be used to find articles in that newspaper.

Newspapers are generally printed in several **sections**, folded separately.

The **banner** is the place where the newspaper's name is printed. It contains the date the paper was printed and the price.

The **headlines** are printed in large letters over an article and tell what the article is about. Headlines may be scanned to find articles of interest.

The **lead story** is the front page news which the editor feels would be of most interest to most people, so the paper will sell well.

**Pictures** highlight the important news and contain **captions** which tell briefly what the picture is about.

The **index** is usually found on the first or second page of a newspaper. It tells where to find various features of the newspaper by section and page number.

---

| **Rafting the Mighty Matanuska** Sports D-1 | **Anchorage Teachers SPEAK OUT about Education** Opinions E-3 | **How to BEAT the High Cost of Housing** Lifestyles F-1 |
| --- | --- | --- |

The Susan C. Anthony

# *Chronicle*

Christmas 1984    Anchorage, Alaska    Price: $1.00

## Car Demolished by Unmanned Vehicle

*December 8, 1983*—A beige 1977 Subaru station wagon, owned by Mrs. Susan Anthony, was repeatedly bashed and knocked 45' across a median by an unmanned Eagle in the back parking lot of Chinook Elementary School, where Mrs. Anthony is employed.

The Eagle, owned by PTA Executive Board member Kay Smithe, had been parked across from Anthony's car and left idling in neutral. An 11 year old girl waiting in the car presumably knocked the Eagle into reverse. It took off at a high speed in a tight circle, crashing into the Subaru's door, then circling around and around, hitting it again and again. The Subaru bounced against another car, owned by Mrs. Nancy Brandt-Erichsen, and caused $1500 damage to it.

The child had jumped out of the car and run to "get help." Mrs. Smithe, seeing the situation, panicked and ran to try and stop her car. It was going too fast for her to get in the open door. She was knocked down and her legs were run over. Not seriously hurt, she got up to try again. Finally, after several attempts, she wedged her feet under the tire and brought the car to a stop.

Although the Subaru still ran, body damage was estimated at over $3000.00.

The Eagle sustained slight damage to the rear bumper and a broken tail light.

One onlooker commented, "I guess it really *is* true that American cars are better built."

Another, musing, suggested that the Eagle may have mistaken Anthony's car for a Rabbit.

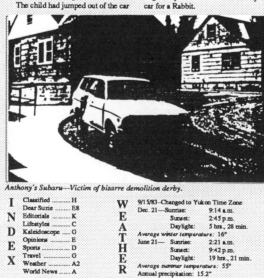

*Anthony's Subaru—Victim of bizarre demolition derby.*

### Freak Accident Just The Beginning...

*December 9*—Subaru's body damage estimated at $3000.
*December 14*—Insurance company refused to pay more than $1950 for totaled car.
*December 16*—Replacement vehicle bought for $1995-blue 1977 Subaru station wagon with 50,000 miles.
*January 3*—New hood ordered for blue car for $100. (Old hood was buckled.)
*February 16*—Fuse for headlights burned out. Car was rendered unusable on the big morning of Mrs. Anthony's first inservice presentation to teachers.
*March 6*—Accelerator stuck and blue car took off. The road was black ice, with cars and a stop sign ahead. The car crashed into a large snowbank, turned on its side and then righted itself, perched atop 5' of snow and ice.
*March 7*—Mechanics informed Mrs. Anthony that blue car had no compression in one cylinder and needed a valve job.
*March 11*—Traffic light turned too fast.
*March 22*—Driver's Ed. class taken to cancel traffic ticket.
*April 5*—Insurance company released a check for $1950. Windshield wiper fell off during a heavy rain.
*May*—Blue car sent to Mr. Alton Smith, who agreed to replace the engine for $700. The newly installed engine had no power and backfired. Smith spent 4 months trying to fix it, taking the engine out and replacing it 5 times, having it computer analyzed and checked by other mechanics. No luck.
*June 20*—Gear shift lever on beige car pulled out by the roots on the morning before a planned trip to Fairbanks. Mr. Smith fixed it at no charge, apologizing for the delay on the other car.
*September 2*—Smith informed Anthony that the blue car was ready for pickup. He had finally bought another car and transferred the engine.
*September 7*—Blue car was picked up-complete with new engine and new hood.
*September 8*—Hood latch came loose at 45 mph. Hood flew up and buckled over top of car. Car had a flat tire within hours.
*September 9*—Windshield of beige car demolished by an unhitched trailer.
*September 19*—Brand new 1984 Subaru 4wd station wagon purchased, covered by 5-yr. warranty and comprehensive insurance. Whew!
*(Hopefully NOT "To Be Continued")*

**I N D E X**

| | |
| --- | --- |
| Classified | H |
| Dear Suzie | E8 |
| Editorials | K |
| Lifestyles | C |
| Kaleidoscope | G |
| Opinions | E |
| Sports | D |
| Travel | G |
| Weather | A2 |
| World News | A |

**W E A T H E R**

9/15/83—Changed to Yukon Time Zone
Dec. 21—Sunrise:  9:14 a.m.
         Sunset:   2:45 p.m.
         Daylight: 5 hrs., 28 min.
*Average winter temperature:* 16°
June 21— Sunrise:  2:21 a.m.
         Sunset:   9:42 p.m.
         Daylight: 19 hrs., 21 min.
*Average summer temperature:* 55°
Annual precipitation: 15.2"

# ORGANIZATION OF A NEWSPAPER

Newspapers contain four major types of information: news, opinions, features and advertisements.

I. **News** is factual information about things that have happened. Its purpose is to keep readers informed. A news story answers six basic questions: who, what, where, when, how and why in the first paragraph. The rest of the article gives details and more in-depth information. Minor details are saved for last in case the story has to be cut in length to fit in the paper.

   A. **Headline news**
      1. World and National News is sent by wire services over Teletype and telephoto machines. The chief wire services in the United States are UPI (United Press International) and AP (Associated Press)
      2. State and Local News is written by reporters of the newspaper

   B. **News which is covered daily**
      1. Sports
      2. Weather
      3. Vital Statistics—births, deaths, engagements, marriages, divorces
      4. Entertainment—TV guide, movies, plays, symphonies, etc.
      5. Business—stock market index, foreign currency exchange rates
      6. Crime—police report and court report
      7. Announcements—community meetings, etc.

II. **Opinions** are written by the editor or others to try to persuade the reader to see and take the point of view of the writer.

   A. **Editorials**

   B. **Letters to the Editor** may be written by anyone. The address for writing to the editor is on the page where these letters are printed.

   C. **Political cartoons**

III. **Features** are articles written to entertain or inform the reader.
   A. Travel
   B. Health
   C. Real Estate
   D. Finance
   E. Food
   F. Lifestyles
   G. Humor
   H. Human Interest
   I. Gardening
   J. Cartoons, Crosswords, Puzzles
   K. Advice Columns

IV. **Advertisements** are a major source of income for a newspaper. Companies or individuals pay for ads.

   A. **Display ads** are generally paid for by a business.

   B. **Classified ads,** or want ads, are often paid for by individuals.
      1. Personals
      2. Lost and Found
      3. Jobs
      4. Services
      5. For Sale (houses, cars, land, equipment)
      6. For Rent
      7. Legal Notices

# PERIODICALS

**Periodicals**, or **magazines**, are publications that appear regularly but not every day. They contain articles and stories of current interest, and are generally illustrated and have many advertisements. They are a good source of up-to-date information.

Over 25,000 periodicals are published in the United States. The five which have the largest circulations are Modern Maturity, NRTA/AARP News Bulletin, Reader's Digest, TV Guide, and National Geographic Magazine.

Information can be located in a periodical by referring to an **index**. Some indexes, such as those listed below, are in book form. Others are published on microfiche or may be found on a computer. Indexes are kept in the reference department of most libraries.

## READER'S GUIDE

The **Reader's Guide to Periodical Literature** is an index to articles published in common magazines. One hardbound book is issued each year and there is a small supplement for each month during the year.

> **DRUG abuse**
> Broader attack on drug abuse, to dry up the flow of drugs. il U S News 68:38 Mr 23 '70

**Entry.** DRUG abuse. Alphabetized by subject.
**Title of article.** Broader attack on drug abuse, to dry up the flow of drugs.
il means the article is illustrated.
**Periodical name.** U S News. Names are abbreviated to save space. A key is in the front of the index.
**Volume, page number.** 68:38
**Date.** Mr 23 '70, abbreviation for March 23, 1970

## NATIONAL GEOGRAPHIC INDEX

The **National Geographic Index** lists articles found in the National Geographic magazine. Only a few hardbound editions have been printed. There is a small supplement for each year since the last hardbound edition.

> **HUMMINGBIRDS**
> The Man Who Talks to Hummingbirds. By Luis Marden. Photos by James Blair. 80-99, Jan 1963

**Entry.** HUMMINGBIRDS. Alphabetized by subject.
**Title of article.** The Man Who Talks to Hummingbirds
**Author.** Luis Marden
**Photographer.** James Blair
**Pages.** 80-99
**Date of Magazine.** January 1963

# TELEPHONE DIRECTORY

A **telephone directory** lists names, addresses and phone numbers of individuals and businesses. It also contains advertisements and listings for government agencies.

Most telephone books contain useful information in the front of the book including the rates at various times of the day (it is cheaper to call long distance at night). They also contain white pages, yellow pages, and blue pages. The **white pages** list businesses and individuals alphabetically by last name. They are most useful if you know the name of the person or business you want to call. The **yellow pages** are arranged by subject and contain advertisements. They are most useful if you need a product or service and want to find out where to go. The **blue pages** contain government listings, and are organized by level of government and agency.

**The White Pages**

Martin R C  280 Maple Ct........428-6915

**The Yellow Pages**

**MUSIC MAN**
FINE HAND CRAFTED
INSTRUMENTS
DISCOUNTS AND RENTALS
See Our Ad at Music Instruction
2890 W 80th Ave..........479-2836

## SPECIAL NUMBERS

**911**  Emergency number, to be used only when human life or property is in danger.

**0**  Operator. The operator can help if you have trouble placing a call, or if you wish to call collect or bill your call to another number.

**411**  Directory Assistance. This is useful if there is no telephone directory nearby or if the number has just been listed.

**(Area code) 555-1212**  Long distance information. Area codes for places in the United States are generally listed in the front of the phone directory.

## HOT LINES

Runaway Hot Line. 800-231-6946. Gives referrals to shelter, counseling, medical help, etc., and sends messages home without revealing a runaway's location.

Child Find of America. 800-I-AM-LOST. Help for lost or kidnapped children.

Crime Tips Hot Line, WeTIP. 800-73-CRIME. Anonymous tips are relayed to police. The purpose is to eliminate major crime and drug trafficking. Arrests will be made only after a full police investigation.

**Note:** In many places, you must dial **1** before long distance, 800 and special numbers.

## LONG DISTANCE CALLS AND SERVICES

**Person-to-person calls** may be made if you wish to talk with a certain person. You are not charged if the person is not there.

**Station-to-station calls** are less expensive than person-to-person calls.

**Direct dialed calls** are those a person dials without the help of an operator. A direct dialed, station-to-station call between 11:00 p.m. and 8:00 a.m. weekdays or anytime on weekends is the least expensive kind of call.

**Operator assisted calls** are more expensive than direct dialing, but are necessary when you wish to call collect, bill the call to your home number, or have the operator give you time and charges for your call.

# TYPES OF LITERATURE

**Fiction** is literature with imaginary characters and events. It is made up by the author.

**Poetry** is a form of literature which expresses experiences, ideas or emotions in a powerful, concentrated and imaginative style. Many poems are written with rhyme and rhythm. Poems may also be written in *free verse,* without a set rhythm.

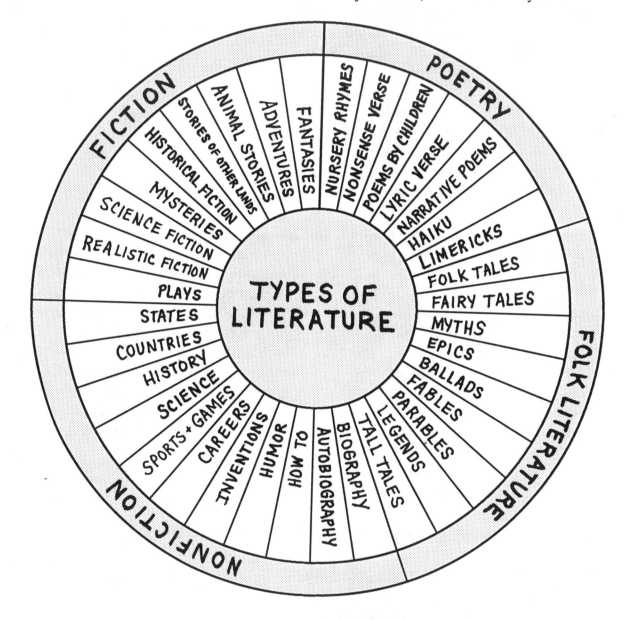

**Nonfiction** is literature about real events and people or factual information. It is not made up by the author.

**Folk literature** is based on the traditional beliefs and stories of a group of people. Most folk literature was passed down by word of mouth from generation to generation before being written down.

# STORY ELEMENTS

## CHARACTERS

**Characters** are the people in the story. **Main characters** are the most important people, and generally face a problem which must be resolved. **Minor characters** are people who have little to do with the main action of the story. Authors create characters by describing their looks, speech, thoughts, actions, attitudes and motives.

## SETTING

**Setting** is the place and time in which a story takes place. The place could be, for example, in the country, in the city, in outer space, or in a fantasy land. The time may be the time of day, season, or a time in history. A story is always set in the past, the present, or the future.

## STYLE

An author's **style** is his way of using words.

## PLOT

The **plot** is the action of a story, or what happens in the story. It is built around a series of **events,** or happenings. A plot generally has four parts:

1. **Exposition**—the background and situation of the story.
2. **Rising action**—events which create suspense in the reader.
3. **Climax**—the highest point of interest, at which time the outcome becomes clear.
4. **Denouement**—the end or conclusion of the story.

## THEME

The **theme** is the basic idea or statement about life which the author wishes to convey. For example, a story could show that crime doesn't pay, that standing up for what you believe is worthwhile, or that an individual can make a difference in the world.

# BOOKS IN SERIES

**The Chronicles of Narnia**
by C.S. Lewis
1. The Lion, the Witch and the Wardrobe
2. Prince Caspian
3. The Voyage of the "Dawn Treader"
4. The Silver Chair
5. The Horse and His Boy
6. The Magician's Nephew
7. The Last Battle

**The Pooh Books**
by A. A. Milne
1. Winnie the Pooh
2. House at Pooh Corner

**The Lord of the Rings**
by J.R.R. Tolkien
1. The Hobbit
2. The Fellowship of the Ring
3. The Two Towers
4. The Return of the King

**The Prydain Chronicles**
by Lloyd Alexander
1. The Book of Three
2. The Black Cauldron
3. The Castle of Llyr
4. Taran Wanderer
5. The High King

**Little House Books**
by Laura Ingalls Wilder
1. Little House in the Big Woods
2. Little House on the Prairie
3. Farmer Boy
4. On the Banks of Plum Creek
5. By the Shores of Silver Lake
6. The Long Winter
7. Little Town on the Prairie
8. These Happy Golden Years
9. The First Four Years

# CALDECOTT AWARD WINNING BOOKS

Both the Newbery and Caldecott awards were established by Frederic G. Melcher. The Caldecott Medal is awarded annually for the most distinguished picture book for children published during the previous year. It was named after Randolph Caldecott, an English illustrator of children's books. The Newbery Medal is given each year to the most distinguished contribution to American children's literature. It was named after John Newbery, an English publisher and bookseller.

The award-winning illustrators, not the authors, are listed below. Look up the title in a library.

| Year | Illustrator | Title |
|------|-------------|-------|
| 1938 | Dorothy P. Lathrop | Animals of the Bible |
| 1939 | Thomas Handforth | Mei Li |
| 1940 | Ingri & Edgar d'Aulaire | Abraham Lincoln |
| 1941 | Robert Lawson | They Were Strong and Good |
| 1942 | Robert McCloskey | Make Way for Ducklings |
| 1943 | Virginia Lee Burton | The Little House |
| 1944 | Louis Slobodkin | Many Moons |
| 1945 | Elizabeth Orton Jones | Prayer for a Child |
| 1946 | Maude & Miska Petersham | The Rooster Crows |
| 1947 | Leonard Weisgard | The Little Island |
| 1948 | Roger Duvoisin | White Snow, Bright Snow |
| 1949 | Berta & Elmer Hader | The Big Snow |
| 1950 | Leo Politi | Song of the Swallows |
| 1951 | Katherine Milhous | The Egg Tree |
| 1952 | Nicolas Mordvinoff | Finders Keepers |
| 1953 | Lynd K. Ward | The Biggest Bear |
| 1954 | Ludwig Bemelmans | Madeline's Rescue |
| 1955 | Marcia Brown | Cinderella; or The Little Glass Slipper |
| 1956 | Feodor Rojankovsky | Frog Went A-Courtin' |
| 1957 | Marc Simont | A Tree is Nice |
| 1958 | Robert McCloskey | Time of Wonder |
| 1959 | Barbara Cooney | Chanticleer and the Fox |
| 1960 | Marie Hall Ets & Aurora Labastida | Nine Days to Christmas |
| 1961 | Nicolas Sidjakov | Baboushka and the Three Kings |
| 1962 | Marcia Brown | Once a Mouse |
| 1963 | Ezra Jack Keats | The Snowy Day |
| 1964 | Maurice Sendak | Where the Wild Things Are |
| 1965 | Beni Montresor | May I Bring a Friend? |
| 1966 | Nonny Hogrogian | Always Room for One More |
| 1967 | Evaline Ness | Sam, Bangs, & Moonshine |
| 1968 | Ed Emberley | Drummer Hoff |
| 1969 | Uri Shulevitz | The Fool of the World and the Flying Ship |
| 1970 | William Steig | Sylvester and the Magic Pebble |
| 1971 | Gail E. Haley | A Story—A Story |
| 1972 | Nonny Hogrogian | One Fine Day |
| 1973 | Blair Lent | The Funny Little Woman |
| 1974 | Margot Zemach | Duffy and the Devil |
| 1975 | Gerald McDermott | Arrow to the Sun: A Pueblo Indian Tale |
| 1976 | Leo & Diane Dillon | Why Mosquitoes Buzz in People's Ears: A West African Tale |
| 1977 | Leo & Diane Dillon | Ashanti to Zulu: African Traditions |
| 1978 | Peter Spier | Noah's Ark |
| 1979 | Paul Goble | The Girl Who Loved Wild Horses |
| 1980 | Barbara Cooney | Ox-Cart Man |
| 1981 | Arnold Lobel | Fables |
| 1982 | Chris Van Allsburg | Jumanji |
| 1983 | Marcia Brown | Shadow |
| 1984 | Alice and Martin Provensen | The Glorious Flight |
| 1985 | Trina Schart Hyman | St. George and the Dragon |
| 1986 | Chris Van Allsburg | The Polar Express |
| 1987 | Richard Egielski | Hey, Al |
| 1988 | John Schoenherr | Owl Man |
| 1989 | Stephen Gammell | Song and Dance Man |
| 1990 | Ed Young | Lon Po Po |

# NEWBERY AWARD WINNING BOOKS

| Year | Author | Title |
|---|---|---|
| 1922 | Henrik Van Loon | The Story of Mankind |
| 1923 | Hugh Lofting | The Voyages of Dr. Dolittle |
| 1924 | Charles Hawes | The Dark Frigate |
| 1925 | Charles Finger | Tales from Silver Lands |
| 1926 | Arthur Chrisman | Shen of the Sea |
| 1927 | Will James | Smoky, the Cowhorse |
| 1928 | Dhan Mukerji | Gay-Neck, the Story of a Pigeon |
| 1929 | Eric P. Kelly | The Trumpeter of Krakow |
| 1930 | Rachel Field | Hitty, Her First Hundred Years |
| 1931 | Elizabeth Coatsworth | The Cat Who Went to Heaven |
| 1932 | Laura Adams Armer | Waterless Mountain |
| 1933 | Elizabeth Lewis | Yung Fu of the Upper Yangtze |
| 1934 | Cornelia Meigs | Invincible Louisa |
| 1935 | Monica Shannon | Dobry |
| 1936 | Carol Ryrie Brink | Caddie Woodlawn |
| 1937 | Ruth Sawyer | Roller Skates |
| 1938 | Kate Seredy | The White Stag |
| 1939 | Elizabeth Enright | Thimble Summer |
| 1940 | James Daugherty | Daniel Boone |
| 1941 | Armstrong Speery | Call It Courage |
| 1942 | Walter D. Edmonds | The Matchlock Gun |
| 1943 | Elizabeth Janet Gray | Adam of the Road |
| 1944 | Esther Forbes | Johnny Tremain |
| 1945 | Robert Lawson | Rabbit Hill |
| 1946 | Lois Lenski | Strawberry Girl |
| 1947 | Carolyn Bailey | Miss Hickory |
| 1948 | William Pène du Bois | The Twenty-One Balloons |
| 1949 | Marguerite Henry | King of the Wind |
| 1950 | Marguerite de Angeli | The Door in the Wall |
| 1951 | Elizabeth Yates | Amos Fortune, Free Man |
| 1952 | Eleanor Estes | Ginger Pye |
| 1953 | Ann Nolan Clark | Secret of the Andes |
| 1954 | Joseph Krumgold | ...And Now Miguel |
| 1955 | Meindert DeJong | The Wheel on the School |
| 1956 | Jean Lee Latham | Carry On, Mr. Bowditch |
| 1957 | Virginia Sorensen | Miracles on Maple Hill |
| 1958 | Harold V. Keith | Rifles for Watie |
| 1959 | Elizabeth George Speare | The Witch of Blackbird Pond |
| 1960 | Joseph Krumgold | Onion John |
| 1961 | Scott O'Dell | Island of the Blue Dolphins |
| 1962 | Elizabeth George Speare | The Bronze Bow |
| 1963 | Madeleine L'Engle | A Wrinkle in Time |
| 1964 | Emily Neville | It's Like This, Cat |
| 1965 | Maia Wojciechowska | Shadow of a Bull |
| 1966 | Elizabeth Borton de Trevino | I, Juan de Pareja |
| 1967 | Irene Hunt | Up a Road Slowly |
| 1968 | Elaine Konigsburg | From the Mixed-Up Files of Mrs. Basil E. Frankweiler |
| 1969 | Lloyd Alexander | The High King |
| 1970 | William H. Armstrong | Sounder |
| 1971 | Betsy Byars | Summer of the Swans |
| 1972 | Robert C. O'Brien | Mrs. Frisby and the Rats of NIMH |
| 1973 | Jean Craighead George | Julie of the Wolves |
| 1974 | Paula Fox | The Slave Dancer |
| 1975 | Virginia Hamilton | M. C. Higgins, the Great |
| 1976 | Susan Cooper | The Grey King |
| 1977 | Mildred D. Taylor | Roll of Thunder, Hear My Cry |
| 1978 | Katherine Paterson | Bridge to Terabithia |
| 1979 | Ellen Raskin | The Westing Game |
| 1980 | Joan Blos | A Gathering of Days: A New England Girl's Journal |
| 1981 | Katherine Paterson | Jacob Have I Loved |
| 1982 | Nancy Willard | A Visit to William Blake's Inn |
| 1983 | Cynthia Voigt | Dicey's Song |
| 1984 | Beverly Cleary | Dear Mr. Henshaw |
| 1985 | Robin McKinley | The Hero and the Crown |
| 1986 | Patricia MacLachlan | Sarah, Plain and Tall |
| 1987 | Sid Fleischman | The Whipping Boy |
| 1988 | Russell Freedman | Lincoln: A Photobiography |
| 1989 | Paul Fleischman | Joyful Noise: Poems for Two Voices |
| 1990 | Lois Lowry | Number the Stars |

# LONG TIME FAVORITES

| Year | Title | Author |
|------|-------|--------|
| 1883 | The Adventures of Pinocchio | Carlo Collodi |
| 600 B.C. | Aesop's Fables | Aesop |
| 1865 | Alice in Wonderland | Lewis Carroll |
| 1947 | Anne Frank: Diary of a Young Girl | Anne Frank |
| 1908 | Anne of Green Gables | L. M. Montgomery |
| 1873 | Around the World in 80 Days | Jules Verne |
| 1941 | The Black Stallion | Walter Farley |
| 1903 | The Call of the Wild | Jack London |
| 1964 | Charlie and the Chocolate Factory | Roald Dahl |
| 1952 | Charlotte's Web | E. B. White |
| 1855 | Fairy Tales | Hans Christian Anderson |
| 1823 | Grimm's Fairy Tales | Jacob & Wilhelm Grimm |
| 1865 | Hans Brinker, or, The Silver Skates | Mary Elizabeth Mapes Dodge |
| 1881 | Heidi | Johanna Spyri |
| 1966 | The Hobbit | J. R. R. Tolkien |
| 1961 | The Incredible Journey | Sheila Burnford |
| 1902 | Just So Stories | Rudyard Kipling |
| 1886 | Kidnapped | Robert Lewis Stevenson |
| 1950 | The Lion, the Witch and the Wardrobe | C. S. Lewis |
| 1932 | Little House in the Big Woods | Laura Ingalls Wilder |
| 1935 | Little House on the Prairie | Laura Ingalls Wilder |
| 1868 | Little Women | Louisa May Alcott |
| 1934 | Mary Poppins | Pamela L. Travers |
| 1946 | Merry Adventures of Robin Hood | Howard Pyle |
| 1959 | My Side of the Mountain | Jean Craighead George |
| 1904 | Peter Pan | James M. Barrie |
| 1719 | Robinson Crusoe | Daniel Defoe |
| 1911 | The Secret Garden | Frances Hodgson Burnett |
| 1807 | Tales From Shakespeare | Charles & Mary Lamb |
| 1697 | Tales of Mother Goose | Charles Perrault |
| 1901 | Tales of Peter Rabbit | Beatrix Potter |
| 1469 | The Death of (King) Arthur | Sir Thomas Malory |
| 1876 | Tom Sawyer | Mark Twain |
| 1883 | Treasure Island | Robert Lewis Stevenson |
| 1898 | War of the Worlds | H. G. Wells |
| 1972 | Watership Down | Richard Adams |
| 1969 | Where the Lilies Bloom | Vera & Bill Cleaver |
| 1961 | Where the Red Fern Grows | Wilson Rawls |
| 1908 | Wind in the Willows | Kenneth Grahame |
| 1926 | Winnie the Pooh | A. A. Milne |
| 1938 | The Yearling | Marjorie Rawlings |

# THE
# ENGLISH
# LANGUAGE

# THE ALPHABET

An **alphabet** is the letters of a language arranged in order. The word comes from the first two letters of the Greek alphabet, *alpha* and *beta*. Long ago, people could communicate only by speaking or making gestures. Early civilizations, including the Ancient Egyptians, used a system of **hieroglyphic** writing. Many of the early symbols were **pictographs**. For example, a picture of a man would stand for a man. An **ideograph** was a symbol which stood for an idea. Gradually, the system of writing changed so that certain symbols stood for certain sounds. Then the same symbols could be used in many different words. Most modern languages have an alphabet. Chinese and languages based on Chinese never developed alphabets, however. There are about 50,000 **characters**, or symbols, which are used by the Chinese for writing.

The English language developed over a very long time and each letter has its own history. The Romans changed older letter forms into those we use today, and were the first to use small letters and punctuation in writing. English has 26 letters—19 consonants and 5 vowels: *a, e, i, o,* and *u.* Two other letters, *y* and *w,* are also sometimes used as vowels. The list on the right below shows the order of frequency of use.

## HANDWRITING EXAMPLES

| ORDER OF FREQUENCY | |
|---|---|
| 1 | E |
| 2 | T |
| 3 | A |
| 4 | O |
| 5 | N |
| 6 | I |
| 7 | R |
| 8 | S |
| 9 | H |
| 10 | L |
| 11 | D |
| 12 | C |
| 13 | U |
| 14 | M |
| 15 | F |
| 16 | P |
| 17 | Y |
| 18 | G |
| 19 | W |
| 20 | B |
| 21 | V |
| 22 | K |
| 23 | X |
| 24 | J |
| 25 | Q |
| 26 | Z |

Manuscript

Aa Bb Cc Dd Ee Ff Gg
Hh Ii Jj Kk Ll Mm Nn Oo
Pp Qq Rr Ss Tt Uu Vv Ww
Xx Yy Zz

Cursive

Aa Bb Cc Dd Ee Ff
Gg Hh Ii Jj Kk Ll Mm
Nn Oo Pp Qq Rr Ss Tt Uu
Vv Ww Xx Yy Zz

Combinations

br ou ve wr

# SPECIAL ALPHABETS

**Braille** is a coded alphabet of raised dots that can be read by touch. It was developed in 1824 by Louis Braille, a 15-year-old blind Frenchman, and is the alphabet used most often by the blind.

A B C D E F G H I J

K L M N O P Q R S T

U V W X Y Z ch gh sh th

wh ed er ou ow and for of the with

The **International Phonetic Alphabet** is used by the military and by airplane pilots around the world to stand for letters of the alphabet. A pilot whose airplane number is N6837E would say November 6837 Echo.

**Sign language** is a system of communicating with hand gestures. The American Manual Alphabet below can be used to spell out words and is generally understood by deaf people.

Alpha
Bravo
Charlie
Delta
Echo
Foxtrot
Golf
Hotel
India
Juliet
Kilo
Lima
Mike
November
Oscar
Papa
Quebec
Romeo
Sierra
Tango
Uniform
Victor
Whiskey
X-Ray
Yankee
Zulu

A B C D E F
G H I J K
L M N O P
Q R S T U
V W X Y
Z Period Comma
? Start Wait End
Error Understand SOS
1 2 3
4 5 6 7
8 9 0

**Morse code** was developed by the inventor of the telegraph, Samuel Morse. It was used extensively in the past to transmit telegraph messages and news.

# ALPHABETS FROM OTHER LANDS

Many different languages can be written with a single alphabet. Nevertheless, some 65 alphabets are used in the world today, almost half of them in India. The longest alphabet is Cambodian, with 74 letters. The shortest is Rotakas, from the South Pacific, with only 11 letters.

**Greek alphabet:** The Greek alphabet dates from around 700 B.C. and most of the alphabets in modern Europe are based on it. In fact, the word "alphabet" comes from the first two letters of the Greek alphabet, *alpha* and *beta*. It has 24 letters.

Α Β Γ Δ Ε Ζ Η Θ Ι Κ Λ Μ Ν Ξ Ο Π Ρ Σ Τ Υ Φ Χ Ψ Ω

**Cyrillic alphabet:** The Cyrillic alphabet was invented by two missionaries, one named Cyril, in the 800's A.D. They based it on the Greek alphabet and the Slavic language. Russian, Bulgarian, and some other Slavic people use this alphabet. It has 33 letters.

А Ъ В Г Д Е Ё Ж З И Й К Л М Н О П Р С Т У Ф Х Ц Ч Ш Щ Б Ы Ь Э Ю Я

**Arabic alphabet:** The Arabic alphabet is used throughout the Middle East and Northern Africa. Arabic is the language of the Islam religion. It is read from right to left, and has 28 consonants. Vowels are shown by dots called vowel points written near the letters.

**Hebrew alphabet:** Hebrew is the language of the Bible and of the Jewish religion. It has 32 consonants, and is written from right to left.

ס ן נ ם מ ל ך כ י ט ח ז ו ה ד ג ב א
ת ת שׁ שׁ ר ק ץ צ ף פ ע

# COMPUTER KEYBOARD

A typewriter keyboard is almost the same as a computer keyboard, except it does not have certain special keys.

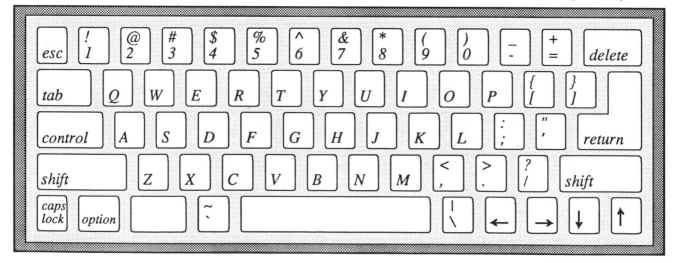

# ABBREVIATIONS

| MEANING | ABBREVIATION |
|---|---|
| *anno Domini* (in the year of our Lord) | A. D. |
| *ante merediem* (before noon) | a.m. |
| as soon as possible | ASAP |
| Avenue | Ave. |
| before Christ | B.C. |
| before Christian era or before common era (means same as B.C.) | B.C.E. |
| Boulevard | Blvd. |
| care of (in care of) | c/o |
| cash on delivery | COD |
| Central Intelligence Agency | CIA |
| Chief Executive Officer | CEO |
| Christian era or common era (means same as A.D.) | C.E. |
| Circle | Cir. |
| Company | Co. |
| continued | cont. |
| Corporation | Corp. |
| Court | Ct. |
| Department | Dept. |
| Doctor | Dr. |
| Drive | Dr. |
| *et cetera* (and other things) | etc. |
| *exempli gratia* (for example) | e.g. |
| Federal Bureau of Investigation | FBI |
| Fort | Ft. |
| General | Gen. |
| Governor | Gov. |
| Heights | Hts. |
| Highway | Hwy. |
| hour | hr. |
| *id est* (that is to say) | i.e. |
| I owe you | I.O.U. |
| Incorporated | Inc. |

| MEANING | ABBREVIATION |
|---|---|
| intelligence quotient | I.Q. |
| Internal Revenue Service | IRS |
| Junior | Jr. |
| Lane | Ln. |
| Limited | Ltd. |
| *medicinae doctor* (medical doctor) | M.D. |
| miles per hour | mph |
| minute | min. |
| Missus | Mrs. |
| Mister | Mr. |
| Miz | Ms. |
| Mount | Mt. |
| not applicable | N/A |
| number | no. (#) |
| page | pg. |
| Park | Pk. |
| Place | Pl. |
| Point | Pt. |
| *post meridiem* (after noon) | p.m. |
| Post Office | P.O. |
| postscript | P.S. |
| President | Pres. |
| public address | P.A. |
| *respondex, s' il vous plait* (answer, if you please) | R.S.V.P. |
| *requiescat in pace* (rest in peace) | R.I.P. |
| Reverend | Rev. |
| Road | Rd. |
| Room | Rm. |
| Route | Rt. |
| Saint | St. |
| second | sec. |
| Senior | Sr. |
| Square | Sq. |
| Street | St. |
| unidentified flying object | UFO |
| United Kingdom | U.K. |
| United States of America | U.S.A. |
| University | Univ. |
| versus (against) | vs. |
| very important person | V.I.P. |
| Vice President | V.P. |

**Abbreviations for:**
**Days**—page 11
**Months**—page 12
**State names**—page 101
**Parts of speech**—page 152
**Measurement units**—pages 206-207

# PUNCTUATION

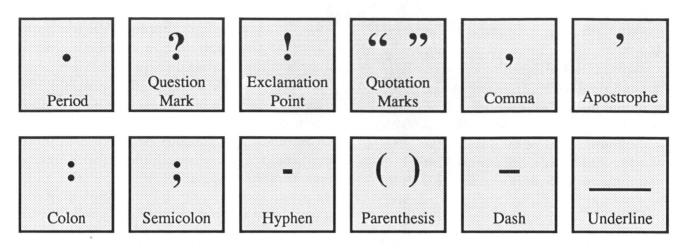

The following rules are for using the punctuation marks most often needed. Complete rules of punctuation may be found in most dictionaries.

## PUNCTUATION TO END SENTENCES

1. To end a **statement**, a sentence which tells, use a period. .
2. To end a **question**, a sentence which asks, use a question mark. ?
3. To end an **exclamation**, a sentence which expresses strong feeling, use an exclamation point. !
4. To end a **command**, a sentence which tells someone to do something, use a period. .

## USES OF PERIODS .

Use periods:
1. To end statements or commands. *Please come here.*
2. In bibliography cards or entries. See page 229.
3. After initials. *A. R. Smith*
4. After most abbreviations. *A.D., B.C., Mr.* See page 169 for a list of common abbreviations.
5. After numbers or letters of a list.

## USES OF APOSTROPHES '

Use apostrophes:
1. In contractions, to show letters have been left out. *didn't, o'clock*
2. To show possession. *Mary's book* Use *s'* with plural nouns. *the boys' coats*
3. To pluralize a number or letter. *5's, B's*

## USES OF COLONS :

Use colons:
1. After the salutation in a business letter. See page 195.
2. Between place of publication and publisher in a bibliography entry. See page 229.
3. To introduce a long list of items.

## USES OF HYPHENS -

Use hyphens:
1. In writing numbers from *twenty-one* to *ninety-nine*.
2. To divide words at the end of a line. Be careful. The rules for correctly dividing words at the end of a line are complicated. If avoidable, do not divide words.

## PUNCTUATION OF DIRECT QUOTATIONS

1. Use quotation marks " " to enclose the **exact words** a person says in a direct quotation. Remember: Capitalize the first word of a direct quotation.
   *"This book is interesting," said Jane.*
   *Jane said, "This book is interesting."*
   *"This book," said Jane, "is interesting."*

2. Use a comma , to set off direct quotations from expressions such as *he said* and *she replied.* See page 155 for words to use instead of "said."

3. Use a period . placed inside the quotation marks when the end of a quoted sentence is the end of the written sentence.
   *Martha said, "I think this is the right way."*

4. Replace the period at the end of a direct quotation with a comma , when the end of a quoted statement is **not** the end of the sentence. The comma is placed inside the quotation marks.
   *"I think this is the right way," said Martha.*

5. When the quoted sentence is a question or exclamation, use a question mark ? or exclamation point ! placed inside the quotation marks even if the end of the quotation is not the end of the sentence.
   *"Look out!" shouted Jane.*
   *Steven asked, "Where are my skates?"*

### PARENTHETICAL PHRASES

| | |
|---|---|
| for example | to begin with |
| for instance | at this point |
| in fact | at the same time |
| in one case | in conclusion |
| furthermore | as a result |
| in addition | therefore |
| also | consequently |
| meanwhile | for this reason |
| eventually | on the other hand |
| at last | however |
| in the meantime | nevertheless |

## USES OF COMMAS ,

Use commas:

1. In direct quotations. See "Punctuation of Direct Quotations," to the left.

2. In letters. See page 193-195.

3. In bibliography cards or entries. See page 229.

4. Between the day of the week and the date. *Monday, March 4*

5. Between the date and the year. *July 4, 1776*

6. Between city and state. *Tampa, Florida*

7. Between city and country. *London, England*

8. After a person's last name when written before the first name (as in the telephone book or encyclopedias). *Lincoln, Abraham Smith, Larry*

9. Between items in a series of three or more. *She can sing, dance, and play the saxophone.*

10. After words which introduce a sentence, such as *yes, no, oh, well, first* and so on. *Well, I guess so.*

11. Before certain words that end a sentence, such as *etc., too,* and *also. May I come, too?*

12. To separate the name of the person to whom you are talking from the rest of the sentence. *Mom, are you ready to go?*
    *I understand what you mean, Mr. Jones.*
    *This, Mike, is for you.*

13. Before such words as *and, but* and *or* in a compound sentence (a sentence made by combining two shorter sentences). *The roads are icy, and there have been several accidents.*

14. To separate "parenthetical" words or phrases, such as *of course, however.* See chart to the left for examples. These words and phrases add meaning, but the sentence would be a complete sentence without them. *This book, however, is very useful. You are right, of course.*

# CAPITALIZATION

**CAPITALIZE:**

1. The first word in a sentence. *Did you enjoy the show?*
2. The first word in a direct quotation. *John said, "Let's go!"*
3. The first word in a line of poetry. *Swift things are beautiful:*
4. The first word in each part of an outline.
5. The pronoun *I*. *Jeff and I are twins.*
6. The first word and all important words in titles. *Gone With the Wind.* See **Titles** below for further examples.
7. All proper nouns—special names of people, places, animals, things, or groups of people. See **Proper Nouns** below for examples.
8. Titles used before a name or in place of a name, including family titles. *Senator Smith, Mother*
9. Initials and many abbreviations. *B.C., A.D., A. W. Smith*
10. The names of days, months, and holidays, but **not** seasons. *Monday, March, Christmas, spring*
11. Historical documents, events and periods. *Constitution, Civil War, Middle Ages*
12. All words, including pronouns, which refer to God, the Holy Family, or Scripture.

For capitalization in **letter writing**, see page 194-195.

**TITLES** are the names of:

Books. *Winnie the Pooh*
Magazines. *Reader's Digest*
Newspapers. *New York Times*
Stories. *Jack and the Beanstalk*
Chapters. *Chapter II- The Gypsy Band*
Articles. *Anchorage: A Dream Reborn*
Poems. *Poem of Praise*
Plays. *Camelot*
Television Shows. *Sesame Street*
Movies. *Star Wars*
Songs. *America the Beautiful*
Paintings or other works of art. *The Night Watch*

**PROPER NOUNS** are special names of specific people, places, animals, things or groups of people. They include the following:

**People, Animals, Groups of People**
Names of people (and initials). *Mary Johnson*
Names of pets. *Rover*
Nationalities and languages. *French*
Religions. *Catholic*
Political groups. *Democrats*
Organizations, clubs, societies. *Boy Scouts*
Special groups of people. *Beatles*

**Geographical Locations**
Continents. *Asia*
Countries. *Brazil*
Geographical Regions (**not** directions). *Middle East*
States and provinces. *Florida*
Cities and towns. *Los Angeles*
Streets, highways, roads, avenues, etc. *Highway 7*
Parks. *Yellowstone Park*

## Bodies of Water

Oceans. *Indian Ocean*
Seas. *North Sea*
Bays. *Hudson Bay*
Rivers. *Colorado River*
Waterfalls. *Niagara Falls*
Lakes. *Great Salt Lake*

## Land Forms

Mountains. *Mt. Hood*
Valleys. *Bear Valley*
Canyons. *Grand Canyon*
Caves or caverns. *Mammoth Cave*
Forests. *Black Forest*
Islands. *Barter Island*
Deserts. *Sahara Desert*

## Heavenly Bodies

Planets. *Jupiter*
Stars. *Alpha Centauri*
Constellations. *Big Dipper*
(Note:  Earth, Sun and Moon are **not** capitalized unless used in a list of other planets or heavenly bodies.)

## Buildings and Other Structures

Bridges. *Golden Gate Bridge*
Schools. *Deer Park Elementary*
Stores. *Safeway*
Museums. *Western Heritage Museum*
Hospitals. *Memorial Hospital*
Churches. *First Baptist Church*
Hotels, motels, inns. *Ramada Inn*
Libraries. *Library of Congress*
Restaurants. *Dan's Pancake House*

## Things

Ships. *Queen Elizabeth II*
Trains. *Midnight Express*
Airplanes. *Boeing 747*
Autos. *Ford Mustang*
Registered Trademarks. *Kleenex*

Do **not** capitalize:
Seasons. *spring, autumn*
Directions. *east, north, southeast*
Names of school subjects—*math, science*— unless they are languages or numbered course titles—*English, Math 201*

---

## SPELLING MEMORY HELPS

| | | | |
|---|---|---|---|
| beauty | <u>Be a</u> <u>beauty</u>. | niece | My n<u>ie</u>ce is n<u>ice</u>. |
| believe | Don't bel<u>ie</u>ve a <u>lie</u>. | parallel | <u>All</u> lines are not par<u>all</u>el. |
| business | Bu<u>sy ness</u>. | piece | Have a p<u>iece</u> of p<u>ie</u>. |
| cemetery | You go to the c<u>e</u>m<u>e</u>t<u>e</u>ry with "e"s (ease). | pleasant | Picnics are pleas<u>ant</u> for an <u>ant</u>. |
| | | prairie | There is <u>air</u> on the pr<u>air</u>ie. |
| familiar | He is a famil<u>iar</u> <u>liar</u>. | principal | The princi<u>pal</u> is my <u>pal</u>. |
| February | You say "<u>br</u>" in Fe<u>br</u>uary. | prison | Her <u>son</u> is in pri<u>son</u>. |
| foreign | Kings <u>reign</u> in fo<u>reign</u> countries. | secretary | A <u>secret</u>ary can keep a <u>secret</u>. |
| friend | You'll be my fri<u>end</u> to the <u>end</u>. | stationery | Use station<u>ery</u> to write a lett<u>er</u>. |
| grammar | <u>Gramma</u> knows <u>grammar</u>. | together | to get her - They went <u>together</u> <u>to get her</u>. |
| hear | You h<u>ear</u> with your <u>ear</u>. | | |
| independent | There is a <u>dent</u> in indepen<u>dent</u>. | tomorrow | Tom or row. |
| innocent | in no cent | weird | <u>We</u> are w<u>ei</u>rd. |

See pages 177-179 for more information on spelling.

# HOMONYMS AND TROUBLESOME WORDS

**Homonyms** are words with the same pronunciation but different meanings, origins and usually different spellings. The list below is to help readers remember which word is which. For complete definitions, consult a dictionary.

**accept - except**
accept (v) - to receive willingly
except (prep) - other than

**access - excess**
access (n) - right to enter or use
excess (adj) - more than enough

**acts - ax**
acts (v) - behaves, takes action
ax (n) - a chopping tool

**ad - add**
ad (n) - advertisement
add (v) - to combine by addition

**addition - edition**
addition (n) - result of adding
edition (n) - a version or issue of
a publication

**affect - effect**
affect (v) - to influence
effect (n) - a result or outcome

**allowed - aloud**
allowed (v) - permitted
aloud (adv) - out loud

**are** (see "hour")

**ate - eight**
ate (v) - past tense of *to eat*
eight (adj) - the number 8

**ax** (see "acts")

**bare - bear**
bare (adj) - without covering
bear (n) - a large animal
(v) - to carry

**be - bee**
be (v) - to exist
bee (n) - an insect

**beat - beet**
beat (v) - to hit again and again
beet (n) - a vegetable

**berry - bury**
berry (n) - an edible fruit
bury (v) - to hide beneath the
earth

**blew - blue**
blew (v) - past tense of *to blow*
blue (adj) - a color

**board - bored**
board (n) - a flat piece of lumber
bored (v) - filled with boredom

**brake - break**
brake (n) - something which
slows or stops motion
break (v) - to split into pieces

**bury** (see "berry")

**buy - by - bye**
buy (v) - to purchase
by (prep) - near or beside
bye (interj) - short for
"goodbye"

**capital - capitol**
capital (adj) - of most
importance: *capital city,
capital letter*
capitol (n) - the building in
which Congress meets

**ceiling - sealing**
ceiling (n) - opposite of *floor*
sealing (v) - closing, shutting,
fastening

**cell - sell**
cell (n) - a small room, such as
in a prison
sell (v) - to exchange something
for money

**cent - sent - scent**
cent (n) - a penny
sent (v) - past tense of *to send*
scent (n) - a smell

**chews - choose**
chews (v) - crushes or grinds
with the teeth
choose (v) - to select

**clothes - close**
clothes (n) - clothing
close (v) - to shut

**council - counsel**
council (n) - a group of people
counsel (v) - to give advice

**creak - creek**
creak (v) - to make a grating or
squeaking sound
creek (n) - a small stream

**dear - deer**
dear (adj) - used in letters: *Dear
Jim,*
deer (n) - an animal

**dew - do - due**
dew (v) - moisture in small
drops
do (v) - to carry out, finish
due (adj) - owed and payable

**desert - dessert**
desert (n) - a dry, sandy region
(v) - to leave or abandon
dessert (n) - a sweet course at
the end of a meal

**die - dye**
die (v) - to stop living
dye (v) - to change the color of
using *dye*

**do - due** (see "dew")

**edition** (see "addition")

**effect** (see "affect")

**eight** (see "ate")

**except** (see "accept")

**excess** (see "access")

**fair - fare**
fair (adj) - just and honest
fare (n) - money paid to travel
on bus or train

**fir - fur**
fir (n) - a kind of tree
fur (n) - soft, thick animal hair

**flew - flu**
flew (v) - past tense of *to fly*
flu (n) - a sickness, short for
*influenza*

**flour - flower**
flour (n) - fine powder: wheat
*flour* is used in bread
flower (n) - a blossom

**flu** (see "flew")

**forth - fourth**
forth (adv) - forward
fourth (adj) - 4th, the one after
third

**for - fore - four**
for (prep) - with the purpose of:
a pencil is *for* writing
fore (adv) - toward the front of a
ship, opposite of *aft*
four (adj) - the number 4

**fur** (see "fir")

**grate - great**
grate (v) - to grind into shreds
great (adj) - very good

**groan - grown**
groan (n) - a deep sound of pain
grown (adj) - from the word
*grow*

**guessed - guest**
guessed (v) - made a guess
about
guest (n) - a person entertained
in one's house

**hair - hare**
hair (n) - the growth covering
people's heads
hare (n) - an animal like a rabbit

**hay - hey**
hay (n) - cut and dried grass for
animal food
hey (interj) - an exclamation to
attract attention

**heal - heel**
heal (v) - to make healthy again
heel (n) - the back part of the
foot

**hear - here**
hear (v) - to hear with the ear
here (adv) - in this place,
opposite of *there*

**heard - herd**
heard (v) - past tense of *to hear*
herd (n) - a group of cattle or
large animals

**here** (see "here")

**hey** (see "hay")

**higher - hire**
higher (adj) - taller, more
elevated
hire (v) - to take on an employee

**hole - whole**
hole (n) - a *hole* in the ground
whole (adj) - complete

**hour - our - are**
hour (n) - sixty minutes
our (adj) - belonging to us
are (v) - form of "to be" (we are)

**its - it's**
its (adj) - belonging to it
it's - contraction of *it is*

**knew** (see "new")
**knight** (see "night")
**knot** (see "not")
**know** (see "no")
**knows** (see "nose")

**lead - led**
lead (n) - a gray metal
led (v) - past tense of *to lead*

**loose - lose**
loose (adj) - not tight
lose (v) - to misplace

**made - maid**
made (v) - past tense of *to make*
maid (n) - a girl

**mail - male**
mail (n) - letters and packages
handled by the Post Office
male (adj) - man or boy

**main - Maine - mane**
main (adj) - the most important
Maine (n) - a state of the U.S.
mane (n) - long heavy hair on
the neck of some animals

**meat - meet**
meat (n) - food
meet (v) - to come together: to
*meet* a person

**missed - mist**
missed (v) - failed to hit or felt
the absence of
mist (n) - a haze of water vapor
in the air, similar to fog

**new - knew**
new (adj) - not old
knew (v) - understood, past
tense of *to know*

**night - knight**
night (n) - opposite of *day*
knight (n) - a military man in the
Middle Ages who wore armor

**no - know**
no (adv) - opposite of *yes*
know (v) - to understand

**none - nun**
none (pron) - not any
nun (n) - a woman of the
Catholic church

**nose - knows**
nose (n) - a part of the face
knows (v) - understands

**not - knot**
not (adv) - no
knot (n) - a fastening made by
tying

**one - won**
one (adj) - the number 1
won (v) - past tense of *to win*

**oh - owe**
oh (interj) - an exclamation
owe (v) - to have a debt

**our** (see "hour")

**pail - pale**
pail (n) - a small bucket
pale (adj) - without much color

**pain - pane**
pain (n) - hurt
pane (n) - division of a window

**pair - pare - pear**
pair (n) - two
pare (v) - to cut or trim away
pear (n) - a fruit

**passed - past**
passed (v) - past tense of *to pass*
past (adj) - gone by, ended

**patience - patients**
patience (n) - ability to wait
without complaining
patients (n) - two or more people
under a doctor's care

**pause - paws**
pause (v) - stop temporarily
paws (n) - feet of some animals

**peace - piece**
peace (n) - freedom from war
piece (n) - a part

**peak - peek**
peak (n) - top of a mountain,
highest place
peek (v) - to glance at something
without being seen

**peal - peel**
peal (n) - a loud ringing of bells
peel (v) - to cut away the skin or
covering of something

**piece** (see "peace")

**plain - plane**
plain (adj) - simple, ordinary,
clear
plane (n) - short for *airplane*

**principal - principle**
principal (n) - first in rank: the
school *principal,* or the
amount of a debt, not
including interest
principle (n) - a fundamental
truth

**quiet - quite**
quiet (adj) - not noisy
quite (adv) - really

**rain - rein - reign**
rain (n) - water falling from the
sky
rein (n) - part of a horse's bridle
reign (v) - to rule: Kings and
queens *reign*

**raise - rays**
    raise (v) - to lift
    rays (n) - lines of light which
        radiate from something bright

**rap - wrap**
    rap (v) - to tap
    wrap (v) - to wind or fold a
        covering around something

**read - red**
    read (v) - past tense of *to read*
    red (adj) - a color

**real - reel**
    real (adj) - genuine
    reel (n) - a fishing *reel*

**rein - reign** (see "rain")

**right - rite - write**
    right (adj) - correct
    rite (n) - a ceremonial custom or
        ritual
    write (v) - to *write* a letter

**ring - wring**
    ring (n) - a circular object such
        as a wedding *ring*
        (v) - to sound or cause a
        ringing sound
    wring (v) - to squeeze or twist to
        get water out

**road - rode**
    road (n) - a highway
    rode (v) - past tense of *to ride*

**rote - wrote**
    rote (n) - routine
    wrote (v) - past tense of *to write*

**sail - sale**
    sail (n) - canvas sheet of a
        sailboat
    sale (n) - having to do with
        selling

**scene - seen**
    scene (n) - scenery
    seen (v) - from *to see:* I have
        *seen* her.

**scent** (see "cent")

**sea - see**
    sea (n) - body of salt water, like
        an ocean
    see (v) - look at

**sealing** (see "ceiling")

**seam - seem**
    seam (n) - the line made by
        sewing two pieces of cloth
        together
    seem (v) - to appear

**seen** (see "scene")

**sell** (see "cell")

**sense - since**
    sense (n) - ability to think or feel
    since (adv) - from then to now

**sent** (see "cent")

**sew - so - sow**
    sew (v) - to join with a needle
        and thread
    so (adv) - very: It's *so* good.
    sow (v) - to plant seeds

**since** (see "sense")

**some - sum**
    some (pron) - Example: *Some*
        people came early.
    sum (n) - The result of addition.

**son - sun**
    son (n) - a male child
    sun (n) - the *sun* in the sky

**stake - steak**
    stake (n) - a short post: tent
        *stake*
    steak (n) - a thick slice of meat

**stationary - stationery**
    stationary (adj) - not moving
    stationery (n) - writing paper
        and envelopes

**steal - steel**
    steal (v) - to rob
    steel (n) - a kind of metal

**stair - stare**
    stair (n) - a step in a staircase
    stare (v) - to look fixedly at
        something

**tacks - tax**
    tacks (n) - small, short nails with
        broad heads
    tax (n) - money paid to the
        government

**tail - tale**
    tail (n) - an animal's *tail*
    tale (n) - story

**their - there - they're**
    their (adj) - belonging to them
    there (adv) - in that place,
        opposite of *here*
    they're - contraction of *they are*

**threw - through**
    threw (v) - past tense of *to throw*
    through (prep) - in one side and
        out the other

**to - too - two**
    to (prep) - toward, for, as far as:
        Go *to* the store.
    too (adv) - more than enough:
        *too* much
    two (adj) - the number 2

**toad - towed**
    toad (n) - a frog-like animal
    towed (v) - pulled with a rope or
        chain

**toe - tow**
    toe (n) - a part of the foot
    tow (v) - to pull with a rope or
        chain

**wade - weighed**
    wade (v) - to walk through water
    weighed (v) - past tense of *to
        weigh*, meaning to find out
        how heavy something is

**waist - waste**
    waist (n) - middle part of the
        body
    waste (v) - to use up needlessly

**wait - weight**
    wait (v) - to stay in one place
        and *wait* for something
    weight (n) - the heaviness of
        something

**way - weigh**
    way (n) - Examples: the right
        *way,* clear the *way*
    weigh (v) - to find the heaviness
        of something with a scale

**weak - week**
    weak (adj) - not strong
    week (n) - seven days

**weather - whether**
    weather (n) - rain, storms, etc.
    whether (conj) - Example:
        *whether* or not

**which - witch**
    which (pron) - Example: *Which*
        one?
    witch (n) - an evil woman

**whole** (see "hole")

**were - we're**
    were (v) - past tense of *are* :
        They *were* gone.
    we're - contraction of *we are*

**wood - would**
    wood (n) - from trees
    would (v) - from the word *will:*
        He *would* not say.

**won** (see "one")

**wrap** (see "rap")

**wring** (see "ring")

**write** (see "right")

**wrote** (see "rote")

**your - you're**
    your (adj) - belonging to you
    you're - contraction of *you are*

# SPELLING

English is a difficult language to spell because sounds can be represented by more than one letter and letters can be represented by more than one sound. Most "rules" have many exceptions. Some words must simply be memorized. This section includes one method for studying spelling, a list of rules which have few exceptions, and a list of frequently misspelled words. See page 173 for some spelling **mnemonics**, or memory helps, for difficult words.

## HOW TO STUDY A SPELLING WORD

Once a method for studying new words is learned, all words can be practiced using it. Here is one possible method:

1.  Look at the word. Make sure you understand its meaning, use and pronunciation.
2.  Read the word and note its form.
3.  Spell the word aloud while pointing to each letter.
4.  Write the word, spelling it aloud as you write.
5.  Proof the word you wrote by:
    a.  Pointing to each letter of the model while spelling it aloud.
    b.  Pointing to each letter of the word you wrote while spelling it aloud.
6.  Correct any errors in the word you wrote.
7.  Close your eyes and visualize the word. Spell it aloud to yourself.

Repeat the procedure as many times as needed to master the word. Use the word in writing.

Long ago in England, people spelled words the way they sounded. There was no one correct spelling for a word. In fact, some people took pride in creative spelling. William Shakespeare spelled his name several different ways. Some of the common ways to spell *cliff* were, *clif, clief, cleove, cleo, cluf, clive, clef* and *cleve*. The idea of "correct" spelling came with the printing of books and the dictionary.

## SPELLING RULES

The following rules in English spelling have very few exceptions:

1.  When a word ends in silent *e,* drop the *e* before adding a suffix beginning with a vowel. *(make + -ing* is *making)*
    Keep the silent *e* before adding a suffix beginning with a consonant. *(time + -ly* is *timely)*

2.  When a word ends in a consonant and *y,* change the *y* to *i* before adding a suffix, unless the suffix begins with *i.* *(happy + -ly* is *happily,* but *hurry + -ing* is *hurrying)*
    When a word ends in a vowel and *y,* do not change the *y* to *i. (play + -ed* is *played)*

3.  When a one-syllable word ends with a short vowel and a single consonant, double the final consonant before adding a suffix beginning with a vowel. *(swim + -ing* is *swimming)*
    When a word has more than one syllable, double the final consonant only if the word is accented on the last syllable. *(begin + -ing* is *beginning)*

4.  The letter *q* is always followed by a *u* except in some foreign words. *(question, quite)*

5.  English words do not end with the letter *v* . *(receive, live)*

# FREQUENTLY MISSPELLED WORDS

| | | | | | |
|---|---|---|---|---|---|
| absence | awful | completely | disappoint | experience | happier |
| absorb | beautiful | concentrate | discipline | extremely | happiest |
| accept* | beauty | conscientious | discuss | familiar | happily |
| accidentally | because | conscience | discussion | families | happiness |
| accommodate | before | conscious | disease | fascinate | hear* |
| accompany | beginning | continue | dissatisfy | fasten | height |
| accuse | believe | continuous | doctor | fatigue | here* |
| ache | benefit | control | does | favorite | heroes |
| achieve | bicycle | convenience | doesn't | February | history |
| acquaintance | biscuit | convenient | dropped | fiction | hoping |
| acquire | boundary | corner | dropping | fictitious | hospital |
| address | brake* | counterfeit | during | field | humor |
| affect* | break* | countries | easier | finally | humorous |
| afraid | Britain | courage | easiest | first | hungry |
| against | brilliance | courageous | easily | forecast | hurrying |
| aggression | brilliant | courteous | effect* | forehead | identify |
| aggressive | bureau | cried | eighth | foreign | imagine |
| all right | business | cries | either | foresee | immediate |
| almost | calendar | criticism | embarrass | forest | immediately |
| a lot | captain | criticize | enemy | foretell | immensely |
| already | career | curiosity | enough | formerly | incident |
| always | carrying | debt | entertain | forty | independence |
| amateur | cemetery | deceive | envelope | fourth* | independent |
| ambition | certain | decide | environment | fragile | Indian |
| among | challenge | decision | equipment | freight | innocent |
| answer | character | definite | equipped | friend | instead |
| apology | chief | definitely | escape | front | intelligence |
| apparent | children | descend | especially | fulfill | intelligent |
| appearance | chocolate | describe | etc. | further | interest |
| appeared | chosen | description | everybody | genius | interpret |
| appreciate | Christian | desert* | everything | getting | interrupt |
| appreciation | cinnamon | desperately | everywhere | government | introduce |
| approach | climb | dessert* | exaggerate | governor | its* |
| arctic | climbed | destroy | exceed | grabbed | it's* |
| argument | climbing | develop | excellence | grammar | jealous |
| article | clothes | diarrhea | excellent | grateful | judgment |
| associate | colonel | dictionary | except* | group | knew* |
| athlete | college | didn't | excited | guarantee | know* |
| athletic | column | different | excitement | guard | knowledge |
| attendance | coming | difficult | exciting | guess | laboratory |
| attendant | commercial | dinner | existence | guest | laid |
| attitude | committee | dining | expense | handsome | later |
| author | complete | disappear | experiment | happen | laughed |

*These words may be confused with other English words. See HOMONYMS AND TROUBLESOME WORDS, pages 174-176.

# FREQUENTLY MISSPELLED WORDS

| | | | | | |
|---|---|---|---|---|---|
| leisure | occur | prairie | rendezvous | stepped | trouble |
| library | occurred | precede | repetition | stepping | truly |
| lightning | occurrence | preferred | repellent | stopped | two* |
| literature | occurring | prejudice | reservoir | stopping | unique |
| lonely | often | preparation | restaurant | stories | unnecessary |
| loose* | omitted | pretty | ridiculous | straight | until |
| lose* | opinion | principal | rhyme | strengthen | unusual |
| lying | opportunity | principle | rhythm | stretch | usually |
| magazine | opposite | prison | ridiculous | studied | vaccinate |
| magnificent | original | privilege | running | studies | vacuum |
| many | other | probably | safely | studying | vegetable |
| marriage | pageant | procedure | safety | succeed | very |
| mathematics | paid | proceed | Saturday | success | village |
| maybe | pamphlet | profession | scene* | successful | villain |
| meant | parallel | professor | scent* | sugar | weather* |
| medicine | parents | pronunciation | schedule | suggest | Wednesday |
| millionaire | parliament | prophecy | scissors | summarize | weight* |
| miniature | particular | psychologist | search | summary | weird |
| minute | passed* | psychology | secret | superintendent | went |
| mischievous | pastime | pursue | secretary | suppose | were |
| misspell | peculiar | pursuit | seize | surprise | wc're |
| model | perform | quantity | semester | suspense | where |
| modern | period | quiet* | sense* | suspicion | whether* |
| month | permanent | quite* | sentence | swimming | which* |
| mosquito | persuade | raspberry | separate | synagogue | whole* |
| motor | phenomenon | realize | separation | temperament | who's* |
| mountain | physical | really | sergeant | their* | whose* |
| muscle | piece* | receipt | servant | themselves | witch* |
| mystery | pilot | receive | shepherd | there* | woman |
| narrative | plain* | receiving | shining | therefore | women |
| necessary | plane* | recess | similar | they | wonder |
| neighbor | planned | recognize | since* | they're* | wonderful |
| nervous | planning | recommend | sincerely | thief | would* |
| niece | pleasant | reference | soldier | thorough | wreck |
| night | pneumonia | referred | something | thoroughly | write* |
| nineteen | poem | referring | sophomore | thought | writer |
| ninety | poison | rein* | spaghetti | through | writing |
| notice | possess | reign* | speak | tobacco | written |
| noticeable | possessed | relative | speech | together | wrote* |
| nuisance | possession | relief | sponsor | tomorrow | yacht |
| obedience | possible | religion | squirrel | too* | yolk |
| obstacle | practical | religious | stationary* | tragedy | your* |
| occasion | practically | remember | stationery* | tried | you're* |

*These words may be confused with other English words. See HOMONYMS AND TROUBLESOME WORDS, pages 174-176.

# GREEK AND LATIN WORD ROOTS

**Word roots** from Greek and Latin are helpful in figuring out the meanings of unfamiliar words. Experts estimate that about 60% of common English words come from Latin or Greek.

| Root | Meaning | Examples |
|------|---------|----------|
| -aqua- | water | aquarium |
| -aud- | hear | audience, audition |
| -biblio- | book | bibliography |
| -cede- -ceed- | go | exceed, precede |
| -cept- | take | intercept, reception |
| -chrom- | color | monochrome |
| -chron- | time | chronic, synchronize |
| -cred- | believe | incredible, credit |
| -cide- | kill | suicide, decide |
| -clud- | shut | seclude, include |
| -dent- | tooth | indent, dentist |
| -derma- | skin | epidermis |
| -dict- | say | dictator, contradict |
| -duce- | bring forth lead | conduct, product |
| -fid- | faith | fidelity, confidence |
| -flam- | fire | flammable |
| -flor- | flower | florist, florid |
| -flu- | flow | fluent, influence |
| -gram- | letter | telegram, grammar |
| -graph- | writing | autograph, telegraph |
| -gress- | step | progress, aggression |
| -homo- | same | homonym |
| -ject- | throw | eject, reject, inject |
| -journ- | day | journey, adjourn |
| -junct- | join | junction, conjunction |
| -leg- | law | legal, legislature |
| -loc- | place | locate, locus |
| -man- | hand | manufacture, manual |
| -mis- | send | missionary, dismiss |
| -mit- | send | transmit, admit |
| -mort- | death | mortal, mortician |
| -pan- | all | panacea, panorama |
| -pan- | bread | pantry, companion (eat bread together) |
| -path- | feeling | telepathy, sympathy |
| -ped- | foot | pedal, pedestrian |

| Root | Meaning | Examples |
|------|---------|----------|
| -pel- | drive | compel, repel |
| -pend- | hang | depend, pendulum |
| -phil- | love | philosophy |
| -phobia- | fear | claustrophobia |
| -phono- | sound | phonics, telephone |
| -photo- | light | photography |
| -physis- | nature | physics, physical |
| -pod- | foot | tripod, podiatrist |
| -port- | carry | portable, transport |
| -pot- | power | potent, potential |
| -press- | press | impress, depress |
| -psych- | mind | psychology, psychic |
| -rupt- | break | disrupt, interrupt |
| -sci- | know | science, conscience |
| -scend- | climb | ascend, descent |
| -scope- | observe detect | microscope, telescope |
| -scribe- | write | describe, subscribe |
| -script- | write | prescription, scripture |
| -sect- | cut | dissect, intersection |
| -serve- | watch over guard | conserve, observe |
| -spect- | look, see | inspect, spectator |
| -stella- | star | constellation |
| -struct- | build | construct, structure |
| -syn- | same | synonym, synthetic |
| -tain- | hold | maintain, retain |
| -tend- | stretch, pull | pretend, tendency |
| -therapy- | treatment | psychotherapy |
| -thermo- | heat | thermometer, thermal |
| -tort- | twist | distort, torture |
| -tract- | draw, pull | tractor, subtract |
| -ven- | come | convention, intervene |
| -vert- | turn | convert, divert |
| -vis- | see | visible, supervise |
| -vit- | live | vitality, vitamin |
| -viv- | live | survive, revive |
| -voc- | call | vocal, vocation |

# PREFIXES

A **prefix** is a word part that can be added to the beginning of a base word to change its meaning or to form a new word.

| Prefix | Meaning | Examples |
|---|---|---|
| ab- | from | abnormal, absent |
| ad- | toward, to | admit, advance |
| aero- | air | aerobatics, aerospace |
| alti- | high | altitude, altimeter |
| ante- | before | antedate, anteroom |
| anti- | against | antiseptic, antiaircraft |
| anthropo- | human | anthropology |
| astro- | stars | astronomy, astronaut |
| auto- | self, own | autograph, automatic |
| bi- | two | bicycle, biweekly |
| bio- | life | biography, biology |
| cardio- | heart | cardiology, cardiac |
| centi- | hundred | centigram, centipede |
| circum- | around | circumference |
| co- | together | cooperate, coordinate |
| com- | together | combine, compete |
| con- | together | connect, conversation |
| contra- | against | contradiction |
| cosmo- | universe | cosmonaut |
| counter- | against | counteract, |
| deca- | ten | decade, decimal |
| de- | reduce, from | defrost, deform |
| demo- | people | democracy, demon |
| dis- | not | disagree, dishonest |
| | opposite of | disappear, disconnect |
| en- | put into | entangle, ensure |
| | cause to be | enjoy, enlarge |
| equi- | equal | equator, equilateral |
| ex- | out, from | explode, extend |
| ex- | former | ex-teacher |
| fore- | before | forewarn, forefathers |
| | in front of | forehead, forearm |
| geo- | earth | geology, geography |
| hydro- | water | hydroelectric |
| hyper- | too much | hyperactive |
| il- | not | illegal, illogical |
| im- | not | impossible, impolite |
| in- | not | incorrect, invisible |

| Prefix | Meaning | Examples |
|---|---|---|
| inter- | between | interrupt, intercept |
| ir- | not | irregular |
| mal- | bad | malfunction |
| mega- | great | megaphone, megaton |
| micro- | small | microscope, microbe |
| mid- | middle | midnight, midsection |
| milli- | thousand | millimeter, millipede |
| mini- | small | miniskirt, miniscule |
| mis- | wrong, bad | misspell, mistrust |
| mono- | one | monotone, monopoly |
| multi- | many | multicolored |
| non- | not | nonmember |
| omni- | all | omnivore |
| out- | more than | outnumber, outdo |
| over- | too much | oversleep, overflow |
| poly- | many | polygon, polychrome |
| post- | after | postscript, postdate |
| pre- | before | prefix, preschool |
| pro- | for | prolabor |
| quad- | four | quadruple, quadrant |
| re- | back | refill, repay |
| | again | rebuild, reconsider |
| retro- | back | retroactive, retrospect |
| semi- | partly | semicircular, semisoft |
| sub- | below | submarine, subzero |
| | part | subcontinent, subtotal |
| super- | above | superpower |
| sym-, syn- | together | sympathy, synonym |
| tele- | far away | telephone, television |
| trans- | across | transport |
| tri- | three | tricycle, triangle |
| ultra- | beyond | ultralight, ultrashort |
| un- | not | unlucky, unsafe |
| | opposite of | unplug, uncover |
| under- | below | underground |
| | not enough | undercooked |
| uni- | one | universe, uniform |
| up- | up | uplift, uphill |

# SUFFIXES

A **suffix** is a word part that is added after a base word to change its meaning or form a new word.

| Suffix | Meaning | Examples | Part of Speech |
|---|---|---|---|
| -able, -ible | capable or worthy of being | washable, reversible | adjective |
| -an | one born or living in | American, African | noun, adjective |
| -ance, -ancy | a thing that is | inheritance | noun |
| -ant | a person or thing that | accountant | noun |
| | causing or being | observant | adjective |
| -ary | connected with | dictionary, imaginary | noun, adjective |
| -ate | to become or cause to become | activate, evaporate | verb |
| | filled with | proportionate | adjective |
| -dom | state of being | wisdom | noun |
| -ed | past tense | liked, wanted | verb |
| -eer | person having to do with | engineer, mountaineer | noun |
| -en | become, cause to be or have | darken, brighten | verb |
| | made of | wooden, woolen | adjective |
| -er | more | taller, wider | adjective |
| | a person or thing which | miner, roller | noun |
| -ery | the act of | robbery | noun |
| -ese | native of, language of | Chinese, Japanese | adjective |
| -ess | female | lioness, actress | noun |
| -est | most | biggest, highest | adjective |
| -ful | full of, having | colorful, careful | adjective |
| -fy | make or cause to become | simplify, glorify | verb |
| -hood | condition of | childhood, likelihood | noun |
| -ian | someone who | musician, politician | noun |
| -ing | continuous action | listening, running | verb |
| -ion, -tion | result of, state of being | permission, action | noun |
| -ish | like, somewhat | childish, foolish | adjective |
| -ist | person who | novelist, artist | noun |
| -ity | state of being | necessity, possibility | noun |
| -less | without | helpless, restless | adjective |
| -like | similar to | childlike, doglike | adjective |
| -logy | science of | geology, biology | noun |
| -ly | like, in a manner that is | friendly, loudly | adverb |
| -ment | result of being | punishment, pavement | noun |
| -ness | quality or state of being | happiness, sickness | noun |
| -ous | full of, having | humorous, dangerous | adjective |
| -or | person who | actor, sailor | noun |
| -s, -es | more than one | boys, boxes | noun |
| -tion | the act or state of | graduation, correction | noun |
| -y | like, full of | dusty, wavy | adjective |

# GRAMMAR AND PARTS OF SPEECH

Note:   It would be impossible to include a thorough explanation of our complex English language in a short space.  This section is intended to provide a simplified framework from which learning can progress, and is not intended to be comprehensive.

## NOUNS

**Definition:**  A **noun** names a person, place, thing, quality, act or feeling. *(girl, city, desk, honesty, sadness)*
Nouns may be made up of more than one word: *(Dr. Smith, Pikes Peak)*

**Proper nouns and common nouns:**
A **proper noun** names someone or something in particular and is capitalized. *(Mary)*
A **common noun** is any noun that is not a proper noun. *(girl)*

**Singular nouns and plural nouns:**
A **singular noun** names <u>one</u> person, place, thing, quality, act or feeling. *(hat)*
A **plural noun** names more than one. *(hats)*
**Rules for pluralizing words:**
1.  To form the plural of most nouns, add *-s*. *(dogs)*
2.  For nouns ending in *-s, -x, -z, -sh, or -ch,*  add *-es*. *(foxes)*
3.  For nouns ending in *-o*, add *-s* or *-es*. *(potatoes, radios)*
4.  For nouns ending with a vowel and *-y*, add *-s*. *(toys, monkeys)*
    For nouns ending with a consonant and *-y*, change the y to *i* and add *-es*. *(berries, babies)*
5.  Some nouns form irregular plurals, including the following:

    | | | |
    |---|---|---|
    | *moose - moose* | *child - children* | *mouse - mice* |
    | *deer - deer* | *man - men* | *goose - geese* |
    | *fish - fish* | *woman - women* | *foot - feet* |
    | *sheep - sheep* | *person - people* | *tooth - teeth* |

**Possessive nouns**
**Possessive nouns** show ownership. *(<u>Mike's</u> book)*
**Rules for forming possessives:**
1.  To form the possessive of most singular nouns, add *'s. (Mary* becomes *Mary's—Mary's car is red.)*
2.  To form the possessive of a plural noun that ends in *-s*, add *'. (boys* becomes *boys'—The boys' mothers were all at school.)*
3.  To form the possessive of a plural noun which does not end in *-s*, add *'s. (children* becomes *children's—The children's hats were gone.)*

## PRONOUNS

**Definition:**  A **pronoun** is a word that takes the place of **a** noun.

**Personal pronouns**
A **personal pronoun** refers to a specific person or thing.
Singular pronouns refer to one person, plural pronouns to more than one.
First person pronouns refer to the person speaking or writing.
Second person pronouns refer to the person being spoken or written to.
Third person pronouns refer to any other person or object.
Subject pronouns replace a noun in the subject of the sentence (person or thing doing the action).
Possessive pronouns replace a possessive noun.
Object pronouns replace a noun which is receiving the action of a sentence.

**Indefinite pronouns** do not refer to a specific person or thing.

| | | | |
|---|---|---|---|
| *anybody* | *anyone* | *anything* | *whatever* |
| *everybody* | *everyone* | *everything* | *whoever* |
| *somebody* | *someone* | *something* | *one* |
| *nobody* | *no one* | *nothing* | *you* |

**Reflexive pronouns** refer back to the subject.

| | |
|---|---|
| *myself* | *ourselves* |
| *yourself* | *yourselves* |
| *himself* | *themselves* |
| *herself* | |
| *itself* | |

| CHART OF PERSONAL PRONOUNS | | | | | | |
|---|---|---|---|---|---|---|
| | SINGULAR | | | PLURAL | | |
| | Subject | Object | Possessive | Subject | Object | Possessive |
| First Person | *I* | *my* *mine* | *me* | *we* | *our* *ours* | *us* |
| Second Person | *you* | *your* *yours* | *you* | *you* | *your* *yours* | *you* |
| Third Person | *he* *she* *it* | *his* *her(s)* *its* | *him* *her* *it* | *they* | *their* | *them* |

## ADJECTIVES

**Definition:** An **adjective** describes, or modifies (limits the meaning of), a noun or pronoun. *(Three angry people were arguing. She was happy to come home.*

**Articles.** The **articles** are *a, an,* and *the.*
Use *a* before singular nouns beginning with a consonant: *a dog*
Use *an* before singular nouns beginning with a vowel sound: *an egg*
Use *the* before any noun, to refer to a specific noun: *the milk*

**Comparative and superlative adjectives.**
**Rules for forming comparative and superlative adjectives:**
1.  For most adjectives of one or two syllables, add *-er* or *-est* to form comparative and superlative adjectives.
    *John is tall.*
    *Janet is taller than John.*
    *Mike is the tallest of the three.*
2.  For longer adjectives, use *more* or *most* to form comparative and superlative adjectives.
    *Monica is discouraged.*
    *I am more discouraged than Monica.*
    *Mrs. Miller is the most discouraged of all.*
3.  A few common adjectives form irregular comparatives and superlatives.
    *good, better, best*
    *bad, worse, worst*
    *many, more, most*
    *little, less, least*

### CONTRACTIONS

**Contractions** are formed with nouns or pronouns and auxiliary verbs or verbs which express a state of being or having.

| | | |
|---|---|---|
| | | I would - I'd |
| | | you would - you'd |
| | | he would - he'd |
| | | she would - she'd |
| | | it would - it'd |
| | | we would - we'd |
| | | they would - they'd |
| I am - I'm | I will - I'll | is not - isn't |
| you are - you're | you will - you'll | are not - aren't |
| he is - he's | he will - he'll | was not - wasn't |
| she is - she's | she will - she'll | were not - weren't |
| it is - it's | it will - it'll | will not - won't |
| we are - we're | we will - we'll | would not - wouldn't |
| they are - they're | they will - they'll | can not - can't |
| | | could not - couldn't |
| I have - I've | I had - I'd | should not - shouldn't |
| you have - you've | you had - you'd | has not - hasn't |
| he has - he's | he had - he'd | have not - haven't |
| she has - she's | she had - she'd | had not - hadn't |
| it has - it's | it had - it'd | does not - doesn't |
| we have - we've | we had - we'd | do not - don't |
| they have - they've | they had - they'd | did not - didn't |

## VERBS

**Definition:** A **verb** expresses action, either physical or mental, or it expresses a state of being.
Examples of action verbs: *sing, think, like, make, do*
Examples of verbs to express a state of being: *am, is, are, was, were, be, being, been*

**Verb phrases** are made up of a main verb and one or more helping or auxiliary verbs. The main verb is the last verb in the phrase. *Mr. Jones might hire me tomorrow. They could have been on vacation.*
The main auxiliary verbs are *can, may, should, might* and *must.*
Forms of the verbs *do, be,* and *have* are often used as auxiliary verbs: *She has been working a lot.*

**Verb tenses** show different time, or tense.
Present tense:          *I look.*
Past tense:             *I looked.*
Future tense:           *I will look.*
The **present participle** is used in progressive forms to show continuing action.
Present progressive tense:   *I am looking.*
Past progressive tense:      *I was looking.*
Future progressive tense:    *I will be looking.*
The **past participle** shows finished action. It is used in the passive voice.
Present tense:   *It is being drawn.*
Past tense:      *It was drawn.*
Future tense:    *It will be drawn.*
**Perfect** tenses show when an ongoing action started. They consist of forms of the word and the past participle.
Present perfect tense:   *I have looked.*
Past perfect tense:      *I had looked.*
Future perfect tense:    *I will have looked.*

**Principal parts of verbs** are the verb, the present participle, the past and the past participle.

**Regular verbs** are verbs which form the past and past participle by adding *-ed.*

| Present | walk |
|---|---|
| Present Participle (add *-ing*) | walking |
| Past (add *-ed*) | walked |
| Past participle (add *-ed*) | walked |

**Spelling rules for forming the parts of regular verbs:**
1.  For words ending in silent *e*, drop the *e* before adding *-ed* or *-ing. (live, lived, living)*
2.  For words ending in a short vowel and a single consonant, double the final consonant before adding *-ed* or *-ing. (drop, dropped, dropping)*

**Irregular verbs** form the past and the past participle in a variety of ways. The present participle is formed the same as for regular verbs. See the Chart of Irregular Verbs for examples.

# CHART OF IRREGULAR VERBS

| PRESENT | PAST | PERFECT | PRESENT | PAST | PERFECT |
|---|---|---|---|---|---|
| beat | beat | beaten | let | let | let |
| begin | began | begun | lie | lay | lain |
| bend | bent | bent | lose | lost | lost |
| bite | bite | bitten | make | made | made |
| blow | blew | blown | meet | met | met |
| break | broke | broken | put | put | put |
| bring | brought | brought | raise* | raised* | raised* |
| build | built | built | read | read | read |
| burst | burst | burst | ride | rode | ridden |
| buy | bought | bought | ring | rang | rung |
| catch | caught | caught | rise | rose | risen |
| choose | chose | chosen | run | ran | run |
| come | came | come | say | said | said |
| cost | cost | cost | see | saw | seen |
| cut | cut | cut | sell | sold | sold |
| dig | dug | dug | set | set | set |
| dive | dived, dove | dived | shake | shook | shaken |
| do | did | done | shoot | shot | shot |
| drag* | dragged* | dragged* | show | showed | shown |
| draw | drew | drawn | shrink | shrank | shrunk |
| drink | drank | drunk | sing | sang | sung |
| drive | drove | driven | sink | sank | sunk |
| eat | ate | eaten | sit | sat | sat |
| fall | fell | fallen | sleep | slept | slept |
| feel | felt | felt | slide | slid | slid |
| fight | fought | fought | speak | spoke | spoken |
| fit | fit | fit | spend | spent | spent |
| fly | flew | flown | spread | spread | spread |
| forget | forgot | forgotten | spring | sprang | sprung |
| freeze | froze | frozen | stand | stood | stood |
| get | got | gotten | steal | stole | stolen |
| give | gave | given | sting | stung | stung |
| go | went | gone | swear | swore | sworn |
| grow | grew | grown | sweep | swept | swept |
| hang | hung | hung | swim | swam | swum |
| have | had | had | swing | swung | swung |
| hear | heard | heard | take | took | taken |
| hide | hid | hidden | teach | taught | taught |
| hit | hit | hit | tear | tore | torn |
| hold | held | held | tell | told | told |
| hurt | hurt | hurt | think | thought | thought |
| is/are | was/were | been | throw | threw | thrown |
| keep | kept | kept | understand | understood | understood |
| know | knew | known | wear | wore | worn |
| lay | laid | laid | win | won | won |
| lead | led | led | wind | wound | wound |
| leave | left | left | wring | wrung | wrung |
| lend | lent | lent | write | wrote | written |

*These words are regular but are often mistaken for irregular verbs.

## ADVERBS

**Definition:** An **adverb** modifies (qualifies or limits the meaning of) a verb, adjective or another adverb. Adverbs usually tell *where, when, how,* or *to what extent.* Adverbs may consist of more than one word.

Examples: Where *here, inside, nearby, somewhere*
When *tomorrow, earlier, frequently, lately*
How *quietly, quickly, well, carefully*
(Many adverbs that tell how end in *-ly.*)
To what extent (these may also be called intensifiers) *extremely, very, quite, so*

## PREPOSITIONS

**Definition:** A **preposition** shows a relationship between a noun or a pronoun and another word in the sentence. A preposition is often more than one word.

| | | |
|---|---|---|
| *about* | *beside* | *near* |
| *above* | *besides* | *next to* |
| *according to* | *between* | *of* |
| *across* | *beyond* | *on* |
| *after* | *by* | *onto* |
| *against* | *down* | *over* |
| *ahead of* | *during* | *through* |
| *along* | *except* | *throughout* |
| *among* | *for* | *to* |
| *around* | *from* | *toward* |
| *at* | *in* | *under* |
| *because of* | *in back of* | *until* |
| *before* | *in front of* | *up* |
| *behind* | *instead of* | *with* |
| *below* | *into* | *within* |
| *beneath* | *like* | *without* |

## CONJUNCTIONS

**Definition:** **Conjunctions** are used to connect words, phrases or sentences. *(and, but, or, however, therefore, so, if, when, except, because, though, although, unless)*

## INTERJECTIONS

**Definition:** **Interjections** are special words which often express emotion, or serve as fillers or attention-getters. The word "interjection" comes from Latin and means "thrown in between." Most interjections are followed by commas or exclamation points.

*Ouch! Whew! Oh! Hey!*
*Why, I know what you mean!*
*Well, I guess I'd better go.*
*Say, I have an idea.*
*Oh, I suppose it's all right.*

# WORD USAGE IN STANDARD ENGLISH

**bring, take**—*Bring* means to carry or lead someone or something **here**. *Please bring the newspaper to me.* *Take* means to carry or lead someone or something **there**. *Please take this with you to school tomorrow.*

**can, may**—*Can* shows the ability to do something. *She can play tennis well.* *May* asks or gives permission to do something. *May I use your telephone?*

**did, done**—*Did* is used to show past tense of *do. We did our work. Done* is used after a form of *have. She has done her chores.*

**doesn't, don't**—*Doesn't* is used with *he, she* and *it. Janet doesn't like ice cream. Don't* is used with *I, you, we* and *they. We don't have to leave until 9:00.*

**good, well**—*Good* describes something or someone. *That is a good apple. Well* describes an action. *He writes well.*

**in, into**—*In* means a location inside of something. *We drove in a car. Into* means motion or direction to a place within. *We drove into a car.*

**lay, lie**—*Lay* means to put or place something down. *Lay the books on the table, please. Lie* means to put or place yourself down. *I think I'll lie down and rest.*

**learn, teach**—*Learn* means to acquire or get knowledge. *He wants to learn French. Teach* means to give or impart knowledge. *The professor teaches history.*

**leave, let**—*Leave* means to go away. *They have to leave now. Let* means to permit. *He let me borrow a car.*

**lend, borrow**—*Lend* means to allow another person to use something of yours with the understanding that it be returned. *She will lend you a pen. Borrow* means to take something belonging to another person with the understanding that it will be returned. *May I borrow your hammer?*

**raise, rise**—*Raise* means to cause something to move upward. *It's time to raise the flag. Rise* means to move upward. *The sun will rise at 5:38 a.m. today.*

**set, sit**—*Set* means to place or put something in a certain position. *Please set the table. Sit* means to put yourself in a sitting position. *I will sit on the bench.*

# WRITING, MUSIC AND ART

# THE WRITING PROCESS

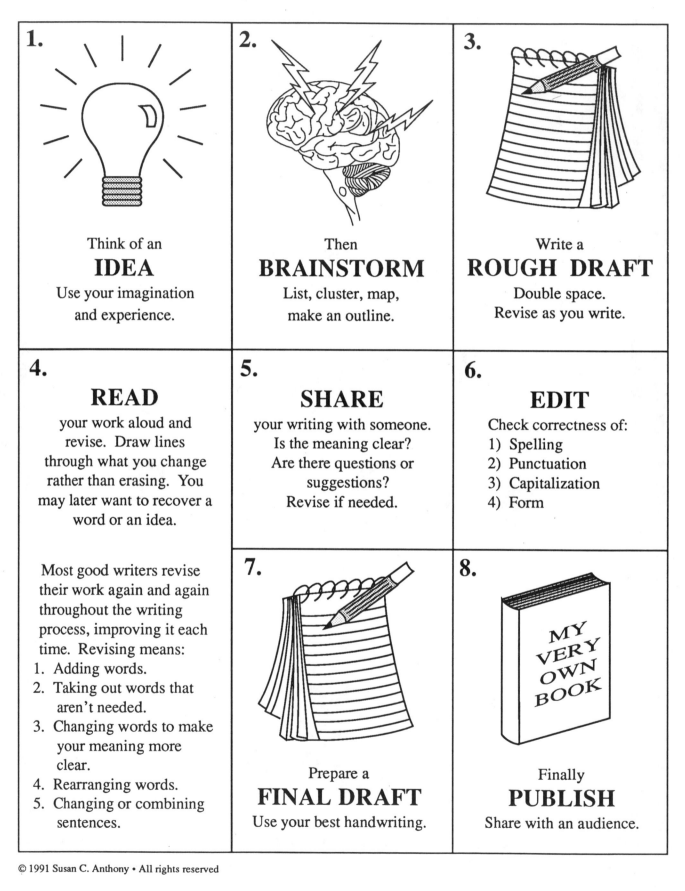

**1.**

Think of an
## IDEA
Use your imagination
and experience.

**2.**

Then
## BRAINSTORM
List, cluster, map,
make an outline.

**3.**

Write a
## ROUGH DRAFT
Double space.
Revise as you write.

**4.**

## READ
your work aloud and
revise. Draw lines
through what you change
rather than erasing. You
may later want to recover a
word or an idea.

Most good writers revise
their work again and again
throughout the writing
process, improving it each
time. Revising means:
1. Adding words.
2. Taking out words that
   aren't needed.
3. Changing words to make
   your meaning more
   clear.
4. Rearranging words.
5. Changing or combining
   sentences.

**5.**

## SHARE
your writing with someone.
Is the meaning clear?
Are there questions or
suggestions?
Revise if needed.

**6.**

## EDIT
Check correctness of:
1) Spelling
2) Punctuation
3) Capitalization
4) Form

**7.**

Prepare a
## FINAL DRAFT
Use your best handwriting.

**8.**

MY VERY OWN BOOK

Finally
## PUBLISH
Share with an audience.

# TO WRITE

advertisements
advice columns
animal stories
announcements
apologies
autobiographies
awards

beauty tips
bedtime stories
biographies
books
book jackets
book reviews
bumper stickers

campaign speeches
cartoon captions
cereal boxes
character sketches
codes
comparisons
comic strips
complaints
congratulations
conversations
crossword puzzles

definitions
descriptions
dialogues
diaries
diets
directions
directories
dramas
dream scripts

editorials
epitaphs
essays
exaggerations
explanations

fables
fairy tales
fantasies
folk tales
fortunes

game rules
get well notes
good & bad news
greeting cards
grocery lists
gossip

headlines
horoscopes

inquiries
interviews
introductions
invitations

jokes
journals

labels
legends
letters
lies
lists

magazine articles
memories
menus
messages
monologues
movie reviews
mysteries
myths

newscasts
newspapers
notebooks
notes

observations
opinions
orders

persuasive letters
plays
poems
post cards
posters
predictions
problems
problem solutions
product descriptions
puppet shows
puzzles

quizzes
questionnaires
questions
quotations

ransom notes
realistic fiction
rebus writing
recipes
reports
requests
research papers
riddles

sales notices
schedules
science fiction
secrets
self descriptions
signs
silly sayings
soap operas
songs
speeches
spook stories
sports stories
stories
superstitions

TV commercials
TV guides
TV programs
tall tales
thank you notes
tongue twisters
travel folders

want ads
wanted posters
warnings
wills
wishes
weather reports

Before beginning to write, think about your **purpose** and your intended **audience.** Your audience may be yourself, your friends, a teacher, the readers of a newspaper or someone else. Your **purpose** may be one of the following:

| | |
|---|---|
| to report | to inspire |
| to evaluate | to prove learning |
| to summarize | to clarify thoughts |
| to explain | to record |
| to share | to question |
| to inform | to create |
| to persuade | to discover yourself |

# PREWRITING

**Thinking** is the most important part of good writing. Thinking of a good topic is the first challenge.

It may help to close your eyes and visualize possible topics until you find one that interests you and that you can write about. Some writers make a list of possible topics just before writing. Others keep an ongoing "idea notebook" in which they write possible topics whenever they think of them. This provides a "bank" of ideas to review and choose from when it is time to write.

After choosing a topic and before beginning a rough draft, note as many ideas as possible about the topic. This helps with two important steps:

1.  Capturing specific ideas on paper and clarifying them.
2.  Organizing thoughts.

Each writer eventually discovers his/her own best methods for prewriting. The following are some suggestions to try.

## CLUSTERING

1.  Write the topic in a big circle in the middle of a page.
2.  As you think about the topic, write one or two words to remind you of each idea or thought about it.
3.  When writing, group related ideas as much as possible. Circle and connect ideas that have something in common.

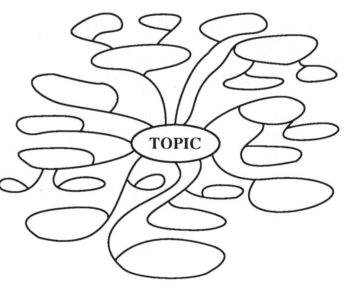

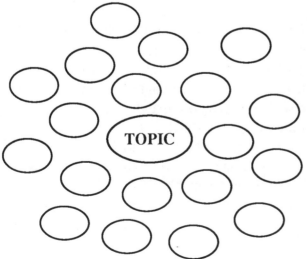

## BUBBLING

Similar to clustering, but the circles are not connected. After writing all ideas, go back and use color to highlight and group ideas which belong together.

## MAPPING

Mapping is a form of outlining.
1. Write the topic in a circle in the middle of the page.
2. Write main ideas on lines connected to the circle.
3. Write supporting ideas on lines connected to the main ideas.
4. Write details connected to supporting ideas.
5. When finished, go back and number the main ideas, supporting ideas, and details to indicate a sequence to use for writing.

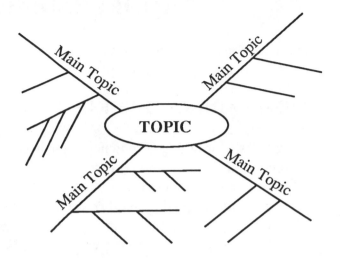

## OUTLINING

An outline is a formal map.  Other prewriting activities can help organize thoughts into an outline.

The **title** of the outline is the main subject.
**Roman numerals** are used for the main headings, which may be sections of a report or topics of paragraphs.  The first ten Roman numerals are: I, II, III, IV, V, VI, VII, VIII, IX, and X.
**Capital letters** show subheadings:  A, B, C, D, E, F, etc.
**Arabic numerals** show the details about the subheadings:  1, 2, 3, 4, 5, etc.
**Small letters** can be used under Arabic numerals to show details about details: a, b, c, d, e, etc.

Either phrases or sentences may be used in outlines, but the structure should be kept consistent.  Generally, if there is a **I.**, there must be a **II.**  If there is an **A.**, there must be a **B.**, and so on.

| TITLE OF OUTLINE | POISONOUS SNAKES OF THE U.S. |
|---|---|
| I. **Main Heading** <br>   A. **Subheading** <br>     1. **Detail** <br>       a. **Sub-detail** <br>       b. **Sub-detail** <br>     2. **Detail** <br>   B. **Subheading** <br>   C. **Subheading** <br> II. **Main Heading** <br>   A. **Subheading** <br>   B. **Subheading** | I. **Pit vipers** <br>   A. Rattlesnake <br>     1. Characteristics <br>       a. Size <br>       b. Rattle <br>     2. Range <br>   B. Water mocassin <br>   C. Copperhead <br> II. **Coral snakes** <br>   A. Eastern coral snake <br>   B. Western coral snake |

## LISTING

1. Write all the ideas you can think of about the topic in a list.
2. Go back through the list and group related ideas.  You might use color to highlight ideas which belong together, or use another sheet of paper and rewrite by main topic.

## USING CARDS

1. Use 3x5 index cards and write one idea per card.
2. When finished, group cards with related ideas into piles.  Name each group of cards (these will be main topics).
3. Put the cards in each group in order.

# PROOFREADING AND EDITING

The purpose for proofreading and editing is to prepare a piece of writing for a final draft or for publication by making sure it is correct in all details.

## PROOFREADING CHECKLIST

1. Is the first word of each sentence capitalized?
2. Are margins straight and correct?
3. Are paragraphs indented?
4. Are all words spelled correctly? See pages 178-179, FREQUENTLY MISSPELLED WORDS, or use a dictionary.
5. Are homonyms and confusing words spelled correctly? See pages 174-176, HOMONYMS AND TROUBLESOME WORDS.
6. Do all sentences end with correct punctuation?
7. Is all other punctuation correct? See pages 170-171, PUNCTUATION.
8. Are words capitalized correctly, including proper nouns and titles? See pages 172-173, CAPITALIZATION.
9. Are correct verb forms used? See page 185, CHART OF IRREGULAR VERBS.
10. Are all sentences complete? Are there any run-on sentences?

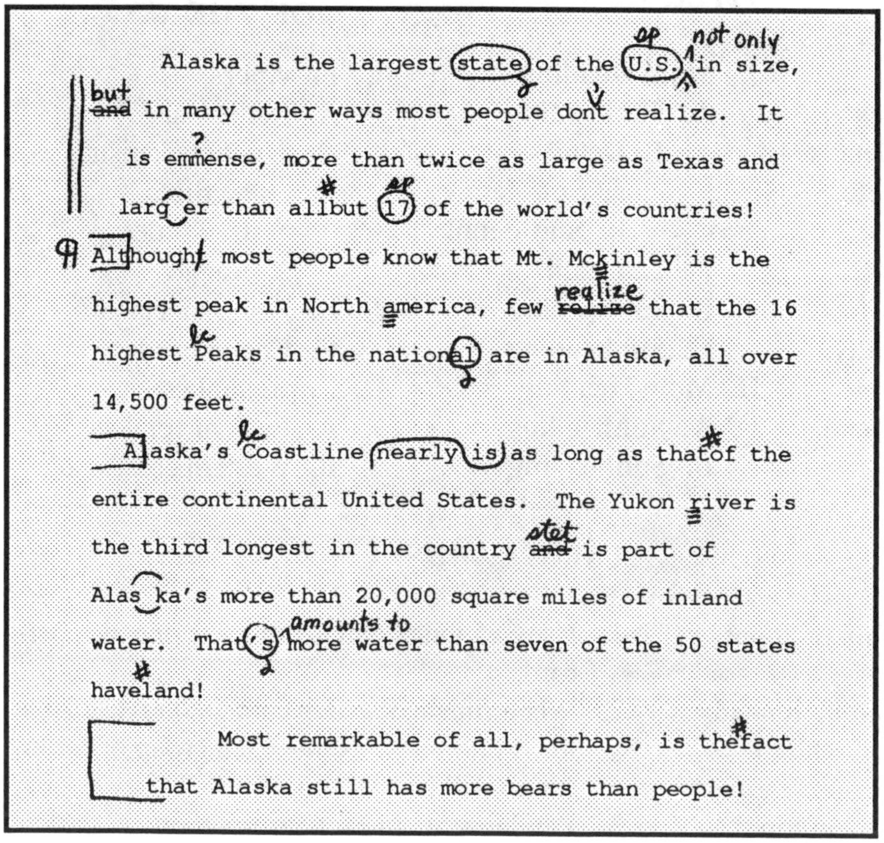
sp
not only
Alaska is the largest state of the U.S. in size,
but
and in many other ways most people dont realize. It
?
is emmense, more than twice as large as Texas and
#
sp
larg er than allbut 17 of the world's countries!
Althought most people know that Mt. Mckinley is the
realize
highest peak in North america, few relize that the 16
lc
highest Peaks in the nationsl are in Alaska, all over
14,500 feet.
lc
Alaska's Coastline nearly is as long as thatof the
entire continental United States. The Yukon river is
stet
the third longest in the country and is part of
Alas ka's more than 20,000 square miles of inland
amounts to
water. That's more water than seven of the 50 states
haveland!
Most remarkable of all, perhaps, is thefact
that Alaska still has more bears than people!

## PROOFREADERS' MARKS

**Proofreaders' marks** show changes that must be made in the proof, or rough draft. The short essay on the bottom left shows the use of proofreader's marks.

- delete (take out)
- / delete
- ^ insert
- insert period
- insert comma
- insert apostrophe
- insert quotation marks
- # insert a space
- delete a space
- transpose
- move left
- move right
- || straighten
- ¶ begin a new paragraph
- ≡ capitalize
- lc use lower-case letters
- sp spell out
- ? check to see if correct
- stet let it stand the way it was before it was marked

# LETTER WRITING

A **letter** is a written message addressed to a person or organization and most often sent through the **postal system**. There are two types of letters, friendly letters and business letters.

| | FRIENDLY LETTER | BUSINESS LETTER |
|---|---|---|
| **Sent to** | Friends<br>Relatives<br>Pen Pals | Companies<br>Editors<br>Government officials |
| **Purpose** | Keep in touch<br>Make friends (pen pals)<br>Say thank you<br>Say congratulations<br>Apologize<br>Send birthday or holiday greetings | Express an opinion<br>Make a complaint<br>Praise something good<br>Ask for information<br>Request materials<br>Order a product |
| **Writing** | Usually handwritten | Usually typed |
| **Return address** | Sometimes is not included | Often is part of printed letterhead stationery |
| **Date** | May be abbreviated | Never abbreviated |
| **Inside address** | Never included | Always included. Use the exact address which will be on the envelope. |
| **Greeting** | Follow with a comma ,<br>Normally use the person's first name | Follow with a colon :<br>Use a person's title and last name. If unknown, use, *Dear Sir or Madame:* or *To Whom It May Concern:* |
| **Body** | Indent the first line of each paragraph | Skip lines between paragraphs. Paragraphs are sometimes not indented. |
| **Closing** | *Your friend,*<br>*Love,* | *Sincerely,*<br>*Sincerely yours,*<br>*Yours truly,* |
| **Signature** | Sign with first name only, or first and last name. | Always sign in ink with both first and last names. |
| **Typed name** | Never included. | Always included in typewritten business letters. Usually, it is four spaces below the closing. |

## POSTAL RATES

**First class letters** (up to 12 ounces airmail)
    U.S. and Mexico..25¢ for the first ounce
                20¢ for each additional ounce
    Canada ................30¢ for the first ounce
                22¢ for each additional ounce
    All other places....45¢ for each **half** ounce

**Aerogrammes** ..............39¢

**Postcards**
    U.S. and Mexico...15¢
    Canada..................21¢
    All other places ....36¢ airmail

## FRIENDLY LETTER

2860 Park Avenue — Return address
Denver, Colorado 80215
June 16, 1991 — Date

Dear Mary Jane, — Greeting

We arrived at my grandmother's house late last night. It was a long drive from California! The weather wasn't bad, but I'm glad we had air conditioning. The Rocky Mountains were beautiful. I'm looking forward to our camping trip next week in the mountains.

I miss you already. I'm going swimming this afternoon and it won't be the same without you.

Write soon and tell me what's happening with you.

— Body

Your friend, — Closing
Jill — Signature

P.S. I forgot to ask if you are going to camp. Send me your camp address if you are.

*P.S.* means *postscript*. It is used when the writer forgot something important and does not want to recopy an entire revised letter.

## FINDING A PEN PAL

Letters are a good way to make new friends from almost anywhere in the world. To be matched with a pen friend overseas, send a self-addressed, stamped envelope to: International Friendship League, State House, P.O. Box 127, Boston, MA 02133. Include in the letter your full name, home address with zip, date of birth, sex, special interests or hobbies, and languages known including English. Everyone on the foreign lists knows English, or you may correspond in another language. Include $5.00 for a lifetime registration if you are under age 18, and $10.00 if you are 18 or older. Indicate if you are interested a certain area or country.

## BUSINESS LETTER

3920 6th Street
Anchorage, Alaska  99502 ——— Return address
December 3, 1990 ——————————— Date

John C. Withers, Editor
Anchorage Tribune
P.O. Box 2693 ——————————— Inside Address
Anchorage, Alaska  99510-2693

Dear Mr. Withers: ————————————————— Greeting

    Opening wilderness areas of Alaska to oil and gas development need not be now or never.  We should think again about the wisdom of our frenzied push to squander petroleum resources wastefully and as quickly as possible.  Oil under the ground is oil in safekeeping for future generations.

    Americans already consume far more than a fair share of the earth's fossil fuels, creating pollution, acid rain, and greenhouse gasses which could forever change the world.  We should be developing clean, renewable sources of energy, now! ——— Body

    I say leave the wilderness undeveloped for now.  In 50 or 100 years, people may finally appreciate the true value of both wilderness <u>and</u> oil.  Both are irreplaceable once gone.

Yours truly, ————————————————— Complimentary close

————————————————— Signature

Sandra Sutherland ——————————————— Typed signature.

Stamp

## ADDRESSING AN ENVELOPE

Return address—

Sandra Sutherland
3920 6th Street
Anchorage, Alaska 99502

Always include a zip code in the return address and address.

Address—

John C. Withers, Editor
Anchorage Tribune
P.O. Box 2693
Anchorage, Alaska  99510-2693

The address (not return address) should be typed double spaced if it has only three lines.

# JOURNAL WRITING

Journals can help you think, learn, remember and discover yourself. Write in a journal often, every day if possible. Be sure to note the date of each entry. Occasionally, read back through your journal and write your thoughts about that!

Whenever possible, write about today or right now. When you have more time or want to write about something else, consider the other ideas below.

## TODAY OR RIGHT NOW

Places you went
People with whom you spent time
Things you did
Things people said
Things you bought or were given
Special events at home, school, work
First impressions about someone or something new
Stories in the news and your reaction
Things you learned today

**Observations of nature**—
temperature, weather, the first robin, the first snow

**What you see, hear, smell or feel** at this moment

**Today's** feelings, thoughts, problems, opinions, ideas, decisions, goals, accomplishments

## LISTS

**Make lists of:**
things you love or hate
things for which you are thankful
things about which you wonder
things which hurt
things which don't make sense
things to which you look forward

## ABOUT YOURSELF

What your name means and how you got that name
What you know about your ancestors
Events and memories of your childhood
Stories people tell about you
Things you want to do or be someday
Your parents' work

Your appearance
Your good or bad habits
The best or worst things about you
Things of which you are proud

Your interests
Your daily or weekly schedule
Chores or your job
Sports
Hobbies
Clubs

Places you've lived
Pets you've had
People you admire
Things you've lost or found.

Birthdays or holidays
Dreams or nightmares

## BEST & WORST

**When were you:**
Happiest
Saddest
Sickest
Silliest
Angriest
Guiltiest
Loneliest
Laziest
Most afraid
Most grateful
Most disgusted
Most determined
Most envious
Most courageous
Most cowardly

## OPINIONS

On: Advice
Cheating
Divorce
Haircuts
Homework
Lying
Smoking
Stealing
Teenagers
Unfair rules
War
Being your age
Crying
Writing

## DESCRIPTIONS

**Describe the people in your life.** Write about their appearance, feelings, clothing, actions, beliefs. What do they say? How do they talk? What do others say about them?

Write about: family, friends, teachers

**Describe the places in your life.** Write about:
your room
the view from your window
your house
your neighborhood
your classroom
your school
Draw floor plans or maps of some of the places!

## FEELINGS

**What are your feelings about:**
how you look
getting your way
getting pushed around
getting up early
making mistakes
failing or losing
growing older
being ignored
being teased
being cheated
being tricked
being bothered
succeeding or winning
not being invited
not being understood
love, happiness, kindness
friendship, trust, death

## FAVORITES

**Your favorites and why.**
activity
animal
article of clothing
birthday
book
cartoon character
color
day of the week
dessert
flower
food
holiday
invention
movie
music
person
place
pet
restaurant
school subject
sport
story
time of the year
TV commercial
TV program

## IF

**If only...**
If you had $10,000...
If you had three wishes...
If you had a time machine...
If you had three minutes on television...
If you could go anywhere...
If you could keep only five things ...
If you could change the world...
If you lived in the past...
If you lived in the future...
If you were...someone else
something else
the boss

## EXPERIENCES AND MEMORIES

**Firsts.** Write about:
Your first day of school
Your first haircut
Your first home run
Your first memory
Your first performance
Your first report card
Your first speech
Your first swimming lesson

**Experiences.** Write about:
Being homesick
Being in trouble
Dressing up
Getting something new
Going to the doctor or dentist
Losing a friend
Making a friend
Riding the bus
The beach
A camping trip
The circus
Parades
Parties
Plays
Vacations

**Special events:** Write about:
A big storm
A disaster
An encounter with a dangerous animal
A time you felt understood
A time you got revenge
A time you helped someone
A phase you went through
A wish which came true

# MUSIC

**Music** consists of sounds and silences arranged and combined in patterns. **Sound** is produced by the vibrations of an object. All music has five basic elements.

## ELEMENTS OF MUSIC

1. **Pitch** is the highness or lowness of a sound and is based on the **frequency**, or speed, of the vibrations. The faster an object vibrates, the higher the pitch. Pitch is shown with **notes**.

2. **Rhythm** is the regular arrangement of strong and weak sounds and **rests**, or silences. It is measured in **beats**.

3. **Melody** is the **tune**, or order of sounds and silences.

4. **Harmony** is the sounding of two or more notes at the same time. Three or more notes sounded together are a **chord**.

5. **Tone color** is the quality of a musical sound. The difference in sound between a trumpet and a violin playing the same note is tone color.

## MUSICAL NOTATION

Music is written using **musical notation**, or symbols for notes and rests on a **grand staff**. The grand staff is a combination of the **treble clef** for high notes and the **bass clef** for low notes. A **clef** consists of five lines and the four spaces between them.

## PITCH IN MUSICAL NOTATION

Each line or space on the clef represents a certain pitch. The notes are named using the letters A through G.

The distance between two notes with the same name is an **octave**. On a piano, the keys which are an octave apart look the same. Notes raised one-half tone form a **sharp**, shown with the symbol . Notes lowered one-half tone are **flat**, shown with the symbol . A **natural** cancels a sharp or flat. The **key signature** shows which sharps or flats are always played.

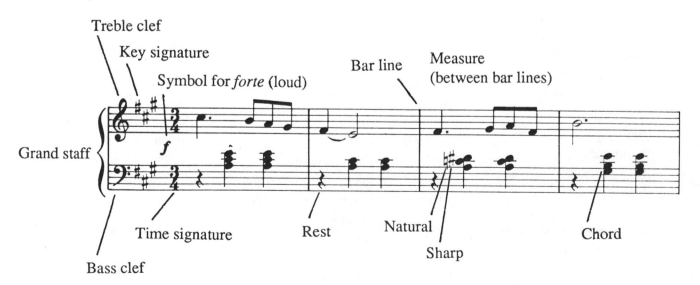

Treble clef
Key signature
Symbol for *forte* (loud)
Bar line
Measure (between bar lines)
Grand staff
Time signature
Rest
Natural
Sharp
Chord
Bass clef

## RHYTHM IN MUSICAL NOTATION

Rhythm is shown by the shape of the notes and by **rests**, which have the same time value as notes. The rests show silences which have the same time value as the notes.

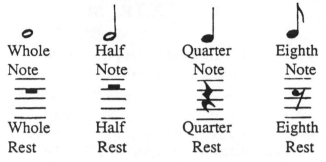

| Whole Note | Half Note | Quarter Note | Eighth Note |
| --- | --- | --- | --- |
| Whole Rest | Half Rest | Quarter Rest | Eighth Rest |

A whole note or rest has the same **duration**, or time value, as two half notes, four quarter notes, or eight eighth notes.

Notes and rests are grouped into **measures**, which are evenly spaced units of time. **Bar lines** separate the measures.

A **time signature** is a fraction. The numerator, or top number, shows how many beats are in a measure and the denominator, or bottom number, shows which kind of note (quarter note, half note, eighth note) receives one beat.

## EXPRESSION IN MUSICAL NOTATION

Composers also note "expression," or their ideas about how the music should be performed. Some of the terms used to show expression and dynamics are:

| | | | |
| --- | --- | --- | --- |
| *adagio* | slow | *allegro* | fast |
| *piano* | soft | *forte* | loud |
| *legato* | smooth | *staccato* | abrupt |
| *crescendo* | growing louder | *diminuendo* | growing softer |

## MUSICAL INSTRUMENTS

Musical instruments are grouped according to the source of the sound vibration. Some examples of each type are given.

I. **Chordophones** are stringed instruments.
   A. Bowed—violin, viola, cello, bass
   B. Plucked—guitar, harp, banjo
   C. Keyboard—piano, harpsichord

II. **Aerophones** are wind instruments.
   A. Woodwind—recorder, flute, reed instruments such as clarinet and oboe
   B. Brass—horn, trumpet, trombone, tuba
   C. Keyboard—pipe organ

III. **Membranophones** are some of the percussion instruments.
   A. Drums
   B. Tamborines

IV. **Idiophones** are also percussion instruments.
   A. Cymbals
   B. Gongs

V. **Electrophones** have electrically produced sounds.
   A. Synthesizer
   B. Electronic keyboard

## VOCAL MUSIC

Vocal music is produced by the vibration of people's vocal chords in song. Voices are classified by the **range** of tones, high to low, which a person can sing. **Lyrics** are the words of a song. **Accompaniment** is the instrumental part played with a song.

| | |
| --- | --- |
| *soprano* | highest female voice |
| *alto (contralto)* | lowest female voice |
| *tenor* | high adult male voice |
| *baritone* | middle male voice |
| *bass* | lowest male voice |

# ART AND COLOR

**Art** is the use of skill and creativity in the making of beautiful objects. Some of the **fine arts** are drawing, painting and sculpture. **Graphic arts** include printing, etching and photography.

## PRINCIPLES OF ART
Rhythm
Balance
Unity
Variety
Emphasis

## ELEMENTS OF DESIGN
Line
Shape
Color
Texture
Form

## THE SPECTRUM

A **prism**, which is a triangular piece of glass, divides light into a **spectrum** of colors. Visible light has in it all of the colors of the rainbow in this order: red, orange, yellow, green, blue, indigo and violet. **Ultraviolet** light is beyond violet and **infrared** is beyond red. People cannot see these colors but some animals can.

## THE COLOR WHEEL

**Primary colors** are yellow, blue and red.

**Secondary colors** are orange, violet and green. They are made by mixing the primary pigments. **Pigment** is the coloring material in paint.

**Complementary colors** are opposite each other on the color wheel, such as green and red.

**Adjacent colors** are next to each other on the color wheel, such as yellow and green.

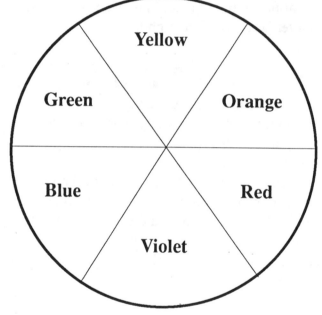

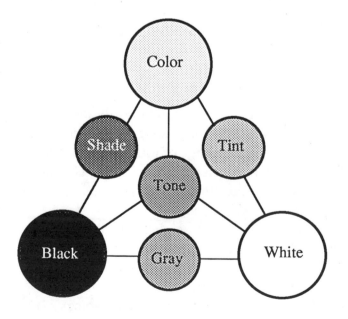

## TINTS AND SHADES

A **shade** is made by mixing any color and black.

A **tint** is made by mixing any color and white.

**Gray** is the result of mixing black and white.

A **tone** is made by mixing a color with both black and white.

# MATH
# AND
# NUMBERS

# MATHEMATICS

**Mathematics** is the science of numbers. **Arithmetic** is a branch of mathematics which deals with numbers and their computations. **Geometry** is another branch of mathematics, dealing with points, lines, angles, surfaces and solids. Some other branches of mathematics are **algebra**, **calculus** and **trigonometry**.

A **number** is an amount. A **numeral** is the symbol we use to show that amount. Although most places in the world use our numeration system, with 0, 1, 2, 3, 4, 5, 6, 7, 8, and 9 as the numerals, some systems are different. For example, people in Egypt use the following symbols for the numbers 1 to 9.

> ١ ٢ ٣ ٤ ٥ ٦ ٧ ٨ ٩

## ROMAN NUMERALS

**Roman numerals** were widely used until the A.D. 1500's, and are still used today sometimes on the faces of clocks, in outlines, and to record dates on monuments.

$$
\begin{aligned}
I &= 1 \\
V &= 5 \\
X &= 10 \\
L &= 50 \\
C &= 100 \\
D &= 500 \\
M &= 1000
\end{aligned}
$$

**Addition rule:** Add the values for the symbols from left to right: **XVII** = 10+5+1+1 = 17

**Subtraction rule:** When a symbol for a smaller number is written to the *left* of a symbol for a larger number, subtract the smaller number from the larger and add the result as usual:
**IV** (1 before 5) = 5-1 = 4
**XXIX** (1 before 10) = 10+10+(10-1) = 29

## COMMON MATH SYMBOLS

| | |
|---|---|
| + plus (addition) | > greater than |
| − minus (subtraction) | < less than |
| X times (multiplication) | % percent |
| ÷ divided by (division) | $ dollars |
| = equals | ¢ cents |
| ≠ does not equal | |

## SUGGESTIONS FOR SOLVING MATH WORD PROBLEMS

1. **Read** the problem carefully. What does it ask you to find?
2. **Think** about the problem. Try using these strategies.
   *Visualize what is happening in your mind.
   *Draw a picture or diagram.
   *Restate the problem in your own words.
   *Make a list or chart to organize the facts.
   *Act out the problem.
3. Notice any **key words**.
   Key words which may signal addition are: *total, in all, all together, sum, together.*
   Key words which signal subtraction are: *how many more, how many less, difference, greater than, fewer than, left, more than, less than, change.*
4. **Decide** how to solve the problem and put the facts into a number sentence, such as 18 x 45 =____.
5. **Solve** the number sentence.
6. **Label** the answer.
7. **Check** the math for accuracy. Then think about the problem again. Does the answer make sense?

# PLACE VALUE

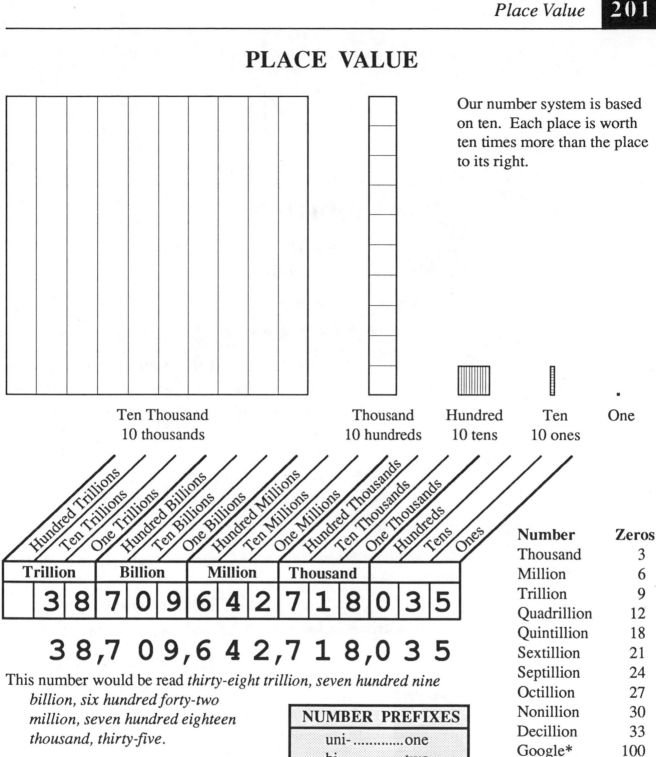

Our number system is based on ten. Each place is worth ten times more than the place to its right.

| Ten Thousand | Thousand | Hundred | Ten | One |
|---|---|---|---|---|
| 10 thousands | 10 hundreds | 10 tens | 10 ones | |

| | Trillion | | | Billion | | | Million | | | Thousand | | | | | |
|---|---|---|---|---|---|---|---|---|---|---|---|---|---|---|---|
| Hundred Trillions | Ten Trillions | One Trillions | Hundred Billions | Ten Billions | One Billions | Hundred Millions | Ten Millions | One Millions | Hundred Thousands | Ten Thousands | One Thousands | Hundreds | Tens | Ones |
| | 3 | 8 | 7 | 0 | 9 | 6 | 4 | 2 | 7 | 1 | 8 | 0 | 3 | 5 |

## 3 8,7 0 9,6 4 2,7 1 8,0 3 5

This number would be read *thirty-eight trillion, seven hundred nine billion, six hundred forty-two million, seven hundred eighteen thousand, thirty-five.*

| Number | Zeros |
|---|---|
| Thousand | 3 |
| Million | 6 |
| Trillion | 9 |
| Quadrillion | 12 |
| Quintillion | 18 |
| Sextillion | 21 |
| Septillion | 24 |
| Octillion | 27 |
| Nonillion | 30 |
| Decillion | 33 |
| Google* | 100 |

*At one time, there was no name for a one with 100 zeros after it. An American mathematician, Edward Kasner, asked his 9-year-old nephew to name it. He called it a "googol" and that is what mathematicians call it today!

### NUMBER PREFIXES

| | |
|---|---|
| uni- | one |
| bi- | two |
| tri- | three |
| quadri- | four |
| quint- | five |
| sex- | six |
| sept- | seven |
| oct- | eight |
| non- | nine |
| deci- | ten |

A hundred seconds is 1⅔ minutes.
A thousand seconds is about 17 minutes.
A million seconds is more than 11½ days.
A billion seconds is over 31½ years.
A trillion seconds is 31,710 years!

```
0 +  0 =  0      1 +  0 =  1      2 +  0 =  2      3 +  0 =  3      4 +  0 =  4      5 +  0 =  5      6 +  0 =  6
0 +  1 =  1      1 +  1 =  2      2 +  1 =  3      3 +  1 =  4      4 +  1 =  5      5 +  1 =  6      6 +  1 =  7
0 +  2 =  2      1 +  2 =  3      2 +  2 =  4      3 +  2 =  5      4 +  2 =  6      5 +  2 =  7      6 +  2 =  8
0 +  3 =  3      1 +  3 =  4      2 +  3 =  5      3 +  3 =  6      4 +  3 =  7      5 +  3 =  8      6 +  3 =  9
0 +  4 =  4      1 +  4 =  5      2 +  4 =  6      3 +  4 =  7      4 +  4 =  8      5 +  4 =  9      6 +  4 = 10
0 +  5 =  5      1 +  5 =  6      2 +  5 =  7      3 +  5 =  8      4 +  5 =  9      5 +  5 = 10      6 +  5 = 11
0 +  6 =  6      1 +  6 =  7      2 +  6 =  8      3 +  6 =  9      4 +  6 = 10      5 +  6 = 11      6 +  6 = 12
0 +  7 =  7      1 +  7 =  8      2 +  7 =  9      3 +  7 = 10      4 +  7 = 11      5 +  7 = 12      6 +  7 = 13
0 +  8 =  8      1 +  8 =  9      2 +  8 = 10      3 +  8 = 11      4 +  8 = 12      5 +  8 = 13      6 +  8 = 14
0 +  9 =  9      1 +  9 = 10      2 +  9 = 11      3 +  9 = 12      4 +  9 = 13      5 +  9 = 14      6 +  9 = 15
0 + 10 = 10      1 + 10 = 11      2 + 10 = 12      3 + 10 = 13      4 + 10 = 14      5 + 10 = 15      6 + 10 = 16

7 +  0 =  7      8 +  0 =  8
7 +  1 =  8      8 +  1 =  9
7 +  2 =  9      8 +  2 = 10
7 +  3 = 10      8 +  3 = 11
7 +  4 = 11      8 +  4 = 12
7 +  5 = 12      8 +  5 = 13
7 +  6 = 13      8 +  6 = 14
7 +  7 = 14      8 +  7 = 15
7 +  8 = 15      8 +  8 = 16
7 +  9 = 16      8 +  9 = 17
7 + 10 = 17      8 + 10 = 18

9 +  0 =  9     10 +  0 = 10
9 +  1 = 10     10 +  1 = 11
9 +  2 = 11     10 +  2 = 12
9 +  3 = 12     10 +  3 = 13
9 +  4 = 13     10 +  4 = 14
9 +  5 = 14     10 +  5 = 15
9 +  6 = 15     10 +  6 = 16
9 +  7 = 16     10 +  7 = 17
9 +  8 = 17     10 +  8 = 18
9 +  9 = 18     10 +  9 = 19
9 + 10 = 19     10 + 10 = 20
```

# ADDITION

**Addition** tells the total when two or more sets, or groups of things, are put together.

♣♣♣♣♣♣♣♣♣♣♣   **11**   addend
♣♣♣♣♣♣♣♣   **+ 8**   addend
           **19**   sum

Check addition by doing the problem again, perhaps with the addends in a different order. The two answers should be the same.

> Addition and subtraction facts can be grouped. For example:
>
> **5 + 8 = 13**       **8 + 5 = 13**
> **13 − 5 = 8**       **13 − 8 = 5**

**Subtraction** tells how many are left when some of a set, or group of things, is taken away.

⬭⬭⬭⬭⬭⬭⬭⬭⬭⬭   **19**   minuend
⬭⬭⬭⬭⬭⬭⬭⬭   **− 8**   subtrahend
           **11**   difference

Check subtraction by adding the difference and the subtrahend. The answer should equal the minuend.

# SUBTRACTION

```
0 -  0 =  0      1 -  1 =  0
1 -  0 =  1      2 -  1 =  1
2 -  0 =  2      3 -  1 =  2
3 -  0 =  3      4 -  1 =  3
4 -  0 =  4      5 -  1 =  4
5 -  0 =  5      6 -  1 =  5
6 -  0 =  6      7 -  1 =  6
7 -  0 =  7      8 -  1 =  7
8 -  0 =  8      9 -  1 =  8
9 -  0 =  9     10 -  1 =  9
10 - 0 = 10     11 -  1 = 10

2 -  2 =  0      3 -  3 =  0
3 -  2 =  1      4 -  3 =  1
4 -  2 =  2      5 -  3 =  2
5 -  2 =  3      6 -  3 =  3
6 -  2 =  4      7 -  3 =  4
7 -  2 =  5      8 -  3 =  5
8 -  2 =  6      9 -  3 =  6
9 -  2 =  7     10 -  3 =  7
10 - 2 =  8     11 -  3 =  8
11 - 2 =  9     12 -  3 =  9
12 - 2 = 10     13 -  3 = 10
```

```
4 -  4 =  0     5 -  5 =  0      6 -  6 =  0      7 -  7 =  0      8 -  8 =  0      9 -  9 =  0     10 - 10 =  0
5 -  4 =  1     6 -  5 =  1      7 -  6 =  1      8 -  7 =  1      9 -  8 =  1     10 -  9 =  1     11 - 10 =  1
6 -  4 =  2     7 -  5 =  2      8 -  6 =  2      9 -  7 =  2     10 -  8 =  2     11 -  9 =  2     12 - 10 =  2
7 -  4 =  3     8 -  5 =  3      9 -  6 =  3     10 -  7 =  3     11 -  8 =  3     12 -  9 =  3     13 - 10 =  3
8 -  4 =  4     9 -  5 =  4     10 -  6 =  4     11 -  7 =  4     12 -  8 =  4     13 -  9 =  4     14 - 10 =  4
9 -  4 =  5    10 -  5 =  5     11 -  6 =  5     12 -  7 =  5     13 -  8 =  5     14 -  9 =  5     15 - 10 =  5
10 - 4 =  6    11 -  5 =  6     12 -  6 =  6     13 -  7 =  6     14 -  8 =  6     15 -  9 =  6     16 - 10 =  6
11 - 4 =  7    12 -  5 =  7     13 -  6 =  7     14 -  7 =  7     15 -  8 =  7     16 -  9 =  7     17 - 10 =  7
12 - 4 =  8    13 -  5 =  8     14 -  6 =  8     15 -  7 =  8     16 -  8 =  8     17 -  9 =  8     18 - 10 =  8
13 - 4 =  9    14 -  5 =  9     15 -  6 =  9     16 -  7 =  9     17 -  8 =  9     18 -  9 =  9     19 - 10 =  9
14 - 4 = 10    15 -  5 = 10     16 -  6 = 10     17 -  7 = 10     18 -  8 = 10     19 -  9 = 10     20 - 10 = 10
```

| | | | | | | |
|---|---|---|---|---|---|---|
| 0 x 0 = 0 | 1 x 0 = 0 | 2 x 0 = 0 | 3 x 0 = 0 | 4 x 0 = 0 | 5 x 0 = 0 | 6 x 0 = 0 |
| 0 x 1 = 0 | 1 x 1 = 1 | 2 x 1 = 2 | 3 x 1 = 3 | 4 x 1 = 4 | 5 x 1 = 5 | 6 x 1 = 6 |
| 0 x 2 = 0 | 1 x 2 = 2 | 2 x 2 = 4 | 3 x 2 = 6 | 4 x 2 = 8 | 5 x 2 = 10 | 6 x 2 = 12 |
| 0 x 3 = 0 | 1 x 3 = 3 | 2 x 3 = 6 | 3 x 3 = 9 | 4 x 3 = 12 | 5 x 3 = 15 | 6 x 3 = 18 |
| 0 x 4 = 0 | 1 x 4 = 4 | 2 x 4 = 8 | 3 x 4 = 12 | 4 x 4 = 16 | 5 x 4 = 20 | 6 x 4 = 24 |
| 0 x 5 = 0 | 1 x 5 = 5 | 2 x 5 = 10 | 3 x 5 = 15 | 4 x 5 = 20 | 5 x 5 = 25 | 6 x 5 = 30 |
| 0 x 6 = 0 | 1 x 6 = 6 | 2 x 6 = 12 | 3 x 6 = 18 | 4 x 6 = 24 | 5 x 6 = 30 | 6 x 6 = 36 |
| 0 x 7 = 0 | 1 x 7 = 7 | 2 x 7 = 14 | 3 x 7 = 21 | 4 x 7 = 28 | 5 x 7 = 35 | 6 x 7 = 42 |
| 0 x 8 = 0 | 1 x 8 = 8 | 2 x 8 = 16 | 3 x 8 = 24 | 4 x 8 = 32 | 5 x 8 = 40 | 6 x 8 = 48 |
| 0 x 9 = 0 | 1 x 9 = 9 | 2 x 9 = 18 | 3 x 9 = 27 | 4 x 9 = 36 | 5 x 9 = 45 | 6 x 9 = 54 |
| 0 x 10 = 0 | 1 x 10 = 10 | 2 x 10 = 20 | 3 x 10 = 30 | 4 x 10 = 40 | 5 x 10 = 50 | 6 x 10 = 60 |

| | | | |
|---|---|---|---|
| 7 x 0 = 0 | 8 x 0 = 0 | | |
| 7 x 1 = 7 | 8 x 1 = 8 | | |
| 7 x 2 = 14 | 8 x 2 = 16 | | |
| 7 x 3 = 21 | 8 x 3 = 24 | | |
| 7 x 4 = 28 | 8 x 4 = 32 | | |
| 7 x 5 = 35 | 8 x 5 = 40 | | |
| 7 x 6 = 42 | 8 x 6 = 48 | | |
| 7 x 7 = 49 | 8 x 7 = 56 | | |
| 7 x 8 = 56 | 8 x 8 = 64 | | |
| 7 x 9 = 63 | 8 x 9 = 72 | | |
| 7 x 10 = 70 | 8 x 10 = 80 | | |
| 9 x 0 = 0 | 10 x 0 = 0 | | |
| 9 x 1 = 9 | 10 x 1 = 10 | | |
| 9 x 2 = 18 | 10 x 2 = 20 | | |
| 9 x 3 = 27 | 10 x 3 = 30 | | |
| 9 x 4 = 36 | 10 x 4 = 40 | | |
| 9 x 5 = 45 | 10 x 5 = 50 | | |
| 9 x 6 = 54 | 10 x 6 = 60 | | |
| 9 x 7 = 63 | 10 x 7 = 70 | | |
| 9 x 8 = 72 | 10 x 8 = 80 | | |
| 9 x 9 = 81 | 10 x 9 = 90 | | |
| 9 x 10 = 90 | 10 x 10 = 100 | | |

# MULTIPLICATION  X

**Multiplication** of 6 x 3 tells how many total there would be in 3 sets, or groups, of 6 each.

3 times
6 in each group

6 multiplicand
x 3 multiplier
18 product

Check multiplication by doing the problem again. Perhaps reverse multiplicand and multiplier. The two answers should be the same.

> Multiplication and division facts can be grouped. For example.
>
> 7 x 9 = 63      9 x 7 = 63
> 63 ÷ 9 = 7      63 ÷ 9 = 7

**Division** of 14 ÷ 4 tells how many sets, or groups, of 4 are in 14, and how many are left over.

$$4\overline{)14}$$

divisor · quotient 3 · dividend 14 · 12 · remainder 2

There are 3 sets of 4 with 2 left over.

Check division by multiplying the quotient by the divisor, then adding the remainder if there is one. The answer should equal the dividend.

# DIVISION ÷

| | | |
|---|---|---|
| 0 + 0 | I | 0 + 1 = 0 |
| 1 + 0 | M | 1 + 1 = 1 |
| 2 + 0 | P | 2 + 1 = 2 |
| 3 + 0 | O | 3 + 1 = 3 |
| 4 + 0 | S | 4 + 1 = 4 |
| 5 + 0 | S | 5 + 1 = 5 |
| 6 + 0 | I | 6 + 1 = 6 |
| 7 + 0 | B | 7 + 1 = 7 |
| 8 + 0 | L | 8 + 1 = 8 |
| 9 + 0 | E | 9 + 1 = 9 |
| 10 + 0 | | 10 + 1 = 10 |

| | |
|---|---|
| 0 + 2 = 0 | 0 + 3 = 0 |
| 2 + 2 = 1 | 3 + 3 = 1 |
| 4 + 2 = 2 | 6 + 3 = 2 |
| 6 + 2 = 3 | 9 + 3 = 3 |
| 8 + 2 = 4 | 12 + 3 = 4 |
| 10 + 2 = 5 | 15 + 3 = 5 |
| 12 + 2 = 6 | 18 + 3 = 6 |
| 14 + 2 = 7 | 21 + 3 = 7 |
| 16 + 2 = 8 | 24 + 3 = 8 |
| 18 + 2 = 9 | 27 + 3 = 9 |
| 20 + 2 = 10 | 30 + 3 = 10 |

| | | | | | | |
|---|---|---|---|---|---|---|
| 0 + 4 = 0 | 0 + 5 = 0 | 0 + 6 = 0 | 0 + 7 = 0 | 0 + 8 = 0 | 0 + 9 = 0 | 0 + 10 = 0 |
| 4 + 4 = 1 | 5 + 5 = 1 | 6 + 6 = 1 | 7 + 7 = 1 | 8 + 8 = 1 | 9 + 9 = 1 | 10 + 10 = 1 |
| 8 + 4 = 2 | 10 + 5 = 2 | 12 + 6 = 2 | 14 + 7 = 2 | 16 + 8 = 2 | 18 + 9 = 2 | 20 + 10 = 2 |
| 12 + 4 = 3 | 15 + 5 = 3 | 18 + 6 = 3 | 21 + 7 = 3 | 24 + 8 = 3 | 27 + 9 = 3 | 30 + 10 = 3 |
| 16 + 4 = 4 | 20 + 5 = 4 | 24 + 6 = 4 | 28 + 7 = 4 | 32 + 8 = 4 | 36 + 9 = 4 | 40 + 10 = 4 |
| 20 + 4 = 5 | 25 + 5 = 5 | 30 + 6 = 5 | 35 + 7 = 5 | 40 + 8 = 5 | 45 + 9 = 5 | 50 + 10 = 5 |
| 24 + 4 = 6 | 30 + 5 = 6 | 36 + 6 = 6 | 42 + 7 = 6 | 48 + 8 = 6 | 54 + 9 = 6 | 60 + 10 = 6 |
| 28 + 4 = 7 | 35 + 5 = 7 | 42 + 6 = 7 | 49 + 7 = 7 | 56 + 8 = 7 | 63 + 9 = 7 | 70 + 10 = 7 |
| 32 + 4 = 8 | 40 + 5 = 8 | 48 + 6 = 8 | 56 + 7 = 8 | 64 + 8 = 8 | 72 + 9 = 8 | 80 + 10 = 8 |
| 36 + 4 = 9 | 45 + 5 = 9 | 54 + 6 = 9 | 63 + 7 = 9 | 72 + 8 = 9 | 81 + 9 = 9 | 90 + 10 = 9 |
| 40 + 4 = 10 | 50 + 5 = 10 | 60 + 6 = 10 | 70 + 7 = 10 | 80 + 8 = 10 | 90 + 9 = 10 | 100 + 10 = 10 |

# FRACTIONS

A **fraction** is an equal part of a whole.

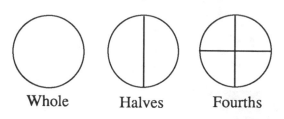

Whole          Halves          Fourths

The **numerator** tells how many parts are being counted or referred to.

$$\frac{1}{2}$$

**Numerator**

**Denominator**

The **denominator** tells into how many equal parts the whole is divided.

**Equivalent fractions** are different ways of naming the same amount.

$$\frac{1}{2} = \frac{2}{4} = \frac{3}{6}$$

To change a fraction to an equivalent fraction, multiply both numerator and denominator by a common multiple. To **reduce**, or change to lowest terms, divide both numerator and denominator by a common factor.

## FACTORS CHART

| | | | | | | | | | |
|---|---|---|---|---|---|---|---|---|---|
| **1** | 1 | | | | | | | | |
| **2** | 1 | 2 | | | | | | | |
| **3** | 1 | 3 | | | | | | | |
| **4** | 1 | 2 | 4 | | | | | | |
| **5** | 1 | 5 | | | | | | | |
| **6** | 1 | 2 | 3 | 6 | | | | | |
| **7** | 1 | 7 | | | | | | | |
| **8** | 1 | 2 | 4 | 8 | | | | | |
| **9** | 1 | 3 | 9 | | | | | | |
| **10** | 1 | 2 | 5 | 10 | | | | | |
| **11** | 1 | 11 | | | | | | | |
| **12** | 1 | 2 | 3 | 4 | 6 | 12 | | | |
| **13** | 1 | 13 | | | | | | | |
| **14** | 1 | 2 | 7 | 14 | | | | | |
| **15** | 1 | 3 | 5 | 15 | | | | | |
| **16** | 1 | 2 | 4 | 8 | 16 | | | | |
| **17** | 1 | 17 | | | | | | | |
| **18** | 1 | 2 | 3 | 6 | 9 | 18 | | | |
| **19** | 1 | 19 | | | | | | | |
| **20** | 1 | 2 | 4 | 5 | 10 | 20 | | | |
| **21** | 1 | 3 | 7 | 21 | | | | | |
| **22** | 1 | 2 | 11 | 22 | | | | | |
| **23** | 1 | 23 | | | | | | | |
| **24** | 1 | 2 | 3 | 4 | 6 | 8 | 12 | 24 | |
| **25** | 1 | 5 | 25 | | | | | | |
| **26** | 1 | 2 | 13 | 26 | | | | | |
| **27** | 1 | 3 | 9 | 27 | | | | | |
| **28** | 1 | 2 | 4 | 7 | 14 | 28 | | | |
| **29** | 1 | 29 | | | | | | | |
| **30** | 1 | 2 | 3 | 5 | 6 | 10 | 15 | 30 | |
| **31** | 1 | 31 | | | | | | | |
| **32** | 1 | 2 | 4 | 8 | 16 | 32 | | | |
| **33** | 1 | 3 | 11 | 33 | | | | | |
| **34** | 1 | 2 | 17 | 34 | | | | | |
| **35** | 1 | 5 | 7 | 35 | | | | | |
| **36** | 1 | 2 | 3 | 4 | 6 | 9 | 12 | 18 | 36 |
| **37** | 1 | 37 | | | | | | | |
| **38** | 1 | 2 | 19 | 38 | | | | | |
| **39** | 1 | 3 | 13 | 39 | | | | | |
| **40** | 1 | 2 | 4 | 5 | 8 | 10 | 20 | 40 | |
| **41** | 1 | 41 | | | | | | | |
| **42** | 1 | 2 | 3 | 6 | 7 | 14 | 21 | 42 | |
| **43** | 1 | 43 | | | | | | | |
| **44** | 1 | 2 | 4 | 11 | 22 | 44 | | | |
| **45** | 1 | 3 | 5 | 9 | 15 | 45 | | | |
| **46** | 1 | 2 | 23 | 46 | | | | | |
| **47** | 1 | 47 | | | | | | | |
| **48** | 1 | 2 | 3 | 4 | 6 | 8 | 12 | 16 | 24 48 |
| **49** | 1 | 7 | 49 | | | | | | |
| **50** | 1 | 2 | 5 | 10 | 25 | 50 | | | |
| **75** | 1 | 3 | 5 | 15 | 25 | 75 | | | |
| **100** | 1 | 2 | 4 | 5 | 10 | 20 | 25 | 50 | 100 |

**Factors** of a number divide into it evenly.

**Common factors** are any factors two numbers have in common.

The **greatest common factor** is the largest factor two numbers have in common.

A **prime number** has only itself and 1 as factors.

A **composite number** has factors other than itself and 1.

**Common multiples** are any multiples two numbers have in common.

The **least common multiple** is the smallest multiple two numbers have in common.

## MULTIPLES CHART

| 1 | 2 | 3 | 4 | 5 | 6 | 7 | 8 | 9 | 10 |
|---|---|---|---|---|---|---|---|---|---|
| 2 | 4 | 6 | 8 | 10 | 12 | 14 | 16 | 18 | 20 |
| 3 | 6 | 9 | 12 | 15 | 18 | 21 | 24 | 27 | 30 |
| 4 | 8 | 12 | 16 | 20 | 24 | 28 | 32 | 36 | 40 |
| 5 | 10 | 15 | 20 | 25 | 30 | 35 | 40 | 45 | 50 |
| 6 | 12 | 18 | 24 | 30 | 36 | 42 | 48 | 54 | 60 |
| 7 | 14 | 21 | 28 | 35 | 42 | 49 | 56 | 63 | 70 |
| 8 | 16 | 24 | 32 | 40 | 48 | 56 | 64 | 72 | 80 |
| 9 | 18 | 27 | 36 | 45 | 54 | 63 | 72 | 81 | 90 |
| 10 | 20 | 30 | 40 | 50 | 60 | 70 | 80 | 90 | 100 |

# DECIMAL FRACTIONS

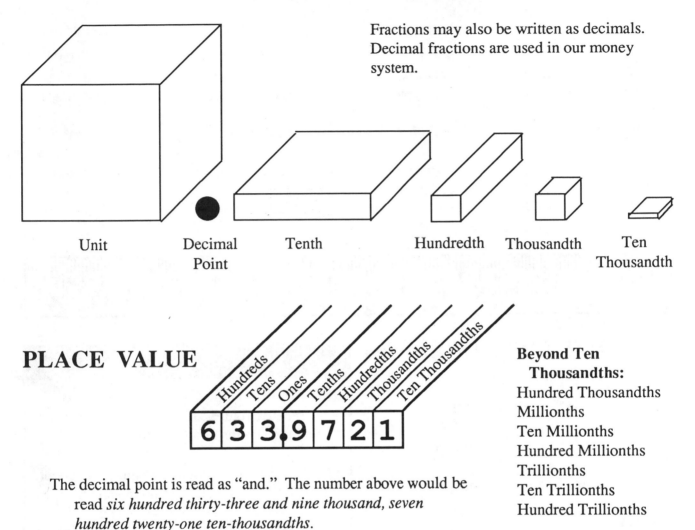

Fractions may also be written as decimals. Decimal fractions are used in our money system.

Unit  Decimal Point  Tenth  Hundredth  Thousandth  Ten Thousandth

## PLACE VALUE

| Hundreds | Tens | Ones | Tenths | Hundredths | Thousandths | Ten Thousandths |
|----------|------|------|--------|------------|-------------|-----------------|
| 6 | 3 | 3. | 9 | 7 | 2 | 1 |

**Beyond Ten Thousandths:**
Hundred Thousandths
Millionths
Ten Millionths
Hundred Millionths
Trillionths
Ten Trillionths
Hundred Trillionths

The decimal point is read as "and." The number above would be read *six hundred thirty-three and nine thousand, seven hundred twenty-one ten-thousandths.*

## FRACTION DECIMAL EQUIVALENTS

| | | | | |
|---|---|---|---|---|
| $\frac{1}{2} = .5$ | $\frac{3}{4} = .75$ | $\frac{4}{5} = .8$ | $\frac{3}{8} = .375$ | $\frac{3}{10} = .3$ |
| $\frac{1}{3} = .33*$ | $\frac{1}{5} = .2$ | $\frac{1}{6} = .167*$ | $\frac{5}{8} = .625$ | $\frac{7}{10} = .7$ |
| $\frac{2}{3} = .67*$ | $\frac{2}{5} = .4$ | $\frac{5}{6} = .833*$ | $\frac{7}{8} = .875$ | $\frac{9}{10} = .9$ |
| $\frac{1}{4} = .25$ | $\frac{3}{5} = .6$ | $\frac{1}{8} = .125$ | $\frac{1}{10} = .1$ | *Approximate |

# METRIC MEASUREMENT

| | PREFIX | LENGTH | VOLUME | WEIGHT |
|---|---|---|---|---|
| x 1000 | **kilo-** | kilometer (km) | kiloliter (kl) | kilogram (kg)* |
| x 100 | **hecto-** | hectometer (hm) | hectoliter (hl) | hectogram (hg) |
| x 10 | **deca-** | decameter (dam) | decaliter (dal) | decagram (dag) |
| **BASIC UNIT** | | **METER** (m) | **LITER** (l) | **GRAM** (g) |
| x .1 | **deci-** | decimeter (dm) | deciliter (dl) | decigram (dg) |
| x .01 | **centi-** | centimeter (cm) | centiliter (cl) | centigram (cg) |
| x .001 | **milli-** | millimeter (mm) | milliliter (ml) | milligram (mg) |

*1000 kilograms equals one metric ton.

# ENGLISH MEASUREMENT

## LENGTH

| | | |
|---|---|---|
| 12 inches (in. or ") | = | 1 foot (ft. or ') |
| 3 feet (ft.) | = | 1 yard (yd.) |
| 5,280 feet (ft.) | = | 1 land mile (mi.) |
| 3 land miles | = | 1 league |
| 1.15 land miles | = | 1 nautical mile |

## VOLUME

| | | |
|---|---|---|
| 3 teaspoons (tsp.) | = | 1 tablespoon (tbsp.) |
| 2 cups (c.) | = | 1 pint (pt.) |
| 4 cups (c.) | = | 1 quart (qt.) |
| 2 pints (pt.) | = | 1 quart (qt.) |
| 2 quarts (qt.) | = | 1 half-gallon |
| 4 quarts (qt.) | = | 1 gallon (gal.) |
| 8 quarts (qt.) | = | 1 peck (dry measure) |
| 4 pecks | = | 1 bushel |

## WEIGHT

| | | |
|---|---|---|
| 16 ounces (oz.) | = | 1 pound (lb.) |
| 2000 pounds (lb.) | = | 1 short ton |

## USING MEASUREMENT

**PERIMETER** is the distance around a geometric figure. To find the perimeter, add the lengths of all the sides.

**AREA** is the number of square units that cover a geometric figure. To find the area:
*Rectangle:* length x width (l x w)
*Triangle:* ½ base x height (½ b x h)
Some units of English measurement are used only for area:

| | | |
|---|---|---|
| 4,840 square yards | = | 1 acre |
| 640 acres | = | 1 square mile |
| 1 square mile | = | 1 section |
| 36 square miles | = | 1 township |

**VOLUME** is the number of cubic units that fill a three-dimensional solid. To find the area of a rectanglar solid, multiply:
length x width x height (l x w  x h)

# CONVERSION CHARTS

*Conversions are approximate:*

## ENGLISH TO METRIC

| When you know | Multiply by | To find |
|---|---|---|
| inches (in.) | 2.5 | centimeters (cm) |
| feet (ft.) | 30 | centimeters (cm) |
| yards (yd.) | 0.9 | meters (m) |
| miles (mi.) | 1.6 | kilometers (km) |
| teaspoons (tsp.) | 4.93 | milliliters (ml) |
| tablespoons (tbsp.) | 14.79 | milliliters (ml) |
| cups (c.) | 0.24 | liters (l) |
| pints (pt.) | 0.47 | liters (l) |
| quarts (qt.) | 0.95 | liters (l) |
| gallons (gal.) | 3.8 | liters (l) |
| ounces (oz.) | 28 | grams (g) |
| pounds (lb.) | 0.45 | kilograms (kg) |
| short tons | 0.9 | metric tons |

## METRIC TO ENGLISH

| When you know | Multiply by | To find |
|---|---|---|
| millimeters (mm) | 0.04 | inches (in.) |
| centimeters (cm) | 0.4 | inches (in.) |
| meters (m) | 3.3 | feet (ft.) |
| meters (m) | 1.1 | yards (yd.) |
| kilometers (km) | 0.6 | miles (mi.) |
| liters (l) | 2.1 | pints (pt.) |
| liters (l) | 1.06 | quarts (qt.) |
| liters (l) | 0.26 | gallons (gal.) |
| grams (g) | 0.035 | ounces (ox.) |
| kilograms (kg) | 2.2 | pounds (lb.) |
| metric tons | 1.1 | short tons |

## TEMPERATURE CONVERSIONS

Fahrenheit to Celsius—subtract 32, multiply by 5 and divide by 9. To estimate, subtract 30 and divide by 2.

Celsius to Fahrenheit—multiply by 9, divide by 5 and add 32. To estimate, double the Celsius reading and add 30.

# TEMPERATURE

The Celsius, or Centigrade, temperature scale is part of the metric system, and is used in most parts of the world today. The Fahrenheit scale is still more common in the United States.

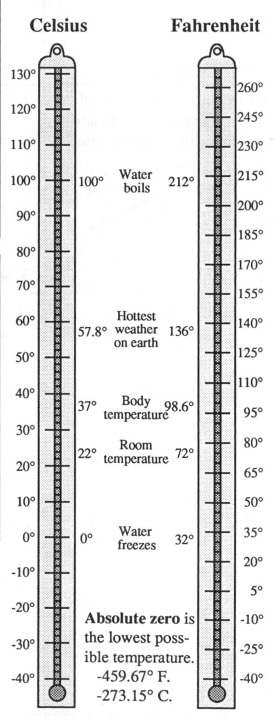

| Celsius | | Fahrenheit |
|---|---|---|
| 100° | Water boils | 212° |
| 57.8° | Hottest weather on earth | 136° |
| 37° | Body temperature | 98.6° |
| 22° | Room temperature | 72° |
| 0° | Water freezes | 32° |

**Absolute zero** is the lowest possible temperature. -459.67° F. -273.15° C.

# GEOMETRIC TERMS

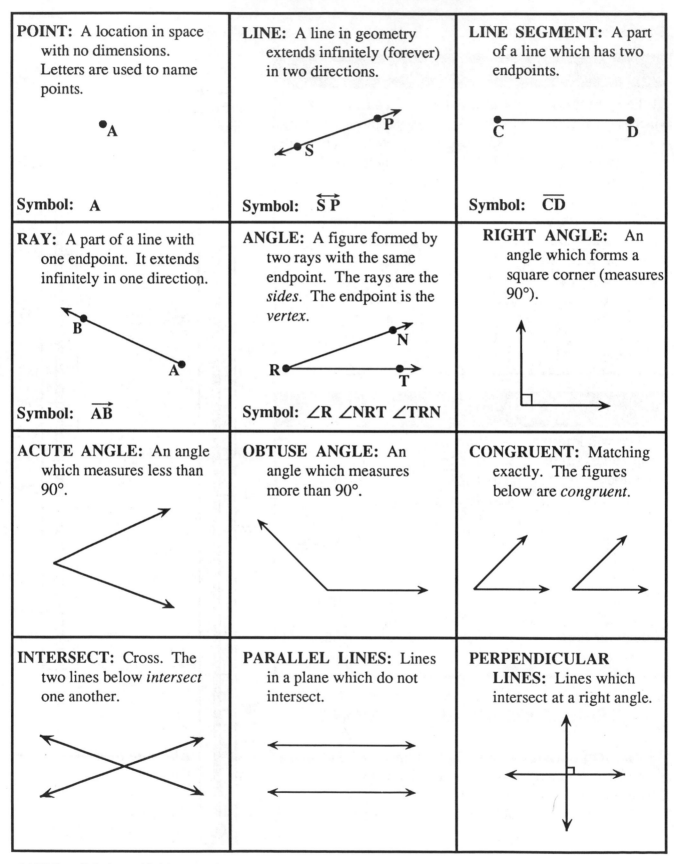

**POINT:** A location in space with no dimensions. Letters are used to name points.

Symbol: **A**

**LINE:** A line in geometry extends infinitely (forever) in two directions.

Symbol: $\overleftrightarrow{S\,P}$

**LINE SEGMENT:** A part of a line which has two endpoints.

Symbol: $\overline{CD}$

**RAY:** A part of a line with one endpoint. It extends infinitely in one direction.

Symbol: $\overrightarrow{AB}$

**ANGLE:** A figure formed by two rays with the same endpoint. The rays are the *sides*. The endpoint is the *vertex*.

Symbol: ∠R  ∠NRT  ∠TRN

**RIGHT ANGLE:** An angle which forms a square corner (measures 90°).

**ACUTE ANGLE:** An angle which measures less than 90°.

**OBTUSE ANGLE:** An angle which measures more than 90°.

**CONGRUENT:** Matching exactly. The figures below are *congruent*.

**INTERSECT:** Cross. The two lines below *intersect* one another.

**PARALLEL LINES:** Lines in a plane which do not intersect.

**PERPENDICULAR LINES:** Lines which intersect at a right angle.

# GEOMETRIC FIGURES

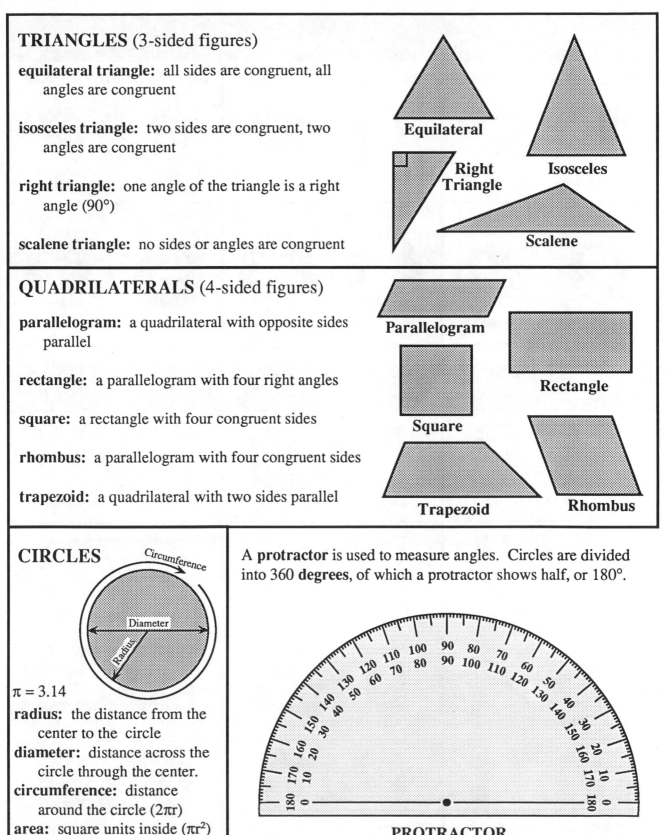

## TRIANGLES (3-sided figures)

**equilateral triangle:** all sides are congruent, all angles are congruent

**isosceles triangle:** two sides are congruent, two angles are congruent

**right triangle:** one angle of the triangle is a right angle (90°)

**scalene triangle:** no sides or angles are congruent

**Equilateral**

**Right Triangle**

**Isosceles**

**Scalene**

## QUADRILATERALS (4-sided figures)

**parallelogram:** a quadrilateral with opposite sides parallel

**rectangle:** a parallelogram with four right angles

**square:** a rectangle with four congruent sides

**rhombus:** a parallelogram with four congruent sides

**trapezoid:** a quadrilateral with two sides parallel

**Parallelogram**

**Rectangle**

**Square**

**Trapezoid**

**Rhombus**

## CIRCLES

Circumference

Diameter

Radius

$\pi = 3.14$

**radius:** the distance from the center to the circle

**diameter:** distance across the circle through the center.

**circumference:** distance around the circle ($2\pi r$)

**area:** square units inside ($\pi r^2$)

A **protractor** is used to measure angles. Circles are divided into 360 **degrees**, of which a protractor shows half, or 180°.

**PROTRACTOR**

# UNITED STATES MONEY

## COINS

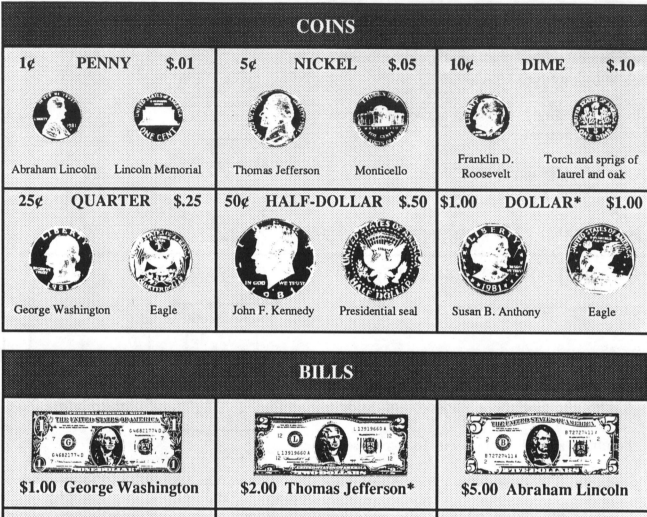

| | | |
|---|---|---|
| 1¢ **PENNY** $.01 | 5¢ **NICKEL** $.05 | 10¢ **DIME** $.10 |
| Abraham Lincoln — Lincoln Memorial | Thomas Jefferson — Monticello | Franklin D. Roosevelt — Torch and sprigs of laurel and oak |
| 25¢ **QUARTER** $.25 | 50¢ **HALF-DOLLAR** $.50 | $1.00 **DOLLAR*** $1.00 |
| George Washington — Eagle | John F. Kennedy — Presidential seal | Susan B. Anthony — Eagle |

## BILLS

| | | |
|---|---|---|
| $1.00 George Washington | $2.00 Thomas Jefferson* | $5.00 Abraham Lincoln |
| $10.00 Alexander Hamilton | $20.00 Andrew Jackson | $50.00 Ulysses S. Grant |
| $100.00 Benjamin Franklin | $500.00 William McKinley* | $1,000 Grover Cleveland* |
| $5,000 James Madison* | $10,000 Salmon P. Chase* | $100,000 Woodrow Wilson* |

* No longer produced.

# HANDBOOK

# FIRST AID

**First aid** is emergency treatment for injury or sudden illness which is given before regular medical care is available. Correct knowledge and action by the first person on the scene of a major medical emergency can save a life. Knowing what *not* to do is as important as knowing what to do. Mistakes can make things much worse. The best trained person available should take charge in an emergency.

This section is a short guide to first aid for major emergencies. It may be used as a guide if well-trained persons or first aid books are not available.

## WHAT TO DO IN EVERY EMERGENCY

1. Stay calm. Call or send for help. In most places, call 911.
2. Go to the victim only if it is safe. *Do not put yourself in danger*.
3. Check for breathing. (See BREATHING.)
4. Stop any heavy bleeding. (See BLEEDING.)
5. Prevent further injury. In general, *do not* move a person who may have broken bones, especially of the back or neck. Move other victims only as much as is necessary to treat them.
6. Treat the injury. Only do as much as you know is right.
7. Treat for shock in *all* major medical emergencies. (See SHOCK)

## BLEEDING

1. Apply direct pressure to the wound with a sterile dressing or a piece of clean cloth for at least ten minutes.
2. If the cloth becomes soaked with blood, put a new cloth on top of it. Do not remove the old cloth.
3. If there is no reason to suspect broken bones, a wounded arm or leg may be raised to help slow bleeding.
4. Treat for shock and make sure help has been called.

## BREATHING

1. If a victim is not breathing, quickly call or send for help.
2. Place the victim on his back with his face to the side. Kneel beside his head.
3. Listen for breathing. *Do not* give artificial respiration to a person who is breathing.
4. Clear the mouth with your fingers.
5. Clear the airway. Using two fingers on the forehead and two fingers under the chin, tilt the head back to clear the airway. The tongue should not be blocking the throat.
6. Listen again for breathing. Clearing the airway may allow the person to breathe on his own. If it does, *do not* give artificial respiration. If it does not, continue.
7. Pinch the nose and blow into the person's mouth until the chest rises.
8. When the chest rises, stop blowing. Turn your head to the side and listen for the air to be exhaled while you breathe.
9. Repeat. Give one breath every five seconds for adults, and a smaller breath every three seconds for young children.
10. Continue artificial respiration until the victim breathes for himself or is pronounced dead by a doctor.

It is recommended that everyone receive first aid training and that all homes and businesses have a complete up-to-date first aid handbook. For information, contact your local chapter of the American Red Cross.

# BROKEN BONES

1. If broken bones are suspected, a victim should *not* be moved.
2. Use ice packs to reduce pain and swelling.
3. Get help and treat for shock.

# BURNS

1. Wash your hands with soap and water before treating a burn. Burns are easily infected.
2. Put the burned part in a pan or sink of cold water for at least five minutes. Do not use ice.
3. Do not touch a serious burn or put ointment on it.
4. Put a sterile dressing or clean sheet over the burn if medical help will not be coming quickly. This may help prevent infection.
5. Treat for shock. All serious burns will cause shock, and more deaths result from the shock than from the burns themselves.
6. Make sure help has been called.

# DROWNING

1. Call for help.
2. *Never* swim to a drowning person unless you are certified in lifesaving.
3. Toss a rope, or push a board, oar or towel to the person and pull her to shore.
4. Give artificial respiration if needed. (See BREATHING.)
5. Treat for shock and make sure help is coming.

# ELECTRIC SHOCK

1. Disconnect the plug or turn off the electric current. *Do not* touch the victim if there is a live current.
2. If it is not possible to turn off the electricity, use a dry stick to push apart the victim and the wire. Be sure your hands are dry and you are standing on a dry surface.
3. Once the person is away from the current, check for breathing. Give artificial respiration if necessary. (See BREATHING.)
4. Treat the burned areas. (See BURNS.)
5. Treat for shock and make sure help is coming.

# POISONING

1. Look for the poison. If there is a container, read the label for directions.
2. Call a doctor, 911, or the Poison Control Center.
3. If the victim is unconscious, do not give liquids.
4. If the victim is conscious, dilute the poison by having her drink water or milk.
5. Watch the victim's breathing. If she stops breathing, give artificial respiration. (See BREATHING.)
6. Treat for shock and make sure help is coming.

# SHOCK

Shock is a result of poor blood circulation caused by the body's reaction to a severe injury. Shock can cause death even when the injuries are not life-threatening. Remember, do not move a person if bones may be broken.

1. Treat the injury first.
2. Keep the victim lying down on his back.
3. Keep the victim warm but not hot. Cover him with a blanket or coat.
4. Help the victim get comfortable. Loosen tight clothing.
5. In general, do not give the victim anything to drink unless for treatment.
6. Talk calmly to the victim and reassure him that help is coming.

# ETIQUETTE

**Etiquette** is another word for manners, or being polite. Knowing the basic rules of etiquette will help you know what to do in situations with other people, such as eating out and meeting new people. The purpose for manners is to show courtesy and consideration for others. People generally enjoy being around a person with good manners, and are poorly impressed with bad manners. The most important rules of etiquette are to be thoughtful about how your words and actions will affect other people, and to treat others as you would like to be treated.

## VERY IMPORTANT WORDS

**PLEASE.** Say *Please* when you are asking for something.

**THANK YOU.**
Say *Thank you*
—when others are courteous or helpful to you.
—when you receive praise or a compliment.
—when you receive a gift.
—when you've enjoyed a good time with someone.
—when you've been to someone's home.

**EXCUSE ME** or **I'M SORRY**
Say *Excuse me* or *I'm sorry*
—when you bump someone.
—when you interrupt.
—when you spill or break something.
—when you are late.
—when you yawn.
—when you forget something.
—when you must leave a group.
—when you don't hear or understand something.
—when you have hurt or embarrassed someone.

**MAY I?\***
Say *May I?*
—when you are asking permission.
—when you are asking someone to pass something to you at the table.

*\*May I?* asks permission. *Can I?* asks if you are able. For example: *Can I drive your car?* asks if you know how to drive. *May I drive your car?* asks if the person will allow you to borrow it.

## INTRODUCTIONS

Always make introductions when two or more people are meeting for the first time. The best introductions lead easily into conversations. Think of what interests or experiences people might have in common and mention them in the introduction.

### INTRODUCING OTHERS

1. Say, *Mrs. Smith, this is John.* Or, more formally, *Mrs. Smith, this is my cousin, John. John, this is my neighbor, Mrs. Smith.*

2. It is best to tell something about the people so it is easy for them to begin a conversation. For example, *John is visiting us this week from California.*

3. Remember:
   1. Say a woman's name before a man's.
   2. Say an adult's name before a child's.
   3. Say a more important person's name before a less important person's.

### INTRODUCING YOURSELF

1. Say, *Hello, my name is _____.*
2. Ask the other person's name.
3. Begin a short conversation.

## WHEN YOU'RE INTRODUCED

1. Stand if the other person is standing.
2. Look at the person and smile. Shake hands.
3. Say, *Hello. How are you?* or *Nice to meet you.*
4. Say the other person's name and make sure you are pronouncing it correctly.
5. Use the person's name and try to remember it. If you forget, say, *I'm sorry, could you tell me your name again?*
6. Young people should use an adult's title and last name unless asked to do otherwise. For example, *Mr. Johnson* not *Dick.*

# CONVERSATIONS

## BEGINNING A CONVERSATION

1. Say something about what's going on around you.
2. Ask a general question.
3. Give an honest compliment.
4. Ask a question or make a comment about something the person has said or something you've noticed about them.

## HAVING A CONVERSATION

1. Take turns talking and listening.
2. Listen and pay attention to the other person. Don't let your eyes or mind wander.
3. Ask questions, but don't ask about things which are none of your business, such as personal affairs or finances. If someone asks you a question you don't want to answer, say, *I'm sorry, but I'd rather not talk about that.*
4. Find things you both have in common and talk about them.
5. Talk about your interests and experiences, especially those which seem to interest the other person.

6. Don't interrupt. If you must interrupt for some reason, say, *Excuse me for interrupting, but _____.*
7. Don't brag or exaggerate.
8. Don't criticize others or say untrue or unkind things.
9. Don't whisper to someone in front of someone else.
10. Don't talk or laugh so loudly that people outside the conversation are disturbed.

## ENDING A CONVERSATION

1. Say something like,
*It's been great talking with you.*
*Well, have a nice day.*
*Take care of yourself.*
2. Smile, say goodbye, and leave.

# TELEPHONE ETIQUETTE

## MAKING A CALL

1. Don't call when the other person is likely to be sleeping or having a meal.
2. Let the phone ring at least seven times.
3. When someone answers, say, *Hello, this is _____. May I speak to _____, please?*
4. Speak clearly and loudly enough to be heard. Talk right into the phone.
5. Keep calls short. Someone else may need the phone.
6. If you want to have a long conversation, ask the person if she has time to talk.
7. When finished, say something like, *It was nice to talk with you.*
8. If you reach an answering machine, leave a short message that you called.
9. If the person you want isn't there, ask to leave a message or say you'll call back later.
10. If you think you've reached a wrong number, ask, *Is this 342-9168?* If not, say, *I'm sorry to have bothered you.*

## RECEIVING A CALL

1. Say, *Hello.*
2. **If** the person asks for someone else, say, *Just a moment, please.* Put the receiver down quietly and go get the person, or cover the receiver and call her to the phone.
3. **If** the person asks for someone who is not there, say, *I'm sorry. She's not here right now. May I take a message?*
4. **If** the person is busy and can't come to the phone for **any** reason, or if a young person doesn't want the caller to know he's home alone, say *I'm sorry. He can't come to the phone right now. May I take a message or have him call you back?* Don't tell the caller the reason the person can't come to the phone.
5. **If** someone calls when you have company, say, *I'd love to talk to you, but I have a guest. May I call you back later?*

## TABLE MANNERS

There are many rules for good table manners. The most important thing to remember is to be considerate of others. If you don't know what to do, watch your host or hostess and do as they do.

### BEFORE A MEAL

1. Wash your hands and face before coming to the table.
2. Be on time.
3. Put the napkin on your lap.
4. Sit up straight at the table. Don't slouch or tilt the chair.

### SERVING

1. Pass the whole serving dish.
2. Use the serving spoon or fork, not your own.
3. Don't reach in front of someone to get a serving dish. Ask the person nearest it to pass it.
4. If you don't like some of the food, take a small amount or say, *No, thank you.* Always take some of the main dish.
5. If you don't know if you'll like something, take a small amount and try it. If you like it, take more later.
6. Don't take so much of something you like that there isn't enough left for the other people.
7. Wait until everyone is served to begin eating. Wait until the host or hostess begins.
8. Compliment the cook or say nothing. Never say anything negative or critical.

### EATING

1. Chew with your mouth closed.
2. If food is too hot, let it cool. Don't blow on it.
3. If you take a bite of something which is too hot, quickly drink some water and say nothing.
4. Don't put too much food in your mouth at once.
5. Don't take a drink with your mouth full. Use the napkin before drinking to avoid getting food on the glass.
6. Don't talk with your mouth full.
7. Avoid distasteful conversation.
8. Don't make loud eating noises.
9. If you find something in your food, such as a hair, try to put it aside without being noticed and say nothing.
10. If you must sneeze or cough, turn your head away from the table and cover your nose and mouth with the napkin.
11. If you spill some food, scoop it up with a knife or spoon and put it on the side of your plate. Say *I'm sorry* if someone has noticed.

12. If you must take something out of your mouth, take it out the same way you put it in. For example, take olive pits out with your fingers, but fish bones out with your fork. Put these things on the side of your plate.
13. Don't comb your hair, pick your teeth, or otherwise groom yourself at the table.
14. If you must leave the table, say, *Excuse me, I'll be right back.* Don't explain your reasons.

## AFTER A MEAL

1. Leave the utensils on the plate.
2. Lay the napkin on the table next to your plate. Don't crumple or fold the napkin.
3. Thank the host and hostess.
4. Ask to be excused if you need to leave the table before everyone else leaves.

# SAYING "NO"

Sometimes people ask you to do things which are wrong. It is important to be assertive—to be able to say "no" and keep your friends, have fun and stay out of trouble.

1. Ask questions. Be sure you know exactly what the person has in mind.
2. Name the trouble. "You mean you want me to help you steal something?"
3. Identify the consequences. "If I do that, I could get caught and arrested!"
4. Suggest an alternative. "Instead, why don't we see if we can earn some money and buy what we want? My dad needs some help in his shop, and he'd be happy to pay us."
5. Move away. Begin moving away from the person and the situation while still talking. Don't allow them a chance to argue.
6. Sell your idea. "Dad's shop is great, and it would be fun working with you."
7. Leave the door open. "I'll be at the shop in about an hour. Come on over!"

## PARTIES

### PLANNING A PARTY

1. What kind of party will it be? Some kinds of parties are birthday, surprise, Christmas, costume, and picnic.
2. Where will it be held? Some possible places are the dining room, backyard, or park.
3. When will it be? What day, date and time of day?
4. How many people will come and who? Make a guest list. Don't leave out one or two people who are part of a group.
5. What refreshments will be served?
6. What activities or entertainment will there be? Some ideas are games, contests or music.
7. What decorations are needed?
8. Who will help set up and clean up?

### INVITATIONS

Invite people in person, by telephone or in writing a week or so ahead of time. Be sure they know your name, the date and time of the party, the location of the party and anything special, such as what to bring or wear.

### AT THE PARTY

1. Greet the guests at the door.
2. Take their hats and coats.
3. Make introductions.
4. Make sure everyone has a good time and no one is left out.
5. Walk people to the door when they leave.
6. Say, *Thank you for coming.*

### AFTER THE PARTY

1. Be sure to clean up and take down any decorations.
2. Send thank you notes for any gifts.

# PROBLEM SOLVING

1. **Define the problem.** Put the problem in words. Who's problem is it, really? Is it within your power to change?

2. **Research the problem.** Get all the information available.

3. **Brainstorm solutions.** Think of as many ideas as possible. Don't judge them at all at this stage. The wilder the ideas, the better.

4. **Analyze solutions.** Which ideas are possible? Combine and change ideas while searching for the best solution.

5. **Choose a solution.** Think about the possible outcomes of the different solutions. Who might be hurt? What are the pros and cons of each? What seems most likely to work?

6. **Make a plan.** Follow through on your plan.

7. **Evaluate** whether the solution is working after some time has passed. If not, think about trying another solution.

# DISCUSSIONS

The leader:
1. Introduces the topic.
2. Makes sure everyone has a chance to speak.
3. Summarizes what was said at the end.

Participants:
1. Ask questions.
2. Answer questions.
3. Tell personal experiences.
4. Restate what someone else has said.
5. Summarize what others have said.
6. Tell ideas.
7. Introduce other topics.
8. Retell what was read.
9. Tell feelings.
10. Give examples.
11. Read or give supporting evidence.
12. Relate the discussion to other learning.

## COURTESY IN DISCUSSIONS

1. Move to the discussion area quickly and quietly.
2. Listen as others speak.
3. Look at the speaker.
4. Keep your mind on the discussion.
5. Speak clearly.
6. Talk about the topic.
7. Respect others who have ideas different from yours.
8. Tell others when and why you like what they said.
9. Let others have a turn to speak.
10. Summarize and participate well.

# READING ORALLY

1. Stand straight and face the audience.
2. Read loudly enough for everyone to hear.
3. Speak clearly and use correct pronunciation.
4. Hold the book down so the audience can see your face.
5. Hold your head up so your voice will not be blocked.
6. Look up often and make eye contact with someone in the audience.
7. Read smoothly and use good expression.

# PREPARING A SPEECH

1. **Decide on the purpose of the speech.**
   * To entertain. You want your audience to simply enjoy themselves.
   * To inform. You want your audience to learn or understand something.
   * To create a feeling. You want your audience to feel inspired, angry, or enthusiastic.
   * To convince. You want your audience to change their minds to agree with you.
   * To move to action. You want your audience to do something, such as vote for someone.

2. **Think about the audience and the occasion.**

3. **Choose and narrow the subject.**
   * Choose a subject about which you already know something and in which you are interested.
   * Think about what will be interesting to the audience.
   * Know the time limit of your speech and narrow the subject to fit.

4. **Gather material, such as facts, stories or examples.**
   * Think about your personal experience.
   * Talk to other people.
   * Read and study to find out more about your subject than anyone in your audience will know.
   * Consider gathering maps, pictures, charts, models, or other visual aids.

5. **Organize your material.**
   * Introduction.
     a. Give the subject of the speech.
     b. Get the attention of your audience, perhaps with a joke or surprising fact.
   * Body.
     a. List your three or four main points.
     b. Put your main points in order.
   * Conclusion.
     a. Summarize the main ideas.
     b. Recommend action if you want your audience to do something.

6. **Prepare the speech.**
   * Write the speech or practice saying it.
   * Make sure you know the correct pronunciation of words you plan to use.
   * Practice the speech again and again until you feel very comfortable with it. Practice in front of a family member, friends or a mirror.

# DELIVERING A SPEECH

Before you stand up, take a deep breath and imagine yourself doing an excellent job. Imagine your audience responding just as you want.

1. Stand tall and straight.
2. Speak loudly, clearly and slowly enough for everyone to hear and understand you.
3. Talk in a lively, conversational way.
4. Make eye contact with people in the audience.
5. Use movements and gestures.
6. Avoid unnecessary movements.
7. Use your notes as a guide but do not read from them.
8. Pay attention to your audience. Watch their reactions.

# PRESENTING A FORMAL PLAY

1. **Make basic planning decisions.**
   * Who will present the play? How many people will be involved?
   * Who will be the audience?
   * Who will be the director?
   * Is there a theme or special occasion ?
   * Should the play be serious or humorous? Is a musical appropriate?
   * How long should the play be?
   * How much time is available for practice?
   * Where can the play be held? Is there a stage, curtains or lighting?
   * How much money can be spent?

2. **Locate potential scripts.**
   * Check with a librarian.
   * Write your own script.

3. **Select a script.** Keep these questions in mind while reading scripts:
   * How many characters are required?
   * Are speaking parts distributed?
   * Is the play interesting?
   * Are vocabulary and subject matter good for the cast and the intended audience?
   * Can the set, costumes, and props be done with the time, space and money?
   * Are the stage directions clear?

4. **Conduct a first reading.**
   * Make sure there is an underlined copy of the script for each character.
   * Read through the script, taking parts.
   * Discuss the characteristics of each character.

5. **Cast the play.**
   * Have tryouts and select main characters first, then others.
   * Choose understudies if needed.
   * Choose a stage crew and prompters.

6. **Characters begin to memorize lines.**
   Here are tips for memorizing:
   * Read the play several times and know the order of events.
   * Say your character's cues and lines again and again, out loud and in your mind. Visualize the play. Once in a while, rest and do something else, then repeat the lines to yourself again.
   * Practice while relaxed, such as just before sleeping.
   * Have someone read the other parts, especially your cues, while your practice your lines with expression.

7. **Plan the setting.**
   * Decide what different scenes or backgrounds are needed.
   * Sketch possible stage arrangements and backdrops.
   * Plan for a backstage area, if needed.
   * Decide how to change scenes.
   * Begin work on the backdrops.

8. **Plan costumes.**
   * Consider the time period and place in which the play takes place.
   * Begin gathering and making costumes.

9. **Walk through the play, reading the scripts.**
   * Speak loudly, slowly and distinctly.
   * Face the audience as much as possible.

10. **Rehearse.**
    * Practice entrances, exits, speech, actions, gestures, expressions, sound effects and use of props.

11. **Advertise and make programs.**

12. **Perform the play for the audience** and enjoy the results of all your work.

# INTERVIEWING A PERSON

An **interview** is a meeting with a person for the purpose of asking about his knowledge, ideas, or experiences. A reporter or writer may interview a person to get information for a story. A person applying for a job may have an interview. Sometimes the best way to find information on a subject is to interview an expert in the field. Here are ideas for setting up and conducting an interview.

I. **Know your purpose.** Choose the best person based on your purpose.

II. **Make arrangements** in person or by telephone.
    A. Introduce yourself.
    B. Ask for an interview and tell its purpose.
    C. Tell the person about how long the interview will take. Most interviews should be for no longer than an hour.
    D. Set a time and place to meet.
    E. If you would like to use a tape recorder or videocamera, ask at this time.

III. **Read background information** on the person and the topic of the interview. Use what you learn to help prepare questions.

IV. **Write questions** you would like to have answered.
    A. Avoid yes/no questions. Write open-ended questions which will lead the person into talking about what interests you. One example of an open-ended question is, "What do you think about...?"
    B. Avoid personal questions or questions which are none of your business.
    C. List the questions in some order and mark the most important ones. If you run short of time, skip the less important ones.

V. **Beginning the interview.**
    A. Be on time. Have your list of questions, your notebook and a pencil.
    B. Smile, shake hands, introduce yourself and thank the person for taking time to talk with you.
    C. Talk with the person for a few minutes before beginning the questions so you will both feel more comfortable.

VI. **Conducting the interview.**
    A. Ask your questions one at a time.
    B. Listen carefully and show interest.
    C. Take notes on what the person says. See page 224, TAKING NOTES.
    D. Don't keep so closely to the list of questions that the interview is stiff and uncomfortable.
    E. Don't allow the person to wander *too* far from the subject.

VII. **Ending the interview.**
    A. Toward the end of the time planned, say, "I have one last question." Then ask it.
    B. Before finishing, ask if the person has any final comments or suggestions for you.
    C. Close the interview by thanking the person again.

VIII. **After the interview.**
    A. As soon as possible, read your notes and fill them in.
    B. **Always** send a thank you note.

# TAKING NOTES

**Notes** are words, phrases and numbers written quickly for the purpose of assisting or jogging the writer's memory. A person may take notes on reading materials, speeches, films, or her own thoughts.

With practice, note taking becomes easy and natural. The following ideas may help as you find your own best way of taking notes.

1. Date notes and write the source. Write the name of a speaker, the title of a film, or bibliographic information on reading material. Bibliographic information includes the author, title, and copyright date of the book. See page 229, BIBLIOGRAPHIC FORM.

2. Leave large margins so more can be written to fill in the notes later.

3. Write key words and phrases. Do not use complete sentences. Leave out unimportant words. When deciding what to write, ask yourself, "Is this really important?"

4. Use abbreviations you understand. Some common ones are ＋ for "and," **@** for "at" or "around," **#** for "number," **%** for "percent," and **w/** for "with."

5. Write clearly enough that you can read the notes later, but don't waste time trying to use your best handwriting.

6. Write numbers, statistics, and important facts. These are especially hard to remember without notes.

7. Skip a line between major ideas.

8. Underline or put a star by the most important points.

9. Don't copy words exactly without using quotation marks and giving credit to the author.

10. If possible, read over your notes soon after taking them and fill them in while your memory is fresh.

## ORGANIZING NOTES AND PAPERS

As important as taking notes is organizing them so you can find them when needed. Different systems work for different people. Here are some suggestions:

1. Use a different color for each school subject. Have all spiral notebooks or folders for that subject the same color.

2. Use a separate spiral notebook for each subject. Use a new page for each new day and be sure to write the date.

3. Use loose leaf paper and a folder. One advantage to this system is it is easy to keep handouts with your notes. The disadvantage is papers may get lost or out of order.

4. Use a three-ring binder to keep notes for all subjects together. Use dividers to separate the subjects. Keep the notebook neat and avoid tearing papers out.

# HOMEWORK AND STUDYING

Nearly all students will be required to study on their own or do homework. Successful students make a habit of studying regularly, and know how to use their time well. One of the most important things is to learn to **concentrate**, or focus your mind. Here are suggestions to help as you work to find your own best methods of studying.

I. **Set up a place for studying.**
   A. Find a quiet spot where you will not be interrupted.
   B. Make sure there is enough light, a good chair, a desk or table, and a clock.
   C. Gather study materials and keep them together in a desk, drawer or box. At the least, have paper, pencils and pens. General reference books, such as a dictionary, a thesaurus, and *Facts Plus* are also good to have.

II. **Choose a regular time** for homework and study based on your schedule and preferences.

III. **Know what you are doing.**
   A. Pay attention in class and ask questions if something is not clear.
   B. Write down all assignments when they are given. Include page numbers, special requirements, and dates due.
   C. Put assignment notes and books you will need at home in a backpack or special place immediately so they will not be forgotten at the end of the day.

IV. **Use your study time wisely.**
   A. Get into a good frame of mind. Focus your attention.
   B. Plan your time. Learn to estimate how long each assignment will take.
   C. Begin study time with a review of what you've already learned.

   D. Study reading materials, such as textbook chapters.
      1. Survey the chapter quickly. Read the title, headings, chapter summary, and questions. Look at the illustrations.
      2. Have a purpose for reading. What do you need to learn?
      3. Read the chapter section by section. Concentrate.
      4. After each section, review in your mind the important points. Later, review it again by paging through and trying to remember important points. Review again within 24 hours. The more often you review, the better. Always review before tests.
   E. Do daily assignments.
      1. Work carefully and neatly.
      2. Put completed assignments and books in a backpack or special place immediately so they will not be forgotten in the morning.
   F. Work on long term projects or assignments.
      1. List all of the small jobs which need to be done and keep the list up to date.
      2. Make a timeline for yourself and set goals.
      3. Do a little on the project each day.

   G. Congratulate yourself at the end of each study time. Reward yourself for progress toward your goals.

# IMPROVING YOUR MEMORY

**Memory** is the ability to recall or remember information after a period of time during which you were not thinking about it. To have a good memory, you must be able to get information into your mind, store it in your memory, and then be able to get it out when you need it.

**Getting the information.** You must "get" it before you can forget it (or remember it). The amount you learn depends directly on the amount of time you spend learning. You must practice, or rehearse, new knowledge again and again, or it will be forgotten. Generally, people forget 40% of what they learn within 20 minutes, and more than half of it within an hour. To avoid this forgetting, practice and recite new learning again and again. Check yourself a lot at first, then gradually increase the time between practices. For best long-term memory, keep practicing long after you think you know it perfectly. Use times when your mind is free to practice, such as when you're washing up, waiting for a bus, or waiting in line. Practice a little at a time and often for best results.

**Storing the information.** You must store what you learn in some organized and meaning-ful way or it will be difficult or impossible to recall. Your mind is like a huge library. If information is not organized and stored, it is like having all of the books in a pile on the floor. To store information, you connect it to things you already know. The more connections, the better.

**Find and retrieve the information.** Unless knowledge is completely mastered and used a lot, this will mean scanning your memory. As in a library, you may look through several categories before finding what you want. Practice finding and retrieving information.

## TIPS FOR BETTER MEMORY

1. Keep notes, lists, calendars and diaries to jog your memory.
2. Decide what is most important to remember. Always look for main ideas.
3. Classify information and make categories. Things can be classified by:
   a. Time—winter, snow, cold, storms
   b. Place—school, office, classrooms, gym
   c. Similarities—hat, cap, bonnet
   d. Differences—mountains, valleys
   e. Wholes to parts—kitchen, sink, stove
   f. Scientific groups—birds, robin, eagle
4. Look for patterns. For example, the first letters of the five Great Lakes spell **H O M E S**, **H**uron, **O**ntario, **M**ichigan, **E**rie, **S**uperior. Sometimes you can make a sentence which will remind you of the first letters of words you need to remember in order. For example, the lines on the treble clef from bottom to top are **E G B D F**, **E**very **G**ood **B**oy **D**oes **F**ine.
7. Associate new learning with what you already know. If there is no association, make one up. For example, you might picture a person whose name is Bailey bailing out a sinking boat.
7. Make up a rhyme or use rhythm. Rhythm is probably how you learned the alphabet.
8. Visualize the information in your mind. Make bright, exaggerated and interesting pictures that get your attention.
   a. See it clearly and in vivid color.
   b. Exaggerate and enlarge things.
   c. See it in three dimensions.
   d. Put movement and action in the picture.
   e. Put yourself in the picture.
9. Create a story about the information to link it together and give it meaning.
10. Use the information. Relate it to new things you see and learn. Imagine yourself needing it in a funny or unusual situation.

# TAKING STANDARDIZED TESTS

**Standardized tests** are tests which have been used and revised many times until they give consistent results. Generally, they are **norm-referenced**. This means the test was given to a large group of people before being published to find a norm, or average standard of achievement. In most cases, standardized tests are scored by the publishers of the tests, who then compare your results with the norm. The results are often given as **percentiles**, which compare your scores with the norm for your age group. The 50th percentile is average. Below the 50th percentile is below average and above the 50th percentile is above average. If the test is very good, half of the people who take the test will score below the 50th percentile and half will score above.

It is important to do your best on standardized tests to show what you truly know and what you still need to learn. Here are suggestions for doing your best.

I. **Before the test.**
   A. Know the purpose of the test.
   B. Get a good night's sleep.
   C. Eat breakfast.
   D. Don't drink many fluids.
   E. Get into a good frame of mind. Picture yourself as calm, confident and successful.
   F. Get to the testing location on time. Plan to avoid stress and rushing.
   G. Have two sharp #2 pencils with good erasers.
   H. Get drinks and go to the restroom before or between tests, so that the testing time will be uninterrupted.
   I. Make sure you are seated comfortably and can see the clock.

II. **During the test.**
   A. Concentrate. Focus your mind.
   B. Do not talk or make distracting noise.
   C. Listen carefully. Ask questions if the directions are not clear.
   D. Watch the time and know when the test will end. Pace yourself but don't worry too much about not finishing.
   E. Work through all the questions in order. If a question is especially hard, skip it and come back to it when you have finished the test. Be sure to skip the answer space if you do this.
   F. Read all of the possible answers for each question before choosing an answer.
   G. Quickly discard any answers which are clearly wrong and choose from the others. Words like "always" and "never" often signal that an answer is false.
   H. Make your best guess if you don't know. If you have a strong hunch, you may be right.
   I. If questions are based on a reading passage, it is best to read the questions, then the passage. Then try to answer the questions. Scan back through the passage again to make sure your answer is correct.
   J. When you finish, go back through the test a second time and check all answers for careless mistakes. Change answers only if you are *sure* they were wrong or if you have a very strong feeling they were wrong.
   K. Do the hard questions you skipped the first time through. Don't be afraid to guess. Even a wild guess has a chance of being correct.
   L. Use all of the time allowed to check and recheck your work. Congratulate yourself for having done your best when the test is over.

# THE RESEARCH REPORT

The **research report** is a common school assignment which provides experience in locating and organizing information. There is no single correct way to do such a report. With practice, people find what works best for them.

I. **Choose a topic**
   A. List several topics, then choose one.
   B. Make sure the topic is not too broad. *The United States* is an example of a topic which is too broad.
   C. Make sure enough information is available about the topic. *Multnomah Falls* is an example of a topic about which limited information may be available in a small library.

II. **Think about the topic.**
   A. Write what you already know about the topic.
   B. Write what you would like to learn.
   C. Begin thinking of categories of information. For a report on a country, for example, you might think of categories such as the land, the people, and the government.

III. **Locate information and begin a bibliography.**
   A. Think of key words which would describe the topic.
   B. Go to the card catalog. Write titles and call numbers, then locate the books to choose those which seem the most valuable.
   C. Use the encyclopedia and almanac for general background information.
   D. Check atlases, periodical indexes, and the vertical file.
   E. Make a bibliography card for every book or source of information. See page 229 for examples of bibliography entries.

IV. **Select and gather information. Take notes.** Notes are brief records written to help you remember something.
   A. Write only as much as you need to remember the ideas.
   B. Do not write complete sentences.
   C. Write in your own words. Do not copy. Copying words written by someone else and representing them as your own is a crime called **plagiarism**.
   D. Notes may be taken on notebook paper, but it may be easier to organize them on 3x5 cards. Write only one idea, or "note" on each card.

V. **Organize the information and begin an outline.**
   A. Think about the information and how it fits together.
   B. Think of a title which tells the topic.
   C. Put note cards into piles by category. The names of the categories are the **main headings** of the outline.
   D. Put the cards in each pile into a sequence, or order, which makes sense. The information on the cards may be **subheadings** or **details** of the outline.
   E. Write an outline. See page 191 for an example of complete outline form.

VI. **Write the report.**
   A. Write a rough draft. Skip lines on the paper to leave room for revisions. Each main heading on the outline should be a new paragraph.

B. Read your work and revise as you write. Revising means adding words, taking out unnecessary words, moving words or combining sentences to make writing communicate better.

C. Edit the report for spelling, punctuation, capitalization and sentence sense.

D. Write a final draft. Include such things as maps, diagrams and pictures.

E. Make a cover, title page, table of contents and bibliography. The main part of the report should come between the table of contents and the bibliography.

**VII. Presenting the report orally.**

A. Study the information and know it well. Begin the report with some fascinating facts or information.

B. Do not read the report to your audience. Use the outline and notes to talk about it.

C. Stick to the subject. Follow the outline so you can end on time.

D. Speak loudly and clearly. Look at the audience.

E. Use visual aids such as maps and pictures to interest the audience.

F. See MAKING A SPEECH, page 221, for more hints.

# BIBLIOGRAPHIC FORM

A **bibliography** is a list of books and other materials on a specific subject which have been used by a writer. When doing a research report, it is important to keep track of sources of information by recording the author, title, place of publication, name of publisher, and copyright date of each source. The bibliography, or list of sources, should be alphabetized and listed at the end of a report. If bibliography cards have been kept, they can be alphabetized and copied in order.

Punctuation is very important in a bibliography, and different types of reference materials have slightly different bibliographic forms. If a piece of information, such as the author's name, is not available, leave it out and write the next piece of information. See below.

### BIBLIOGRAPHY

"Handwriting: How Important Is It?" Good Housekeeping, Vol. 283 (March 1987), p. 9.
Iverson, William J. "Handwriting." The World Book Encyclopedia. 1984. Vol. 9.

## BOOK

Todd, Alden. Finding Facts Fast. New York: William Morrow & Company, 1972.

Author. Title. Place of Publication: Publisher, Date.

## MAGAZINE ARTICLE

Jeffery, David. "Yellowstone: The Great Fires of 1988," National Geographic, Vol. 175 (February 1989), p. 255.

Author. "Title of Article," Periodical Name, Volume (Month and Year), Page Number.

## ENCYCLOPEDIA

Iverson, William J. "Handwriting." The World Book Encyclopedia. 1984. Vol. 9.

Author. "Title of Article." Name of Encyclopedia. Date. Volume.

# SCIENCE PROJECTS

A **science project** is most often done to present at a **science fair.** Its purpose is to give students a chance to practice being scientists by using scientific skills and processes to investigate a problem or question. The final product is a display which includes a written report.

## SKILLS OF SCIENTISTS

1. **Observing** is using the senses of sight, hearing, smell, taste or touch.
2. **Classifying** is identifying and arranging things by similarities or differences.
3. **Measuring** is finding such things as length, weight, temperature, pressure or time.
4. **Communicating** means telling or writing data, such as numbers or words.
5. **Predicting**, or **hypothesizing**, means making an educated guess about what will happen before an experiment takes place.
6. **Inferring** is suggesting reasons, causes or explanations for what happened. It is done after the experiment.
7. **Experimenting** is setting up a way of testing a hypothesis in order to answer a question. It is important to test only *one* thing at a time—one variable. All other variables must stay the same. In most experiments, there should be a **control**, or one sample which is not tested. The tested samples can then be compared to it.

## TYPES OF SCIENCE PROJECTS

1. **Collection.** The student gathers and arranges objects, such as rocks.
2. **Model.** The student builds a model, or example, of something to show a scientific fact or idea such as a model of a volcano.
3. **Demonstration.** The student shows how something works, often using a **working model**, or model with moving parts. For example, a homebuilt model of a simple electric motor could be used to demonstrate how a motor works.

4. **Experiment.** The student investigates a problem using the scientific method. An experiment could be set up, for example, to see which colors absorb the most light.

## DOING A SCIENCE PROJECT

1. Choose a topic and form a question.
2. Do background reading and talk to others.
3. Develop a hypothesis, or educated guess, based on the background information.
4. Decide on methods and procedures.
5. List and then gather materials.
6. Do the experiment and collect data.
7. Organize the data using tables, graphs or charts.
8. Draw conclusions. Was your hypothesis correct?
9. Write the research report. Include your question, hypothesis, list of materials, methods used, results, conclusions, and a bibliography of books and other sources.
10. Design and construct your exhibit. It should be freestanding, neat and uncluttered. Use photographs, drawings, charts or graphs. In front of the standing backboard, show samples, results or measuring devices.

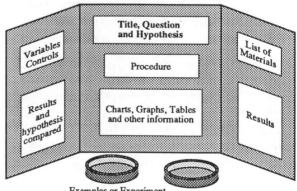

Examples or Experiment

# SOURCES AND NOTES

p. 7, 8, 10 — **Veterans Day** was observed as a legal holiday between 1971 and 1978, on the fourth Monday in October. This was unpopular and the official date was changed back to November 11.

p. 12 — Since 1972, scientists have been adjusting the calendar periodically with **leap seconds**, which are added or subtracted as needed to compensate for irregularities in earth's movements.

p. 13 — "B.C.E." is also called "before Christian era."

p. 15, 16 — The **speed of light** is a vacuum is 186,282.42 ± 0.2 miles per second, according to the General Assembly of the International Scientific Radio Union. In air on a standard day, it is about 52 miles per second slower than in a vacuum.

p. 15 — **Distances to stars** varied greatly from source to source. These figures are from the World Book Encyclopedia.

p. 16 — **Rotation of sun** varies by latitude because the sun is a ball of gas. 22 days is an average.

p. 17 — The **earth's rotation period** is actually 23 hours and 56 minutes as measured by fixed stars. This is the *sidereal day*. Because of the earth's motion around the sun, the time from noon to noon is 24 hours.

p. 17 — In the chart of **Planets of the Solar System**, both **distance from sun** and **speed in orbit** vary because orbits around the sun are eliptical, not circular. The *apogee* is the point furthest from the sun. For earth, it is 94.5 million miles; for Pluto, it is 4,571 million miles. The *perigee* is the point closest to the sun. For earth it is 91.4 million miles; for Pluto, it is 2,748 million miles. The speed at the perigee is faster than at the apogee.

p. 22 — **Layers of the atmosphere.** The temperature 30 miles above the earth is higher than at lower elevations because of the absorption of heat by the ozone layer. At this altitude, there is so little air that it would not "feel" warm.

p. 24 — The **speed of sound** depends on the substance through which the sound waves travel. In a vacuum, no sound can be heard because there is no medium. The speed of 1,116 feet per second is for a standard day (59° at sea level). The speed increases as air temperature rises. Through water at 77°, sound travels about 4,908 feet per second; through steel, 17,100 feet per second.

p. 25 — The **fastest winds** not in a tornado were recorded at Mt. Washington in New Hampshire on April 12, 1934. The wind speed was 231 miles per hour.

p. 28 — The lengths and beginnings of **geological periods** are scientific estimates which overlap and vary and to some degree from source to source. The **Pennsylvanian** and **Mississippian** periods are together called the **Carboniferous** in some sources.

p. 31 — According to Dr. David Stone at the University of Alaska Fairbanks, the **Richter Scale** shown is based on an old formula. New versions take into account energy that is hard to record. On the new scale, Chili's 1961 earthquake is the largest well-recorded event with a magnitude of 9.5. The 1964 Alaska quake is second largest at 9.2.

p. 33 — The **decibel scale** was compiled from several sources with the assistance of an audiologist at Gallaudet College in Washington, D.C. The true intensity of a sound depends on distance from the source. Although 0 to 15 dB is considered the threshold of normal hearing,

some people can hear sounds in the -15dB range. Continuous exposure to sounds of 90dB or higher can cause hearing loss. Impact sounds such as gunshots are most likely to cause damage.

p. 34 — The **number of known elements** varies by source. According to Dr. Glenn Shaw at the Geophysical Institute at the University of Alaska Fairbanks, atoms with atomic numbers higher than 107 are so unstable that it is hard to know when you have them.

p. 35 — **Melting** and **boiling points** are rounded to the nearest degree. **Steel** is an **alloy** of iron and other materials. **Stainless steel** contains about 8% nickel, 18% chromium and 74% iron.

p. 38 — The **speeds of animals** are not easily tested and recorded. The speeds listed are generally the fasted recorded speeds I could locate for any species of the group, and are mostly estimates for short distances, not speeds that can be sustained.

p. 38 — The 188dB **sound** of a blue whale carries 530 miles in *water*. It would not travel so far in air.

p. 43-45 — The **recommended daily allowances** for vitamins and minerals are generally the highest given, except for sodium. To find recommendations based on age and sex, consult a source with more in-depth information.

p. 46 — The **outline of drugs** is based on classifications shown in *The Encyclopedia of Drug Abuse,* by Dr. Robert O'Brien and Dr. Sidney Cohen. **Anabolic steroids** do not fit into the classes. They are derivatives of testosterone, a natural male hormone.

p. 48 — **Depth and pressure chart.** A column of salt water one inch square and 33 feet deep weighs the same as a column of the atmosphere at sea level (14.7

pounds). Fresh water weighs less–a column *34* feet deep weighs 14.7 pounds. The pounds per square inch on the depth and pressure chart include the weight of both air and sea water. About half of the weight of the atmosphere is in the 18,000 feet nearest the earth. Mountain climbers at 18,000 feet experience only about 7.4 pounds of air pressure on the average.

p. 49 — The heights of **waterfalls** are for total drops, not single drops. Some have several drops.

p. 54-70 — **Countries of the World.** For capital, language, currency and literacy rate, the *World Factbook 1990*, compiled by the Central Intelligence Agency, was used. For area, population, population growth rate, population density, per capita GNP, average life expectancy, infant mortality rate and location, the source was the *1990 World Population Data Sheet*, compiled by the Population Reference Bureau, Inc. In cases where per capita GNP was missing from the *World Population Data Sheet*, information from the *World Factbook* was used. Latitudes and longitudes were taken from the *World Book Great Geographical Atlas*. For comparison purposes, here are statistics on the entire world:
**Area:** 196,683,760 sq. mi.
139,252,100 sq. mi. water (70.8%)
57,431,657 sq. mi. land (29.2%)
**Population:** 5,321,000,000
**Population Growth Rate:** 1.8%
**Population Density:** 93
**Per capita GNP:** $3,470
**Average life expectancy:** 64
**Infant Mortality Rate:** 73
**Literacy Rate:** 71% (77% men, 66% women)

— Up-to-date figures for united **Germany** were not available. The figures given were reached by combining information from East and West Germany.

— **Capital cities. Germany:** Although **Berlin** is the official capital of the united Germany, as of this publication, the seat of government is in the old West German capital of **Bonn**. The **Netherlands: Amsterdam** is the official capital, the seat of government is **The Hague**. **Philippines: Quezon City** is the official capital, **Manila** is the de facto capital. **South Africa** has three capitals, legislative, executive and judicial. Other countries may have more than one capital, the one listed is the one most frequently cited.

— **Populations of capital cities** are the most recent available from the Population Reference Bureau. They generally refer only to populations within the city proper, although in some cases information for metropolitan areas is given. Dates vary between 1970 and 1989; most are within the decade of the 80's. The numbers shown will therefore give only a general idea of the true size of the city.

— **Languages** include official languages and others most used. In some countries, hundreds of separate languages and dialects are spoken.

— **Currency.** These are the basic units of currency only.

— **Populations** are 1990 mid-year estimates. Almost half of the world's people live in the four largest countries–China, India, the Soviet Union and the U.S.

— **Population growth rates** shown are rates of natural increase, or the birth rate minus the death rate. They show rates of population growth without counting net immigration or emigration.

— **Population density** is population divided by total area. The figures are rounded to the nearest whole number. Countries with high densities can be thought of as more crowded than those with low densities. It is important to

remember that the type of land influences how many people can live there. Fewer people can live in a desert than on fertile farmland.

— **Per capita GNP.** These are per capita gross national products for 1988 in equivalent U.S. dollars. The GNP is the value of all goods and services produced within a country, plus income earned abroad, minus income earned by foreigners within the country. This is *not* the per capita income. Average people do not actually earn this much. Income is generally distributed unevenly. Poor people would have a much lower per capita income than this figure indicates.

— **Average life expectancy** is the average number of years to be lived by a group of people born in the same year if mortality at each age remains constant in the future. These figures are a combined average for both sexes. Generally, women have a longer life expectancy than men.

— **Infant mortality rate (IMR)** is the number of deaths of infants under one year of age in a given year per 1000 live births in the same year. It is considered an important indicator of the general health of a society. If a country has an IMR of 50 or more, it indicates a societal problem of hunger and starvation. Figures are rounded.

— **Literacy rate** is an estimate of the percentage of people who are able to read and write at all, and does not indicate any set level of competence. For this reason, these figures may appear higher than might be expected. Numbers are rounded.

p. 72-77 — The **time line of history** is intended to be a general overview of western history. It is merely a starting place for studying the rich histories of thousands of cultures and peoples of the world. It should be noted that eras did not suddenly start or stop during the years indicated on the time line, but gradually grew and declined.

p. 78-83 — **Notable people** were chosen to highlight individual contributions from a wide variety of people of different races and backgrounds. Those listed have articles written about them in standard encyclopedias. In the short space of 6 pages, many notable people are not listed. As with the time line, this is a starting place for further learning.

p. 84-87 — **Inventions and discoveries** were chosen on the basis of both importance and understandability.

p. 88 — **Lengths of canals** are rounded to the nearest mile.

p. 88 — **Bridges** included in the chart have the longest main spans in the world The longest total length, including bridge and approaches, is the Rio-Niterói Bridge in Brazil, at 45,604 feet. The main span is 984 feet. It is a plate and box girder bridge. The longest cable-stayed bridge is the Alex Fraser near Vancouver, British Columbia, with a main span of 1,526 feet. The longest continuous truss bridge is the Astoria in Oregon/Washington at 1,232 feet. The longest concrete arch bridge is the KRK in Yugoslavia, at 1,280 feet.

p. 90 — **Heights of skyscrapers** are heights to the roof. The total height may be quite a bit more.

p. 94-101 — **States of the Union.** Information is from the Council of State Governments *Book of the States, 1990-91*, the U.S. Bureau of the Census, the U.S. Bureau of Economic Analysis, and the U.S. Geological Survey. For comparison purposes, here is information on the United States as a whole from those sources:
**Population:** 249,022,783
**Population density:** 69
**Area:** 3,618,770
**Highest point:** 20,320 ft.
**Lowest point:** -282 ft.

— **Populations of capital cities** are official 1980 census figures for the cities themselves, not the metropolitan areas. 1990 figures are not yet available.

— **Governors** include those elected in November 1990.

— **Population** figures are from the 1990 United States Census, and indicate the number of people in residence as of April 1, 1990.

— **Population density** is population divided by total area and rounded to the nearest whole number.

— **Per capita income** is from the U.S. Bureau of Economic Analysis for 1988. These figures refer to before tax income.

— **Areas** include both land and inland water areas.

p. 103-105 — **Largest cities of the United States.** This is 1988 information from the U.S. Bureau of the Census, based on the 1980 Census of Population and unpublished data. The areas were provided by the municipalities and include areas annexed or detached.

p. 105 — **Largest urban areas of the world.** For this list, urban areas are defined as population clusters of continuous built-up area with a population density of 5,000 persons per square mile. Political and administrative boundaries were disregarded in determining these populations. Figures are rounded to the nearest 100,000, so Manila (9.88) is larger than Cairo (9.85). The most densely populated city in the world is Hong Kong, with 247,004 persons per square mile. The source was the *World Population Profile, 1989*, prepared by the U.S. Bureau of the Census. These are estimates for mid-1990.

p. 106-109 — Many parks first entered the **National Park System** as national monuments. Others were authorized several years before they were established. The date given is the date *established*. Most parks have

undergone numerous boundary changes. The acreages given are those of December 31, 1988. Some parks have had name changes. The date given is the date established under any name. Haleakala National Park was originally part of Hawaii Volcanoes National Park, and was separated on Sept. 13, 1960.

p. 110-111 — Information about **Indians** presented on these pages is a general framework for studying native American cultures. Not all tribes in a group are listed, and not all information given about the group applies to each tribe. Tribes listed have individual articles in standard encyclopedias. Information is for traditional and customary use before the adaptation of modern ways, and will generally not apply to the present day. Many tribes no longer live in their traditional homeland. **Staple foods** are foods most constantly and generally eaten. Information on **Indians of the Plains** reflects the lifestyle after Europeans come to the Americas, bringing the horse. Before then, people farmed corn, beans and squash, and men generally hunted deer and elk because buffalo were difficult to hunt on foot. The lifestyle of following buffalo herds and hunting on horseback lasted only about 200 years. The great buffalo herds disappeared by about 1890, the date of the last battle with the Sioux at Wounded Knee.

p. 162 — **Long-time favorites** were chosen to represent books and authors which have been read and enjoyed by children of several generations and which are not on the Newbery list.

p. 164 — The **frequency of letters** is from *The Cambridge Encyclopedia of Language* by David Crystal and is based on letter counts from a very large number of sources.

# PARTIAL BIBLIOGRAPHY OF SOURCES

Caney, Steven. *Steven Caney's Invention Book.* New York: Workman Publishing, 1985.

*Chase's Annual Events, 1990.* Chicago: Contemporary Books, Inc., 1989.

Conlin, Joseph R. *The Morrow Book of Quotations in American History.* New York: William Morrow & Company, Inc., 1984.

Council of State Governments. *The Book of the States, 1990-91.* Lexington, Kentucky: The Council of State Governments, 1990.

Council of State Governments. *State Administrative Officials Classified by Function, 1989-90.* Lexington, Kentucky: The Council of State Governments, 1989.

Crystal, David. *The Cambridge Encyclopedia of Language.* New York: Cambridge University Press, 1987.

*Encyclopedia Americana (1990 edition).* Danbury, Connecticut: Grolier Incorporated, 1989.

Ensminger, Audrey H. and others, *Foods and Nutrition Encyclopedia.* Clovis, California: Pegus Press, 1983.

Gunston, Bill and others. *The Guiness Book of Speed Facts and Feats.* Enfield, Middlesex: Guiness Superlatives, 1984.

Hatch, Jane M. *The American Book of Days, 3rd edition.* New York: H.W. Wilson Company, 1978.

Hurlbut, Cornelius S., Jr., *The Planet We Live On, An Illustrated Encyclopedia of the Earth Sciences.* New York: Harry N. Abrams, Inc., 1976.

*The Incredible Machine.* Washington, D.C.: National Geographic Society, 1986.

Jenkins, Francis A. and Harvey E. White. *Fundamentals of Optics, 4th edition.* New York: McGraw-Hill Book Company, 1976.

Lide, David R. *Handbook of Chemistry and Physics, 71st edition, 1990-91.* Boca Raton, Florida: CRC Press, Inc., 1990

McFarlan, Donald and others. *1990 Guiness Book of World Records.* New York: Sterling Publishing Company, Inc., 1989.

*Merit Student's Encyclopedia.* New York: Macmillan Educational Company, 1985.

*The New Encyclopædia Britannica.* Chicago: Encyclopædia Britannica, Inc., 1986.

*New York Public Library Desk Reference.* New York: Simon & Schuster, Inc., 1989.

*The 1990 Information Please Almanac.* Boston: Houghton Mifflin Company, 1990.

O'Brien, Robert and Sidney Cohen, M.D. *The Encyclopedia of Drug Abuse.* New York: Facts on File, Inc., 1984.

Simpson, J. A. and E. S. C. Weiner. *The Oxford English Dictionary.* Oxford: Clarendon Press, 1989.

Population Reference Bureau. *1990 World Population Data Sheet.* Washington, D.C.: Population Reference Bureau, 1990.

*Reader's Digest Guide to Places of the World, A Geographical Dictionary.* London: Reader's Digest Association, 1987.

Ridpath, Ian. *Illustrated Encyclopedia of Astronomy and Space.* New York: Crowell, 1976.

Sebel, Peter and others. *Respiration, The Breath of Life.* New York: Torstar Books, 1985.

*Small Inventions That Make a Big Difference.* Washington, D.C.: National Geographic Society, 1984.

*The Statesman's Year-Book, 1990-91, 127th edition.* New York: St. Martin's Press, 1990.

U.S. Central Intelligence Agency. *The World Factbook 1990.* Washington, D.C.: U.S. Government Printing Office, 1990.

U.S. Congress. *1989-1990 Congressional Directory, 101st Congress.* Washington, D.C.: U.S. Government Printing Office, 1989.

U.S. Department of Commerce, Bureau of the Census. *Statistical Abstract of the United States: 1990, 110th edition.* Washington, D.C.: U.S. Government Printing Office, 1990.

U.S. Department of Commerce, Bureau of the Census. *World Population Profile 1989.* Washington, D.C.: U.S. Government Printing Office, 1989.

U.S. Department of the Interior, National Park Service. *The National Parks Index 1989.* Washington, D.C.: U.S. Government Printing Office, 1989.

*Washington Information Directory, 1988-89.* Washington, D.C.: Congressional Quarterly, Inc., 1988.

*Webster's New Geographical Dictionary.* Springfield, Massachusetts: Merriam-Webster, Inc., 1984.

Whitford, H.C. *A Dictionary of American Homophones and Homographs.* New York: Teacher's College Press, 1966.

Willoughby, David P. "Running and Jumping," *Natural History,* (March 1974), p. 69-72.

*The World Almanac and Book of Facts, 1990.* New York: Pharos Books, 1989.

*World Book Encyclopedia, 1990 edition.* Chicago: World Book, Inc., 1989.

Wulffson, Don L. *Extraordinary Stories Behind the Invention of Ordinary Things.* New York: Lothrop, Lee & Shepard Books, 1981.

# INDEX